Transitional Justice

Genocide, Political Violence, Human Rights Series

Edited by Alexander Laban Hinton, Stephen Eric Bronner, and Nela Navarro

Transitional Justice

Global Mechanisms and Local Realities after Genocide and Mass Violence

EDITED BY

ALEXANDER LABAN HINTON

RUTGERS UNIVERSITY PRESS

NEW BRUNSWICK, NEW JERSEY, AND LONDON

First paperback printing, 2011

LIBRARY OF CONGRESS CATALOGING-IN-PUBLICATION DATA

Transitional justice : global mechanisms and local realities after genocide and
mass violence / edited by Alexander Laban Hinton.
   p. cm. — (Genocide, political violence, human rights)
   Based on a conference held in 2007 in Newark, N.J.
   Includes bibliographical references and index.
   ISBN 978-0-8135-5068-8 (pbk. : alk. paper)
   ISBN 978-0-8135-4761-9 (hardcover : alk. paper)
   1. Transitional justice. 2. Crimes against humanity. I. Hinton, Alexander Laban.
   JC571.T6994 2010
   364.15′1—dc22   2009036232

A British Cataloging-in-Publication record for this book is available from the
British Library.

A version of "(In)Justice: Truth, Reconciliation, and Revenge in Rwanda's *Gacaca*"
by Jennie E. Burnet was previously published as "The Injustice of Local Justice:
Truth, Reconciliation, and Revenge in Rwanda" in *Genocide Studies and Prevention* 3,
no. 2 (2008): 173–193. Reprinted with permission of the journal editors.

Visit our Web site: http://rutgerspress.rutgers.edu

Manufactured in the United States of America

CONTENTS

PART THREE
Voice, Truth, and Narrative

FOREWORD

This book has an ambitious goal: to design outlines of the anthropology of transitional justice. Reading it brings insight into the complexities and complications that emerge when postconflict societies seek a path forward after mass violence.

As Alex Hinton points out, even if the area of transitional justice is still emerging, actors in this field have produced a broad range of reflections, tools, reviews, tentative theoretical approaches, and have used a combination of different disciplines, including history, law, sociology, anthropology, philosophy, and religious studies. Moreover, institutions are being created and staffed by so-called transitional justice professionals, where courses are being organized and degrees awarded. Budgets are being allocated and new market niches are being developed, with the usual competition between institutions, including the export—sometimes imposition—of experts from north to south. Additionally, dialogue between theory and practice is being established, albeit with varying degrees of success.

In this context, and as this volume illustrates, the effort to analyze transitional justice from an anthropological perspective is not only useful but also indispensable. *Transitional Justice* demonstrates that we must analyze this field from multiple perspectives. Who conceptualizes, decides, defines, benefits from (and finances) the programs, projects, and strategies of transitional justice? What is the impact of transitional justice measures? And how is transitional justice perceived by different stakeholders? Such issues need to be analyzed on both the local and global levels—from a center-periphery perspective, from the vantage of victims and perpetrators, through the lens of gender, and from the vantage of different social institutions, power centers, and actors. Transitional justice also has to be studied temporally to discern long-term patterns and outcomes.

This collection shows that it is also important to deconstruct key concepts and to question the vocabulary used in this new field of expression, where we encounter quasi-redemptive terminology (the healing of a society), ontological terms (reconciling society), normative expressions (reestablishing the rule of law), ethical terms (reestablishing human dignity), legal terms (condemning and judging), philosophical-psychological terms (establishing the truth, healing), and political terms (reforming institutions).

Transitional justice has emerged as a field of reflection and theory because some complex and real problems need to be solved—problems that go beyond the answers given to the victims or the sanctions imposed on the perpetrators. For the struggle against impunity to have more impact, it is necessary to "produce society" (as we anthropologists very often say), a social bond that cultivates accountability and promotes civic trust and equality of citizens and opportunity at all levels. The issue of the relationship between the production of society and impunity is present throughout this book.

Overall, one conclusion emerges with blinding clarity in this book: transitional justice is not a universal panacea. By itself it cannot resolve anything and it cannot be an end in itself. Nevertheless, transitional justice can be a useful link when combining different strategies that contribute to a stronger strategic vision when designing policies against impunity. It can also help the actors progress beyond purely legalist thinking and contribute to the process of construction and reestablishment of civil confidence in a variety of forms.

Reflection in the context of societies where odious and large-scale crimes have occurred is difficult, because one must deal directly with a very complex universe of victims, grasp the logics and trajectories of perpetrators and states, and grapple with the frequent absence of political will on the part of governments and even the international community.

One of the tasks of an emerging "anthropology of transitional justice" should be to contribute to the process of reflection by exploring these issues and by using anthropological analysis, when appropriate, to help shape the more effective strategies. This collection of articles is a valuable step in that direction.

Mô Bleeker

ACKNOWLEDGMENTS

The origins of this project date back to a 2007 symposium, "Local Justice: Global Mechanisms and Local Meanings in the Aftermath of Mass Atrocity," held at Rutgers University–Newark. I would like to thank the Office of the Chancellor at Rutgers–Newark for supporting this event. Several participants later presented papers in a session at the July 2007 meeting of the International Association of Genocide Scholars, which was held in Bosnia and Herzegovina. I would also like to thank the participants and audience members for their thoughtful remarks.

My editorial efforts were greatly facilitated by grants from the Rutgers Research Council and the United States Institute of Peace. The opinions, findings, and conclusions or recommendations expressed in this book are those of the authors and do not necessarily reflect the views of the United States Institute of Peace.

I'd also like to thank the editors of the journal *Genocide Studies and Prevention* for permission to reprint a revised version of Jennie Burnet's "The Injustice of Local Justice: Truth, Reconciliation, and Revenge in Rwanda," *Genocide Studies and Prevention* 3, no. 2 (2008): 173–193.

I am grateful to Marlie Wasserman for her editorial vision for this volume. I'd also like to thank my colleagues Steven Bronner, Nela Navarro, and Tom LaPointe for their collegiality and support. Finally, I would like to thank W. L. Hinton, Monica Phillips, Alison Hack, Marc Sherman, the external reviewers, and, especially, Nicole Cooley for their helpful thoughts and suggestions about this volume.

Transitional Justice

Introduction

Toward an Anthropology of Transitional Justice

ALEXANDER LABAN HINTON

How do societies come to terms with the aftermath of genocide and mass violence? And how might the international community contribute to this process? In recent years, transitional justice mechanisms such as tribunals and truth commissions have emerged as a favored means of redress, one that is now the focus of international workshops, academic conferences, UN reports, foreign relations and diplomacy, nongovernmental organizations, and scholarly research.

This volume argues that, however well-intentioned, transitional justice needs to more deeply grapple with the messiness of global and transnational involvements and the local, on-the-ground realities with which they intersect, complexities that are too often glossed over, due in part to the privileging of a cluster of liberal normative goods, such as the rule of law, peace, reconciliation, civil society, human rights, combating impunity, and justice.

Specifically, this intersection of justice and locality, or what might be called "local justice," is concerned with the ways in which justice is experienced, perceived, conceptualized, transacted, and produced in various localities, ranging from village-level interactions between former victims and perpetrators, to offices of nongovernmental organizations, to the courtrooms of international tribunals.[1]

Because justice is so frequently assumed to be something almost transcendent and universal, epitomized by due process, legal rights, and international norms, it is critical to explore how a sense of justice (or the lack thereof) after genocide and mass violence is always negotiated within particular localities enmeshed with global and transnational flows of ideas and ideologies, legal mechanisms, human rights regimes, capital, electronic media, and so forth (Appadurai 1996; see also Stover 2005; Stover and Weinstein 2004; Wilson 2001). The nexus of justice and locality is therefore frequently one of "friction" (Tsing 2005), the dynamic intersection of a varying combination of local, regional, national, transnational, and global processes in particular contexts.

This book, then, seeks to explore the local justice dynamic by considering what justice means and how it is negotiated in different localities where transitional justice efforts are under way (or related rhetorics and processes are in play) after genocide and mass atrocity. In doing so, it seeks to envision what an anthropology of transitional justice might look like.

After examining the emergence of transitional justice, this introduction explores three dimensions of the anthropology of transitional justice: the messiness of these initiatives ("transitional frictions"), the ways in which transitional justice is negotiated and understood on the ground ("justice in the vernacular"), and how transitional justice initiatives foreground and background different groups and perspectives ("voice, truth, and narrative").

Transitional Justice

The field of transitional justice is relatively new, emerging in the wake of the cold war amid euphoria about the "new world order" and the possibilities of humanitarianism, human rights, and international law. Indeed, the term "transitional justice" is thought to have been coined as recently as 1991 (Teitel 2008, 1; see also Arthur 2009). Transitional justice is often defined as the process of redressing past wrongs committed in states shifting from a violent, authoritarian past toward a more liberal, democratic future—though more recently the term has been defined in a broader manner (for example, a more general "response to systematic or widespread violations of human rights")[2] and extended to encompass a larger set of outcomes, such as advancing development and social justice (Mani 2008).

Transitional justice is strongly informed by at least three key streams of experience (Neier 1999; Teitel 2003). One key current was the post–World War II attempt to deal with the atrocities committed by Nazi Germany and Japan (Bass 2000; Teitel 2003). While some people, including Winston Churchill, argued that the crimes of the former leaders of these regimes were so egregious and obvious that they should be summarily executed, others argued that it was important to "stay the hand of vengeance" and try them in a court of law (Moghalu 2008, 30).

The latter side won out, resulting in the creation of two international tribunals, the 1945 International Military Tribunal at Nuremberg (Nuremberg Trials) and the 1946 International Military Tribunal for the Far East (Tokyo War Crimes Trials). While these tribunals were momentous in a number of respects, they were particularly significant for expanding the applicability of international law to individuals (as opposed to only states) and for prioritizing international law over domestic law—a move that undermined the doctrine of sovereignty that had largely guided international relations since the 1648 Treaty of Westphalia.

Second, even as the Nuremberg and Tokyo war crimes tribunals were being held, the international community began building a new corpus of international human rights law that went far beyond preexisting laws, such as the Geneva and Hague conventions. Almost immediately after the creation of the United Nations, which foregrounded human rights in its charter, delegates passed the 1948 Universal Declaration of Human Rights and 1948 Convention on the Prevention and Punishment of the Crime of Genocide. Over the next few decades, the infrastructure of the human rights regime was laid with the promulgation of a number of other treaties covering discrimination, torture, and civic, cultural, economic, political, and social rights; the founding of regional human rights courts in Africa, Europe, and Latin America; and the establishment of international human rights organizations like Amnesty International and Human Rights Watch (Kelly and Dembour 2007; Smith 2007).

And, third, transitional justice took shape in the 1980s as a number of countries in Africa (e.g., Uganda, Zimbabwe), and especially Latin America (e.g., Argentina, Bolivia, El Salvador, Uruguay), that had been ruled by dictators or military regimes moved toward democratic rule (Hayner 2002; Kritz 1995a, 1995b; O'Donnell and Schmitter 1986). In many cases, the previous government insisted upon amnesties or pardons as a precondition for stepping aside. If the new governments were constrained in their ability to prosecute former perpetrators, they were able to establish commissions that sought to explain what had happened—which was critical to societies that had suffered through a reign of fear and terror epitomized by death squads and "disappearances" (Neier 1999). In this volume, Antonius Robben explores perhaps the most well known of these early truth commissions, the National Commission on the Disappeared, established in 1983 in Argentina, where up to 30,000 people had "disappeared" under military rule beginning in 1976.

All of these strands began to converge in the late 1980s with the end of the cold war. On the world stage, Presidents Mikhail Gorbachev and George H. W. Bush, invoking a phrase used by Woodrow Wilson in the wake of World War I, spoke of a "new world order" that would be uplifted by international peace and cooperation, democratization, the rule of law, respect for human rights, and humanitarian intervention. A giddiness about the possibilities of liberal emancipation was partly linked to an ongoing "third wave of democratization" (Huntington 1991), one that was suddenly catalyzed by democratization in Eastern European countries that had formerly been part of the Soviet bloc. As in Latin America and Africa, these postsocialist states were confronted by the dilemma of how a repressive and violent past should be dealt with as the country attempted to democratize (Borneman 1997).

It was in this context that the field of transitional justice began to take shape. If debates about accountability frequently centered on issues of truth and justice (Arthur 2009), in practice these early initiatives, partly influenced by the 1980s truth commissions in Argentina and elsewhere, tended to foreground truth. Truth inquiries and commissions continued to proliferate, culminating in perhaps the most renown instantiation, the 1995–2000 Truth and Reconciliation Commission (TRC) in South Africa (Hayner 2002; Rotberg and Thompson 2000). Other emerging transitional justice practices included lustration (administrative purges of those associated with the prior regime), memorialization, and reparation programs.

While trials have long been recognized as an important means of redress, the rise of this second key engine of transitional justice was linked to the Bosnian and Rwandan genocides. In contrast to the disappearances in Argentina, the violent acts committed during these conflicts were witnessed by the entire world. What seemed to be needed was a form of justice that would hold the perpetrators accountable while individualizing guilt and thereby undermining accusations of group blame that could perpetuate the conflict. To this end, the International Criminal Tribunal for the former Yugoslavia (ICTY) and Rwanda (ICTR) were set up in 1993 and 1994, respectively. This swing toward justice was furthered by the 1998 Rome Statute and subsequent creation of the International Criminal Court (Moghalu 2008).

By the turn of the twentieth century, transitional justice was emerging as a field, one that has grown rapidly over the last decade. Today, it is linked to a set of practices (prosecutions, truth commission, memorialization, lustration and vetting, reparations, amnesties, and pardons) and institutional structures such as international humanitarian law, international tribunals and courts, the United Nations Development Program (UNDP), and nongovernmental organizations, including the International Center for Transitional Justice that, since its establishment in 2001, has grown to a staff of more than 100 people working all over the world.[3] In academia, transitional justice is now linked to a set of foundational texts (e.g., Hayner 1994; Kritz 1995a, 1995b; Minow 1998; Orentlicher 1991; Teitel 2000) associated with a large literature,[4] and it is the subject of numerous courses and studied at university centers, seminars, conferences, and working groups.[5] It is even the focus of a new periodical, the *International Journal of Transitional Justice*.

An editorial in the lead issue of *International Journal of Transitional Justice* (2007) notes that the field, if initially the concern primarily of legal and human rights scholars/practitioners, is now interdisciplinary and the concern of a combination of scholars, practitioners, and activists (Weinstein 2007; see also Bell 2009). This range is manifest in the first issue, which includes essays from all three perspectives and fields as diverse as anthropology, law, political science, education, geography, and sociology.

The editorial also notes that the purview of transitional justice has been expanding, a claim reflected by subsequent special issues on "Gender and Transitional Justice" and "Transitional Justice and Development." In the development issue, the guest editorial argues that transitional justice also should be concerned with development and social justice issues (e.g., inequality, discrimination, marginalization, structural violence, war economies, and corruption) that impact the long-term success of transitional justice initiatives (Mani 2008).

Yet another new direction noted by the editorial is the growing recognition of the importance of the local. In some sense, the local has always lurked in the background of transitional justice studies, as some scholars and practitioners have argued that each situation is different and demands a locally attuned response. This line was perhaps most famously asserted by Desmond Tutu, who argued that the South African experience required a South African response emphasizing restorative justice, with its focus on restoring social balance, over "more Western" retributive justice (see Minow 1998, 81; Waldorf 2006). But even courts like the ICTY and ICTR have come under critique in recent years for being too slow, expensive, and distant from the victims. In response, a new genre of more local "hybrid" or mixed tribunals, comprising a mixture of national and international personnel, were subsequently established in places like Cambodia, East Timor, Kosovo, and Sierra Leone (Dickinson 2003; Linton 2001; Romano et al. 2004).

But some transitional justice scholars have argued that, while effective in ways, tribunals often fall short of their goals because expectations for them are too high and they are not accompanied by a matrix of other strategies meant to facilitate social repair (Fletcher and Weinstein 2002; Stover and Weinstein 2004), a claim that dovetails with calls for transitional justice to address issues of development and social justice (Mani 2008). At a minimum, transitional justice needs to at least ask whether the universalistic assumptions about the benefits of justice accord with what people think on the ground (Stover and Weinstein 2004). Ideally, the field would actively take into account "the impact of non-Western cultures and different beliefs . . . [and] . . . ask ourselves about local practices of justice" (Weinstein 2007, 2). While most of the attention has centered on one of these "traditional" practices, the *gacaca* hearings in Rwanda (see Burnet, this volume), there is a small but growing number of studies on how conflict is dealt with on the local level in places like Guatemala, Timor Leste, and Uganda, where transitional justices initiatives have been launched (e.g., Arriaza and Roht-Arriaza

2008; Baines 2007; Roht-Arriaza and Mariezcurrena 2006; see Waldorf 2006 for a review).[6]

Toward an Anthropology of Transitional Justice

If transitional justice has increasingly recognized the importance of taking local realities into account, anthropology has been largely silent on the topic of transitional justice. A handful of anthropologists have directly engaged this literature, often in relationship to local understandings of justice (e.g., Clarke 2009; Coxshall 2005; Shaw 2007a; Theidon 2007; see also Dembour and Kelly 2007) and/or the assumptions and efficacy of transitional justice mechanisms in places like Aceh (Drexler 2006); Guatemala (e.g., Sanford 2003; O'Neill 2005), post-Socialist Europe (e.g., Borneman 1997, 2002); Rwanda (e.g., Burnet 2008; Eltringham 2008, Magnarella 2000), and South Africa (e.g., Feldman 2002; Ross 2003; Wilson 2001, 2003). One can skim through much of the "canonical" literature on transitional justice and find little inclusion of or reference to the work of anthropologists. Similarly, a 2006 review of "Anthropology and International Law" includes a penultimate section on "International Tribunals and Transitional Justice" that includes only a few references. A 2009 keyword search on "transitional justice" in the anthropology database AnthroSource yields no results. Most often the connections between anthropology and transitional justice have been tangential or indirect through related literatures on the anthropology of genocide, political violence, human rights, social suffering, and international law.

Undoubtedly, there are a number of reasons for this lack of direct anthropological engagement with the transitional justice literature. Transitional justice is a new field, one whose emergence has been more closely linked to legal studies and political science. Anthropology, in turn, was somewhat slow to come to the study of the aforementioned related topics of genocide, human rights, international law, and political violence.[7]

An important part of the anthropological hesitation about transitional justice, however, may stem from the latter's normative associations. The very term "transitional justice" suggests a hierarchy and a teleology, with an implicitly more "backward" or "barbaric" society using the tools of liberalism to "develop" into a more modern, "civilized," liberal, democratic state (see O'Donnell 1996; Teitel 2000). Sometimes these discourses are acknowledged in a relatively open way, such as when the "before" condition is described using terms such as "barbaric" (Bhargava 2000) or "a failed state" (Helman and Ratner 1993). Most often they are tacit, implied by opposition to the "ultimate goal, which is the transition to a democratic state that governs through law and that thereby guards human rights" (Hesse and Post 1999a, 20–21). In this conception, transitional justice is depicted as leading toward an idealized "post" state of liberalism defined by a cluster of key terms, such as "rule of law," "civil society," "legal culture," "civilized," "human rights," "democratic," "pluralistic," "free market," and "liberal" (see, for example, Bass 2000; Hesse and Post 1999b; Neier 1998).

For anthropologists, such language is reminiscent of late nineteenth and early twentieth century "stage theory," which posited that all human culture naturally progresses from a relatively simple state of savagery to one of civilization, this higher state being characterized by progress, complexity, and rationality (see Morgan 1909; Tylor 1874; Adams 1998). As both theory and ideological justification, stage theory was often used to legitimate imperial and colonial projects as the "white man's burden" to uplift more "primitive" peoples, who were alternatively conceived as "noble savages" and violent "brutes" (see, for example, the different conceptions of Hobbes 2003 and Rousseau 2002).

While stage theory has long been discredited, derivative conceptions perdure in popular culture (e.g., *Lord of the Flies*), discussions of "progress," "civilization," and "development," and even contemporary humanitarian missions (Razack 2000; see also Dwyer, Hitchcock and Babchuk, Wagner, and Woolford, this volume). This notion has traction within transitional justice, though those writing in the vein of what might be called "critical transitional justice studies" have critiqued the field for this discursive strand (e.g., Bell 2009; Teitel 2000). Such scholars are wary of potentially enabling a sort of neoimperialism that, in a situation of unequal power, produces, via transitional justice mechanisms, certain forms of knowledge (for example, human rights discourses, liberal ideals, new histories), persons (for example, democratic, law-abiding citizens), and practices (for example, voting, free market economics, due process procedures). To facilitate this transformation, international actors and local elites are often said to be selecting from a "toolkit" or "menu" of transitional justice items, metaphors that tacitly depict them as engineers or mechanics who have the expertise and knowledge to rebuild the "broken society" or "failed state."

Even as it serves as an arena in which knowledge is produced, transitional justice may also foster a shrinkage, as time is truncated and sociocultural complexity is reduced into more manageable (and, often, controllable) categories. As signified by its modifying adjective, transitional justice implies a passage as the society in question is depicted as moving from one state (of illiberal violence and conflict) into another (of peace, reconciliation, and democracy). The transitional justice phase itself constitutes a kind of "zero time" by which past and present are foreshortened and reframed (see also Wagner, this volume). Long, complicated histories are reduced to an immediate past of conflict; future horizons are delimited by the promised end of the transition, an idyllic state of civilized democracy.

Transitional justice also produces a certain category of being, as people are seemingly transformed into liberal subjects who, as "autonomous" citizens imbued with "freedom," "equality," and "rights" engage in demo-cratic, social, juridical, and political practices. Thus, in a trial, due process rights are afforded to defendants, while judges, lawyers, and monitors work to ensure that the proceedings accord with "international standards." By enacting this legal process, the trial produces the category of liberal democratic, rights-bearing citizens who are simultaneously safeguarded and regulated by the "rule of law" (see Sanford and Lincoln, this volume, for a discussion of how police and judicial corruption in a postconflict phase undermine such aspirations). The very act of placing people into such liberal democratic identity categories, however, shapes and shrinks the understanding of the past. For example, the juridical parsing of people into the singular categories of victims, perpetrators, and witnesses often glosses over the ambivalent, dual, and ambiguous actions performed by given individuals and warring groups in the violent past (see also Drexler, this volume; Ea and Sim 2001).

More broadly, this production of knowledge and being in a context of transition closely resembles a rite of passage (Turner 1967; van Gennep 1960; see also Osiel 1997; Teitel 2001), as the society in question moves from a preexisting conflict situation into a liminal phase of transition before emerging into a new state of liberalism. Like rites of passage, trials, truth commission, memorializations, and other transitional justice mechanisms are highly symbolic. On a performative level, they not only enact liberal ide-als and subjectivities but also signify a purification of the social body, which is symbolically moved from a contaminating state of conflict and illiberalism to a condition of liberal democratic purity. During this process, new collec-tive narratives are forged, ones that seek to delineate the violent past in a manner that increases the social cohesion of the fractured society and legiti-mates the postconflict government initiating the transitional justice process (Osiel 1997). These narratives are often far from hegemonic, though they may shift alternative narratives and perspectives into an "off-stage" position, as several essays in this volume illustrate (see the chapters by Burnet, Dwyer, Hitchcock and Babchuk, Casey, Robben, and Wagner)

It is precisely the emergence of critical transitional justice studies that provides a point of entrée for anthropology to engage with this new field. This volume constitutes an initial attempt to illustrate what this anthropol-ogy of transitional justice might look like. In contrast to those who might assume some sort of straightforward relationship between transitional justice mechanisms and outcomes (for example, many of the charters of international tribunals suggest that the trials will deliver a host of social goods, including advancing the rule of law, combating impunity, promoting peace and reconciliation, revealing the truth, helping people heal, and so forth), anthropologists are more oriented to the complexities of the encounter between global/transnational mechanisms and the local realities on the ground. This book is divided into three sections that explore this messiness: the friction of the global-local encounter, one that often has unanticipated and problematic consequences; the ways in which global conceptions and mechanisms of justice are experienced, perceived, and translated on the ground; and how transitional justice initiatives involve contestation and negotiations about the past, as different voices and narratives are privileged and backgrounded. Many of the essays speak across these themes, of course, even if they have been placed within a topical section about which they have much to say.

Transitional Frictions

Even as they may be initiated with the best of intentions, transitional justice mechanisms almost always have unexpected outcomes that emerge out of the "frictions" between these global mechanisms and local realities. Anna Tsing uses the term "friction" to refer to "the awkward, unequal, unstable, and creative qualities of interconnection across difference" (2005, 4). If she applies this metaphor to the spread of capitalism and environmental imperatives to distant locales like Indonesia, it is also a productive way of thinking about transitional justice, which likewise brings universalist aspirations to bear in radically different contexts. The chapters in the first part of this volume explore these sorts of "transitional frictions," which, in the extreme, may even facilitate new sorts of violence and impunity as opposed to combating them.

Sarah Wagner's "Identifying Srebrenica's Missing: The 'Shaky Balance' of Universalism and Particularism" explores such issues in Bosnia and Herzegovina, the sites of two central transitional justice mechanisms—the ICTY and the International Commission on Missing Persons (ICMP), which works on exhuming and identifying the remains of the dead. Wagner's essay focuses on ICMP, which is often described in terms of a bundle of transitional justice rhetorics of social repair that are expressed through terms like "reparation," "rehabilitation," and "restoration."

As an allegedly apolitical institution, ICMP was supposed to serve as a model of how an ethnically divided country might be "rehabilitated." But, Wagner shows, the very act of identifying and returning remains is ethnicized, as the bodies become part of ethnic commemorations and former antagonists are reminded of the ethnic violence of the past. For Wagner, this contradiction illustrates the tension between the universalist ideals of transitional justice and the complex, particularist realities on the ground that do not mesh with this singular, homogenizing impulse. Like Drexler, Wagner is also critical of the ideological underpinnings of "reparation politics" and transitional justice, noting that they tend to produce a certain sort of truth, reaffirm a global hierarchy, assert a "civilizing" trajectory and "foreshortened time horizon" that truncates and glosses over complex histories, and make an almost clichéd set of assumptions about social repair.

In "The Failure of International Justice in East Timor and Indonesia," Elizabeth F. Drexler explores some of the "unintended consequences" of transitional justice initiatives in East Timor, where there has been a Commission for Truth and Reception, community reconciliation hearings, and an ad hoc tribunal (held in Jakarta). Drexler's essay delivers a devastating critique of these initiatives, arguing that, as opposed to "delivering justice" and establishing "the truth," they have undermined law and contributed to a sense of impunity by not prosecuting the Indonesian military leaders and allied militia leaders who masterminded and implemented the violence. Because of their limited jurisdiction, these mechanisms (with the exception of the final report of the Commission for Truth and Reception) have also produced a skewed account of the past that constructs the conflict as a civil war between Timorese—precisely the narrative that the Indonesian military seeks to promote to occlude its long history of involvement in the violence.

Besides ignoring the historical and sociopolitical context of the violence, such a narrative also glosses over the many ways in which many East Timorese lived in a situation of structural indeterminacy amidst social disruption, mistrust, betrayal, and uncertainty, and how, during the conflict, East Timorese might occupy varying and even conflicting roles that shifted across context and time. This "doubleness" lacks a role in the master narrative, which imports the reductive legalistic conception of "victim" and "perpetrator." Drexler calls for greater attention to narratives that diverge from this master narrative of "civil war," ones that take account of silenced voices, ambiguous positions, and the larger historical context that implicates the Indonesian military and international community. Moreover, as opposed to simply burying the past, as some Timorese political leaders suggest, East Timor might benefit from an international tribunal with the jurisdiction to hold the masterminds accountable. The danger of localizing transitional justice, she warns, is that these mechanisms may inadvertently create a narrative that localizes the origins and dynamics of a conflict and thereby ignores the larger context in which it emerged.

Victoria Sanford and Martha Lincoln's "Bodies of Evidence: Feminicide, Local Justice, and Rule of Law in 'Peacetime' Guatemala" explores yet another dimension of "transitional friction": gendered violence and the long-term efficacy of transitional justice mechanisms like the truth commission held after the genocide in Guatemala (Sanford 2003). Centering their discussion around the case of Claudina, a young woman murdered in

Guatemala in 2005, Sanford and Lincoln's essay questions the assumption that such mechanisms buttress the "rule of law" and combat nonviolence in any straightforward manner. Claudina's death is illustrative of a disturbing pattern in Guatemala, where female homicides have escalated dramatically in recent years. Following the judicial audit initiated by Claudina's father, Sanford and Lincoln compare the steps that reasonably should be expected in such a criminal investigation to what actually happened in Claudina's case. Not only did the investigators fail to ask basic questions, investigate obvious leads, and gather crucial evidence, but they appear to have done so with indifference and even intent. Remarkably, more than half of the murders of women in the country are simply never investigated.

When asked about these murders, officers often blamed the victim, suggesting that the violence was a response to their loose morals, provocative dress, or bodily signifiers of prostitution (for example, body piercings or tattoos), a legitimating rhetoric that also emerges in Casey's study of youth violence in northern Nigeria. Sanford and Lincoln characterize such violence against women as "feminicide," a term that not only denotes the killing of women but also holds responsible "male perpetrators . . . [and] the state and judicial structures that normalize misogyny," ranging from institutional silence or indifference to an atmosphere of impunity due to failure to properly investigate cases and seek justice for the victims. This situation bears uncanny similarity to the genocide of the early 1980s, when the Guatemalan state trained people to assault, mutilate, rape, and kill female "subversives," a term that has resurfaced in descriptions of female murder victims. Most of these genocidal perpetrators were never punished and some remain in positions of power, Sanford and Lincoln note, a situation that may very well contribute to feminicide in the present.

Justice in the Vernacular

If transitional justice initiatives are often said to promote a host of seeming universal goods, including the rule of law, justice, and peace and reconciliation, these ideas frequently do not accord with local understandings. As noted earlier, transitional justice scholars and practitioners have increasingly acknowledged the importance of taking such local understandings into account, usually through attempts to draw upon local traditions of conflict resolution such as *gacaca*. Much less attention has been paid to the ways in which transitional justice concepts are transmitted and translated into local idioms. This process of "vernacularization," as Sally Merry (2006a, 2006b) calls it, is often a messy process, involving negotiation between transnational actors (e.g., the UN, transnational nongovernmental organizations [NGOs]), mediators (e.g., local NGOs and outreach officers), and local actors (e.g., community leaders, witnesses, family members, civil parties, and victims).

Consequently, vernacularization also involves friction, as the meaning and form of transitional justice idioms are mediated, appropriated, translated, modified, misunderstood, ignored, or even rejected in everyday social practice (e.g., Dembour and Kelly 2007; Goodale and Merry 2007; Merry 2006b; Wilson 2001). The essays in this section consider these sorts of justice in the vernacular from a range of perspectives both within and beyond the usual purview of transitional justice

In "Local (In)Justice: Truth, Reconciliation, and Revenge in Rwanda's *Gacaca*," Jennie E. Burnet examines one of the most ambitious transitional justice attempts to localize justice, the traditional *gacaca* courts in Rwanda that the government is using to alleviate massive overcrowding in the country's jails and to supplement prosecutions at the ICTR, foreign courts, and the Rwandan national courts. Burnet's fieldwork suggests that the success of *gacaca* varies widely, but broadly it has had the unfortunate effect of exacerbating ethnopolitical tensions, sometimes even in communities in which antagonists have attained a degree of reconciliation.

Part of the problem stems from the government's politicization of *gacaca*, as the government has coupled it with an education campaign that asserts the state's master narrative, which depicts the genocide as perpetrated by Hutus against Tutsis. Such a master state narrative omits the fact that moderate Hutus were targets of violence and that some Hutus did not participate. Burnet's informants sometimes made public statements that accorded with this state narrative but would tell her something quite different in more private settings. More troubling, Burnet finds that people are also using *gacaca* to settle old grudges or for personal gain, motives that intensify intracommunal tensions. If *gacaca* has been lauded by some as a local mechanism that will help Rwandans attain a sense of justice, the realities on the ground are much more complex and suggest that *gacaca* may be having precisely the opposite effect, disrupting already fragile relations between former perpetrators and victims.

Conerly Casey's "Remembering Genocide: Hypocrisy and the Violence of Local/Global 'Justice' in Northern Nigeria" explores the vernacularization of liberal ideals associated with transitional justice in northern Nigeria. If youth violence might initially appear as vigilantism, Casey, echoing Hitchcock and Babchuk, Drexler, Wagner, and others in this volume, argues that it is in fact enmeshed in complicated histories and social dynamics. Reacting against the push of liberal universalism, the inequalities and injustices they observe in their own lives, and a global war on terror (replete with images from Guantanamo, Iraq, Afghanistan, and Abu Ghraib that look like a war on Muslims), many northern Nigerian youths seek what Casey calls "affective citizenship," or an ethnoreligious "feeling of belonging to, and having agency within, the state" that is linked to their structural positionings and local affordances, including a postcolonial history of ethnic conflict and the 1999–2000 implementation of Sharia law in twelve states in northern Nigeria.

Ironically, youth violence is often legitimated as an attempt to uphold the constitution and Sharia law. One of the axes upon which this violence has revolved is gender, as Muslim youths sometimes attack or rape women whose moral virtue is in question, even if this simply means these "prostitutes" are unmarried or participate in capitalist activities. This sort of "cultural justice" extends to other areas, such as raiding hotels and restaurants where alcohol is served. Casey argues that the actions of these youths cannot be explained away as due to the irrational exuberance or "victimized innocence" of their age. Instead, these youth, enmeshed in the intersection of liberal universalism, Sharia law, the Nigernian constitution, and their on-the-ground observations of the world, actively construct their identity, moral and social status, and market position through a violence they assert as just.

In "Genocide, Affirmative Repair, and the British Columbia Treaty Process," Andrew Woolford focuses on a transitional justice process that is understudied in the field: treaty negotiations with First Nations peoples. Specifically, Woolford examines the British Columbia Treaty Process, which has been ongoing between First Nations and the governments of British Columbia and Canada since 1992. If government representatives claim that the negotiations are about unresolved land claims, First Nations peoples foreground an array of other issues, including the genocidal past. Emphasizing the importance of taking local knowledge into account, Woolford notes that Aboriginal understandings of genocide, particularly with regard to identity and territoriality, do not fit neatly into the categories used in the 1948 UN Genocide Convention, such as its group definitions of nationality, ethnicity, race, or religion. Moreover, the very attempt to place them within such a homogenizing framework—for example, through the "imagined general property of 'Indian-ness'"—replicates genocidal practices of assimilation that were perpetrated against First Nations in past contexts like the infamous Canadian residential schools.

Woolford argues that a similar logic underlies the British Columbia Treaty Process itself. Using their position of structural power, government representatives have attempted to use legalistic rules and terminology to delimit outcomes and what can and cannot be discussed during negotiations. For First Nations peoples, for example, justice is linked to an acknowledgment of past wrongs. By refusing to discuss compensation, which implies moral wrong and illegality, or asserting that the treaty process must follow legalistic principles of "modification and release" and "full and final settlement," government representatives attempt to render such claims irrelevant.

Woolford notes that such practices not only subject First Nations to a sort of symbolic violence but replicate genocidal patterns of the past by seeking to assimilate them into neoliberal capitalism, a contemporary analog of the residential schools.

Robert K. Hitchcock and Wayne A. Babchuk's "Local Justice and Legal Rights among the San and Bakgalagadi of the Central Kalahari, Botswana" similarly explores the efforts of indigenous peoples who have suffered through genocide to seek redress for the abuses of the past. Their piece focuses on the Central Kalahari Legal Case, in which a group of indigenous peoples brought suit in 2002 against the government of Botswana for evicting them from their ancestral lands inside the Central Kalahari Game Reserve. Like Drexler, Hitchcock and Babchuk note that it is important to attend to the sociocultural and historical complexities underlying the case in order to understand it more fully.

Historically, the San and Bakgalagadi have occupied the bottom of the social hierarchy, enduring mistreatment and even servitude. During the legal case, some nongovernmental groups even accused the Botswana government of perpetrating genocide, an accusation that resonates with past treatment of these indigenous groups. Hitchcock and Babchuk trace out the history and local conceptions of land ownership that informed the perspective of the indigenous groups and Botswana government. Ironically, the government defended itself by noting that it had drawn upon indigenous systems of justice, consultation, and the *kgotla*, a public legal space, prior to removing the San and Bakgalagadi. The case itself illustrates the intersection of the local, regional, and international discourses about justice, as traditional San and Bakgalagadi practices were invoked, international media and nongovernmental organizations decried the relocations, and human rights norms informed the proceedings. Although the court ruled in favor of the San and Bakgalagadi, Hitchcock and Babchuk note that their situation remains tenuous, though their plight may have been buffered by the 2007 passage of the UN Declaration on the Rights of Indigenous Peoples.

Voice, Truth, and Narrative

Transitional justice initiatives are almost always entangled in fields of politics and power, ranging from the authority of the United Nations and the international community to dynamics on the local level. Structurally, these initiatives are established in a manner that foregrounds certain groups and narratives. The quest to establish the "truth," for example, is often circumscribed by political considerations that influence who is heard, what sorts of information may be considered, how that information is used in a final report or verdict, and so forth. Thus, the focus of an international tribunal is bound by temporal and personal jurisdiction, which may lead to the

elision of important parts of the past or certain segments of the population. Anthropologists have long been concerned with such issues of voice,
truth, and narrative, particularly with regard to exploring those whose voices
or understandings of the past have been backgrounded, muted, or even
silenced. The essays in this section examine this issue—which again highlights the messiness of the global-local encounter—in a variety of contexts,
ranging from the courtrooms of an international tribunal to a memorial in
a family compound in Bali.

Antonius C.G.M. Robben's "Testimonies, Truths, and Transitions of Justice in Argentina and Chile" focuses on the Southern Cone of Latin America,
where some of the first transitional justice initiatives were undertaken in
Argentina and Chile after the fall of violent dictatorships. Robben illustrates
how justice in the aftermath of violent dictatorship may diverge strongly
based on a country's objective, sociopolitical situation (particularly with
regard to the structural position of the former perpetrators), and political
actors. Thus, in Argentina, where the military retained less influence than in
Chile, the National Commission on Disappeared Persons (CONADEP) focused
more than the Chilean National Commission on Truth and Reconciliation
(the "Rettig Report") on riveting testimonial narrative (vs. flattened, muted
accounts or even silences), retributive (vs. restorative) justice, and issues of
truth and accountability (vs. reconciliation and reparation).

These orientations contributed to the production of different sorts of
narrative voice. The CONADEP report, which relied on riveting survivor
testimony, asserted a master narrative that placed blame largely on the military. Not surprisingly, the report was met with disbelief by people who knew
little about the violence and with denial by the military and its supporters,
who advanced an alternative narrative depicting the violence as the unfortunate but necessary response to the dire sociopolitical threat posed by
enemy subversives. Argentina's government tried to steer a middle course by
promoting a "two-demons" narrative that blamed both sides. In Chile, where
the population was more split and the former perpetrators retained greater
influence, the Rettig report was less divisive, spreading blame and focusing
on reconciliation and reparation. Even as it relied more on testimony and
acknowledged the military's responsibility for the violence, Chile's later
National Commission about Political Imprisonment and Torture (Valech
report) also ultimately emphasized reconciliation. Through this comparison,
Robben illustrates how truth narratives are constructed and undergo change
in transitional justice initiatives, how voice is differentially enabled and
silenced, and how "truth" and "justice" are bound up with political goals,
situational conditions, and issues of legitimacy.

In "Judging the 'Crime of Crimes': Continuity and Improvisation at the
International Criminal Tribunal for Rwanda," Nigel Eltringham considers the

issue of voice in a very different setting, the courtrooms of the ICTR. Eltringham illustrates how such international courts develop their own micro-
practices through negotiation, agency, and performance. For example, the
simple act of "standing" in the courtroom chamber is a non-verbal behavior
that asserts the right to speak and more broadly connotes power, voice and
authority. As opposed to following a singular dictate about when to stand,
international lawyers have different understandings of and opinions about
standing and engage in this practice in ways that are also influenced by per-
sonality and legal tradition.

This sort of analysis is at the heart of Eltringham's essay, which, through
the careful study of micropractices at the ICTR, a major ad hoc international
tribunal, seeks to explore the assumptions underlying "international justice"
and to challenge its often-assumed universality. "Standing" illustrates how
"naturalized cultural forms from non-international judicial contexts" (for
example, local variants of the regional civil and common law traditions)
shape the structure and functioning of "international justice." For Eltringham, "international justice" is always ultimately embedded in local performative and symbolic spaces and "remains a social activity dependent upon
socially acquired assumptions and expectations." Justice, in other words,
remains local even in the most seemingly universal of contexts, an ad hoc
international tribunal.

Leslie Dwyer's "Building a Monument: Intimate Politics of 'Reconciliation' in Post-1965 Bali" directly explores the relationship between voice,
truth, narrative, and the violent past in her examination of the issues that
arose when a group of Indonesian youths in Bali decided to build the "1965
Park" in their extended family compound to commemorate relatives who
died during the 1965–1966 genocide, an event about which people had only
recently begun to speak. In doing so, these youths explicitly drew upon
global discourses of transitional justice, stating that the 1965 Park would
contribute to social repair, closure, acknowledgment, healing, and reconciliation. When some people did not fully embrace the idea of the memorial,
they sometimes were mocked as "backward" in contrast to the "advanced"
or cosmopolitan identity they were asserting.

While unpacking the assumptions of this youth identity, which often
centered around a homogenized conception of victimhood, Dwyer points
out the ways in which other groups in the family compound chose not to
participate or were excluded or even silenced by the dominant voice of the
youths. Many elders, who had lived through the decades during which it was
dangerous to mention the genocide, preferred to remember the past through
religious conceptions of ancestral respect, ritual trance, divination, and karmic justice. Besides this generational gap, there was also a gendered dimension to the reception of the park, as the voices of women, many of whom

were victimized by bodily "examinations" and sexual assault, were often marginalized. At one point the youths dismissed as too apolitical the suggestion of some women that they place an ancestral shrine on one corner of the park. Completely absent from the debates was a consideration of the spaces where women did speak about such political topics, such as during group weaving. For Dwyer, the events surrounding the 1965 Park illustrate not just how global conceptions and instruments of transitional justice are localized, but how, with their expansive promises of peace, justice, healing, and reconciliation, such initiatives may dominate, silence, or elide alternative mechanisms, voices, coping strategies, and understandings of the violent past (see also Drexler and Burnet on this point).

A KEY ARGUMENT of this book is that justice is always enmeshed with locality and that transitional and other justice initiatives are often quite messy and often fail to attend to critical on-the-ground realities, ranging from social structure, to local knowledge, to complex histories, and to the assumptions that underlie such endeavors. Whose truth is asserted or denied? Whose voice is heard or silenced? What does justice mean across space and through time? And what interests and/or structures of power drive transitional justice initiatives? As we have seen, from an anthropological perspective, it is critical to consider on-the-ground realities to fully answer such questions, even if such answers reveal the messiness of the intersection of global mechanisms with complex, on-the-ground realities.

As Roger Duthie notes in his afterword, "The Consequences of Transitional Justice in Particular Contexts," transitional justice initiatives often have admirable goals even if they are plagued by unintended consequences. Thus, attempts to seek "a more accurate record of the events of the past" may be unable to take account of local complexities and dynamics, and efforts to create a new, unifying narrative may break down due to local agendas and identifications. For Duthie, the chapters in the volume do not simply reveal the complexities and difficulties of transitional justice and related initiatives but suggest that our expectations for them should be modest and realistic and that we should expect unintended consequences. Transitional justice is a tool that, despite its limitations, can still potentially bring about positive social change, particularly if it more fully takes account of justice and locality. As the essays in this volume demonstrate, it is precisely at this juncture that an anthropology of transitional justice emerges.

NOTES

Research for this essay was supported, in part, by grants from the Rutgers Research Council and the United States Institute of Peace. The opinions, findings, and conclusions or recommendations expressed in this essay are those of the author and do not necessarily reflect the views of either institution. I would like to thank W. L. Hinton, Monica Phillips, the reviewers, and, especially, Nicole Cooley for their helpful thoughts and suggestions about this essay.

1. By local justice, I do not mean vigilante or popular justice; though, if analyzed from an experience-near perspective, what we often explain away with the term "vigilante justice" might very well fit under the rubric of local justice (see Casey, this volume; Gordon 2004). Likewise, I do not use the term "local justice" just to refer to traditional mechanisms of conflict resolution and adjudication, though again these fall under the umbrella of local justice (see Waldorf 2006). My use is closest to that of Merry (2006b), who includes "local justice" in the subtitle of her volume *Human Rights and Gender Violence: Translating International Law into Local Justice.*

2. "What Is Transitional Justice?" International Center for Transitional Justice, http://www.ictj.org/en/tj/.

3. See the International Center for Transitional Justice at http://www.ictj.org/en/index.html.

4. See, for example, the University of Wisconsin's Transitional Justice Data Base Project bibliography of 2,344 scholarly works, at http://users.polisci.wisc.edu/tjdb/bib.htm.

5. See, for example, David Baker's list of more than 140 courses, at http://sitemaker.umich.edu/backer/transitional_justice_resources.

6. As this book was going to press, the International Journal for Transitional Justice was also working on a special issue on "Global and Local Approaches to Transitional Justice."

7. See, e.g., Cowan, Dembour, and Wilson (2001); Goodale (2009); Goodale and Merry (2007); Dembour and Kelly (2007); Hinton (2002a, 2002b, 2009); Merry (1992, 2006a); Scheper-Hughes and Bourgois (2004).

REFERENCES

Adams, William Yewdale. 1998. *The Philosophical Roots of Anthropology.* Stanford: CSLI Publications.

Appadurai, Arjun. 1996. *Modernity at Large: Cultural Dimensions of Globalization.* Minneapolis: University of Minneapolis Press.

Arriaza, Laura, and Naomi Roht-Arriaza. 2008. "Social Reconstruction as a Local Process." *International Journal of Transitional Justice* 2:152–172.

Arthur, Paige. 2009. "How 'Transitions' Reshaped Human Rights: A Conceptual History of Transitional Justice." *Human Rights Quarterly* 31 (May): 321–367.

Baines, Erin K. 2007. "The Haunting of Alice: Local Approaches to Justice and Reconciliation in Northern Uganda." *International Journal of Transitional Justice* 1 (1): 91–114.

Bass, Gary J. 2000. *Stay the Hand of Vengeance: The Politics of War Crimes Tribunals.* Princeton: Princeton University Press.

Bell, Christine. 2009. "Transitional Justice, Interdisciplinarity and the State of the 'Field' or 'Non-Field.'" *International Journal of Transitional Justice* 3 (1): 5–27.

Bhargava, Rajeev. 1999. "Restoring Justice to Barbaric Societies." In *Truth v. Justice: The Morality of Truth Commissions,* ed. Robert I. Rotberg and Dennis Thompson, 45–67. Princeton: Princeton University Press.

Borneman, John. 1997. *Settling Accounts: Violence, Justice and Accountability in Postsocialist Europe.* Princeton: Princeton University Press.

———. 2002. "Reconciliation after Ethnic Cleansing: Listening, Retribution, Affiliation." *Public Culture* 14:281–304.

Burnet, Jennie E. 2008. "The Injustice of Local Justice: Truth, Reconciliation, and Revenge in Rwanda." *Genocide Studies and Prevention* 3 (2): 173–193.

Call, Charles T. 2004. Is Transitional Justice Really Just? *Brown Journal of World Affairs* 11 (1): 101–113.

Clarke, Kamari Maxine. 2009. *Fictions of Justice: The International Criminal Court and the Challenge of Legal Pluralism in Sub-Sahara Africa*. New York: Cambridge University Press.

Cowan, Jane K., Marie-Bénédicte Dembour, and Richard Wilson, eds. 2001. *Culture and Rights: Anthropological Perspectives*. New York: Cambridge University Press.

Coxshall, Wendy. 2005. "From the Peruvian Reconciliation Commission to Ethnography: Narratives, Relatedness, and Silence." *POLAR: Political and Legal Anthropology Review* 28 (2): 203–222.

Dickinson, Laura A. 2003. "The Promise of Hybrid Courts." *American Journal of International Law* 97 (2): 295–310.

Dembour, Marie-Bénédicte, and Tobias Kelly, eds. 2007. *Paths to International Justice: Social and Legal Perspectives*. New York: Cambridge University Press.

Drexler, Elizabeth. 2006. "History and Liability in Aceh, Indonesia: Single Bad Guys and Convergent Narratives." *American Ethnologist* 33 (3): 313–326.

Ea, Meng-Try, and Sorya Sim. 2001. *Victims and Perpetrators? Testimony of Young Khmer Rouge Cadres*. Phnom Penh: Documentation Center of Cambodia.

Elstser, Jon. 2004. *Closing the Books: Transitional Justice in Historical Perspective*. New York: Cambridge University Press.

Eltringham, Nigel. 2008. "A War Crimes Community: The Legacy of the International Criminal Tribunal for Rwanda Beyond Jurisprudence." *New England Journal of International and Comparative Law* 14 (2): 309–318.

Feldman, Allen. 2002. "Strange Fruit: The South African Truth Commission and the Demonic Economies of Violence." *Social Analysis* 46 (3): 234–265.

Fletcher, Laurel E., and Harvey M. Weinstein. 2002. "Violence and Social Repair: Rethinking the Contribution of Justice to Reconciliation." *Human Rights Quarterly* 24:573–639.

Goodale, Mark, ed. 2009. *Human Rights: An Anthropological Reader*. Malden, MA: Blackwell.

Goodale, Mark, and Sally Engle Merry, eds. 2007. *The Practice of Human Rights: Tracking Law between the Global and the Local*. New York: Cambridge University Press.

Gordon, Robert. 2004. "Popular Justice." In *A Companion to the Anthropology of Politics*, ed. David Nugent and Joan Vincent, 349–366. Malden, MA: Blackwell.

Hayner, Priscilla B. 1994. Fifteen Truth Commissions 1974–1994: A Comparative Study. *Human Rights Quarterly* 16 (4): 597–655.

———. 2002. *Unspeakable Truths: Facing the Challenge of Truth Commissions*. New York: Routledge.

Helman, Gerald B., and Steven R. Ratner. 1993. "Saving Failed States." *Foreign Policy* 89:3–21.

Hesse, Carla, and Robert Post. 1999a. "Introduction." In *Human Rights in Political Transitions: Gettysburg to Bosnia*, ed. Carla Hesse and Robert Post, 13–36. New York: Zone Books.

———. 1999b. *Human Rights in Political Transitions: Gettysburg to Bosnia*. New York: Zone Books.

Hinton, Alexander Laban. 2005. *Why Did They Kill? Cambodia in the Shadow of Genocide*. Berkeley: University of California Press.

Hinton, Alexander Laban, ed. 2002a. *Genocide: An Anthropological Reader*. Malden, MA: Blackwell.

———. 2002b. *Annihilating Difference: The Anthropology of Genocide*. Berkeley: University of California Press.

Hinton, Alexander Laban, and Kevin Lewis O'Neill, eds. 2009. *Genocide: Truth, Memory, and Representation*. Durham, NC: Duke University Press.

Hobbes, Thomas. 2003. *Leviathan*. Bristol: Thoemmes Continuum.

Huntington, Samuel P. 1991. *The Third Wave: Democratization in the Late Twentieth Century*. Norman: University of Oklahoma Press.

Kelly, Tobias, and Marie-Bénédicte Dembour. 2007. "Introduction: The Social Lives of International Justice." In *Paths to International Justice: Social and Legal Perspectives*, ed. Marie-Bénédicte Demour and Tobias Kelly, 1–25. New York: Cambridge University Press.

Kritz, Neil, ed. 1995a. *Transitional Justice: How Emerging Democracies Reckon with Former Regimes*. Vol. 1, *General Considerations*. Washington, DC: United States Institute of Peace.

———. 1995b. *Transitional Justice: How Emerging Democracies Reckon with Former Regimes*. Vol. 2, *Country Studies*. Washington, DC: United States Institute of Peace.

Lederach, John Paul. 1997. *Building Peace: Sustainable Reconciliation in Divided Societies*. Washington, DC: United States Institute of Peace.

Linton, Suzannah. 2001. "Cambodia, East Timor and Sierra Leone: Experiments in International Justice." *Criminal Law Forum* 12:185–246.

Magnarella, Paul. 2000. *Justice in Africa: Rwanda's Genocide, Its Courts, and the UN Criminal Tribunal*. Aldershop, UK: Ashgate Publishing.

Mani, Rama. 2008. "Editorial: Dilemmas of Expanding Transitional Justice, or Forging the Nexus between Transitional Justice and Development." *International Journal of Transitional Justice* 2 (3): 253–265.

Merry, Sally Engle. 1992. "Anthropology, Law, and Transnational Processes." *Annual Review of Anthropology* 21:357–379.

———. 2006a. "Anthropology and International Law." *Annual Review of Anthropology* 35:99–116.

———. 2006b. *Human Rights and Gender Violence: Translating International Law into Local Justice*. Chicago: Chicago University Press.

Minow, Martha. 1998. *Between Vengeance and Forgiveness: Facing History after Genocide and Mass Violence*. Boston: Beacon.

Moghalu, Kingsley Chiedu. 2008. *Global Justice: The Politics of War Crimes Trials*. Stanford: Stanford University Press.

Morgan, Lewis Henry. 1909. *Ancient Society*. Chicago: Kerr.

Neier, Aryeh. 1998. *War Crimes: Brutality, Genocide, Terror and the Struggle for Justice*. New York: Times Books.

———. 1999. "Rethinking Truth, Justice, and Guilt after Bosnia and Rwanda." In *Human Rights in Political Transitions: Gettysburg to Bosnia*, ed. Carla Hesse and Robert Post, 39–52. New York: Zone Books.

O'Donnell, Guillermo. 1996. "Illusions and Conceptual Flaws." *Journal of Democracy* 7 (4): 160–168.

O'Donnell, Guillermo, and Philippe Schmitter. 1986. *Transitions from Authoritarian Rule: Tentative Conclusions from Uncertain Democracies*. Baltimore: Johns Hopkins University Press.

O'Neill, Kevin. 2005. "Writing Guatemala's Genocide: Christianity and Truth and Reconciliation Commissions." *Journal for Genocide Research* 7 (3): 331–349.

Orentlicher, Diane. 1991. "Settling Accounts: The Duty to Prosecute Human Rights Violations of a Prior Regime." *Yale Law Journal* 100 (8): 2537–2615.

Osiel, Mark. 1997. *Mass Atrocity, Collective Memory, and the Law.* New Brunswick: Transaction.

Razack, Sherene. 2000. "'Clean Snows of Petawawa': The Violence of Canadian Peacekeepers in Somalia." *Cultural Anthropology* 15 (1): 127–163.

Roht-Arriaza, Naomi, and Javier Mariezcurrena, eds. 2006. *Transitional Justice in the Twenty-First Century: Beyond Truth versus Justice.* New York: Cambridge University Press.

Romano, Cesare P. R., Andre Nollkaemper, and Jann K. Kleffner, eds. 2004. *Internationalized Criminal Courts and Tribunals: Sierra Leone, East Timor, Kosovo, and Cambodia.* New York: Oxford University Press.

Roper, Steven D., and Lilian A. Barria. 2006. *Designing Criminal Tribunals: Sovereignty and International Concerns in the Protection of Human Rights.* Burlington, VT: Ashgate.

Ross, Fiona C. 2003. *Bearing Witness: Women and the Truth and Reconciliation Commission in South Africa.* London: Pluto.

Rotberg, Robert I., and Dennis Thompson, eds. 2000. *Truth v. Justice: The Morality of Truth Commissions.* Princeton: Princeton University Press.

Rousseau, Jean-Jacques. 2002. *The Social Contract and The First and Second Discourses.* New Haven: Yale University Press.

Sanford, Victoria. 2003. *Buried Secrets: Truth and Human Rights in Guatemala.* New York: Palgrave.

Scheper-Hughes, Nancy, and Philippe Bourgois, eds. 2004. *Violence in War and Peace: An Anthology.* Malden, MA: Blackwell.

Shaw, Rosalind. 2007a. "Memory Frictions: Localizing the Truth and Reconciliation Commission in Sierra Leone." *International Journal of Transitional Justice* 1:183–207.

———. 2007b. "Displacing Violence: Making Pentecostal Memory in Postwar Sierra Leone." *Cultural Anthropology* 22 (1): 66–93.

Smith, Rhona. 2007. *Textbook on International Human Rights.* Oxford: Oxford University Press.

Stover, Eric. 2005. *The Witness: War Crimes and the Promise of Justice in The Hague.* Philadelphia: University of Pennsylvania Press.

Stover, Eric, and Harvey M. Weinstein, eds. 2004. *My Neighbor, My Enemy: Justice and Community in the Aftermath of Mass Atrocity.* New York: Cambridge University Press.

Teitel, Ruti G. 2000. *Transitional Justice.* New York: Oxford University Press.

———. 2003. "Transitional Justice Genealogy." *Harvard Human Rights Journal* 16:69–94.

———. 2008. "Editorial Note—Transitional Justice." *International Journal of Transitional Justice* 2 (1): 1–4.

Theidon, Kimberly. 2006. "Justice in Transition: The Micropolitics of Reconciliation in Postwar Peru." *Journal of Conflict Resolution* 50 (3): 433–457.

———. 2007. "Transitional Subjects: The Disarmament, Demobilization and Reintegration of Former Combatants in Columbia." *International Journal of Transitional Justice* 1 (1): 66–91.

Tsing, Anna. 2005. *Friction: An Ethnography of Global Connection.* Princeton: Princeton University Press.

Turner, Victor. 1967. *The Forest of Symbols: Aspects of Ndembu Ritual.* Ithaca: Cornell University Press.

Tylor, Sir Edward Burnett. 1874. *Primitive Culture*. Boston: Estes.

Uvin, Peter, and Charles Mironko. 2003. "Western and Local Approaches to Justice in Rwanda." *Global Governance* 9 (2): 219–231.

van Gennep, Arnold. 1960. *The Rites of Passage*. Chicago: University of Chicago Press.

Waldorf, Lars. 2006. "Mass Justice for Mass Atrocity: Rethinking Local Justice as Transitional Justice." *Temple Law Review* 79 (1): 1–88.

Weinstein, Harvey M. 2007. "Editorial Note." *International Journal of Transitional Justice* 1 (1): 1–5.

Wilson, Richard A. 2001. *The Politics of Truth and Reconciliation in South Africa: Legitimizing the Post-Apartheid State*. New York: Cambridge University Press.

———. 2003. "Anthropological Studies of National Reconciliation Processes." *Anthropological Theory* 3 (3): 367–387.

PART ONE

Transitional Frictions

1

▷ ▷ ▷ ▷ ▷ ▷ ▷ ▷ ▷ ▷ ▷ ▷ ▷ ▷ ◁ ◁ ◁ ◁ ◁ ◁ ◁ ◁ ◁ ◁ ◁ ◁ ◁ ◁

Identifying Srebrenica's Missing

The "Shaky Balance" of
Universalism and Particularism

SARAH WAGNER

Return, reconstruction, recognition, reparation. The language of postwar Bosnia and Herzegovina is saturated with a sense of what once was—or what was imagined to be—and the need to bring it back into existence. In these words, Bosnia's recent past serves as the referent for verbs of restoration and rehabilitation as those who employ them attempt to bridge the gap between a pre-genocide, pre-rape, and pre-flight place and an envisioned harmoniously multiethnic and functional society. Such a time-compressing impulse to render order and re-right wrongs is not unique to Bosnia. Rather, as the essays in this volume demonstrate, attempts at redress are part of a larger discourse of international interventionism in postconflict societies that has emerged over the past half century and whose key concepts include reparation politics and transitional justice.[1]

This chapter examines an unusual form of such intervention, a newly fashioned tool of the international postconflict tool kit: the DNA-based technology used to identify mortal remains of persons missing as a consequence of the 1992–1995 war in Bosnia and Herzegovina, specifically the victims of the Srebrenica genocide.[2] Juxtaposing the results of this forensic technology with those of another key international intervention in Bosnia, the International Criminal Tribunal for the former Yugoslavia (ICTY), this discussion maps important tensions and challenges within the project of identifying missing persons. Responses to mass atrocities, including uncovering mass graves, reassembling bodies, and prosecuting war criminals, belong to an ideological framework of justice and reconciliation that emerged from the post–World War II era of international human rights (Teitel 2000, 2003, 2006; Sanford 2003; Fletcher and Weinstein 2002; Joyce and Stover 1991; Pouligny 2005). As such, they fit within contemporary modes of addressing injustices against individual victims as much, if not more, than against states. They are also part of an international grammar of reparation, a term with broad connotations, encompassing "a variety of types of redress, including *restitution, compensation, rehabilitation, satisfaction,* and *guarantees of nonrepetition*" (Hayner 2001, 171).[3] Finally, within this general rubric of reparation, efforts undertaken to identify Bosnia's missing, including the missing of the July 1995 Srebrenica massacre, also entail the specific aim of social reconstruction (Stover and Weinstein 2004; Wagner 2008)—that is, recovering, identifying, and commemorating victims to effect social repair.[4]

How has this technoscientific form of international interventionism fared in postwar Bosnia and Herzegovina, whose population, territory, and governmental structure continue to be divided according to ethnonational identity (e.g., the two entities of the Bosniak and Croat-controlled Federation of Bosnia and Herzegovina and the Bosnian Serb-controlled Republika Srpska, and a presidency that rotates among the three ethnonational political constituencies of Bosnian Serbs, Bosnian Croats, and Bosniaks [Bosnian Muslims])? In answering this question, I use postmortem identification technology to venture comment on moments of engagement between the particularities of a postwar state and the international concepts of order and rights that have given rise to pursuits such as truth and reconciliation commissions and memorial centers. The specific example of Srebrenica's missing illustrates that, beyond the invaluable humanitarian achievement of returning remains to surviving families, the DNA science applied toward postconflict social repair exposes tension—a friction (Tsing 2005) between the ideological prescriptions of modern liberal democracy and the complex circumstances of a society defined both externally and internally along oppositional ethnonational lines. The results of the biotechnology invite us to examine how internationally accepted universals intersect with particular circumstances: "According to Habermas, modern collective identity has involved a *shaky balance* between two products of modernization: universalism and particularism. Universalism refers to ideas of freedom and democracy that are central features of Enlightenment thinking, but these ideas have been pursued, for the most part, through the particularism of nation-states—structures that have also developed during modernization" (italics added; Olick and Coughlin 2003, 50–51). As a postconflict society, Bosnia and Herzegovina is by definition a country in transition, a nation-state still under repair where intersections of universalism and particularism are particularly fraught. Since the end of the war in November 1995, Bosnia's political course has been dominated not only by an awkward division of power among state and local governments but also by an international protectorate presence (the Office of the High Representative established to oversee the implementation of the civilian components of the Dayton Peace Agreement), which is in turn supported by a cluster of influential international organizations, among them the Organization for Security and Co-operation in Europe, the United Nations Development Programme, and the International Committee of the Red Cross. The work of identifying missing persons thus takes place in a society in which the pursuit of universal ideas such as equality, individual freedom, and human rights is shared, and at times thwarted, by several actors: governmental and nongovernmental, local, national, and international alike.

Reflecting the ideals of Western liberalism, recovery and identification efforts in postwar Bosnia, specifically those targeting the victims of the Srebrenica genocide, are nested within a discourse of rights: both the right to know and the right to justice. The "right to know" refers to the right of surviving families to know whether their missing relatives are dead, where the remains are located, and to have those remains returned to them. Officially codified through the national legislation of the Missing Persons Law, which the Bosnian Parliamentary Assembly voted into existence in October 2004, the "right to know" refers to the right of Bosnian nationals regardless of ethnonational affiliation; whether Bosniak, Bosnian Serb, or Bosnian Croat, the beneficiaries of the legislation share the common experience of unaccounted-for human loss. The "right to justice" is less formally institutionalized. It is an ideal pursued through a range of channels, the most important of which for this discussion is the work of the ICTY and the International Commission on Missing Persons (ICMP).

Framing this analysis within and at times beyond the intersection of universalism and particularism helps us to consider what identifying mortal remains means outside of the most important context—that is, what identification means to the surviving relatives—and to examine the sociopolitical ramifications of reassembling, reading, and recognizing bodies of missing persons. The identification technology as a form of international interventionism sheds light on the political metanarrative of a postconflict state and its international arbiters, of universalisms made possible, yet simultaneously contradicted, through the particular circumstances of a country in transition. Finally, this discussion reveals the irony of postwar reconstruction efforts in Bosnia, eager to produce a specific kind of society and citizenry, yet often frustrated in the task by incongruous politics and a foreshortened view of the region's past.

Srebrenica Massacre

The circumstances of the genocide at the UN safe area of Srebrenica in July 1995 are critical to understanding the technology eventually developed to identify its victims. Before the outbreak of war in the spring of 1992, Srebrenica had been a relatively homogenous and quiet community, a resort town whose residents worked in nearby mines and factories or as part of the tourist economy supporting its regionally renown health spa, the Banja Guber. Nestled in the mountains of eastern Bosnia, the city boasted a population of about 5,800, the majority of which were Bosniak.[5]

As Yugoslavia began to disintegrate and violence erupted in Bosnia, Srebrenica's landscape was radically transformed. It soon became an enclave housing 40,000–50,000 Bosniak refugees from the Bosnian Serb–controlled region of the Podrinje Valley, the land to the west of the Drina River, which serves as a natural border between Bosnia and Serbia. Life in wartime Srebrenica was marked by dire humanitarian conditions and isolation, frequent mortar attacks from the surrounding Serb forces, and at times testy relations with the UN peacekeeping forces (Honig and Both 1996; Mustafić 2003; Rohde 1997; Sudetic 1998).

On July 11, 1995, a day now infamous in postwar Bosnia, Bosnian Serb and Serbian forces overtook the enclave and expelled the refugee population, killing more than eight thousand Bosniak men and boys in the process. The majority of the victims were summarily executed and their remains dumped into mass graves. In the months that followed, Bosnian Serb forces returned to the site of those graves and, attempting to hide traces of the war crimes, dug up, transported, and reburied the bodies in secondary mass graves. The conditions of those gravesites, most of them filled with disarticulated and partial skeletal remains, became the impetus for developing the innovative DNA-based technology used to identify not only Srebrenica's missing but also victims from the armed conflicts in former Yugoslavia throughout the 1990s.

Law and Technology

Two primary instances of international intervention have dominated postwar Bosnia's reparation politics and efforts aimed at transitional justice: the proceedings at the ICTY, established by the UN Security Council in May 1993, and the identification process led by ICMP, the international organization founded by U.S. president Bill Clinton in June 1996 to resolve the cases of missing persons, reduce the anguish of their families, and lesson the tension between parties. From the onset, the two institutions and their respective work were closely interconnected, their paths intersecting frequently throughout the postwar period. In the context of Srebrenica, this meant regular collaboration on early attempts at uncovering and exhuming the mass graves scattered throughout the Podrinje region of eastern Bosnia.[6] In more recent years, as work in the graves became more compartmentalized, their respective efforts have followed different, though related, trajectories with ICMP dedicated to identifying individual missing persons in the pursuit of the surviving families' right to know and the ICTY documenting crimes and prosecuting indicted war criminals in the pursuit of international law.[7]

Nevertheless, their mandates share the common aim of document-ing the past in order to pave the way for a more stable future in postwar Bosnia. They operate on different levels: the tribunal compiles evidence to establish "what really happened," apportioning blame and holding indi-viduals responsible for wartime actions; ICMP documents the fate of indi-vidual victims, reattaching names to unrecognizable remains and, when possible, filling in the details of the missing person's final moments of life and death. Occasionally, the documentary proof of DNA-based identifica-tion is used to support ICTY's work. ICMP staff members have been called upon to provide expert testimony before the tribunal, and, in some cases, this has entailed testimony regarding the exhumation and identification of Srebrenica victims. An extension of the pursuit of families' right to know, such testimony fits within the related discourse of the right to justice. The scientific authority of geneticists and forensic anthropologists is levied by both prosecutors and defense council to strengthen, or alternately refute, claims of criminal activity.

With the two interventionist projects linked through overlapping agen-das and regular collaboration during the postwar period, the often politi-cally charged atmosphere surrounding the results of their work has at times undermined their respective public role as arbiters of truth and justice. National political and religious leaders, activists, as well as representatives of the media and the international community have at times used these vehicles for postwar repair to advance their own more short-term and politi-cally expedient aims. This is especially true regarding events leading up to and after the tenth anniversary of the Srebrenica genocide. Things came to a head in June 2005, with the explosive revelation of what soon became dubbed the "Scorpions tape." Having surfaced as part of the prosecution's evidence at the ICTY trial of former Serbian president Slobodan Milošević, the videotape contained footage that documented a Serbian special police unit (the Scorpions or *Škorpioni*) as its members transported, abused, and finally executed six young civilian prisoners from the Srebrenica enclave. It appeared in public one month before the tenth anniversary, reviving anguishing memories for surviving family members and stirring up the pot of public debate yet again about Serbia's involvement in the massacre. Although the lead prosecutor in the case, Geoffrey Nice, explained that the timing (i.e., in the run-up to the July 11 commemoration) was merely coinci-dental, the impact on the Bosnian public was nevertheless enormous.

The following year, the annual commemoration and mass burial of identified victims at the Srebrenica-Potočari Memorial Center became an important backdrop to two other Srebrenica-related proceedings at The Hague: first, the judgment rendered for the Bosniak defendant, Naser Orić, the wartime commander of the Bosniak defense forces in Srebrenica; and, second, the chief prosecutor's opening remarks at the much-awaited collective trial of seven Bosnian Serbs. On June 30, 2006, the tribunal found Orić—a polemical figure among both Bosnian Serbs and Bosniaks—guilty of failing to prevent the murders and cruel treatment of Serb detainees in the enclave's prison in late 1992 and early 1993, but acquitted him on several other counts. The judges sentenced him to two years in prison, a relatively light punishment in view of the prosecutors' recommended eighteen years of incarceration. Having already spent three years in custody in The Hague, Orić was thus free to walk and ten days later free to attend the July 11 commemoration at Potočari—although, in the end, he chose not to in order to avoid "unwanted consequences."

Orić's acquittal on the majority of charges and subsequent release prompted a range of responses back in Bosnia. His supporters openly celebrated in the Federation city of Tuzla. A prominent reporter for the pro-Bosniak newspaper *Dnevni avaz*, Almasa Hadžić, remarked, "I am particularly pleased that he was acquitted of the charges of wanton destruction of Serb property in the villages around Srebrenica because Serbs have often quoted that as the main reason for the subsequent massacre of 8,000 Bosnian Muslims in this town in July 1995. . . . Now they've lost that argument" (Sadović 2006). Few, if any, Bosnian Serbs shared the same satisfaction. "'This is outrageous,' said Igor Gajić, editor-in-chief of the Banja Luka–based magazine *Reporter*. 'You get more than that for a car crash with no human casualties. This will only add to the feeling of distrust Serbs already have for the tribunal'" (Sadović 2006).[8] Rather than providing common ground for a "communicative history," where both Bosniaks and Bosnian Serbs move closer to a "mutual agreement" about the events in question (Torpey 2003, 6), Orić's release, like the Scorpions tape, appeared to heighten tensions already exacerbated by the commemorative ceremony about to take place at Potočari, including the public interment of mortal remains recently identified through the DNA testing procedures.

The controversy stirred by the Orić decision set the tone for the next major Srebrenica-related proceeding at the tribunal one month later. Again, the work of identification and commemoration served as a politically charged backdrop for the pursuit of the right to justice. The event took place during the prosecutor's opening remarks at the first day of the much-anticipated trial of seven Bosnian Serbs indicted for crimes relating to the Srebrenica genocide. In her statement, chief prosecutor Carla Del Ponte referred to her visit to the Srebrenica-Potočari Memorial Center that very week for the eleventh anniversary commemoration and mass burial held on July 11, 2006. Defense lawyers interrupted her, objecting to the "emotive" nature of her remarks. She responded, "No emotion, absolutely no emotion. Facts, my dear defense lawyers, facts" (Simons 2006). For her, the visit and her narration

of the 505 coffins being interred in the memorial center cemetery constituted a set of incontrovertible—not emotionally tainted—facts, which she
levied to strengthen her portrayal of the intensity, scale, and consequences
of the crimes committed at Srebrenica. Invoking the documentary proof of
identified remains returned to surviving families, Del Ponte implicitly fused
the aims of ICTY and ICMP as institutions of transitional justice and social
repair. Moreover, her remarks carried political weight, signaling her allegiance with the victims of Srebrenica, living and dead. It bears mentioning
that Del Ponte announced very publicly her decision the previous year of
not attending the tenth-anniversary commemoration at Potočari in order to
register her dissatisfaction with the fact that both Ratko Mladić and Radovan
Karadžić still remained at large.[9] The following year, her presence at—not
absence from—the memorial center became the political statement.[10]

Beyond illustrating the intersecting procedures and results of the two
international projects of postconflict intervention, these incidents inti-
mated, intentionally or not, that the international community was supporting one postwar narrative over another—namely, Bosniak claims of
victimhood and, by extension, Serb aggression. Part of this impression cor-
relates to the circumstances of the war: a disproportionately higher number
of Bosniaks were missing at the end of the war than Bosnian Serbs or Croats
(87.8 percent, 9.0 percent, and 2.8 percent respectively), and, within the
context of the 1992–1995 war, there is no Bosnian Serb equivalent to the Srebrenica massacre or to the phenomenon of the Srebrenica secondary mass
graves.[11] Indeed, the more frequent and high profile exhumations of Bosniak
graves and the significantly higher number of identifications of Bosniak
missing have tended to reinforce rather than assuage Bosnian Serb concerns
about parity across the identification efforts.

In turn, Bosnian Serb and Serbian political leaders have presented
their constituencies with a very different account of wartime events in the
Srebrenica enclave. Amid all the activities and media coverage of the tenth
anniversary of the genocide, the Bosnian Serb and Serbian public heard just
as much—if not more—news coverage about their victims than the events
of July 1995 (e.g., the 3,000 Bosnian Serb deaths in area of Srebrenica during the three-year war and the infamous "bloody Christmas" massacre of
January 1993, in which Naser Orić's forces were accused of having killed
forty-three Bosnian Serbs in the village of Kravica). Given these competing historical accounts of the region and its victims, the internationally
sponsored efforts to identify bodies and prosecute war criminals have often
polarized Bosnian Serb and Bosniak reactions. Moreover, from the timing of
the public release of the Scorpions tape to Del Ponte's opening statement
in the Bosnian Serb Seven trial, the implicit and explicit links between
the judicial and identification-commemoration processes undermined the

neutrality of these institutional attempts at reparation, at least among the Bosnian Serb public.

Identification as a Tool of Transitional Justice

During this same period of the run-up to the July 11, 2006, commemoration, the International Commission on Missing Persons was engaged in its own public relations activities highlighting its achievements within the framework of transitional justice. In late June, it held a tenth-anniversary celebration in Washington, D.C., where its commissioners gathered to mark the organization's accomplishments of the past decade. The chairman of ICMP and founder of AOL, James Kimsey, addressed the attendees:

> ICMP's work embodies the efforts of society to address the issue of persons missing as a consequence of conflicts and crimes against humanity, for the sake of truth and justice. Society has understood that mass graves are like political minefields, whether they exist in the Former Yugoslavia, South America, Iraq, or South East Asia. For post conflict societies the ability to move forward depends on overcoming the fears of the past. . . . During our first ten years, we have resolved the fate of more than ten thousand missing persons, helping to bring a sense of closure for their families. (ICMP 2006)

Kimsey's language references transitional justice concepts with phrases such as "truth and justice," "moving forward," and "overcoming fears of the past." At the same time, he also employs a term of healing, of closure, that likely resonated more with an audience in Washington, D.C., than with the experiences of families of the missing in former Yugoslavia. Identification and the knowledge it imparts—in all its gritty and harrowing specificity—often opens, rather than closes off, a whole range of new and disturbing facts, images, and emotions for surviving families (Wagner 2008). "Closure" hints at a level of social repair that eludes many of these relatives, even as they gain the knowledge of their loved one's fate and gravesite to tend.

Beyond these phrases of justice and repair, the most striking word used by Kimsey in this address is "society": "Society has understood that mass graves are like political minefields." He speaks of a collective that understands violence, addresses its consequences, and moves forward; yet this abstract "society" bears little resemblance to the divided communities of the very place that prompted the development of ICMP's cutting-edge technology. Indeed, it is hard to reconcile a notion of a unified society with postwar Bosnia, where many Bosnian Serbs, Bosnian Croats, and Bosniaks stake claims to their own territorial integrity, discrete languages with differing scripts, separate media outlets, and so on. Instead, as the work of identifying

Srebrenica's missing reveals, the ideals of truth and justice exist—are championed, pursued, thwarted, rejected—not in the abstract, but through the very concrete and complex circumstances of postconflict societies.

Bureaucracies of Transitional Justice

Though disparate, the events described above share an aspect (aside from timing) characteristic of many of the postwar attempts to address Bosnia's recent and bloody past: they are the fruits of interventionist tools designed to shape Bosnia and Herzegovina according to the mold of a functional democratic state in this internationally sponsored process of nation-building. One is a legal device, the other a scientific instrument. As such, both—law and technology—are human mechanisms of governmentality, mechanisms by which those Western liberal ideals of freedom and equality underwriting projects such as postconflict nation-building are thought to be defined, protected, and advanced. Furthermore, as products of law and science, they are the kinds of artifices employed by governments and international organizations to distinguish "developed" from "developing," "civilized" from "barbarous." As Alex Hinton points out in his introduction to this volume, there is an implicit hierarchy and teleology in the notion that the tools of liberalism can be applied to fashion modern, "civilized," liberal, democratic states from their "backward" or "failed" existence.

In this light, the instruments of transitional justice created for former Yugoslavia present yet another, perhaps more subtle, way to draw those same lines. In establishing the tribunal in The Hague, the UN Security Council sent the message to the warring factions within former Yugoslavia that while it would not bloody its own hands by stopping the killing, it would provide a means for cleaning up afterwards. Likewise, the creation of ICMP was Clinton's postwar humanitarian offering to the region, an institution dedicated to piecing together the disociated bodies and polities of former Yugoslavia.

Through these institutions aimed at repair and reconstruction, the international community was also embracing a discourse of human rights—the right to know and the right to justice—that sought to protect the citizens of postwar Bosnia from the failures of the wartime state. The pursuit of justice through the tribunal and through a DNA-based identification technology rests on a Durkheimian understanding of the individual as a "supremely sacred thing"—a social fact (Durkheim 1982). The legal framework that constitutes the jurisdiction of the ICTY is that of customary international law, specifically a body of law developed in response to the atrocities of World War II and the persecution of a *people*, Jews, not a *state*.[12] By becoming signatories of documents such as the Universal Declaration of Human Rights, states pledged to provide protection to all citizens, all human beings, regardless of where and under whose rule they lived. The DNA-based technology designed to identify bodies of the Srebrenica missing likewise reflects these ideals by which individual citizens, even posthumously, are protected through recovery, recognition, and reburial.

That these two mechanisms of transitional justice were led by international organizations—and in the case of the ICTY, an extraterritorial institution—comes as no surprise. In the immediate postwar period, the territorial successors of the former state of Yugoslavia lacked both the infrastructure and political cohesion to address the injustices of the recent conflicts and, in turn, protect the rights of all citizens in their respective societies. Furthermore, by prosecuting war criminals and identifying the missing, foreign governments with a stake in postwar Bosnia's future gained a say in how its wartime losses and damage were addressed, in some instances ensuring that their own inaction or, worse, complicity remained safely outside the realm of scrutiny or required redress. In this sense, the tribunal and ICMP are necessarily international rather than local or even regional entities, functioning as extensions of the international community rather than the postwar governments of former Yugoslavia. Both systems operate as bureaucracies of an internationally constituted central authority. Their budgets and staff bear this out: the ICTY receives its funding from the UN (arguably the world's largest bureaucracy, which is, in turn, funded by individual states), while ICMP's money comes almost entirely from foreign governments and foundations. The ICTY's staff is composed of judges, lawyers, investigators, and translators from all over the world. Though the body of ICMP's staff is over 90 percent local (from the region of former Yugoslavia), its administration is almost entirely international (led by American, Canadian, British, and German nationals).[13] Most agree this is a necessary structure: aside from questions of forensic (specifically forensic genetics) expertise, the prevailing logic—borne out by the example of the Missing Persons Institute discussed below—dictates that ICMP's role as a neutral party would be compromised by appointing Bosnian nationals to its positions of leadership. Thus, given their high-profile roles, these international staff members are often seen as the public face of the institution, at least to foreign donors; they frequently appear in the local and international media, at international conferences on forensic science, and at fund-raising events such as the tenth-anniversary celebration in Washington, D.C.

The bureaucracies of international intervention in postwar Bosnia arise from an absence of power, from the lack of a *unified* central authority, both during and after the war, and, perhaps most important, from the lack of trust the divided Bosnian public had in its own political leaders. For just as the Bosniaks in the Srebrenica enclave found themselves ceding authority and protection to the centralized power of the UN peacekeeping forces, in the aftermath of the genocide their recourse for justice lay primarily with the institutions fostered in that same climate of international intervention. For what Bosnian Serb official in the years immediately following the end of the war was disclosing the locations of mass graves and handing over the perpetrators of the Srebrenica massacre? And what Federation authority could force the Republika Srpska (RS) government to do so?

Here we approach the conundrum of the late twentieth and early twenty-first century version of Habermas's shaky balance between universalism and particularism. How can a universal human right—be it the freedom of movement or the right to know where one's missing family member is—be guaranteed in a place such as Srebrenica? Within the confines of our debate, the problem with universalisms is not the concepts articulated in them per se, but the fact that they are inextricably bound to the complex particularism of postwar social experience and political order. Often we think of rights being violated or conversely protected by state authorities, which are geographically and ideologically tied to nation-states. And, as noted above, it is state governments that sign on to human rights declarations and protocols, and state governments whose so-called national interests become reasons not to intervene in places like Rwanda, Bosnia and Herzegovina, and Darfur. Yet as the example of postwar Bosnia suggests, this binary of universal ideals and particular nation-states breaks down, and instead we see how concepts such as the right to know or the right to justice become vehicles for intervention that involve citizens, governments (municipal, cantonal, entity-level, etc.), nongovernmental organizations, and international institutions. Social reconstruction and reparation politics eschew the abstract, causing frictions of engagement along the way—the messy effects of intersecting interests and experience.

A Local Successor

Perhaps the best way to grasp the incongruities of universalism and particularism at work in the identification process and subsequent commemorations is to look at one of ICMP's major transitional justice initiatives—the Missing Persons Institute (MPI). As with most internationally funded postconflict reconstruction projects, a long-term aim of ICMP's identification efforts was to develop local capacities to carry out the process. This meant more than just building and equipping mortuaries and DNA extraction and analysis facilities; it also entailed creating a local organ that could continue identifying Bosnia's missing persons long after the well of international funding had dried up and, indeed, when the Bosnian government would assume

full financial and political responsibility for the identification efforts for its
missing citizens. The idea was that ICMP would gradually transfer expertise
and resources to MPI. More to the point, ICMP, as the neutral international
organization, would fashion a local entity in its own image: established in
2000, MPI would be an apolitical organization, with representatives and staff
from all three ethnic groups. In fact, it was to become a successor organization not to ICMP itself, but rather to the entity agencies, the Federation
Commission on Tracing Missing Persons (the body responsible for missing
Bosniaks and Bosnian Croats) and the RS Office on Detained and Missing
Persons (responsible for missing Bosnian Serbs)—the ideal transitional justice output. The entity agencies would be collapsed into MPI with the goal of
eliminating separate political agendas and engendering cooperation between
the two. To ensure this, MPI's creators followed the model of the Dayton
Accords, drafting into its mandate a board of directors, with the feature of a
rotating director general and a collegium of subordinate directors overseeing
reconnaissance and exhumations, administration and records, and examinations and identifications.[14] The configuration promised an impartiality born
from equal representation at the organization's administrative helm. Thus,
the head of the Federation Commission, a political appointee of the leading
Bosniak nationalist party, SDA (Stranka demokratske akcije) and outspoken
critic of the RS government, Amor Mašović, along with his Bosnian Croat
colleague, Marko Jurišić, was soon to share power with his Bosnian Serb
counterpart, Milan Bogdanić.[15] By uniting the entity agencies under one roof
and granting MPI central authority over the various aspects of recovery and
identification, the newly minted bureaucracy would simultaneously stream-
line and render more transparent the overall process.[16]

Beyond simply trying to foster a new sense of cooperation and political
cohesion within the ranks of this successor organization, ICMP and the Bosnian governmental officials supporting MPI intended to transform the way
Bosnian citizens approached the topic of missing persons. Their object was
to move Bosnians beyond the confines of their respective ethnic identity—
and thereby the constraints of their ethnonational political affiliations—by
embracing the discourse of the right to know. There are two ideas under-
girding this aim: people from all three ethnic groups share the experience of
missing a family member, and the path toward a democratic Bosnia entails
a national identity that overrides ethnic difference. At the signing of the
"Agreement on Assuming the Role of Co-founders of the Missing Persons
Institute of Bosnia and Herzegovina" on August 30, 2005, these notions were
echoed by ICMP's chief of staff, Kathryne Bomberger:

> The implementation of the Missing Persons Institute marks a mile-
> stone in the history of both BiH [Bosnia and Herzegovina] and the

International Commission on Missing Persons. By creating a sustainable, state-level structure, BiH has taken an important step forward in addressing the issue of the missing regardless of the ethnic, religious or national origin of the person being searched for. This is no small feat. (ICMP 2005)

They were also invoked by Bosnia and Herzegovina's minister for human rights and refugees, Mirsad Kebo:

The establishment of the Institute implies a scientific approach to this subject. It also implies transparency, accuracy, and unconditional determination towards the truth.

The Institute will search for missing persons regardless of their religious or ethnic background and any form of discrimination. By establishing this Institute we search for institutional solutions and define the work of the Institute as an institution on the level of Bosnia and Herzegovina. . . .

We emphasize the importance of the state institutions, which should lead the process of searching for the missing persons, as well as all the other processes pertinent to the citizens of Bosnia and Herzegovina. (ICMP 2005)

The underlying message is clear: to function as a democratic state and, more concretely, to shore up candidacy for accession to the European Union, Bosnia and Herzegovina would have to stop classifying its citizens (including its missing citizens) according to ethnic differences and instead treat them all uniformly as Bosnians. Only then could it begin to act as a unified polity.

Such calls for systemic change in postwar Bosnia's political order and national consciousness have come in different forms and from different sources over the past fourteen years. Indeed, in many critics' view, Bosnia's European Union membership is closely tied to this transformation. For example, an article that ran in the *Economist* in June 2003 charged that "until [Bosnia] builds genuine cross-community government structures enabling its three groups—Serbs, Croats and Muslims—to co-operate without outsiders needing to hold the ring, it has no chance of joining the club in the foreseeable future" (*Economist* 2003, 52). After years of a more hands-off approach by the Bush administration, U.S. vice president Joe Biden reinvigorated the warning in an address before the Bosnian Parliamentary Assembly on May 19, 2009. Decrying a "sharp and dangerous rise in nationalist rhetoric," Biden exclaimed in one of several unscripted turns in the speech, "God, when will you tire of that rhetoric, stirring up anger and resentment . . . With all due respect, and forgive me for saying this in your parliament, but this must stop" (Bailey 2009). He continued:

Let me be clear: Your only real path to a secure and prosperous future is to join Europe as Bosnia and Herzegovina. Right now, you're off that path. To get back on track, you need to work together across ethnic and party lines so that your country functions like a country—and so that you interact with the rest of the world as a single, sovereign state. . . . You can follow this path to Europe. Or you can choose an alternative course. But you need to understand the consequences. At best, you'll remain among the poorest countries in Europe. At worst, you'll descend into ethnic chaos that defined your country for the better part of a decade. And you will be judged harshly by history and your children. The choice is yours. If you make the right choice, we will stand with you. Making the right choice means that the leaders of this country must stop the pursuit of narrow ethnic and political interests instead of the national interest. (Biden 2009)

As if anticipating this very task and call for change, four years earlier, with the founding of MPI, Kathryne Bomberger had followed her own official statement with a public comment: "That institution is necessary in order to stop the practice that ethnicity serves as the [main] criterion for the victims. Right now Bosniaks search for Bosniaks, Serbs for Serbs, and Croats for Croats, and the same activities are funded three times over. With the establishment of the institute there will be one list of the missing in Bosnia-Herzegovina without any kind of division, because a victim, before all else, is a victim" (Skuletić 2005).

Despite its earnest and optimistic call for change, the rhetoric surrounding the creation of the MPI belied the political tensions that plagued the project of forming a unified local successor agency from the onset. To begin with, its leadership quickly proved politically awkward if not problematic. Several months after its official cofounding with ICMP by the Bosnian presidency in June 2003, the institute's top administrator was appointed. Gordon Bacon became the transitional director general. An Irishman who prior to this appointment had worked as ICMP's chief of staff for three years, Bacon had been intimately involved in the controversial public debate about the events of the Srebrenica massacre, serving as a member of the RS Commission on Srebrenica (alongside people such as the SDA-affiliated academic Smail Čekić). This involvement placed him front and center in the media's coverage of the final report detailing the massacre and indirectly established him as an advocate of the Srebrenica community. Bacon's appointment, moreover, signaled that MPI was not yet ready for domestic leadership, or perhaps that the local leaders were not yet ready to relinquish their own more politically weighty positions as heads of their respective commissions. Indeed, it took a full five years for this "local" institution to be run by locals. In late 2005, with the Bosnian government's full support, Mašović, Jurišić, and Bogdanić become the rotating directors of MPI's collegium.

One of MPI's selling points to the Bosnian public was the fact that a local institution with an independent budget and staffed by representatives from all three ethnic groups would eliminate some of the barriers that had stood between the entity agencies in the past—everything from reconnaissance activities to the transfer and custody of remains. For example, the logic went that by collapsing the entity commissions into one organization, there would be increased access not only to information regarding gravesites but also to their physical locations. This would be especially important for the Srebrenica cases. At long last, Bosnian Serb officials would promote rather than obstruct or slow the investigation of the Srebrenica-related gravesites. Or would they?

Not everyone in Bosnia was as hopeful as MPI's founders about its capacity to foster change. Some staff members of the Podrinje Identification Project, ICMP's facility dedicated specifically to the Srebrenica genocide cases, had reservations. According to ICMP's long-term plans, the Podrinje Identification Project would eventually be enfolded into MPI, a disconcerting prospect for many of its employees. Some of their concerns thus stemmed from their own imminent job insecurity. If the Srebrenica-specific facility became part of MPI, there was no guarantee that they would be hired on by the local organ—despite their extensive experience in the field and good relations with the Srebrenica families.[17] As one person remarked dryly, their jobs would all soon be filled by Mašović's cousins. Furthermore, they also expressed concern about how such a task might be carried out within what they perceived to be an organization potentially more—not less—subject to ethnonationalist politics. Members of the vocal family association, the Women of Srebrenica, echoed this latter concern. The directors of the survivors' advocacy organization had protested the mere presence of Serbian forensic anthropologists at one of the Srebrenica mass graves. How would they respond to Bosnian Serbs potentially participating in the investigation and exhumation of gravesites related to the genocide?

The Srebrenica families were not alone in their skepticism. Indeed, the public debate about appointees to MPI's various boards played out in the media, with representatives of family associations and Bosnian nongovernmental organizations trading barbs over charges of political bias. For example, when Milijana Bojić, president of the Union of Missing and Imprisoned Persons of the Republika Srpska, was named to the advisory board, there was strong backlash from the Bosniak community. President of the Mothers of the Srebrenica and Žepa Enclaves and arguably the most vocal representative of the Srebrenica families, Munira Subašić railed: "She [Bojić] countless times through her actions and false statements insulted our murdered children. Bojić has no respect for the missing persons of other nationalities. With her hate language, she cannot represent all ethnic groups." Bojić, in turn, responded that "[The protests] came after I said that Amor Mašović (president of the Federation Commission for Missing Persons) who is a professional parliamentarian, could not be a member of the MPI's presidency" (Alić 2007).

MPI's slow start also stemmed from charges of obstructionism within its ranks. In June 2008, six months after the Bosnian government formally launched the institute, discord broke out among staff from the separate ethnic commissions now employed by MPI. Salaries had not been paid for five months, and when staff members did finally receive their back pay it was significantly reduced, prompting the Republika Srpska government to revive its own entity-specific commission (the Office on Detained and Missing Persons) and transfer 76,000 euro into its account. A reported nine Bosnian Serb members of MPI quit their jobs to rejoin the RS commission, "citing among their justifications that the MPI was looking only for missing Bosniaks" (Alić 2008). Roundly criticized by Bosnian Serbs, including members of MPI who remained in their jobs, as well as Bosniaks, the temporary mutiny nevertheless undermined MPI's credibility in the eyes of the Bosnian public. One year later, a signal that MPI may have overcome its most challenging period, the chairmanship of the Expert Group on Exhumations and Missing Persons was at long last transferred from ICMP to MPI, thereby placing the leadership of the entire country's efforts at recovering the missing into the hands of a national (rather than international or entity-specific) agency.

MPI thus came to embody the problems inherent in the international community's attempts to develop a kind of collective conscience regarding a perceived universal—the experience of and response to missing persons—without fully appreciating the ethnonationalist political history of the region. Its supporters fell victim to the "foreshortened time horizon" of transitional justice, which views history as starting the day before yesterday (Torpey 2003, 8), by assuming that inter-entity cooperation and an independent budget would enable the discourse of ethnicity-blind rights to take root in the Bosnian public's mind. In urging Bosnian Croats, Bosnian Serbs, and Bosniaks to search for *Bosnians*, MPI's advocates presupposed not only a collective identity that could rise above the recent ethnonational divisions but also a centralized bureaucratic institution that could help foster this identity.

Missing from this optimistic framing of MPI's potentially transformative role was the acknowledgment of the constant spotlight thrown on ethnicity and ethnonational politics by the very acts of identifying and commemorating the victims of violent conflict (Verdery 1999). For although its mechanisms are intended to be apolitical, the work of exhuming and identifying the missing takes place within a highly charged field of competing nationalisms—be they Bosniak, Bosnian Serb, or Bosnian Croat. The often oppositional public rhetoric of the various nationalist leaders influence the way people respond to bodies recovered and commemorated. Leading up to, during, and after the war, nationalist claims of victimhood frequently have drawn from previous historical injustices—whether from World War II, such as the prisoner camp of Jasenovac and Serb reprisal killings, or as far back as 1389 and the battle of Kosovo Polje. Despite international inter-ventionist attempts to bound projects of transitional justice and reparation politics temporally (i.e., limited to the conflicts of the 1990s), exclusionary ethnonational rhetoric within the region of former Yugoslavia often refer-ences more distant past events in attempting to interpret the results of those very projects. Thus, evident in the example of the July 11 ceremonies at the Srebrenica-Potočari Memorial Center and subsequent Bosnian Serb reactions, communal divisions have not dissipated as the graves in the center's cemetery are filled with the remains of identified bodies (Duijzings 2007; Wagner 2008). Instead, as the Srebrenica controversy illustrates, the identification-commemoration process gives rise to *new* forms of ethnona-tionalism on the part of both Bosniaks and Bosnian Serbs. Similar to the "unintended consequences" of transitional justice initiatives in East Timor that Beth Drexler analyzes in her chapter, the results of the identification process—namely, nationalist political leaders' manipulation of the recovery and reburial of missing persons—have reinforced ethnonationalist dis-courses in which graves memorializing one ethnic group in turn document the criminality of the opposing ethnic group.

International Allegiances

Through its financial and political support of the DNA-based identification technology and the memorial center at Potočari, the international com-munity has used its position as a temporary central authority in the politi-cal quagmire of postwar Bosnia to shepherd Bosnia and Herzegovina, the nation-state, and its citizenry along the path toward democracy. Returning bodies to families and ensuring sanctified, witnessed burials constitute a significant aspect of the larger aim of postwar social reconstruction. Yet just as there are ethnonationalist politics shaping and interpreting the "facts" of bodies recovered and reburied at Potočari, members of the international community have their own politically compelling reasons for supporting the identification of missing persons and the commemorations held at the memorial center. Their financial and political backing of both projects also seeks to re-right certain historical injustices of the war for which they, as UN Security Council and NATO member states, hold some responsibility—from creating the safe area to refusing pleas for air strikes and ignoring satellite imagery. In comparison to the other major instrument of transitional justice, the ICTY, the identification of missing persons presents a much more benign and overtly humanitarian avenue for such reckoning. Indeed, the ICTY purposefully circumvents the question of UN culpability, claiming it does not fall within the court's jurisdiction. In a letter written in response to representatives of the Women of Srebrenica regarding this very question, ICTY's chief prosecutor, Carla Del Ponte states:

> After carefully [*sic*] review and investigation of this complex case, I must inform you that I believe that the acts and conduct of, specifically, members of UNPROFOR [United Nations Protection Force] in and around the fall of Srebrenica in 1995 do not amount to a prosecutable violation of crime under the jurisdiction of the ICTY.
>
> I truly regret this stage of affairs, but this is the reality and I must plan and process accordingly. (Del Ponte 2004)

Once assured this protection, countries such as the United States and the Netherlands are left with more palatable methods for redressing their failure to protect the refugees from the Srebrenica enclave. Indeed, the very phrase "international community" loses cohesion upon scrutiny here—the nation-states that constitute what Bosnians call the *međunarodna zajednica* have cultivated different and at times opposing foreign policies for wartime and postwar Bosnia and Herzegovina. Far from disinterested arbiters, certain governments have taken more interest than others in efforts to identify and commemorate Srebrenica's victims. The United States has become ICMP's largest donor; the Netherlands earmarks its donations for the Srebrenica cases and the work conducted by the Podrinje Identification Project. These same governments reinforce their financial support of ICMP's work by sending diplomatic representatives to the July 11 ceremonies. Indeed, their presence among the inner circle of VIP attendees at Potočari on these occasions signals their alliances within the controversy of the Srebrenica massacre (Duijzings 2007, 165). The success of the identification process, driven in large part because of DNA testing, makes it possible for these representatives of the international community to stand shoulder-to-shoulder with the Bosniak community. By aligning themselves with the victims, they draw a strict line between their own responsibility through inaction and that of Bosnian Serbs and Serbians through aggression. Thus, a pattern arises: the Western diplomatic corps attend the state funeral of Bosnian Muslim president Alija Izetbegović and absent themselves from the non–state sponsored funeral of Slobodan Milošević; they attend the July 11 ceremony and mass burial at the Srebrenica-Potočari Memorial Center and ignore the Bosnian Serb commemoration the next day at Kravica. The symmetry is not lost on the Bosnian Serb and Serbian public. As a Serbian daily newspaper article noted after the tenth-anniversary commemoration, "The day before yesterday [July 11, 2005] the whole world was with the Bosniaks, yesterday the Serbs were alone" (Saponjić 2005). The remark hits on the very problem with the transitional justice paradigm's truncated view of history (as beginning the "day before yesterday")—that is, the sense that Bosnia's history began in 1992, at the outbreak of the war, and only certain atrocities merit international attention and commemoration.

General Principles, Particular Cases

A Bosnian Serb in Srebrenica once told me that no one, except for perhaps the killers themselves, would begrudge a mother her right to know where her missing son's bones lie and to give those bones a proper burial. He was talking about a basic human impulse, one that he felt most Bosnians acknowledge whether they are Bosnian Serb, Bosnian Muslim, or Bosnian Croat. He was willing to admit that stripped of all other meanings, the need to have the mortal remains of missing persons returned to their surviving families was something most people understood and respected, regardless of whom they considered to be the war's victims or heroes. In that same conversation he and his wife spoke to me for the first time frankly about how they as Bosnian Serbs saw the unfolding of the war and the postwar period of reconstruction. Conversations such as these were few and far between during my fieldwork in Srebrenica, which took place when the memorial center was just beginning to be filled (2003–2004), because my research was so obviously oriented toward the victims of the genocide. But what I took away from them was invaluable: a glimpse of an entirely different reading of what had happened during the war and the reasons those things happened. Such discussions helped me set aside the events of July 1995 for a moment and, doing my best to suspend judgment, see the anguish of a sister who lost her younger brother to the war, the trying circumstances of a family displaced and living in poverty, and a young woman struggling valiantly to gain the trust of her Bosniak neighbors and fellow-citizens of Srebrenica.

The perspectives of my Bosnian Serb friends, again who were few in number in Srebrenica, added nuance and depth to the picture I was forming of the identification process. Hearing my friend acknowledge that mothers deserve to know their sons' fate and yet insist that Bosnian Serbs had no choice but to go to war crystallized for me the frictions between abstract ideals and particular experiences that shape the lives of Srebrenica's postwar residents. For in his own words, he was articulating what he held to be a tenet of human nature that nevertheless could not help but become distorted by the reality that defined his world. Distinct and in many respects incompatible with the realities of the surviving families of the Srebrenica genocide or chief prosecutor at ICTY, it nevertheless threw into relief the tension between the universal and the particular of postwar Bosnia.

The theologian John Calvin once wrote, "In reply to the general question, every man will affirm that murder is evil. But he who is plotting the death of an enemy contemplates murder as something good. . . . Herein is man's ignorance: when he comes to a particular case, he forgets the general principle that he has just laid down" (McNeil 1960, 282). In the case of Bosnia, its postwar citizens are being asked to apply the general principle but at the same time forget—or at least "move beyond"—the particular case of their recent past experiences and, for some, their present circumstances. And an international community struggles to promote the ideals of human rights and transitional justice without taking into full account the particularisms of Bosnia and Herzegovina, whose past beyond the day before yesterday involves the same competing political forces of expanding nation-state ambition, power, and terrain that have characterized the past two centuries of the community of "civilized" and developed states. In addition to what it reveals about the more intimate experiences of returning mortal remains to surviving families, the identification technology also teaches us about the problematic and often inconsistent goals that underwrite efforts to rebuild and rehabilitate a postwar society. For the mechanisms of reparation politics and transitional justice being developed and promoted in Bosnia are human artifices and, as such, are constantly subject to political re-presentation and interpretation. The DNA-based identification technology illustrates that the general principle, the ideals behind the right to know and the right to justice, inevitably exists within a particular case whose circumstances and actors tend to complicate rather than elucidate that very same principle.

NOTES

1. As Alex Hinton writes in his introduction to this volume, the concept of transitional justice is relatively new, shaped by post–World War II attempts at legal redress and the burgeoning field of international humanitarian law, as well as by the shifting political landscapes of Latin America and Africa in the 1980s. For a comprehensive history of the transitional justice field, see Ruti Teitel (2000, 2003), as well as the edited volumes by Neil Kritz (1995).

2. In her analysis of postconflict Sierra Leone, Rosalind Shaw analyzes truth commissions as a "standard part of conflict resolution 'first aid kits'" (2005, 1–3).

3. As in other postconflict societies, the term "reparation" in Bosnia has been closely tied to debates concerning responsibility for material and human loss, and identification technology has played an important role in those discussions. Numbers of bodies recovered and identified provide concrete evidence of atrocities; the science of DNA analysis promises to separate fact from fiction, truth from propaganda, thereby ensuring that future monetary awards neither inflate nor deflate calculations of human loss suffered by one state at the hands of another.

4. See Mark Duffield's work on the term "social reconstruction" at the intersection of development and security issues (2001, 2002).

5. The prewar ethnonational composition of the city mirrored that of the larger municipality. According to the 1991 census, of the approximately 36,666 residents of the municipality, which stretched over 527 square kilometers, 75.20 percent were Bosniaks, while 22.68 percent were Bosnian Serbs (UNDP 2004).

6. During the initial stages of the identification efforts, ICMP's mandate was carried out by the Boston-based organization Physicians for Human Rights, whose personnel worked closely with ICTY investigators and forensic specialists in the exhumation of the Srebrenica graves.

7. In addition to the international organizations tasked with investigating war crimes and identifying individual sets of remains, the two Bosnian entities (the Federation and the RS) had their own missing persons institutions: The Federation Commission for Missing Persons (Federalna komisija za traženje nestalih) and the RS Office for Tracing Detained and Missing Persons (Канцеларија за тражење несталих и заробљених лица Републике Српске).

8. For an in-depth analysis of responses to the ICTY in Bosnia and Herzegovina, see Lara Nettelfield's *Courting Democracy* (Cambridge, UK: Cambridge University Press, forthcoming).

9. Karadžić was captured in July 2008 and sent to the Netherlands to stand trial at The Hague. Following the model of the Serbian president Slobodan Milošević, Karadžić opted to represent himself and based his defense on the claim that he had been guaranteed immunity from prosecution at The Hague by U.S. diplomat and chief negotiator of the Dayton Peace Agreement, Richard Holbrooke.

10. Controversy again swirled around her decision to attend the annual commemoration ceremony the following year in 2007. This time, it was representatives of the surviving families who decried her presence, angry that she had not done more to capture General Mladić (Nettelfield, forthcoming).

11. These figures (the percentage of deaths by ethnicity) were presented by the Federation government in a resolution about the Fund for Support for Families of the Missing, passed during its forty-third session on January 23, 2008 (Vlada Federacije Bosne i Herzegovine 2008).

12. The offenses that fall within ICTY jurisdiction are outlawed in the Geneva Conventions of 1949, the Genocide Convention of 1948, the Nuremburg Charter of 1945, and the Hague Convention (IV) of 1907.

13. An exception to this pattern, Bosnian Adnan Rizvić has served as deputy director of the forensic sciences division since 2004.

14. According to the Agreement on Assuming the Role of Co-Founders of the Missing Persons Institute of Bosnia and Herzegovina, MPI is governed, managed, and supervised by three main boards: a steering board, a board of directors, and the supervisory board. Tellingly, the chairpersons of the three boards may not belong to the same "constituent people in Bosnia and Herzegovina" (i.e., cannot be of the same ethnic group). Finally, there is also an advisory board made up of six representatives of family associations from throughout the country.

15. During the initial two-year mandate, the position of the collegium director was to rotate every eight months among the three men (Mašović, Jurišić, and Milan

Bogdanić), after which the members of the collegium would elect a director through a public vote.

16. These aspects included investigating and exhuming gravesites, maintaining custody over all remains of the missing, registering all missing persons, and notifying families of identifications.

17. The Agreement on Assuming the Role of Co-founders of the Missing Persons Institute of Bosnia and Herzegovina stipulates that "the initial staff of the Institute will be taken over from the staff employed in the Federation Commission on Tracing Missing Persons and the Republika Srpska Office on Detained and Missing Persons"; no mention is made of ICMP staff, including those working with the Podrinje Identification Project.

REFERENCES

Alić, Anes. 2007. "Missing Persons Politics." *ISN Security Watch*, March 14. http://www.isn.ethz.ch/isn/Current-Affairs/Security-Watch/Detail/?id=52846&lng=en.

———. 2008. "Missing Persons, Ever-Present Divide." *ISN Security Watch*, June 26. http://www.isn.ethz.ch/isn/Current-Affairs/Security-Watch/Detail/?id=88510&lng=en.

Bailey, Holly. 2009. "Biden to Bosnia: Shape Up or Else." *Newsweek*, May 19. http://blog.newsweek.com/blogs/thegaggle/archive/2009/05/19/biden-to-bosnia-shape-up-or-else.aspx.

Biden, Joseph. 2009. "Vice President Joe Biden Address to the Parliament of Bosnia and Herzegovina." Office of the Vice President, May 19. http://www.whitehouse.gov/the_press_office/Prepared-Remarks-Vice-President-Joe-Biden-Addresses-Parliament-of-Bosnia-and-Herzegovina/.

Del Ponte, Carla. 2004. Letter to Ms. Hajra Ćatić. Office of the Prosecutor, International Criminal Tribunal for the former Yugoslavia, The Hague, July 27.

Duffield, Mark. 2001. *Global Governance and the New Wars: The Merging of Development and Security*. London: Zed Books.

———. 2002. "Social Reconstruction and the Radicalization of Development: Aid as a Relation of Global Liberal Governance." *Development and Change* 33 (5):1049–1071.

Duijzings, Ger. 2007. "Commemorating Srebrenica: Histories of Violence and the Politics of Memory in Eastern Bosnia." In *The New Bosnian Mosaic: Identities, Memories and Moral Claims in Post-War Society*, ed. Xavier Bougarel, Elissa Helms, and Ger Duijzings 45–52. Hampshire, UK: Ashgate.

Durkheim, Emile. 1982. "What Is a Social Fact?" In *The Rules of the Sociological Method*, ed. Steven Lukes and trans. W. D. Halls, 50–59. New York: Free Press.

Economist. 2003. "The Regatta Sets Sail: The Balkans and the European Union." 367 (8330): 52–53.

Fletcher, Laura E., and Harvey M. Weinstein. 2002. "Violence and Social Repair: Rethinking the Contribution of Justice to Reconciliation." *Human Rights Quarterly* 24:573–639.

Hayner, Priscilla B. 2001. *Unspeakable Truths: Confronting State Terror and Atrocity*. New York: Routledge.

Honig, Jan Willem, and Norbert Both. 1996. *Srebrenica: Record of a War Crime*. London: Penguin Books.

International Commission on Missing Persons (ICMP). 2005. "Missing Persons Institute Launched on International Day of the Disappeared—State-level Institute Will Search for All Missing Regardless of Ethnic Origin." http://www.ic-mp.org/home.php?act=news&n_id=117&.

————. 2006. "Press Release: Contributing to Truth. Justice and Reconciliation in Post-conflict Societies." June 29

Joyce, Christopher, and Eric Stover. 1991. *Witnesses from the Grave: The Stories Bones Tell.* Boston: Little, Brown.

Kritz, Neil. 1995. *Transitional Justice: How Emerging Democracies Reckon with Former Regimes, Volume I. General Considerations.* Washington, DC: United States Institute of Peace Press.

McNeill, John T., ed. 1960. *Calvin: Institute of the Christian Religion.* Vol. I, trans. Ford Lewis Battles. Louisville, KY: Westminster John Knox Press.

Mustafić, Mirsad. 2003. *Sjećanje na Srebrenicu.* Tuzla: JU NUB "Derviš Sušić."

Nettelfield, Lara. 2010. *Courting Democracy in a Post-Conflict State: The Hague Tribunal's Impact in Bosnia and Herzegovina.* Cambridge, UK: Cambridge University Press.

Olick, Jeffrey K., and Brenda Coughlin. 2003. "The Politics of Regret: Analytical Frame." In *Politics and the Past,* ed. John Torpey. Lanham: Roan & Littlefield.

Pouligny, Beatrice. 2005. "Civil Society and Post-Conflict Peacebuilding: Ambiguities of International Programmes Aimed at Building 'New' Societies." *Security Dialogue* 36 (4): 495–510.

Rohde, David. 1997. *Endgame: The Betrayal and Fall of Srebrenica, Europe's Worst Massacre since World War II.* New York: Farrar, Straus and Giroux.

Sadović, Merdijana. 2006. "Orić Released Following Conviction." Tribunal Update No. 459, June 30. Institute for War and Peace Reporting.

Salimović, Sadik. 2002. *Knjiga o Srebrenici.* Srebrenica: Skupština opštine Srebrenica.

Sanford, Victoria. 2003. *Buried Secrets: Truth and Human Rights in Guatemala.* New York: Palgrave Macmillan.

Shaw, Rosalind. 2005. "Rethinking Truth and Reconciliation Commissions: Lessons from Sierra Leone." *United States Institute of Peace Special Report* 130 (February). http://www.usip.org/pubs/specialreports/sr130.html.

Simons, Marlise. 2006. "Trial over Massacre at Srebrenica Begins." *New York Times,* July 14. http://www.nytimes.com/2006/07/14/world/europe/14iht-hague.2204844.html.

Skuletić, S. 2005. "Mogućnost greške pri identifikaciji je 0,05 posto." *Dnevni avaz,* June 18.

Stover, Eric, and Harvey M. Weinstein. 2004. *My Neighbor, My Enemy: Justice and Community in the Aftermath of Mass Atrocity.* Cambridge: Cambridge University Press.

Sudetic, Chuck. 1998. *Blood and Vengeance: One Family's Story of the War in Bosnia.* New York: Penguin Books.

Šaponjić, Z. 2005. "Srbi sami ožalili svoje." *Glas javnosti,* July 13.

Teitel, Ruti. 2000. *Transitional Justice.* New York: Oxford University Press.

————. 2003. "Transitional Justice Genealogy." *Harvard Human Rights Journal* 16:69–94.

————. 2006. "Transitional Justice: Postwar Legacies." *Cardozo Law Review* 27 (4): 1615–1631.

Torpey, John, ed. 2003. *Politics and the Past: On Repairing Historical Injustices.* Lanham: Rowman & Littlefield.

Tsing, Anna. 2005. *Friction: An Ethnography of Global Connection.* Princeton: Princeton University Press.

United Nations Development Programme (UNDP). 2004. "Rights-Based Municipal Assessment and Planning Project, Municipality of Srebrenica, Republika Srpska, Bosnia and Herzegovina, October 2003–February 2004."

Verdery, Katherine. 1999. *The Political Lives of Dead Bodies.* New York: Columbia University Press.

Vlada Federacije Bosne i Herzegovine. 2008. "Saopćenje o radu" and "43 sjednica Vlade Federacije BiH." *Vlada Federacije Bosne i Hercegovine* (Sarajevo), January 23. http://www.fbihvlada.gov.ba/bosanski/sjednica.php?sjed_id=64&col=sjed_saopcenje.

Wagner, Sarah. 2008. *To Know Where He Lies: DNA Technology and the Search for Srebrenica's Missing.* Berkeley: University of California Press.

2

▶▶▶▶▶▶▶▶▶▶▶▶▶▶▶ ◀◀◀◀◀◀◀◀◀◀◀◀◀◀◀

The Failure of International Justice in East Timor and Indonesia

ELIZABETH F. DREXLER

The global rise in violence over the past two decades has been accompanied by a proliferation of transnational, postconflict, justice, and reconciliation institutions. Justice has become a very powerful normative discourse authorizing interventions, reconfiguring legal subjectivities within and between sovereignties. Institutions of transitional justice, trials and tribunals, no less than truth commissions attempt to develop narratives about past violence intended to settle accounts or fill in missing pieces. It is often assumed that these narratives, and their ability to demonstrate the truth, play a powerful role in legitimating future institutions and mending the social (du Toit 2000; Kritz 1995; Popkin and Roht-Arriaza 1995; Rotberg 2000; for critical reevaluation of this premise, see Roht-Arriaza and Mariezcurrena 2006). An underlying premise of all these strategies is that getting the narrative right contributes to working through the past, by punishing the right perpetrators and aligning social power with legal truths and/or by officially acknowledging victims' truths and realigning social relations. Too often, these issues have been cast in terms of politics and feasibility (Feher 1999) rather than informed by a nuanced understanding of the dynamics of these narratives as they are constructed by transitional institutions.

Analysts have pointed to the importance, as well as the difficulty, of determining what constitutes justice in various social and cultural contexts. Increasingly, international and nongovernmental organizations have supported studies of local forms of justice in the hope of integrating internationally supported institutions with local norms and practices, or in a search for alternative mechanisms to addresses injustices that cannot be attended to by the formal mechanisms. Many scholars have documented the failure of international institutions to attend to local specificities and to achieve their stated goals (Burnet, this volume; Hitchcock, this volume; Ross 2001, 2003;

49

Shaw 2007; Wilson 2001). Like other anthropologists who have pointed to the shortcomings of international institutions where they obscure, distort, or fail to take account of local context and specificities, I am concerned with situating international transitional processes on the ground. Rather than advocate for a more "local" form of justice, or ethnographically map the translation of global justice institutions and processes into local contexts, I explore the complex relationships among narratives, institutions, and legitimacy to examine how the very distinction between international and local justice may produce unintended consequences that ultimately foreclose possibilities for accountability and resolution of past violence. The danger of merely localizing transitional justice lies in ignoring the extent to which the formulation of the conflict by both local actors and international mediators is always embedded in global relations.[1] Transitional justice mechanisms that localize conflicts tend to horizontalize them—that is, to posit conflicts between different groups in society rather than between the state and its citizens. In these interventions, justice is seldom defined in terms of accountability; instead, it is a means to a goal of intergroup or national reconciliation. I suggest examining the imbrications of the global and local rather than cordoning off a zone of local justice as distinct from and opposed to global or international justice.[2]

It is critically important to understand and develop institutions that support the ability of individuals and communities to develop ways of resuming and building everyday lives in the aftermath of violence. Indeed, as Veena Das has argued, in these contexts the "ordinary" can be a remarkable achievement. Her notion of the ordinary does not rely on concepts of closure and reconciliation but rather explores how everyday life is practiced after large-scale violence involving whole communities (Das 2006). Many studies have shown that high-profile tribunals often do very little to ameliorate conditions on the ground (Stover 2007). The limitations of trials and the law are well documented (Roht-Arriaza 2006). I argue, the problem is not so much a gap between international and local conceptions of rights as it is a complex set of linkages that often do not work effectively or constructively. In the case of East Timor and Indonesia, internationalized trials have taken place locally, but the political settlement between the newly recognized nation and its neighboring state has allowed the masterminds to go free. Both this perceived injustice and the narrative of civil conflict that has been substituted for any examination of the Indonesian state's role in generating and fueling violence impede the rebuilding process. What is necessary is not closure but a process of justice that addresses all the dimensions and dynamics of the conflict. Along with the invisible links between justice and violence that Walter Benjamin and others (Agamben 1998; Benjamin 1921; Derrida 1992) have pointed out, we must recognize that justice is never absolute, not simply because it is always arbitrary but also because of its inherent limitations. Too often, our scrutiny of justice does not extend to examining the presuppositions of international actors and the consequences of the assumptions built into transnational or hybrid justice institutions.

In East Timor, multiple internationally funded institutions have addressed past violence but have been constrained from extending their reach into Indonesia despite the major roles played in Timor by various arms of the Indonesian military state. The Timor-Leste Commission for Reception, Truth, and Reconciliation (CAVR) was charged with seeking the truth about violence that occurred in Timor from 1974 to 1999. The CAVR also led Community Reconciliation Hearings (PRK) to foster the reintegration of low-level perpetrators into their communities. At the same time, two tribunals were charged with accounting for violence that occurred during East Timor's referendum for independence from Indonesia in 1999. The Indonesian government tried Indonesian perpetrators in an ad hoc tribunal in Jakarta, and the UN supported a hybrid international tribunal, incorporating international staff but based in Timor. Although these tribunals initially attracted international acclaim, most people I spoke with in Timor were extremely dissatisfied with the entire process and demanded a more powerful international tribunal to redress the injustices that these transitional institutions have perpetuated.[3] Despite its commissions of inquiry concluding that justice had not been served by the hybrid tribunals in Timor, the UN has not created an international tribunal. Subsequently, elites from Timor and Indonesia designed a Commission for Truth and Friendship to restore good relations between the two countries. This commission did not have any powers to prosecute; many argued it was designed simply to provide amnesty and close the case. The CTF report indicated the TNI bore some responsibility for violence in 1999; however, this statement was treated by both governments as the final word to close the case rather than a start for assigning criminal responsibility.

I focus on how these institutions produce narratives about past violence to highlight the problems associated with marking off a sphere of local justice as prior to and distinct from international justice. The multiple failures of justice institutions demonstrate that acts do not always have consequences and that institutional processes may have unintended consequences at odds with their norms and goals. The premise of international justice is to intervene and provide justice to victims where the state itself is incapable of doing so, often because state actors were the perpetrators or at least complicit in mass violence. Impunity in Timor and Indonesia demonstrates pervasive complicity and corruption: the discourse of justice itself is entangled in politics.

The violence that occurred in Timor in 2006 underlines the failure of these institutions to legitimate law and end the use of violence as a way of doing politics.[4] I argue that legal institutions have been corrupted by their failure to establish appropriate relationships between narrative meanings and social consequences. Conditions of pervasive social distrust are the legacies of Indonesia's military occupation and arbitrary governance in Timor. The internationalized courts have not established a legitimate force of law that operates without being ensnared in politics. At the same time that the "truth" of Timor's history—the patterns of how society was militarized and the extent of military operations—has been documented, major actors and local collaborators have escaped prosecution. That there has been no process of accountability for the widely acknowledged violence underlines the impunity of Indonesian forces. The international community, as the guarantor of justice institutions, has neither recognized its own "command responsibility" for knowing and failing to prevent Indonesia's military campaign nor acknowledged its own continued acquiescence to Indonesian impunity. Thus, the problem that remains appears one of local infighting, retribution for past betrayals, and unfinished civil war. Taking the position of neutral arbitrator, the international institutions again exempt their failures from view and address the legacies of Timor's past in such a way that they constantly strive for and advocate the universal principles of justice while failing to deliver in particular cases.

I examine the performative logics at work in the truth commission and tribunals—the ways in which transitional institutions enforce particular narratives so that they have social and political consequences and exclude other narratives so that pervasive patterns of violence are excluded from prosecutorial and social visibility. Such perverse and powerful logics are at work even when these institutions cannot enforce their narratives by rendering judgments. Many of the primary perpetrators were not on trial, and the limited jurisdiction of the tribunals meant that some narratives—especially regarding the central role of the Indonesian military—could not be articulated in the courtroom. Yet some narratives validated by the transitional institutions take on a power and life of their own, shaping the configuration of national and international politics. Moreover, the legally constructed narratives say one thing, yet another is known, and the gap between common knowledge and enforceable truth undermines the legitimacy of legal institutions, whether local or international. In both situations, the linkage between narrative meanings and social consequences is disrupted, and legal institutions become complicit or corrupted.

Historical and Institutional Contexts in East Timor

The Portuguese colonized East Timor for over four hundred years until the 1974 carnation revolution initiated an abrupt decolonization process. The formation of political parties led to coup, countercoup, and brief civil war (Carey 1995; Jardine 1999). In December 1975, in the midst of the global cold war, Indonesian President Soeharto launched a dramatic invasion and sustained occupation to annex the territory. In the first three years of the occupation, an estimated 200,000 Timorese pro-independence figures and ordinary civilians—approximately one-third of the population—were killed directly or indirectly as a result of the Indonesian invasion and occupation. Extensive military and intelligence operations continued throughout the twenty-four-year period of Indonesian occupation. Although Indonesia formalized its annexation of East Timor in July 1976, the United Nations never formally recognized Indonesian claims to sovereignty over East Timor (Anderson 1995; Robinson 2002; Taylor 1999).

For almost two decades, international advocates and Timorese in exile called attention to Indonesia's illegal occupation. Powerful countries did not act against their cold war ally. Soeharto's long authoritarian rule ended in 1998 in the midst of the Asian financial crisis and its aftermath; Indonesia was more susceptible to international pressure as it sought economic assistance.[5] In January 1999, without the support of the powerful Indonesian military (TNI), Soeharto's successor, President Habibie, announced there would be a referendum in East Timor to accept or reject the offer of special autonomy within Indonesia.

The Indonesian military and nationalist elites were outraged by Habibie's announcement. Violence in Timor escalated: incidents that evidenced the collaboration between the Indonesian military (TNI) and militia groups in creating terror and intimidation that threatened the referendum process were well documented. Nevertheless, in May, Portugal, Indonesia, and the UN agreed that Indonesian troops would be responsible for maintaining security during the balloting (Robinson 2002). Defying the campaign waged by the militias affiliated with the TNI, 98 percent of registered Timorese voted on August 30, 1999; 78 percent voted to reject the Indonesian autonomy proposal in favor of independence. Almost a week later, when the results were announced, members of the TNI and the pro-Indonesia militias intensified their killings, rapes, torture, destruction, and forced deportation of significant numbers of Timorese to Indonesian West Timor.[6] The situation remained violent until the International Force East Timor (INTERFET) restored security a month later. A UN Transitional Authority for East Timor (UNTAET) was established by UN Security Council resolution the following month, in October 1999, with the mandate to "exercise all legislative and executive authority, including the administration of justice."[7]

In January 2000, the UN Secretary General received reports from both the UN and the Indonesian investigations that documented the involvement of high-ranking Indonesian military in the 1999 violence.[8] Nevertheless, the

UN accepted Indonesian government promises that military perpetrators would be tried by the ad hoc human rights tribunal in the Indonesian capital, Jakarta. At the same time, UNTAET established both internationalized or hybrid tribunals and a truth commission in Timor. The Special Panels for Serious Crimes were created in Dili, the capital of East Timor, with the dual goals of holding accountable those who had committed war crimes, crimes against humanity, and genocide, or murder, sexual offenses, rape, and torture in 1999 and developing a functional and legitimate justice system for the new nation.[9] The Commission for Reception, Truth and Reconciliation (CAVR) was designed to facilitate the "resettlement of displaced persons, to seek the truth about past violence from 1974 through 1999, and to promote the reconciliation of divided communities."

The Civil War and Double Agents

All three institutions had the effect of increasing impunity for top-ranking Indonesian military leaders and promulgating civil war narratives about violence between Timorese.[10] The narrative produced by the Indonesian ad hoc tribunal attributes the 1999 violence to a civil conflict resulting from tensions within East Timorese society over the results of the referendum for independence. In this narrative, the TNI merely failed to prevent this violence from occurring. The court's limited temporal and geographic jurisdiction made it difficult for prosecutors and victims to demonstrate patterns of violence and collaboration between the TNI and the militia groups, or to examine the relationship of militia violence in 1999 to patterns developed by the TNI during the long period of occupation prior to the referendum.[11]

The special panels for Serious Crimes in Dili indicted high-ranking Indonesian military members for designing, financing, and coordinating the crimes against humanity implemented by militia groups.[12] Suspects were not extradited to Timor for trial; neither were Timorese militia leaders and government officials who chose to remain in Indonesia.[13] The absence of these figures not only compromised justice efforts but also limited the courts' ability to provide critical evidence and testimony about crimes. Neither the indictments nor the hearings captured the genealogy of militia groups in prior security operations. Systematic violence that occurred during the Indonesian occupation was disqualified from judicial examination, as was earlier violence between the Timorese parties. The narrative that emerged in the serious crimes trials portrayed individuals who were complicit in and aware of systematic plans to commit crimes against humanity. The trials reinforced the idea that the powerful were beyond the law, extending patterns in which the law was corrupt and arbitrary. The conviction of almost exclusively Timorese perpetrators reinforced the idea that the conflict was between Timorese.

The failure of both tribunals to hold the TNI accountable for its role in designing and orchestrating violence fueled demands for an international tribunal. Before he was elected Timor's president, Ramos-Horta stated that the new nation would not pursue an international tribunal and that the nation's energies were best spent burying the past and rebuilding a relationship with Indonesia. In addition to noting that Indonesia had changed since 1999, Ramos-Horta pointed to the fact that Timorese were victims not just of Indonesians but also of other Timorese.[14] Emphasis on the Timorese role in perpetrating violence coincides with the Indonesian narrative of a civil war. The "Commission for Truth and Friendship" established by Timorese and Indonesian authorities has formalized both states' desire to foreclose further judicial examination of violence in 1999.

The relationship of the CAVR to impunity differs. The focus on resettlement and reconciliation necessarily highlighted conflict between Timorese. At the same time, the final report provides copious evidence of crimes and makes strong demands for justice, which remain unrealized. The narratives that emerged from the public performances of the CAVR—especially the community reconciliation program (PRK) hearings that occurred in villages throughout Timor—also concerned violence between Timorese.[15] The narrative that emerged in the community reconciliation hearings I attended portrayed individuals being forced by circumstance to commit regrettable acts. Deponents often alleged that they were forced to commit offensive acts; otherwise, they might have been killed. Victims were especially dissatisfied during hearings in which deponents failed to express remorse or to provide answers about what really happened. Indeed the victims often disappeared in the process. Some people complained that the PRK hearings rarely addressed violence prior to the referendum process; acts perpetrated in 1999 were taken out of a longer context of violence and betrayal. Other people complained that acts of violence perpetrated by Falintil, the resistance movement, were rarely discussed in any of the institutions. In specific cases, the Community Reconciliation Process successfully reintegrated low level perpetrators into their communities and helped individuals and communities rebuild lives after the violence. At the same time that he celebrates the Community Reconciliation Process as a hopeful innovation in postconflict reconstruction, Patrick Burgess, principal legal counsel for the CAVR, notes that additional, independent research is necessary to assess its long-term effects (2006).

These institutions, despite their different agendas and constraints, publicly enacted a version of events that emphasizes violence between Timorese in a time of war. While the role of the TNI is not disputed, its connections with the pro-integration militias were not scrutinized. Moreover, these institutions have had direct effects that solidify the narrative of civil war: many Timorese were jailed for crimes that occurred in 1999; deponents reconciled with communities based on "regrettable" acts committed during "excessive" times; TNI have not been held accountable; and leaders of both countries advocate forgetting and restrict public space for contesting the dominant narrative.

The conditions of possibility for such a "civil war" and the process of how it was subtly and systematically developed over two decades remain underrepresented in official institutions of historical and legal truth. The notable exception is the historical narrative produced in the final report of the Commission for Truth and Reception. The report strongly advocates justice. The final report of the CAVR, *Chega!* [Enough!], documented the facts of the occupation in great detail. Given the record of the various justice-seeking mechanisms, this report demonstrates profound and consistent impunity, both for the Indonesian forces and for their international supporters. In 2004, I asked one woman what she thought of the various transitional institutions. She told me they were not getting the right people. I asked if she meant the top-ranking Indonesian generals. She told me that she thought Ford and Kissinger and all the other internationals who stood by while Indonesia invaded were more responsible.[16] Although the civil war narrative emerged powerfully in and through transitional institutions, the production of a civil war narrative to evade accountability for their role in violence was part of the Indonesian intelligence strategy before the invasion took place. This narrative has effectively granted the Indonesian military and intelligence impunity for their role in directly perpetrating violence and in creating conditions of possibility for violence between Timorese.

The CAVR report describes how, even before the invasion and occupation, the Indonesian forces relied on a strategy of "plausible denial" by "developing the myth that the Indonesian soldiers involved in these operations were merely volunteers helping East Timorese return to take control of their homeland" (2005, 20). The report then details the various paramilitary groups commanded primarily by the Indonesian Special Forces troops (Kopassus). Their relationship to the former resistance forces (Falintil) was complex. For instance, one deponent told the commission, "Major Sinaga formed Parrot Team [Tim Lorico] in the village of Oestico Loilubo from former Falintil. He used them for jungle operations, and after they had found a Falintil place ABRI [Indonesian] troops would go in and shoot. . . . After Sinaga left Timor-Leste, members of Tim Lorico disappeared one by one." The report notes that various paramilitaries had close relationships with various military units, especially the Special Forces, "that were often sustained throughout years of the conflict" (22). Civilians were also recruited into civil defense forces. The picture that emerges is of a completely militarized society—not a society in which all civilians were armed, but a society in which all civilians were drawn into conflict. Ordinary interactions and daily life were restructured by suspicion and the possibility of betrayal. Conditions were such that there was no evidence that one was innocent and could avoid possible abuse. Anyone might be accused of association with the rebels, no evidence was required; any association with the rebels was grounds for mistreatment by the security forces. At the same time, anyone might be suspected of betraying the person who suffered at the hands of the security forces. There was no way to prove one had not betrayed their neighbors, family, or fellow members of the resistance.

The CAVR report states that "the widespread use of East Timorese civil defence forces had a dramatic impact on the East Timorese bringing the conflict and the military into people's everyday lives. . . . Intelligence gathering was a pervasive activity, and civil defence force members, either with members of the Indonesian military or on their own, were often involved in direct violations of civilians' rights" (22). The Indonesian military had trouble controlling these forces, and in the mid-1980s, after a "downsizing plan," many civil defence members defected to Falintil (23). The CAVR report documents that the Indonesian military recruited resistance members for intelligence operations and trained civilian defense forces that then "defected" to Falintil. Intelligence operations were insidious and have been underacknowledged by transitional institutions. And yet, such operations were critical to the "eruption" of civil war that is most often narrated through these institutions. To destroy clandestine support for the resistance and linkages between Timorese civilians and the resistance, the Indonesian military followed a strategy of "building a society in which security forces were implanted deeply within each community, observing and relying on East Timorese informants to create a powerful intelligence operation capable of controlling the civilian population and limiting contact with Falintil" (26). The report notes that Timorese were recruited to work as informants in several ways: "Some willingly offered to help the intelligence units, others were offered bribes, and still others recruited by force of threat. The military often sought to 'turn' clandestine members and former Falintil guerillas to work for the Intelligence Task Force" (27).

The indeterminate relationships between the military and resistance are a complex element of Timor's history. As the report notes, "This system of intelligence informants and spies played a large role in creating suspicion among East Timorese. It enabled the military to penetrate the Resistance, as well as enabling it to plant rumours and misinformation. Many East Timorese were forced to play a dangerous double game, and were continually at risk of being suspected by either side. There were large numbers of East Timorese spies and their prevalence meant that civilians rarely knew who was *mauhu* [an intelligence informant] and who was not, who to avoid and who could be trusted. The pervasiveness of the system sowed deep suspicion among the East Timorese population and social bonds and cohesiveness were casualties of this undercover element of the conflict" (27). The intelligence system was widely known to Timorese, who had to negotiate daily life in a context where potentially fatal betrayal lurked everywhere. The failure of transitional justice to address this pattern does not result from lack of knowledge that intelligence operations were polarizing communities, although the pervasiveness of the civil war narrative suggests that this point has not been adequately linked to the 1999 violence. The problem is one of accountability. The TNI has not been held accountable for designing this system and then disavowing its role through the civil war narrative. In Timor, the lack of accountability for both the TNI and Timorese *mauhu* has created a situation of corruption in which leaders and institutions are not to be trusted. Rumors and mistrust continue to proliferate and no institution or authority seems capable of interrupting the destabilizing power of rumor and suspicion.

The constantly repeated refrain that "it was a time of war" implies spontaneous, emotional actions, not calculated decisions and secret acts shaped by a system of intelligence. The TNI relied on its informants, and on festering resentments initiated by political conflicts and extended by betrayal, to implement its operations and to translate state violence into horizontal violence. The statement "Timorese were victims of other Timorese" fails to address or resolve this complicated dynamic.

Transitional institutions did not address collaboration and betrayal between and within two forces or clarify contributions to the resistance. The police, a key component of any functioning judiciary, were recruited primarily from former Indonesian police. Collaboration with the TNI went far beyond low-level operational support by "little people." Many politicians and resistance leaders had complicated relationships to the Indonesian occupying forces. In my interviews in 2003–2004, relationships that might appear contradictory were often glossed as evidence of the individual's cleverness: "the whole time they were in the Indonesian apparatus they were really working for the clandestine movement." In other cases, resentment is palpable: "how could he have betrayed that many people and still have a position now?" Particular individuals are known to have switched sides at different points in the conflict. In some interpretations this pattern of oscillation indexes horrible complicity; in others it indicates necessary survival skills or contributions to the resistance.

The conflict is structured around the positions of resistance with Falintil and alliance with the Indonesian military and its later version of supporting independence or integration, more than by deep fissures in society that map stably onto two distinct groups of Timorese people. The positions and their conflict logic perpetuate violence enacted by individuals who occupy and act in different positions at different moments. When the court endeavors to make sense of these facts and determine intent, it draws on information provided by witnesses who are complicit in similar actions. The court cannot take this dynamic into account in its legal considerations, especially when the conflict is construed as a civil war between Timorese. It entirely fails to address the systematic operations of the TNI that formed the conditions of possibility for violent conflict between Timorese.

Exploring how individuals shifted between positions, in many cases more than once, moves beyond the analysis of people's political beliefs and personal motivations. The law, as a discipline of limits and determination, falters on encountering this doubleness. The legal process produces the stable, bifurcated positions of victim or perpetrator out of much greater indeterminacy. Some people opportunistically rewrite their pasts; others unwaveringly supported consistent political positions. Many are not easily categorized because they oscillated between sides. The morally ambiguous situations generated by years of intelligence operations have not been, and cannot be, resolved with clear narratives of culpability and victimization. The problem of Timor's transitional institutions is not one of failing to provide a context for individuals who occupied multiple conflict positions to clear their names. Rather, it is a failure to judicially examine the social-historical and political contexts in which such ambiguous positions were created to facilitate and extend the reach of state violence. I am not suggesting that individuals should not be held accountable for their choices and actions during political conflict, but rather that considering the ambiguities of collaboration and resistance deepens our understandings of how the law and other mechanisms of accountability work after conflict.

What is missing from the proceedings is the role of the Indonesian military in designing the system. Not only do its architects remain beyond the reach of the court for trial and sentencing, but the narrative that emerges from the tribunals concerns what militias did to their own people in particular incidents, stripped of the longer historical context and of the systematic TNI operations that created the conditions for these acts. From the cold war to the War on Terror, geopolitics and pragmatics have trumped the espoused norms of respect for human dignity that are invoked as the basis for numerous interventions and institutions. Some early theories of transitional justice suggest that prosecutions and punishment restore the dignity of law itself, but in situations where judgments cannot be enforced it is dangerous to attempt trials as they may demonstrate the powerlessness of the law. One of the failures of international justice in Timor is that the role of the Indonesian military in perpetrating violence in Timor has been demonstrated beyond reasonable doubt and has pointed toward the highest echelons of the military and political elite. Indeed, the UN has failed not only to deliver justice as promised to ordinary Timorese victims, it has failed to prosecute those responsible for killing its own uniformed Timorese staff members. Continually reproducing this conflict as a local conflict between different factions of Timorese, while at the same time documenting that their violent acts were orchestrated by the TNI, renders the justice process corrupt. The masterminds are not on trial, and those standing trial are declared guilty at the same time that public knowledge notes they are simply proxies for those immune to justice. They simultaneously occupy the role of perpetrator and victim of the masterminds and leaders not on trial. The narratives and practices that focus simply on the interactions between the militias and TNI marginalize the victims of the conflict.

Focus on violence between Timorese obscures how these animosities developed and were cultivated. The problem is that the Indonesian military forces created the conditions of possibility for the "civil war" in 1999 through their intelligence operations.[17] The dynamics of the intelligence operations are most succinctly represented by the figure of the *mauhu,* who must play a dangerous double game. The *mauhu* system does significant work in displacing violence from the Indonesian military into society: spreading disinformation and rumor, generating distrust and uncertainty, and perpetuating it through the productive indeterminacy in which it is never clear who anyone is. The *mauhu* system, with its legacies of mistrust, suspicion, and social polarization, is precisely what makes the violence appear local and in need of a local process of justice. The figure of the *mauhu* corrupts current efforts to achieve justice because it is never clear where the *mauhu* fits into standard narratives of victims and perpetrators.

The *mauhu* also disrupts the plans for replacing justice with development and rebuilding Timor for the future. The political conflict and violence in 2006 involved problems among a small group of actors who have been involved for thirty years in the liberation of Timor. The legacies of the double game, especially perceptions of who suffered and who benefited, and who betrayed whom, have not been resolved with independence. Institutionally, the police are a good example: police were primarily recruited from those who served as Indonesian police forces. The Falintil soldiers, who spent their lives in the forest without access to education, and have not been successful in gaining political positions in the Timor they fought for. This is probably a typical set of problems after armed struggle, but it may be compounded in Timor by the pattern of playing a double game for three decades in a very small country. The internationalized trials have not explored this problem in depth, nor have they established credible and socially legitimate institutions that could examine and resolve suspicions and rumors that precipitated the 2006 violence. It is not clear, however, that an international tribunal could have resolved this matter, or even that local people stated that they wanted an international tribunal to address it; some may well think that issues involved are too fraught with potential for further violence to be examined openly. The costs of silence are equally high. The civil war narrative benefits the powerful international forces who want avoid examining their points of contact with the highest echelons of the chain of command. As the international community intervenes to deliver justice, it also obscures the fact that Timorese were victims of global geopolitics during the cold war—and again during the War on Terror—and that the chain of command and knowledge as liability extends beyond even Indonesia's borders, perhaps as far as Ford and Kissinger. In sum, the TNI's militarization of Timorese society is continued by the narrative of civil war sanctioned by international institutions, perpetuating conflict while abrogating justice.

International Justice?

Most Timorese and outside observers concur that justice has not been done in Timor. The repeated examination of past violence and production of narratives and evidence about historical grievances has provided no resolution of the conflict. If indeed the problem that needs to be resolved in East Timor was a civil war, as many institutions have suggested, then a "local" form of justice might seem the most appropriate approach. I am arguing, rather, that it is precisely the localization of accountability and liability that forecloses the possibility of justice. The failure of international justice in Timor may be best understood with detailed contextual information, but defining a sphere of local justice simply underlines the lack of accountability for international—that is, Indonesian—actors. Trials that focus on individual perpetrators and specific acts seldom explore the context that made such violations possible except in empty, generalized terms. Here what is most serious is the failure to address the international components of injustice and their implications in the conditions of possibility for specific acts of violence to be perpetrated with impunity.

Arguments have been advanced that the democratically elected leaders of East Timor have spoken against an international tribunal and that any further demands for international justice by outsiders deny Timorese sovereignty. Speaking of Timor and other cases, analysts have argued that there is an overemphasis on prosecutions that risks exaggerating or romanticizing justice (Kingston 2006). I agree that prosecutions alone will not accomplish everything, but lack of prosecutions may hinder other efforts by Timorese to move beyond the past violence.

Many Timorese and Indonesian nongovernmental organizations have argued that the Indonesian military must be held accountable. The CAVR report has advocated for justice. Geoffrey Robinson (2006) has made a well-supported and compelling argument that there must be an international tribunal. He argues that it is the responsibility of the international community to pursue justice because its representatives were also murdered, and because it is impossible to expect Timorese to have the resources to pursue international forms of justice capable of holding still powerful perpetrators accountable. Joseph Nevins (2005) contends that the international community was complicit because they knew what was going on and failed to act.

In Timor, those who do not hold political power seek justice, often articulated as a process that would hold high-ranking perpetrators accountable in an international tribunal, while the elected officials have chosen to seek reconciliation with Indonesia. An amorphous international community continues to suggest that justice was not done and yet cannot summon the political will to pursue trials. Thus, the situation seems to be one of justice deferred or justice as threat. Timorese leaders are criticized for defending reconciliation; the lack of international political will hides in deference to Timorese leaders' preferences. I am concerned that this might suggest that injustice is held in reserve for a later intervention should global geopolitics determine that it is necessary. Justice as threat ensnares justice in the logics of vengeance and politics that it is meant to interrupt.

NOTES

1. For an example of how the Aceh conflict was formulated as ethnocultural separatism, see Drexler (2008).

2. Other essays in this volume point to the ways in which the tools of transitional justice extend old conflicts or produce new forms of conflict; for an excellent example, see Wagner (this volume).

3. I conducted research in East Timor in 2003–2004, during a period in which these institutions were entering the final phases of their work.

4. The 2006 violence does not indicate that Timorese are rent by intractable conflicts. ICG writes: "Timor-Leste's problems are made more difficult by the country's being so small and the political elite even tinier. The entire crisis, its origins and solutions, revolve around less than ten people, who have a shared history going back 30 years" (2006, 1). This statement misses the role that international forces have played in these conflicts.

5. Timorese in exile and global advocacy networks circulated testimony and evidence of military repression and human rights violations to create international pressure on Indonesia to end its occupation of the territory (Aditjondro 1994; Budiardjo 1984; Carey 1995; Gunn 1997; Jardine 1999).

6. An estimated 600,000 Timorese were forcibly relocated to the Indonesian province. Over 1,300 civilians were killed.

7. UN Security Council Resolution 1272/99.

8. In the five months following the referendum, the Indonesian Human Rights Commission on East Timor (KPP–HAM) produced a report linking violence in Timor

to the highest echelons of the TNI, including the commander-in-chief, General Wiranto. International audiences and human rights organizations praised the efficient and credible work of this commission. Subsequently, international criticism of Indonesia was reduced. It is likely that the military cooperated with the KPP–HAM only to ensure that there would be no international tribunal. The International Commission of Inquiry on East Timor (ICIET) produced the UN report.

9. Early analysis praised the integration of individual accountability and community reconciliation (see Stahn 2001).

10. For a detailed analysis of these institutions, see Drexler (2009).

11. For a detailed discussion of the ad hoc court, see ELSAM (2003); for documentation of the overall context of impunity in Indonesia with reference to Timor, see Linton et al. (2009).

12. For a discussion of these "hybrid" tribunals, see Reiger (2006).

13. The special panels prioritized ten cases that indicted 183 individuals, and 168 of these individuals were not extradited to Timor for trial.

14. *Morning Herald* (Sydney), November 7, 2003.

15. In the PRK process individuals (deponents) who had committed offenses and wished to be reconciled with particular communities submitted statements (depositions) of the nonserious crimes they had committed. In the community hearing, deponents testified before and answered questions from the community. The communities involved agreed to accept the deponents and promised not to ostracize the deponents for that crime after they fulfilled the symbolic act of reconciliation (e.g., cleaning the church). In the community reconciliation hearings, the testimony had immediate effects and the community was bound to act as if the narrative at the hearing were true. Several reports of this process were commissioned by international organizations (see, e.g., Kent 2004; Pigou 2003; Zifcak 2004). The community hearings were framed by elements of traditional law, *adat*. The strength of *adat* leaders varies by communities and influences the hearings.

16. As Joseph Nevins writes, "President Gerald Ford and his secretary of state, Henry Kissinger, met with Suharto in Jakarta the day prior to the invasion. They were fully cognizant of Indonesia's plans to invade. According to a transcript of the meeting, Ford assured Suharto that, with regard to East Timor, '[We] will not press you on the issue. We understand the intentions you have'" (2005, 51). Indeed, the United States worked with Indonesia to develop a rationale for using U.S.-made weapons in self-defense against possible communist threats in East Timor.

17. For discussions of Indonesian intelligence operations, see Kammen (1999, 2003), Moore (2001), and Tanter (2001).

REFERENCES

Aditjondro, George J. 1994. *In the Shadow of Mount Ramelau: The Impact of the Occupation of East Timor*. Leiden, The Netherlands: INDOC Indonesian Documentation and Information Center.

Agamben, Giorgio. 1998. *Homo Sacer: Sovereign Power and Bare Life*. Trans. Daniel Heller-Roazen. Stanford, CA: Stanford University Press

Anderson, Benedict. 1995. "East Timor and Indonesia: Some Implications." In *East Timor at the Crossroads: The Forging of a Nation*, ed. Peter Carey and Carter G. Bentley, 137–147. New York: Social Science Research Council.

Benjamin, Walter. 1921. "Critique of Violence." In *Reflections: Walter Benjamin Essays, Aphorisms, Autobiographical Writings*, ed. Peter Demetz, 277–300. New York: Schocken Books, 1986.

Budiardjo, Carmel. 1984. *The War against East Timor*. London: Zed Books.

Burgess, Patrick. 2006. "A New Approach to Restorative Justice—East Timor's Community Reconciliation Processes." In *Transitional Justice in the Twenty-First Century: Beyond Truth versus Justice*, ed. Naomi Roht-Arriaza and Javier Mariezcurrena, 176–205. Cambridge: Cambridge University Press.

Carey, Peter, ed. 1995. *East Timor at the Crossroads: The Forging of a Nation*. New York: Social Science Research Council.

Cohen, David. 2002. "Seeking Justice on the Cheap: Is the East Timor Tribunal Really a Model for the Future?" *Asia Pacific Issues: Analysis from the East West Center* 61:1–8.

Commission for Reception, Truth, and Reconciliation in Timor-Leste (CAVR). 2005. *Chega! The Report of the Commission for Reception, Truth, and Reconciliation in Timor-Leste.* Part 4, *Regime of Occupation.* http://www.cavr-timorleste.org/en/chegaReport.htm.

Das, Veena. 2006. *Life and Words: The Descent into the Ordinary*. Berkeley: University of California Press.

Derrida, Jacques. 1992. "Force of Law: The 'Mystical Foundation of Authority.'" In *Deconstruction and the Possibility of Justice*, ed. Drucilla Cornell, Michel Rosenfeld, and David Gray Carlson, 3–67. New York: Routledge, Chapman and Hall.

Drexler, Elizabeth. 2008. *Aceh, Indonesia: Securing the Insecure State*. Philadelphia: University of Pennsylvania Press.

———. 2009. "Addressing the Legacies of Mass Violence and Genocide in East Timor and Indonesia." In *Genocide: Truth, Memory, and Representation*, ed. Alex Hinton and Kevin Lewis O'Neill, 219–246. Durham: Duke University Press.

du Toit, Andre. 2000. "The Moral Foundations of the South African TRC: Truth as Acknowledgment and Justice as Recognition." In *Truth V. Justice: The Morality of Truth Commissions*, ed. Robert I. Rotberg and Dennis Thompson, 122–140. Princeton: Princeton University Press.

ELSAM (Lembaga Studi Dan Advokasi Masyarakat). 2003. *The Failure of Leipzig Repeated in Jakarta: Final Assessment of the Human Rights Ad-Hoc Tribunal for East Timor*. Jakarta: ELSAM Lembaga Studi Dan Advokasi Masyarakat.

Feher, Michel. 1999. Terms of Reconciliation." In *Human Rights in Political Transitions: Gettysburg to Bosnia*, ed. Carla Hesse and Robert Post, 325–338. New York: Zone Books.

Gunn, Geoffrey C. 1997. *East Timor and the United Nations: The Case for Intervention*. Lawrenceville, NJ: Red Sea Press.

ICG (International Crisis Group). 2006. *Resolving Timor-Leste's Crisis*. Asia Report no. 120. Jakarta and Brussels: International Crisis Group.

Jardine, Matthew. 1999. *East Timor: Genocide in Paradise*. Monroe, ME: Odonian Press.

Kammen, Douglas. 1999. "Notes on the Transformation of the East Timor Military Command and Its Implications for Indonesia." *Indonesia* 67:61–76.

———. 2003. "Master-Slave, Traitor-Nationalist, Opportunist-Oppressed: Political Metaphors in East Timor." *Indonesia* 76:69–85.

Katzenstein, Suzanne. 2003. "Hybrid Tribunals: Searching for Justice in East Timor." *Harvard Human Rights Journal* 16 (6): 245–278.

Kent, Lia. 2004. *Unfulfilled Expectations: Community Views on CAVR's Community Reconciliation Process*. Dili, East Timor: Judicial System Monitoring Programme.

Kingston, Jeffrey. 2006. "Balancing Justice and Reconciliation in East Timor." *Critical Asian Studies* 38 (3): 271–302.

KPP-HAM. 2000. *Executive Summary Report.* Jakarta: Komnas-HAM.

Kritz, Neil J., ed. 1995. *Transitional Justice: How Emerging Democracies Reckon with Former Regimes.* Washington, DC: United States Institute of Peace Press.

Linton, Suzannah. 2001. "Rising from the Ashes: The Creation of a Viable Criminal Justice System in East Timor." *Melbourne University Law Review* 25 (1): 125–180.

Linton, Suzannah, Elizabeth F. Drexler, and Mario Gomez. 2009. "Post-Conflict Justice in Asia." In *Fighting Impunity and Promoting International Justice. European Initiative for Democracy and Human Rights: Promoting Justice and the Rule of Law,* ed. M. Cherif Bassiouni. Siracusa, Italy: International Institute of Higher Studies in Criminal Sciences.

Moore, Samuel. 2001. "The Indonesian Military's Last Years in East Timor: An Analysis of Secret Documents." *Indonesia* 72:9–44.

Nevins, Joseph. 2005. *A Not-So-Distant Horror: Mass Violence in East Timor.* Ithaca, NY: Cornell University Press.

Pigou, Piers. 2003. *Crying without Tears: In Pursuit of Justice and Reconciliation in Timor-Leste: Community Perspectives and Expectations.* New York: International Center for Transitional Justice.

Popkin, Margaret, and Naomi Roht-Arriaza. 1995. "Truth as Justice: Investigatory Commissions in Latin America." In *Transitional Justice: How Emerging Democracies Reckon with Former Regimes,* ed. Neil J. Kirtz, 262–289. Washington, DC: United States Institute of Peace Press.

Reiger, Caitlin. 2006. "Hybrid Attempts at Accountability for Serious Crimes in Timor Leste." In *Transitional Justice in the Twenty-First Century: Beyond Truth versus Justice,* ed. Naomi Roht-Arriaza and Javier Mariezcurrena, 143–170. Cambridge: Cambridge University Press.

Robinson, Geoffrey. 2002. "If You Leave Us Here, We Will Die." In *The New Killing Fields: Massacre and the Politics of Intervention,* ed. Nicolaus Mills and Kira Bruner, 159–184. New York: Basic Books.

———. 2006. *East Timor 1999: Crimes Against Humanity. Report Commissioned by the United Nations Office of the High Commissioner for Human Rights.* Jakarta and Dili: Hak Association & Institute for Policy Research and Advocacy.

Roht-Arriaza, Naomi, and Javier Mariezcurrena. 2006. *Transitional Justice in the Twenty-First Century: Beyond Truth versus Justice.* Cambridge: Cambridge University Press.

Ross, Fiona. 2001. *Bearing Witness: Women and the South African Truth and Reconciliation Commission.* London: Pluto Press.

———. 2003. "On Having Voice and Being Heard: Some After-Effects of Testifying before the South African Truth and Reconciliation Commission." *Anthropological Theory* 3 (3): 325–341.

Rotberg, Robert I. 2000. "Truth Commissions and the Provision of Truth, Justice and Reconciliation." In *Truth V. Justice: The Morality of Truth Commissions,* ed. Robert I. Rotberg and Dennis Thompson, 3–21. Princeton, NJ: Princeton University Press.

Shaw, Rosalind. 2007. "Memory Frictions: Localizing the Truth and Reconciliation Commission in Sierra Leone." *International Review of Transitional Justice* 1 (2): 183–207.

Stahn, Carsten. 2001. "Accommodating Individual Criminal Responsibility and National Reconciliation: The UN Truth Commission for East Timor." *American Journal of International Law* 95 (4): 952–966.

Stover, Eric. 2007. *The Witnesses: War Crimes and the Promise of Justice in The Hague.* Philadelphia: University of Pennsylvania Press.

Strohmeyer, Hansjorg. 2001. "Collapse and Reconstruction of a Judicial System: The United Nations Missions in Kosovo and East Timor." *American Journal of International Law* 95 (1): 46–63.

Tanter, Richard. 2001. "East Timor and the Crisis of the Indonesian Intelligence State." In *Bitter Flowers, Sweet Flowers: East Timor, Indonesia and the World Community*, ed. Mark Selden and Stephen R. Shalom, 189–208. New York: Rowman and Littlefield.

Taylor, John G. 1999. *East Timor: The Price of Freedom*. London: Zed Books.

Wilson, Richard Ashby. 2001. *The Politics of Truth and Reconciliation in South Africa: Legitimizing the Post-Apartheid State*. Cambridge: Cambridge University Press.

Zifcak, Spencer. 2004. *Restorative Justice in East Timor: An Evaluation of the Community Reconciliation Process of the CAVR*. Dili, East Timor: Asia Foundation.

3

▶ ▶ ▶ ▶ ▶ ▶ ▶ ▶ ▶ ▶ ▶ ▶ ▶ ▶ ▶ ◀ ◀ ◀ ◀ ◀ ◀ ◀ ◀ ◀ ◀ ◀ ◀ ◀ ◀ ◀

Body of Evidence

Feminicide, Local Justice, and
Rule of Law in "Peacetime" Guatemala

VICTORIA SANFORD AND MARTHA LINCOLN

The last time Claudina Isabel communicated with her parents was around 11:45 P.M. on August 12, 2005. Around two in the morning on August 13, her parents were awoken by Zully Moreno, the mother of Claudina Isabel's boyfriend, Pedro Samayoa Moreno, who went to their home to inform them that Claudina Isabel was in grave danger. Señora Moreno claimed that Claudina Isabel called her to tell her she was walking home and that this call was cut short by Claudina Isabel's screams for help. Claudina Isabel's parents immediately went out to search for their daughter first at the house where Claudina Isabel had attended a party in the nearby neighborhood of Colonia Panorama. With no results or leads from the partygoers, they began to search the neighborhoods from the party back to their home.

Desperate, they attempted to make a report at the local police station at about 3:00 A.M. on August 13. The police, however, refused to take a report or even listen to the worried parents. They suggested that Claudina Isabel had run off with her boyfriend and that, in any case, they would not receive any reports until Claudina Isabel had been officially missing for twenty-four hours. It was not until 8:30 that morning that the police formally received Claudina Isabel's parents and made an official report that classified Claudina Isabel Velasquez Paiz as missing. This was three and one-half hours after her lifeless body was found on the street on 10th Avenue in Colonia Roosevelt in Zona 11—a neighborhood not more than two miles from the party where she was last seen by friends. Despite the obvious connection between the location of Claudina Isabel's body and her parents' anguished report to the police, she was not identified until much later that day.

In fact, Claudina Isabel's case, like more than five hundred murder cases of women in Guatemala in 2005, was dismissed from the moment her cadaver was found. This was because, as one official acknowledged, "the

crime scene was not developed as it should have been because of preju-
dices about the social origin and status of the victim. She was classified as
a person whose death did not merit investigation" (PDH 2006b, 5). The first
police officers on the scene determined that Claudina Isabel's murder was
"not worthy" of investigation because she had a belly button ring and was
wearing sandals. In the parlance of the Guatemalan police, this meant she
was a gang member or a prostitute.

But Claudina Isabel was not a gang member or a prostitute. Claudina
Isabel Velasquez Paiz was a nineteen-year-old law student. She was beau-
tiful, gregarious, and well-liked by her peers: more than one thousand
people attended her memorial service. Her father, Jorge Velasquez, did not
understand what was happening when several uniformed armed officers in
bullet-proof vests arrived at the memorial service and demanded access to
his daughter's body. When Mr. Velasquez refused, the police threatened to
arrest him and his wife. The coffin was removed from the memorial service and placed in a private room, where police officers unceremoniously
took fingerprints and nail clippings from the body in the coffin. When they
were finished collecting this material for forensic analysis, they handed Mr.
Velasquez a paper bag. In response to his dismay, the officer explained that
the bag contained the clothing Claudina Isabel had been wearing at the
time she was murdered. "Most families bury the clothing in the coffin," the
police explained. Distraught, Mr. Velasquez responded that he would not be
burying it in a coffin, that he would not allow them to ever again disturb
his daughter. Without thinking about the implications, he asked the funeral
home to burn the bag and its contents, which in murder cases throughout
most of the world would be part of the evidence held on file.

Claudina Isabel was one of 518 women murdered in 2005 in Guatemala.
With each year that passes, it is becoming more dangerous to be a woman in
Guatemala. More than six hundred women were killed in 2006. Since 2007,
on average, two women are murdered each day (USDOS 2009). Between 2002
and 2005, the number of women killed increased by more than 63 percent,
and nearly 40 percent of these murders happened in or near Guatemala City.
Most of the women killed are between sixteen and thirty years old. In 2005,
sixty-eight of the female murder victims (13 percent) were under seventeen
years old (PDH 2006a). Indeed, the mortality rate of women in peacetime
Guatemala today is approaching the very high levels of female mortality
recorded in the early 1980s, at the height of the genocidal war that ultimately
claimed the lives of 200,000 men, women, and children (CEH 1999; Sanford
2003a, 2003b).

The cost of these killings in lost lives and lost futures is brutal. As UN
rapporteur Philip Alston notes, "the death toll is only the beginning of the

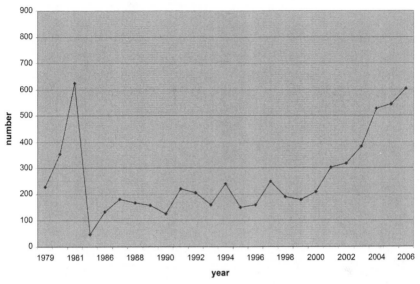

FIGURE 3.1 Female homicides in Guatemala, 1979–2006.
Source: Sanford 2008b.

cost, for a society that lives in fear of killing is unable to get on with its life and business in the ways that it wants" (2007, 5). Moreover, Alston points out that while the female population increased by 8 percent between 2001 and 2006, the female homicide rate increased by more than 117 percent (11).

In this chapter, we examine the costs of these murders for individuals, families, and Guatemalan society by exploring the case of Claudina Isabel Velasquez Paiz within the wider context of transitional justice in Guatemala. Claudina Isabel's murder and the efforts of her father to bring her murderer(s) to justice provide a lens not only into the suffering and loss of an affected family but also offer an up-close appraisal of local justice in peacetime Guatemala. Moreover, by examining the efficacy of the inner workings of the Guatemalan criminal justice system, we contrast the dis- course of judicial reform and transitional justice with the lived experience of citizens seeking justice from a dysfunctional system that has been under internationally driven reform since the 1996 signing of the peace accords.[1] Thus, this chapter offers a critically needed assessment of the specific foibles of the Guatemalan justice system in the context of transitional justice and at the same time offers a gendered analysis of the killing of women in Guatemala, which is grounded in present and past practices of the state and its security institutions (Sanford 2008b).

Background

In December of 1996, the Guatemalan Army and the Guatemalan National Rev-olutionary Union (Union Revolucionario Nacional Guatemalteca—URNG) guer-rillas formally signed peace accords ending more than three decades of armed conflict popularly referred to as La Violencia, or The Violence. The establish-ment of the Commission for Historical Clarification (Comision para el Escla-recimiento Historico or CEH), a truth commission, was one of the outcomes of the peace accords negotiated between the Guatemalan government (still dominated by the army) and the URNG. The parties agreed that institutional responsibility would be assigned for human rights violations, but individual perpetrators would not be named. Though envisioned as an independent com-mission, the majority of investigative staff moved from the United Nations Verification Mission in Guatemala (MINUGUA) office to the CEH. Indeed, many of the MINUGUA staff had previously worked on the United Nations Observer Mission in El Salvador (ONUSAL) and also for the Salvadoran truth commission. Still, unlike the Salvadoran commission, the CEH included a significant num-ber of Guatemalan nationals on its staff, many of whom formerly worked with human rights nongovernmental organizations (Sanford 2002). The mission of the CEH, like other Latin American commissions (see Robben, this volume), was envisaged as an integral contribution to truth, reconciliation, and justice following extreme state violence (see Dwyer, this volume).

The CEH began its work in 1997 and published its final report in 1999. Among the most important findings of the report was a quantification of La Violencia supported by survivors' narratives. These findings included 626 villages massacred, 1.5 million people displaced, 150,000 people seeking ref-uge in Mexico, and more than 200,000 dead or disappeared (CEH 1999).

While these numbers of dead indicate savagery on a massive scale, particularly in a country that had a population of approximately 8 million at the height of the violence in the early 1980s, more shocking still was the attribution of responsibility for these horrific crimes. The CEH determined that the Guatemalan army was responsible for 93 percent of all human rights violations, the guerrillas for 3 percent, and unknown assailants for the remaining 4 percent (CEH 1999, 5:42). Most significant, the CEH found the Guatemalan army and national security state responsible for acts of genocide committed against the Maya—who comprise a majority of the Guatemalan population yet remain politically and economically marginal-ized by poverty, inequality, and discrimination (CEH 1999, 2:315). Defining the massacres as genocidal acts weds truth and justice by emphasizing both the primary role of state institutional structures of violence and the state's international legal obligation to prosecute responsible parties (Sanford 2003a, 2003b, 2008a).

Finding Genocide in Guatemala

Five years after the CEH findings of genocidal acts, on April 29, 2004, the Inter-American Court condemned the Guatemalan government for the July 18, 1982, massacre of 188 Achi-Maya in the village of Plan de Sanchez in the mountains above Rabinal, Baja Verapaz (Corte IDH 2004; Sanford 2003c, 2008a). In this judgment, and for the first time in its history, the court ruled that genocide had taken place and attributed the 1982 massacre and the genocide to Guatemalan army troops. Beyond the importance of this judgment for the people of Plan de Sanchez, the court's ruling is particularly significant. The judgment's key points include a declaration that there was genocide in Guatemala, which was part of the framework of the internal armed conflict when the armed forces of the Guatemalan government applied their National Security Doctrine in their counterinsurgency actions. Moreover, the court placed General Efrain Rios Montt at the helm with command responsibility for the genocide.

Two years and some months later, the Spanish court issued an international arrest order charging various former generals and military officials with genocide, terrorism, torture, assassination, and illegal detention. Those charged include General Efrain Rios Montt (head of state through military coup from March 1982 to August 1983); General Oscar Humberto Mejia Victores (head of state through military coup from August 1983 to January 1986); General Fernando Romeo Lucas Garcia (president of Guatemala from 1978 to March 1982); General Angel Anibal Guevara Rodriguez (minister of defense under Lucas Garcia); Donaldo Alvarez Ruiz (minister of interior under Lucas Garcia); Colonel German Chupina Barahona (director of the National Police (Policia Nacional Civil [PNC]) under Lucas Garcia); Pedro Garcia Arredondo (chief of command of the PNC under Lucas Garcia); General Benedicto Lucas Garcia (army chief of staff during his brother's reign) ("El Juez" 2006). As of March 2007, none of these military officers has been extradited and each has filed numerous appeals to slow the process.[2] Moreover, they continue to make public justifications and/or deny any knowledge of human rights violations. While none of them have been jailed, the country of Guatemala is now their jail because Interpol agreements bind any country receiving a visitor on Interpol's international arrest order list as being immediately extraditable. Still, they continue to argue that self-granted amnesties give them immunity from prosecution, as they live in Guatemala with impunity.

Postconflict Violence

If the generals and their genocidal cronies are the winners of a transitional justice process that guarantees their impunity, the citizens of Guatemala are

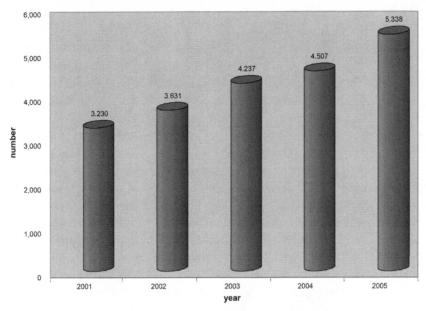

FIGURE 3.2 Homicides in Guatemala, 2001–2005.

Source: PDH 2005, 8.

culture of getting away with murder"

the losers. It is against this backdrop of genocide and impunity that Guatemalans today find themselves living in an extremely violent country with an
astronomically high homicide rate that continues to rise. There were 3,230
murder victims in 2001. By 2005, the number of victims increased to 5,338
(PDH 2005, 8).

In five years of so-called peacetime, there have been 20,943 registered
murders in Guatemala. If the number of murder victims continues to rise at
the current rate, more people will die in the first twenty-five years of peace
than died in the thirty-six-year internal armed conflict and genocide.

The Pan-American Health Organization classifies more than 10 homicides per 100,000 inhabitants as an epidemic and public health concern. In
Japan, there is less than 1 murder per 100,000 inhabitants ("International
Homicide" 2006); in the United States, the murder rate has remained at
roughly 9.8 per 100,000 since 1980 (USDOJ 2009); Venezuela's homicide rate
is 33 per 100,000 (Pan-American Health Organization 2007); and Mexico had
a rate of 14.11 per 100,000 in 2000 (Data 360 2009). In Latin America, the
average number of murders for each 100,000 inhabitants is 30 (PDH 2006a,
5). In 2005, there were 42 homicides for every 100,000 inhabitants in Guatemala. If we narrow our focus to Guatemala City, there were more than 80.
If we focus on Escuintla, the department immediately adjacent to Guatemala

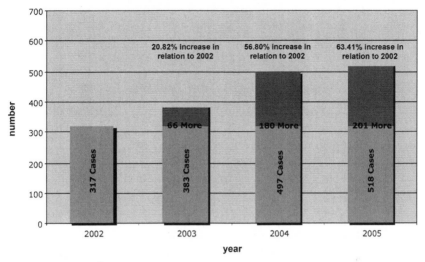

FIGURE 3.3 Rate of feminicide in Guatemala, 2002–2005.
Source: PDH 2005.

City, there were 147 murders per 100,000 inhabitants; some of these murder
victims have been identified as residents of Guatemala City whose bodies
were dumped in Escuintla (PDH 2006a, 5). Between 2002 and 2005, there
were 1,715 female homicides and 15,998 male homicides—a national total of
17,713 people killed in four years (PDH 2005, 9). In such circumstances, how
is local justice understood and conceptualized?

Anthropologies of Local Justice

The terms "local justice" and "community justice" reference a wide spectrum of phenomena, ranging from the establishment of community judicial
bureaucracies to episodes of mob violence where citizens take the law into
their own hands. As such, forms of community justice arise worldwide from
extraordinarily diverse social, legal, and political circumstances. Here we
begin with a review of the literature that (1) elaborates conceptions of local
or community justice in the context of Western jurisprudential theory and
practice; (2) unpacks the tensions between disparate jurisdictional scales
of legal authority; (3) documents the development of community justice
movements in the United States and worldwide; (4) discusses the prospects
of international human rights law for securing community needs for justice;
and (5) provides ethnographic insight into diverse forms of community justice. We conclude with some ethnographic observations about local justice
in Guatemala with the hope of contributing not only to scholarly knowledge

but also to a serious appraisal of postwar reconstruction of judicial systems and the ongoing struggle to establish rule of law within the framework of transitional justice.

Jurisprudence, Geography, and Jurisdiction

While normative justice typically presumes that the individual is the appropriate subject of the law, justice scholar Karen Hegtvedt (2005, 26) explores "the purview of justice research to encompass the group more explicitly." She interrogates philosophical and pragmatic tensions among the concepts of "justice," "individual deserving," and "group." Her discussion encompasses the domains of distributive justice and procedural justice, broadly articulating how concepts of fairness may arise not only out of individual positionality but from group membership or intergroup tensions. Significantly, this intervention brings the concept of "group" into a meaningful tension with established justice frameworks. However, Hegtvedt does not address the rise of social movements aiming to exert local democratic control over key institutions of civil society. Here the concept of community justice calls into question the traditional focus of justice upon individuals and challenges the monopoly of state actors on judicial institutions.

As legal anthropologist Sally Merry points out, the increasing significance of transnational processes and flows, framed by an evolving awareness of the interpenetration of local and global phenomena, has rendered notions of bounded local justice increasingly problematic in the anthropology of law. In view of this complexity, theoretical frameworks that address the coexisting or conjoint legal paradigms that remain in the wake of postcolonial or other transnational processes as legal pluralism appear increasingly inappropriate (Merry 1992, 357).

Nevertheless, the purview of judicial institutions continues to be defined by territorial scales—at least in theory. In the United States, for example, a geographically nested legal hierarchy shares powers between federal and lower-level courts, permitting local courts to exercise semiautonomous authority. This autonomy is not completely sovereign; the federal government reserves the authority to rule on the constitutionality of state and local laws (Fine 1999). Therefore, in the United States there is no purely local justice, nor is federal power necessarily always paramount. Disjunctions and disarticulations between "unequal but mutually constitutive legal orders" can result in slippages and irregularities in the definition and administration of justice (Merry 1992, 358). As Poole (2004) alludes in her work on Peruvian justice systems, friction between court systems functioning at different spatial scales makes theoretical and practical margins visible and meaningful—not only from a philosophical or legal perspective, but for groups or individuals caught between (or beneath) incommensurable legal regimes. A focus on these tensions highlights "the vulnerability of local places to structures of domination far outside their immediate worlds" (Merry 1992, 358).

In the face of inadequate, unresponsive, or elite-controlled justice systems, what are the prospects of popular or local legal paradigms that seek to challenge or supplant higher judicial authorities? What happens in countries where tens of thousands of citizens have suffered rights violations under previous regimes? What recourse do citizens have to justice for violations of the past? What remedies are available to citizens for violations and crimes of the present? Though the pursuit of justice often motivates claimants to seek ever-higher levels of legal authority, a wide range of political and economic situations prevent national—and international—legal frameworks from responding to the justice claims of citizens. Alternative frameworks for justice have developed in many parts of the world as a response to the shortcomings of judicial systems founded and exercised at geographic and political remove. In Great Britain, Australia, the United States, Rwanda, Guatemala, and Mexico—to name just a few places—state-sanctioned, bureaucratized community justice models are being promulgated locally (often with national and/or international technical support and resources), premised upon alternative definitions of justice, punishment, and the roles of various actors within the criminal justice system. While these models do not assume all functions traditionally exercised by municipal, state, and other state-based legal entities, they require higher-level juridical authorities to share or surrender some powers as well as public willingness to resolve disputes through alternative channels.

Writing on restorative justice and community justice models in the United States, Kurki (2000) argues that restorative justice ideals "imply that government should surrender its monopoly over responses to crime to those who are directly affected—the victim, the offender, and the community" (236). Community justice, by contrast, is premised on a reconceptualization of the meaning of crime: not merely an isolated cause for punishment or rehabilitation, but a "social problem that corrodes the quality of life in communities" (236). Within Kurki's framework, community justice models seek not only to administer the punishment and rehabilitation of criminals, but also to design and implement prevention strategies and address neighborhood conflicts that might not normally attract the attention of authorities. Transformations such as these express a response to the shortcomings of judicial forms whose scope is inadequate to address community concerns. But what if, on the one hand, community justice is simply another expression of state monopoly over power? And on the other hand, what if alternative local justice systems are simply another manifestation of international dominance of national governments?

Community Justice Movements

Given their success in challenging the official legal system, some community justice movements have attracted the support and partnership of larger agencies, and nongovernmental organizations have increasingly recognized community justice as an area for funding. The Urban Institute has published white papers on community justice (Roman et al. 2002), and the Open Society Institute (2007) has introduced funding for public interest law groups to "equip legal and non-legal groups to work effectively in legal and public policy spheres to redress injustices and poverty in Baltimore."

While forms of community justice frequently develop without support from think tanks or experts, U.S.-based nongovernmental organizations have become involved in supporting their growth in the Global South. From 2003 to 2005, the International Development Research Center funded a project titled "Community Justice as Restorative Justice in Colombia," which aimed to "contextualize, identify and analyze from the theoretical perspective of restorative justice (. . .) in order to provide elements for future plans for judicial reform, conflict resolution and peaceful co-existence in Colombia" (IDRC 2007). The United States Agency for International Development (USAID) has invested in projects to establish "alternative mechanisms of justice" in Colombia, Guatemala, and Peru; goals include "improved citizen service, access to justice, and quality of service, all with enhanced transparency" (USAID 2007). USAID has also sponsored community justice programs in South Africa (USAID 2007b) and issued a call for proposals to bring community justice resources to the Philippines (USAID 2007a). Guatemala now has some twenty local justice centers that ostensibly provide conflict resolution without recourse to the courts (USDOS 2004). A 2004 U.S. State Department country report on Guatemala describes the justice center's efforts as follows:

> The government's Public Ministry and the Judiciary continued efforts to reform the judicial system. Twenty justice centers, which bring together judges, public defenders, prosecutors, private law practitioners, police, municipal representatives, and civil society in a team approach to dispute resolution and problem solving, provided efficient public service. Clerk of Court offices streamlined case processing, increased transparency, improved customer service, and virtually eliminated corruption in local case management. An analogous system was inaugurated in Guatemala City in the Prosecutor's Office Case Intake Unit. At the Prosecutor's Office Victims Unit in the capital, doctors and nurses were on call 24 hours a day to assist rape and other crime victims and to gather evidence for their cases. (USDOS 2004)

Though these projects appear attractively democratic, the reality of these alternative systems is far more complicated. What these models of local justice leave unresolved are the inherent conflicts and operational *difficulties entailed by the corruption of the state and its formal legal entities. While establishing local justice projects may enable some individuals to bypass the worst abuses of the state courts, do such efforts merely accomplish an end run around a corrupt and untouchable legal system? No doubt, it is far easier to deregulate justice by disarticulating local claims from the larger system than it is to work with legislators and courts to redesign, amend, and overhaul the juridical system—which implies renovating not only the courts but also the investigatory and prosecutorial structures, including police, prosecutors, defenders, and forensic investigators as well as the prison system. * bandard approach

While local justice models may appeal to many rights activists and academics, in many ways supporting these models is akin to supporting the *privatization of justice to communities instead of inhering the responsibility of justice to the state. In effect, the development of local justice models *interesting* *need both* without parallel restructuring of state justice systems amounts to little more than the neoliberal model of gutting state institutions. Given that there are never enough resources to make peace, it is easier to engage this neoliberal model than it is to make the state juridical system function for its citizens. Of course, though the concept of local justice sounds attractive to those who support human rights, in the end there is nothing democratic about it. There is no equality before the law when citizens of the same country are not all equal before the law. Moreover, the already corrupt or ineffective state is off the hook, because state institutions are then no longer responsible for legal outcomes (including equal application of the law), because these outcomes are produced by so-called community traditions. Can community justice function given fundamental inequalities? Is it fair that the poor and marginalized are offered some form of a community justice forum, while the rich have state courts that favor their interests or enjoy recourse to private forms of security and "justice"?

Prospects and Contradictions

While international human rights law aims to establish and operationalize a universal standard of justice, this formulation is not without its difficulties. As Sally Merry points out, interventions by international human rights bodies in the affairs of nation-states can entail "conundrums" on the ground (Merry 2006b). Universalized articulations of "human rights" may map imperfectly onto local formulations of "rights" and "justice." Efforts by international human rights agencies to interface with local, community, or indigenous priorities, values, needs, and culture frequently produce tensions. Incompatibilities between the prerogatives of international human rights models and the particularities of local situations may result in contradictory outcomes, especially when international bodies do not recognize and address the political, cultural, and social realities in a local situation. As Merry notes: "These gaps between global visions of justice and specific visions in local contexts create a fundamental dilemma for human rights practice. There is a struggle between the generalizing strategies of transnational actors and the particularistic techniques of activists working within local contexts. How to negotiate this divide is a key human rights problem" (Merry 2006, 103).

The effects of such misunderstandings may prove pernicious in situations of state-sponsored violence, civil conflict, or a precedent of limited access to justice and other vital social goods. Kathleen Dill's (2005) study of a legal proceeding against the material authors of a rural massacre in Guatemala explores the ramifications of tensions between international human rights bodies and local interests. As Dill points out, while international prosecutors contributed to national-level judicial processes, their failure to address or provide support for local courts seeking to prosecute the intellectual and material authors of human rights violations caused an ultimate failure in the effort to address community interests and needs. Dill argues that "in some cases, local-level trials are an essential component to postwar community reconstruction and these cases should receive support from the international human rights community" (323). Moreover, given the interest of local communities to seek justice, it may very well be a better use of resources to make local courts function, rather than set up parallel but less powerful local justice mechanisms.

As Dill's analysis implies, concepts of human rights codified in international law may also pose challenges to local power relations. Equally paradoxically, Merry observes, the "human rights system challenges states' authority over their citizens at the same time as it reinforces states' power" (Merry 2006, 5). International human rights organizations rely on national governments to administer reforms, even when nation-states demonstrate an unwillingness to protect their citizens' human rights. To some, this may suggest that the creation of local justice mechanisms dedicated to pursuing human rights claims may represent a more direct path to change. When individuals and communities simultaneously lack recourse to state-based legal institutions and are alienated by the premises of international human rights law, creating alternative institutions for defining and obtaining justice may represent a particularly attractive path. Still, as long as local justice systems remain subservient to state institutions and are partial in their coverage and mandate, their efficacy and indeed the very justice they purport to deliver remain in question. As the contributors to this volume indicate, anthropologists have been on the forefront of documenting the development of local justice institutions in scholarly literature.

Ethnographies of Local Justice in Latin America

In her essay "Between Threat and Guarantee: Justice and Community in the Margins of the Peruvian State" (2004), anthropologist Deborah Poole discusses iterations of community or local justice in the context of political and historic factors that shape the lived experience of justice in Peru. As Poole demonstrates, the Peruvian juridical system is predicated on a historically enshrined "de facto form of legal pluralism," in which justice is dispensed unpredictably at multiple, incommensurable levels of the law (42). Poole argues that this situation is corrosive to the state's claims for sovereign authority, but also suggests that the resulting irregularities of justice may be advantageous to empowered state and nonstate agents.

Poole details the roots of privatized local judicial systems: *gamonalismo,* a form of judicial patronage, obtained broadly at the local level in Peru from the 1920s to 1940s. The *gamonal*, Poole argues, represents "both the state and the principal forms of private, extrajudicial, and even criminal power"; despite anti-*gamonalismo* reforms, this contradictory form of violent and "premodern" power still endures (52). Recent internationally backed reforms targeting the apparent corruption of community-based *justicia de paz* sought to create "new arenas of arbitration" with "systems of customary law and community-based dispute resolution" (53). However, as Poole shows, these reforms failed to seize upon the "ambiguous jurisdictional and legal status of justices of the peace"—a haziness that is *de jure* as well as *de facto.* Following the establishment of "conciliation centers" in urban areas, for example, peasants continued to experience the "anxiety and indistinction" (54) characteristic of previous forms of law, and when bringing disputes to law, they continued to be "shuttled back and forth between different instances of the Peruvian judicial system" (60).

As Poole connects local justice models to *gamonalismo*, Rudi Colloredo-Mansfield connects community justice movements in the northern Andes to the interests of "an emerging indigenous economic elite" (638), arguing that grassroots political activism plays a role in the development of new forms of stratification in Andean society. Following the implementation of structural adjustment policies in the region, "states have broken their compacts with the poor"; citing the work of Huggins (1991), Colloredo-Mansfield notes that while crime rates have risen, "national and provincial governments have lost the muscle and legitimacy to track down perpetrators, guarantee fair trials, and generally safeguard civil order" (641). He further points out that no one feels secure in current circumstances: "Members of all segments of Latin American societies feel progressively more insecure. Extralegal justice correspondingly mushrooms, spanning forms that include vigilantism backed by conservative elites, spontaneous beatings of pick-pocketing street kids, and 'communal lynchings' that involve a large part of a neighborhood, ritualized action, and significant coordination" (641). This critical view on community justice elaborates the moral dimension of public punishments, meant to reinscribe an ethos that combines, in Colloredo-Mansfield's estimation, both "colonial-rooted social truths" (642) and the imperatives of neoliberal rationality. It also challenges traditional analyses of social conflict that place crime outside the human rights framework, which tends to divorce local juridical systems' treatment of victims and perpetrators alike from the human rights agenda as well. Rather than an afterthought, juridical treatment of crime victims and perpetrators must be central to analyses of social conflict as well as institutional reform of justice systems.

Vigilantes, Death Squads, and Local Justice

In *Vigilantism and the State in Modern Latin America: Essays on Extralegal Violence*, Martha Huggins defines vigilantism as comprising activities that include "lynching, murders by *justiceiros* [justice-seekers], death squad and paramilitary/parapolice violence, and violence by on-duty police" (6). These types of activities most frequently target citizens and are understood to be "essentially conservative or reactionary" (6). Positioning the actions of lynch mobs and other more or less spontaneous groups of civilians alongside extrajudicial violence by paramilitary groups, Huggins argues that violence and justice in Latin America are conditioned at all scales by the region's dependent, peripheral status. As Sanford has argued, these peripheries are then reproduced at the margins of the state within nation-states (2004). Similarly, Benevides and Fischer Ferreira shed interpretive light on what they term "anonymous lynch actions," which they understand as "another structurally rooted form of contemporary urban violence." Presenting this form of "parallel justice" in the context of seemingly arbitrary police repression of the urban poor, the authors argue that lynchings "represent moments in which citizens' feelings of impotence and rage reach a peak" (Benevides and Fischer Ferreira 1991, 33, 43).

The state's uneven protection of citizens is also theorized as an important contribution to lynching in Bolivia, as Goldstein (2003) claims in his discussion of an episode of community vigilantism against suspected thieves in a poor migrant community. Though lynching has contributed to public perceptions of this region as lawless, Goldstein argues that these forms of violent, spontaneous community justice are "not necessarily antagonistic to the power of the state but, rather, presupposes its existence" (24). In this reading, vigilantes in contemporary urban Bolivia express their "refusal to accept . . . exclusion, . . . claim[ing] their rights as citizens to protect their communities, their property, and their families from predators" (25). The role of the neoliberalizing state in creating the conditions for these forms of violence is not lost on Goldstein, who notes that "the so-called privatization of justice is an ironic response to the lack of official state law enforcement" (24).

In Guatemala, where lynchings have risen as a local practice since the signing of the peace accords, the state has been mostly absent. Indeed, a comprehensive investigation conducted by MINUGUA concluded that the state's weak response to lynchings had become a factor of both legitimation and justification for lynchings: "the idea that lynchings are outside the reach of the law is viewed as a guarantee of impunity by those participating" (MINUGUA 2004, 27).

Likewise, the rise of urban gang violence and organized crime has obscured ongoing death squad activity tied to the PNC that continues to take the lives of Guatemalan citizens through extrajudicial executions and social cleansing. International attention was drawn to the nefarious practices of the PNC in February 2007 when an international investigation determined that three Salvadoran members of the Central American Parliament (PARLACEN) were kidnapped near a major shopping center in Guatemala City, held in a clandestine jail, and taken to a rural location near the Salvadoran border where they were beaten, shot, and burned alive in their vehicle ("Cuatro capturados" 2007). The perpetrators of this extrajudicial execution were none other than the PNC's elite unit designated to investigate organized crime. Five officers were arrested and later slaughtered while held in a maximum security prison. Government officials claimed the implicated officers had been killed by gang members within the prison. Families visiting inmates witnessed the arrival of heavily armed men in black uniforms who stormed the prison shortly before rounds of machine gun fire were heard from within the prison. The chief prosecutor's response to the prison slaying was to conclude that the investigation of the extrajudicial execution of the Salvadorans was over because the implicated officers had been killed (Radiolaprimerisimo 2008).

Beyond illuminating the state's willingness to assassinate their own employees, the case also shed light on the government's tendency to deploy gang violence as a red herring to obscures the political roots of violence. Rather than investigate the murders of young men, government officials tend to blame multiple deaths of young men on gang violence, thus blaming the victim for being a gang member, having ties to gangs, or simply being in the wrong place at the wrong time. Occasionally, the social cleansing is so flagrant that it produces national outrage, as did the case of five young men who were eliminated by PNC officers in September 2007. This crime gained notoriety because the witnesses who reported the crime were a small army patrol and the PNC officers who carried out the social cleansing turned out to be the bodyguards of the PNC director (Prensa Libre 2007). While gangs do have ties to the PNC, they can also be hunted by police, especially if they have not paid their quota of protection money to the police or have simply become too big of a liability. In much the same way, gangs also have ties to drug traffickers and organized crime, which in turn also have ties to the police and military. Many observers believe that the clandestine structures within Guatemala are embedded in the military and police and run by its officers and former officers. So deeply embedded are these parallel powers that the International Commission against Impunity in Guatemala (Comisión Internacional Contra la Impunidad en Guatemala or CICIG) was established through a joint agreement between the United Nations and the government of Guatemala with a mandate to investigate and name the illegal groups, parallel powers, and clandestine security structures; their funding sources; and their ties with government agencies and officials. The PNC and the penitentiary system were among the key institutions identified as priority targets for CICIG investigation, which began its mandate in January 2008 (Nonviolent Peaceforce 2007). In its first report issued in November 2008, CICIG recommended a comprehensive packet of reforms, including judicial reform and greater gun control (Palma 2008).

Local Justice and the Guatemalan Judicial System

Since the signing of the peace accords in 1996, the Guatemalan judicial system has been forced to confront and at least partially prosecute some significant legal cases. These have included the army-ordered assassination of anthropologist Myrna Mack, who investigated massacres in rural Guatemala and the assassination of Bishop Juan Gerardi shortly after the release of the Catholic Church's *Nunca Mas* report, which he led in documenting the thousands of Guatemalans killed by security forces. While the material authors of each murder have been prosecuted, the intellectual authors remain unnamed and at large. Beyond these incomplete cases, there are hundreds of rural massacres from the early 1980s that have now been filed in the courts as criminal cases of murder, with forensic evidence collected by various forensic teams since the 1990s. The courts are also challenged to address numerous recent high-profile cases of corruption, organized crime, and drug trafficking—and thousands of homicides. The end result is an overwhelmed judicial system that is still in the process of adapting to new laws and procedures promulgated in the 1990s to move Guatemala away from a vertical system of justice that was secretive and denied access to most citizens.

Impunity in Guatemala is reinforced by the inefficiency of the judicial system and a legacy of reserving justice for certain groups only. Members of certain elite groups enjoy the privilege of evading the restrictions imposed by the legal system or the consequences of transgression. There is an unwritten norm that some people are "untouchable" by the law. As noted in a recent study on corruption in Guatemala, "legal institutions have been unable to secure the guarantee of equal protection before the law in any satisfactory manner" (FDPL 2007, 204). Elite groups are able to maintain high levels of impunity and further entrench their power through a broad network of influence encompassing the highest levels of government down to the lowest ranks of gangs and private armies or death squads. This framework of influence and racketeering extends to electoral campaigns, elected officials, and judicial appointments (4). Indeed, one lawyer I interviewed in July 2007 in Guatemala City (who requested anonymity) was offered a judgeship, but only if he would agree not to prosecute certain cases awaiting hearings in what would have been his court. This convergence of influence, racketeering, electoral politics, and judicial appointments helps explain why the constitutional court, the highest court in Guatemala, would rule that former military dictator Efrain Rios Montt could run for president, even though the constitution forbids anyone who came to power through military coup (as he did in 1982) from running for office—the court ruled that the law was not retroactive, which means that only those who might come to power through military coup in the future would be banned from seeking elected office after their dictatorships.

One might suggest that the culture of terror that produced genocide in Guatemala in the 1980s has become a culture of impunity in "peacetime." This culture of impunity is systemic and systematic. It begins with the inefficiency of a legal system that has never been able to overcome the formalism of past authoritarian regimes that privileges procedures over the facts of the case. Thus, the legal system as it is currently constituted locates the truth of a case in the execution of written procedures filled in the court, rather than in actual court hearings.

While the transitional postwar revamping of the judicial system included a new emphasis on judicial transparency through the prominence of oral arguments that included USAID-funded trainings for lawyers and judges alike, a decade later the courts have largely reverted back to written cases with little or no oral argument (FDPL 205). Thus, oral arguments and their accompanying transparency clash with an intransigent legal culture that demands form over content and ritual over justice. In such a system, it is difficult to assign responsibility for the resolution of a case when the goals are defined not in terms of legal resolution, but rather in terms of procedural completion. This proceduralism is constituted within a judicial power that is increasingly exercised on the whims of the court and its agents. This ambient power founded in proceduralism and shrouded in ambiguity is then institutionalized in corruption where "justice" can only be achieved after all parties have agreed on a price. The end result is a judicial system based on bureaucratic proceduralism rather than on rule of law.

Murder Investigation Protocol

While there are no binding international standards for murder investigations, basic investigative procedures vary little internationally. In fact, if there is anything remarkable about standard protocols, it is their procedural simplicity and scientific consistency regardless of the complexity of the case. The first task is to secure the crime scene and document all the evidence by mapping, photographing, and collecting everything possible from bloodstains to footprints. The body should then be removed from the scene and taken to the morgue for a complete medico-legal autopsy. The clothing is removed from the victim, painstakingly reviewed for clues, and then retained as evidence. As Dr. Clyde Snow pointed out in an interview with the author in 2007, the victim's clothing "is not returned to the next of kin." Clothing is not returned to the family until after the trial. This, of course, assumes there will be a trial, which assumes there will be an arrest, which assumes there will be an investigation leading to a suspect.

The investigation into Claudina Isabel Velasquez Paiz's murder is riddled with holes, flaws, and inconsistencies. There is no documentation of the names of the paramedics who were the first on the crime scene, nor any record of any manipulation they may have done to her body to either attempt to resuscitate her or determine that she was dead. There is also tremendous confusion about the most basic and critical pieces of forensic information, such as the time of death.

There are also significant discrepancies in the identification of actual injuries sustained by the victim among the various reports. The public prosecutor's (MP) report does not note injuries visible in the crime scene photos and described in the PNC report, including significant bruising to the left eye socket and cheek. The medical examiner also fails to note severe scraping on the left knee and right flank, both of which appear in the photos and are mentioned in the PNC report. There is no documentation indicating the sampling or analysis of blood stains from the victim's clothing or at the crime scene. Although various pieces of Claudina Isabel's clothing had bloodstains, her bra and belt had been removed, her pants zipper was down, and her blouse was on backward, only her blouse was submitted for analysis, and no analysis was done on the rest of her clothing.

The autopsy conducted at the morgue is full of omissions and inconsistencies, beginning with who actually carried out the autopsy. It took the medical examiner more than a year to report the time of death and nearly two months to include Claudina Isabel's name on the report. In the same official correction adding Claudina Isabel's name, the medical examiner wrote that "the time of death was between seven and eleven hours after the autopsy." It was not until June 7, 2006, that the medical examiner corrected this error and indicated that the time of death was between seven and eleven hours before the autopsy. The ballistic analysis fared no better. The ballistic report is dated February 2, 2005, and the MP stamped it "Received," with a date of February 28, 2005. These dates are baffling given that Claudina Isabel was killed six months later.

The MP has made no effort to locate any potential witnesses at the crime scene where Claudina Isabel's body was found. Searches of the homes of primary suspects did not take place until three months after Claudina Isabel's murder. There has been no real search for a weapon.

The prosecutor's office did not even interview Claudina Isabel's family members until one month after her murder, and only then because the family sought out the prosecutor's office to find out what was happening with Claudina Isabel's case. The only statements taken by the MP were those of individuals who voluntarily and randomly presented themselves to the MP to make a declaration. While both MP and PNC carried out interviews, no joint meetings have ever been held among investigators involved in this case to develop strategic lines of inquiry. Thus, all statements have simply been recorded and taken at face value, and contradictions have not been analyzed.

One of the most striking aspects of Claudina Isabel's case is that it is actually being investigated. Most cases end where Claudina Isabel's would have ended had her father not used all of his resources to push for an investigation. Her case would have ended with an autopsy report that did not even include her name. In 2005, the public prosecutor's office conducted only eight successful murder prosecutions, though that year 5,338 men and women were victims of homicide.

Feminicide, Impunity, and Transitional Justice

Who killed Claudina Isabel? Probably someone she knew. If Claudina Isabel was killed by someone who knew her, why place her murder in the category of feminicide? What is feminicide? What does it have to do with impunity and transitional justice? And, how does it help to explain these phenomena? The concept of feminicide builds on the term "femicide," which refers to the murder of women in criminology literature. It also refers to a hate crime against women in the emerging feminist literature addressing the murder of women (Russell and Harmes 2001).

"Feminicide" is a political term. Conceptually, it encompasses more than the term "femicide" because it holds responsible not only the male perpetrators but also the state and judicial structures that normalize misogyny. Feminicide connotes not only the murder of women by men because they are women but also indicates state responsibility for these murders, whether through the commission of the actual killing, tolerance of the perpetrators' acts of violence, or omission of state responsibility to ensure the safety of its female citizens. In Guatemala, feminicide exists because of the absence of state guarantees to protect the rights of women. Impunity, silence, and indifference each play a role in feminicide.

Conclusion

In the 1980s, thousands of women were subjected to sexual violence and torture prior to being assassinated by state agents. In fact, the report of the Commission for Historical Clarification confirms that the state trained its soldiers and other armed agents to rape and terrorize women. During the war, army soldiers and other security officers were responsible for 99 percent of acts of sexual violence carried out against women (Consorcio Actoras de Cambio 2006, 32).

These crimes of the state and its agents have never been brought to justice and have remained in impunity. The state trained killers to rape, mutilate, and murder women during the war. These killers and rapists are free. If the state continues to protect these killers and rapists with impunity, then why would one expect them to search out the murderers of Claudina Isabel Velasquez Paiz or any of the other women who have been killed? Writing about the effects of the wars of the 1980s on women in El Salvador and Guatemala, UN rapporteur Yakin Erturk noted the dire need for government and societal acknowledgment of the systematic use of brutal sexual violence as a weapon of war during the armed conflicts as well as the still unresolved needs of justice and reparations for victims and survivors. Erturk pointed to the imperative of prosecuting perpetrators of previous violent crimes against women as key in the fight against impunity—for justice for victims in the past and as a deterrent to contemporary violence. It is a travesty that more than a decade after the signing of the peace accords, the UN reports that the PNC are the main perpetrators of human rights violations.

UN rapporteur Philip Alston concluded in his special report on extrajudicial executions in Guatemala that the harrowing murder rate is the product of a distinct lack of political will. He wrote, "There are 5,000 or more killings per year, and the responsibility for this must rest with the State. Guatemala is not a failed State and is not an especially poor State" (Alston 2007, 9). Alston also provides the legal framework in which he finds the state

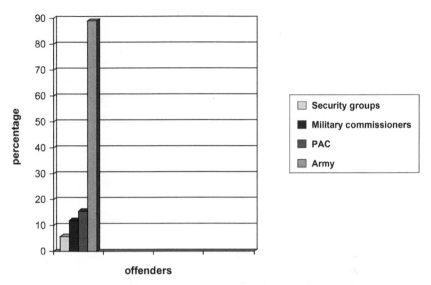

FIGURE 3.4 State agents and sexual violence against women.
Source: Consorcio Actoras de Cambio 2006, 32.

responsible. Under international human rights law, "the failure to establish individual responsibility under domestic criminal law does not absolve the State of responsibility. . . . Under the International Covenant on Civil and Political Rights (ICCPR), the State has legal obligations to both 'respect' and 'ensure' the right to life" (Alston 2007, 10). While Alston notes that as a general rule the state is not responsible for common murders by private persons, he also points out that it is an obligation of the state to "exercise due diligence in preventing such crimes. Once a pattern becomes clear in which the response of the Government is clearly inadequate, its responsibility under international human rights law becomes applicable" (Alston 2007, 11). In order for the state to meets its international obligations, it must "effectively investigate, prosecute and punish perpetrators" (11).

Erturk concluded in her report on Guatemala that "violence against women is met with impunity as authorities fail to investigate cases and to prosecute and punish perpetrators. In this regard, the absence of rule of law fosters a continuum of violent acts against women, including murder, rape, domestic violence, sexual harassment, and commercial sexual exploitation. Security and justice institutions have not responded adequately, particularly by failing to resolve a recent series of brutal murders of women (Erturk 2005, 3).

The international community, including anthropologists, can play a positive role in ending impunity in Guatemala by supporting women's and human rights groups and the Procuraduria de Derechos Humanos de Guatemala (PDH), the human rights ombudsman. Diplomatic missions, concerned citizens, and international aid groups can tie international assistance to ending impunity. Specifically, the international community can pressure the MP to move forward on feminicide and homicide cases; pressure the police to conduct unbiased investigations; pressure the medical examiner's office to complete a consistent forensic protocol on all murder victims regardless of appearance and to include sexual assault as a standard protocol in murder investigations; pressure the Guatemalan government to cooperate with the Spanish court and cooperate with the extradition of the generals for trial in Spain as well as moving forward on the prosecution of hundreds of human rights violations cases currently stagnating in the domestic legal system; and support the dismantling of impunity by full investigation and disclosure on the role of parallel powers in the state. Resolution of the murder of Claudina Isabel would no doubt be an important step in the restoration of justice in the Guatemalan judicial system. Without a functioning juridical system, transitional justice and its attendant internationally supported local justice projects merely reinforce bureaucratic proceduralism that nurtures impunity in Guatemala today.

NOTES

The authors thank Rachel Daniel, Cristina Finan, and Jennifer Sugg for research assistance and database development. Thanks to Silvia Donoso, Alejandro Rodriguez, Brigittine French, Miho Omi, Carlos Aguirre, Zoe Crossland, Heather Walsh-Haney, Clyde Snow, Leyla Renshaw, Lotti Silber, Christa Salamandra, Jane Schneider, Micheline Aharonian-Marcom, and John Wallach for sharing their expertise and comments. Our greatest debt is to Jorge Velasquez for entrusting his daughter's story to us. Special thanks to Alex Hinton for his support of this project and his patience.

1. The World Bank, the IDB, USAID, the United Nations Development Program, the UN Mission in Guatemala, the Organization of American States, the European Union and numerous bilateral donors have contributed millions of dollars to justice reform in Guatemala.

2. General Fernando Romeo Lucas Garcia appears to have died in Venezuela shortly before the arrest order was issued.

REFERENCES

Advancement Project. 2007. "Community Justice Resource Center Newsletter." *Community Justice Resource Center*. http://www.advancementproject.org/cjrc/index.php.

Alston, Philip. 2007. *Civil and Political Rights, Including the Questions of Disappearances and Summary Executions. Mission to Guatemala*. United Nations: Human Rights Council.

Benevides, Maria-Victoria, and Rosa-Maria Fischer Ferreira. 1991. "Popular Responses and Urban Violence: Lynching in Brazil." In *Vigilantism and the State in Modern*

Latin America: Essays on Extralegal Violence, ed. Martha K. Huggings, 33–45. New York: Praeger.

Bureau of International Information Programs, U.S. Department of State. 2007. "New Community Courts Increase Access to Justice in South Africa." http://usinfo.state.gov/xarchives/display.html?p=washfile-english&y=2007&m=May&x=20070523172543AKllennoCcMo.3577997.

Center for Court Innovation. 2007. http://www.courtinnovation.org.

Colloredo-Mansfield, Rudi. 2002. "'Don't Be Lazy, Don't Lie, Don't Steal': Community Justice in the Neoliberal Andes." *American Ethnologist* 29 (3): 637–662.

Comisión para el Esclarecimiento Histórico (CEH). 1999. *Memoria del silencio*. Vols. 1–12. Guatemala City: Comisión para el Esclarecimiento Histórico.

Consorcio Actoras de Cambio. 2006. *Rompiendo el silencio*. Guatemala City: Consorcio Actoras de Cambio y El Instituto de Estudios Comparados en Ciencias Penales.

Corte Interamericana de Derechos Humanos (Corte IDH). 2004. "*Caso Masacre Plan de Sánchez vs. Guatemala.* Sentencia de 29 de abril. Serie C No. 105." http://www.corteidh.or.cr/pais.cfm?id_Pais=18.

"Cuatro capturados por asesinato de disputados al PARLACEN." 2007. *El Periodico* (Guatemala), February 26.

Data 360. 2009. "Homicide Rate by Country." http://www.data360.org/dataset.aspx?Data_Set_Id=1916.

Dill, Kathleen. 2005. "International Human Rights and Local Justice in Guatemala: The Rio Negro (Pak'oxom) and Agua Fria Trials." *Cultural Dynamics* 17 (3): 323–350.

"El Juez Pedraz dictó orden de captura." 2006. *El Periodico* (Guatemala), July 8.

Erturk, Yakin. 2005. *Integration of the Human Rights of Women and Gender Perspective: Violence against Women. Mission to Guatemala.* United Nations: Commission on Human Rights.

Fine, Toni. 1999. "How the U.S. Court System Functions." *Issues of Democracy* 4 (2). http://usinfo.state.gov/journals/itdhr/0999/ijde/fine.htm.

Fundación para el Debido Proceso Legal (FDPL). 2007. *Controles y decontroles de la corrupcion judicial.* Washington, DC: FDPL. http://www.dplf.org/uploads/1196091551.pdf.

Goldstein, Daniel M. 2003. "'In Our Own Hands': Lynching, Justice, and the Law in Bolivia." *American Ethnologist* 30 (1): 11–43.

Hegtvedt, Karen. 2005. "Doing Justice to the Group: Examining the Roles of the Group in Justice Research." *Annual Review of Sociology* 31:25–45.

Huggins, Martha K. 1991. *Vigilantism and the State in Modern Latin America: Essays on Extralegal Violence.* New York: Praeger.

International Development Resource Centre (IDRC). 2007. "Community Justice as Restorative Justice in Colombia." http://www.idrc.ca/en/ev-59364-201-1-DO_TOPIC.html.

"International Homicide Comparisons." 2006. *GunCite.com.* May 20. http://www.guncite.com/gun_control_gcgvinco.html.

Kurki, Leena. 2000. "Restorative and Community Justice in the United States." *Crime and Justice* 27:235–303.

Merry, Sally. 1992. "Anthropology, Law, and Transnational Processes." *Annual Review of Anthropology* 21 (1): 357–379.

———. 2006a. *Human Rights and Gender Violence: Translating International Law into Local Justice.* Chicago: University of Chicago Press.

———. 2006b. "Human Rights, Gender, and New Social Movements: Contemporary Debates in Legal Anthropology." http://www.ciesas.edu.mx/proyectos/relaju/documentos/Merry_Sally.pdf.

Merry, Sally, and Neal Milner, eds. 1993. *The Possibility of Popular Justice: A Case Study of Community Mediation in the United States.* Ann Arbor: University of Michigan Press.

MINUGUA (UN Mission in Guatemala). 2004. *Los linchamientos en Guatemala.* Guatemala City: MINUGUA.

Nonviolent Peaceforce. 2007. "CICIG Opens Dialogue to Establish Its Priorities." http://nonviolentpeaceforce.org/en/guatemalaOct07.

Open Society Institute. 2007. "Community Justice Program." http://www.soros.org/initiatives/baltimore/focus_areas/b_community.

Palma, Claudia. 2008. "CICIG entrega paquete de reformas de ley a la UNE." http://www.elperiodico.com.gt/es/20080923/pais/71585/.

Pan-American Health Organization. 2007. "Statistics on Homicides, Suicides, Accidents, Injuries and Attitudes towards Violence." http://www.paho.org/English/AD/DPC/NC/violence-graphs.htm#homicides-n-sa.

Poole, Deborah. 2004. "Between Threat and Guarantee: Justice and Community in the Margins of the Peruvian State." In *Anthropology in the Margins of the State*, ed. Veena Das and Deborah Poole, 35–65. Santa Fe, NM: School of American Research Press.

Prensa Libre. 2007. "Policias matan a cinco jóvenes." http://www.prensalibre.com/pl/2007/septiembre/26/183477.html.

Procuraduria de Derechos Humanos de Guatemala (PDH). 2005. *Informe de muertes violentas de mujeres.* Guatemala City: PDH.

———. 2006a. *Informe de las caracteristicas de las muertes violentas en el pais.* Guatemala City: PDH.

———. 2006b. *Informe de verificacion sobre la investigacion criminal, caso Claudina Isabel Velasquez Paiz.* Guatemala City: PDH.

Radiolaprimerisimo. 2008. "Asesinato de Fiscal guatemalteco ligado a muerte de salvadorenos." Agencia ACAN-EFE. http://www.radiolaprimerisima.com/noticias/resumen/33575.

Roman, Caterina Gouvis, Gretchen E. Moore, Susan Jenkins, and Keonne M. Small. 2002. "Understanding Community Justice Partnerships: Assessing the Capacity to Partner." http://www.ncjrs.gov/pdffiles1/nij/grants/196552.pdf.

Russell, Diana, and Roberta Harmes, eds. 2001. *Femicide in Global Perspective.* New York: Teachers College Columbia University Press.

Sanford, Victoria. 2002. "Truth Commissions." In *Encyclopedia of Crime and Punishment*, ed. David Levinson, 1637–1641. Thousand Oaks, CA: Sage.

———. 2003a. *Violencia y genocidio en Guatemala.* Guatemala City: F&G Editores.

———. 2003b. *Buried Secrets: Truth and Human Rights in Guatemala.* New York: Palgrave Macmillan.

———. 2003c. "The 'Gray Zone' of Justice: NGOs and Rule of Law in Post-War Guatemala." *Journal of Human Rights* 2 (3): 393–405.

———. 2004. "Contesting Displacement in Colombia: Citizenship and State Sovereignty at the Margins." In *Anthropology in the Margins of the State*, ed. Veena Das and Deborah Poole, 2. Santa Fe, NM: School of American Research.

———. 2008a. "Si hubo genocidio—Yes, There Was a Genocide in Guatemala." In *The Historiography of Genocide*, ed. Dan Stone, 543–576. New York: Palgrave Macmillan.

———. 2008b. "From Genocide to Feminicide: Impunity and Human Rights in 21st Century Guatemala." *Journal of Human Rights* 7 (2): 104–122.

Sierra, Maria Teresa. 2005. "The Revival of Indigenous Justice in Mexico: Challenges for Human Rights and the State." *PoLAR* 28 (1): 52–72.

U.S. Agency for International Development (USAID). 2007a. "USAID: Latin America and the Caribbean—Democracy Programs: Alternative Sources of Justice." http://www.usaid.gov/locations/latin_america_caribbean/democracy/rule/dg_rule8.html.

———. 2007b. "Democracy and Governance Annual Program Statement for FY 07." http://philippines.usaid.gov/documents/rfas/492–07–003-APS.doc.

U.S. Department of Justice (USDOJ). "Homicide Rates." http://www.ojp.gov/bjs/homicide/hmrt.htm.

U.S. Department of State (USDOS). 2004. "Country Reports on Human Rights Practices 2003: Guatemala. Bureau of Democracy, Human Rights, and Labor." http://www.state.gov.

———. 2009. "Norma Cruz Fights to End the Killing of Guatemalan Women Survivors Foundation Aims to Turn the Rising Tide of Violent Deaths." http://www.america.gov/st/democracyhr-english/2009/March/20090306154900ajesromo.1163599.html.

PART TWO

Justice in the Vernacular

4

▶▶▶▶▶▶▶▶▶▶▶▶▶ ◀◀◀◀◀◀◀◀◀◀◀◀◀◀

(In)Justice

Truth, Reconciliation, and Revenge in Rwanda's *Gacaca*

JENNIE E. BURNET

The goal of the *gacacas* was not to parade people before the courts for form, but to try them well!

> –Benoit Kaboyi, executive secretary of Ibuka,
> the National Genocide Survivors Association

The *inyangamugayo* ("people of integrity"/*Gacaca* judges) won't stop until all the educated Hutu are in prison with long sentences.

> –Woman from Northern Province, May 2007

Fifteen years after the 1994 genocide in Rwanda, many genocide survivors and victims are still awaiting justice, although it has been sought through a plurality of mechanisms: an ad hoc international tribunal, foreign courts, Rwandan justice system, and a local justice mechanism known as *Gacaca* (pronounced ga-cha-cha). In a radical departure from precedents in other postconflict countries, where amnesties, truth commissions, selective prosecutions, or some combination thereof, have been used to bring closure to conflict, Rwanda decided to put "most of the nation on trial" (Waldorf 2006, 3). To accomplish this task, the government reinvented a "traditional" conflict resolution mechanism known as *gacaca*.[1] Beginning with a pilot phase in 2001 and a nationwide roll-out in 2005, the entire population has been enlisted to prosecute, defend, testify, and judge an estimated 761,000 suspects accused of genocide as of March 2005 (Reyntjens 2005, 3).

Gacaca has been framed both as transitional justice and local justice (e.g., Uvin and Mironko 2003; Waldorf 2006). According to Hinton,

Transitional justice is often defined as the process of redressing wrongs committed in states shifting from a violent, authoritarian past toward a more liberal, democratic future—though more recently the term has been defined in a broader manner (for example, a more general "response to systematic or widespread violations of human rights") and extended to encompass a larger set of outcomes, such as advancing development and social justice. (Hinton, this volume)

While Rwanda has not moved very far toward "a more liberal, democratic future" in the assessments of most regional specialists (see Longman 2006; Reyntjens 2004, 2006), it has moved a very long way from the genocide crimes and crimes against humanity of the 1994 genocide and the reigning insecurity of the 1990s. According to many economic indicators, Rwanda is developing at a rate far surpassing other postconflict African nations. Yet, characterizing *Gacaca* as transitional justice is problematic, because, as Waldorf (2006) notes, it only adjudicates cases related to the 1994 genocide and does not touch the Rwandan Patriotic Front (RPF) killings. Given that *Gacaca* placed the power of law and justice in the hands of ordinary citizens, it fits the attributes of local justice well (see Hinton, this volume). In public awareness campaigns about *Gacaca*, the Rwandan government portrayed it as a Rwandan solution for a Rwandan problem and as a way to foreground the experiences and voices of genocide survivors.[2] Yet, as with any local process, *Gacaca* is a site of friction where local, regional, national, and international processes intersect (Tsing 2005).

Based on ethnographic fieldwork in urban and rural Rwanda between 1997 and 2003, focus groups and interviews conducted in May and June of 2007, and additional interviews conducted in May 2009, this chapter explores local perceptions of the *Gacaca* process and asks whether *Gacaca* has fulfilled its primary goals to "end impunity," promote reconciliation, and establish the "real truth of what happened during the Genocide" (Official Website of the Republic of Rwanda 2001). My findings indicate that how well *Gacaca* has functioned varies a great deal from community to community. The most important variable appears to be the character of the *inyangamugayo* (people of integrity), who serve as judge and jury in the *Gacaca* system. Regardless of how well *Gacaca* has operated, in the short term it increased (or at least brought to the surface) conflict in local communities and intensified ethnic cleavages. Increased ethnic cleavages in the short term would not necessarily be a negative outcome if the long-term prospects for building a peaceful society were good. By May 2009, nearly a year and a half after the official end of *Gacaca* trials, community-based organizations in some districts have managed to reintegrate released prisoners and reestablish the weft of the social fabric.

The Move toward Local Justice

Since 1994, many justice mechanisms have been used to prosecute the planners and perpetrators of the Rwandan genocide. The new Rwandan government, headed by the RPF,[3] adopted a stance of maximal prosecution: every single participant in the genocide, from the central planners down to coerced peasant farmers or opportunistic looters, would be prosecuted and punished for their crimes. Article 2 of the 1996 genocide code delineated four categories of responsibility in the genocide: (1) "planners, organizers, instigators, supervisors and leaders of the crime of genocide or of a crime against humanity," persons in positions of authority in the government or political parties, "notorious murderers," and "persons who committed acts of sexual torture"; (2) perpetrators or "conspirators of accomplices" of intentional homicide or physical assault causing death; (3) persons guilty of "serious assaults against the person"; and (4) persons who committed crimes against property (Organic Law No. 08/1996). Subsequent amendments to the genocide code, including the laws establishing the *Gacaca* courts and amending their structure and statutes, have maintained this hierarchy of responsibility, with punishments varying in severity by category (Organic Laws No. 40/2000, 08/2004, 16/2004, 28/2006, 10/2007).

On the international plane, the UN Security Council created the International Criminal Tribunal for Rwanda (ICTR) with resolution 955 on November 8, 1994, to prosecute persons responsible for genocide and other serious violations of international humanitarian law committed between January 1, 1994, and December 31, 1994, in Rwanda or in neighboring states. The international human rights community had many hopes for the ICTR. It would allow prosecution of the genocide planners who had fled the country, acknowledge the international scope of the crimes committed in Rwanda, establish a significant repository of testimony and evidence about the 1994 genocide, and help seek justice for genocide survivors. The degree to which the ICTR has lived up to these hopes is debatable.[4] In the early years of its existence, most Rwandan citizens felt completely marginalized by the ICTR, but public information campaigns in Rwanda sponsored by the ICTR, the Hirondelle Foundation, and Internews made most Rwandans aware of the ICTR's activities by the late 1990s and early 2000s. Many Rwandans have followed the progress of the trials via radio news reports, newspapers, or the Internet; in particular, they were interested by the high profile cases such as the media trial, in which owners of the extremist, anti-Tutsi propaganda newspapers and radio were prosecuted, and the military trial, in which several highly placed officers were prosecuted. Yet in terms of "justice in the vernacular" (Hinton, this volume), many Rwandans view the institution as unjust since people prosecuted before the ICTR face lesser penalties than those tried inside Rwanda and enjoy comparatively luxurious prison conditions.[5] In addition, the vast resources invested in the ICTR and its slow progress encouraged additional criticism, and the Rwandan government has, when politically expedient, encouraged negative sentiment toward the ICTR.[6]

Under the principle of universal jurisdiction, several foreign governments have prosecuted Rwandans for genocide crimes. The first example was the trial of a National University of Rwanda professor and four Roman Catholic nuns in Belgium in 2001. All were found guilty and sentenced to imprisonment. More recently, Canada prosecuted Desiré Munyaneza under the Crimes Against Humanity and War Crimes Act, passed in 2000. Munyaneza, the son of a wealthy business man, fled to Canada in 1996 or 1997. In 2005, he was arrested and charged with genocide, crimes against humanity, and war crimes. His trial began in March 2007 and lasted over two years and cost the Canadian government millions of dollars (*Montreal Gazette* 2009). On May 22, 2009, he was found guilty on all counts. Prosecutions of genocide suspects continue before numerous European courts, and the Rwandan government has begun to investigate suspects who fled and are living abroad so that it can request their extradition (CBCNews 2007).

At the national level, the first genocide trials began in Rwanda's Belgian-style court system in December 1996. The Rwandan justice system, itself destroyed in the genocide and its personnel decimated, was overwhelmed and trials moved forward slowly. As of March 2001, the national courts had tried 5,310 people (HRW 2002, 79). In the late 1990s, prison and local jail populations in Rwanda soared to over 130,000, almost all imprisoned on charges of genocide. Even if Rwanda had had the best justice system in the world, it would have been overwhelmed by the problem of trying genocide suspects. Under pressure from the international community to solve the problem, the Rwandan government turned to *gacaca*.

In its traditional form, *gacaca* brought together *inyangamugayo*, who were usually respected elders, the people in dispute, and residents of the hill to establish the facts of the conflict and find a solution. It takes its name from a patch of grass found in the inner courtyard (*igikari*) of a traditional homestead. An inner courtyard was the most private place in a family home and usually only family members entered it. The courtyard was the domain of the wife, and the husband asked permission before entering. Thus, *gacaca* in its traditional form was a private rather than public affair. The deliberations in *gacaca* were considered confidential, and the judgments or decisions of *gacaca* were reported publicly only if such reporting was a specific decision of the *gacaca* process.

Under Belgian colonialism, tribal courts, which were overseen by local chiefs, were established to handle disputes among the indigenous population, and modern Belgian-style courts were established to handle legal disputes involving the foreign (mostly white) population. The laws of ← the colonial state (relegated to the Belgian-style colonial courts) only applied to Europeans and certain categories of other foreigners, while customary law (relegated to the tribal courts) applied to Rwandans and other Africans. *Gacaca* continued to operate during this period, but its decisions were only enforced by local chiefs if these chiefs recognized the legitimacy of a specific *gacaca* and its decisions. In the postcolonial period, the Belgian-style modern courts replaced the tribal courts, yet in some communities local administrators began holding *gacaca* sessions to resolve disputes among rural peasants without involving the modern legal system (Reyntjens 1990). While *gacaca* was used by local officials under the Habyarimana regime, this practice was never codified by Rwandan law, so the exact format and function of *gacaca* varied widely from community to community. In addition, families continued to resolve intrafamilial conflicts through *gacaca* when necessary.

Exactly when *gacaca* was proposed as a possible remedy for Rwanda's postgenocide judicial woes is unclear. In 1996, the UN Human Rights Field Operation in Rwanda (UNHRFOR) commissioned a study of *gacaca* by several Rwandan professors from the National University of Rwanda (Karega et al. 1996). The report documented several forms of *gacaca* throughout the country and even found a few communities who had applied it to solve local disputes in the absence of a functioning judiciary in 1995 and early 1996, but it concluded that *gacaca* was not appropriate as a judicial remedy for the genocide. Political scientist Timothy Longman dates the *gacaca* solution to a conversation between Michele Wagner, a historian of the region and a researcher for Human Rights Watch, and some professors from the National University on the terrace of the Hotel Ibis in Butare in 1995 (T. Longman, pers. comm.). Regardless of the origins of the idea or initial negative studies, *gacaca* emerged as the only possible solution in the eyes of the Rwandan government and many members of the international aid community. International human rights organizations criticized the *Gacaca* courts. Their procedures violated the fundamental rights of the accused because they were prohibited from seeking legal counsel and were not granted full rights to cross-examine or call witnesses for their defense (Penal Reform International 2006, 26–37). As Peter Uvin and Charles Mironko state, "perhaps the strongest element in favor of gacaca is the lack of an alternative" (2003, 227). Given that the codification of *Gacaca* into law was the result of extensive negotiations within the RPF political party and the government of Rwanda (GOR), and among the GOR, international donors, human rights lawyers, and human rights organizations, the *Gacaca* code is an example of friction and awkwardness of working out connections across differences (Tsing 2005, 4).

In January 2001, the original code creating the *Gacaca* courts was passed by the National Assembly. The reinvented *Gacaca* courts changed many of the fundamental aspects of the traditional *gacaca*. The first and most important difference is that the *Gacaca* courts made the proceedings a public affair, with the entire community participating. Second, the foundation of *Gacaca* court proceedings are the testimony of prisoners who confessed to their crimes. In traditional *gacaca*, testimony usually began with the aggrieved stating their case, followed by impartial witnesses providing testimony. The accused testified and were cross-examined by participants based on the accounts provided by the impartial witnesses. Third, the foundation of traditional *gacaca* was not punitive justice, but rather restorative justice. Although the recommendations of a traditional *gacaca* might have included some punishment (for example, the gift of a cow, goat, or other livestock), these punishments were focused on reestablishing social equilibrium between the aggrieved parties and lineages. When a *gacaca* judgment included the gift of livestock, the gift had to be made with all of the ritual ceremony normally accorded to such a gift and with all of the subsequent required countergifts. The *Gacaca* courts have attempted to include aspects of restorative justice through the inclusion of Work of General Interest (known by its French acronym TIG, or *travaux d'intérêt général*), portrayed as a sort of community service but in practice more like prison work camps, and the payment of reparations to the victims' families or to the Genocide Survivors Assistance Funds as part of perpetrators' sentences. Yet, in communities the perception of the *Gacaca* courts is that they were focused on punitive justice, especially since they dealt with property crimes last. The *Gacaca* courts can impose sentences ranging from "civil reparation of damages caused to other people's property" to the death penalty or life imprisonment.[7]

Despite this reinvention of a private conflict resolution mechanism as a public, punitive justice mechanism, the Rwandan population, including survivors, the accused, and families of the accused, maintained hope that the truth might emerge, justice might be served, and the falsely accused might be released. Elections for *inyangamugayo* were held in late 2001, and a pilot phase of *Gacaca* began in 2002. Following its pilot phase from 2001 through 2002, the *Gacaca* statute and entire Rwandan judiciary were reorganized based on the results of the pilot phase. Organic Law No. 16/2004 was promulgated on June 19, 2004, and the *Gacaca* courts began operating nationwide.

Given the RPF's policy of maximal prosecution, the prisons gradually filled following the RPF victory in July 1994. With the return en masse of over one million refugees in late 1996 and early 1997, the prison population ballooned. By 2001, over 130,000 people were accused of genocide and imprisoned (Human Rights Watch 2002). This massive prison population put a strain on state resources; the Rwandan government was unable to provide adequate food, water, or living quarters for prisoners, most of whom were housed in structures originally intended for other purposes. Prisoners' family members were required to bring food and drinking water at least once per week to sustain their imprisoned relatives.

In public statements, the Rwandan government hoped that *Gacaca* would help with the problem of mass incarceration of people accused of genocide: the prisons would be emptied and the drain on state and community resources would be stopped. In early 2003 (a few months before parliamentary and presidential elections), President Kagame provisionally released several thousand prisoners who were elderly, sick, or were minors in 1994. In July 2005, August 2006, and February 2007, authorities released tens of thousands of detainees who were elderly, sick, or had been minors in 1994, or who had confessed to participating in the genocide and had already served the maximum sentence for their category of crimes (HRW 2006; IRIN 2005a, 2005b). Released prisoners attended a six-week reeducation camp (*ingando*) before returning to their home communities. Despite these steps to reduce the prison population, *Gacaca* resulted in an exponential increase in the number of accused genocide suspects. In January 2005, the secretary of state in the Ministry of Justice announced that approximately 761,000 suspects had been identified in the investigation phase of *Gacaca* (Reyntjens 2005, 13). Furthermore, the number of detainees in Rwandan prisons and jails continued to rise from 60,000 at the beginning of 2006 to around 90,000 in May 2007 (Hirondelle News Agency 2007c). In December 2007, Domitille Mukantaganzwa, executive secretary of the National Service of Gacaca Courts, announced that 712,723 cases had been completed out of a total of over 1.12 million cases (Gakwaya 2007). Presumably, many of these cases involved more than one person.

By May 2009, the vast majority of prisoners had either been released or moved into TIG camps. Many of those who had returned home were still required to participate in TIG three days per week. Prisoners remaining in the camps spent six days per week performing TIG and lived in miserable conditions in large structures made from tarps, wood poles, and tin roofing. The stench rising from one camp along the road from Kigali to Muhanga (formerly Gitarama) in May 2009 was stunning. The results of TIG projects are highly visible throughout the country and have included the rehabilitation or construction of roads, the improvement of marshes to increase arable land, and the terracing of hills to increase arable land and reduce environmental degradation.

Putting Justice before Truth

A persisting difficulty for Rwandans in general, and for genocide survivors in particular, is knowing when, where, and how their loved ones died (Burnet

2005; Schotsman 2000). Being the ones who stopped the genocide, the RPF has used its symbolic capital as "the saviors" of Rwanda to legitimate its dictatorial rule. Thus, knowing the truth about the genocide is a political need. Yet, for genocide survivors, this need to know the truth is not merely political or psychological; it is also spiritual and metaphysical. According to traditional Rwandan religious beliefs, the dead inhabit our world as ancestor spirits who cause trouble for the living if they are displeased. Keeping the spirits happy requires a sacred burial and regular ritual offerings of food and drink. While the majority of Rwandans adopted Roman Catholicism at some point during the twentieth century, traditional beliefs still strongly influence Christian converts. Furthermore, Catholic beliefs about purgatory and heaven further emphasize the emotional, psychological, and spiritual need to honor the dead through proper burials.

Gacaca courts were portrayed as a way to uncover the truth about the genocide, and in some communities Gacaca has succeeded in this objective. Chakravarty has documented the complex ways in which the logic of genocide has been deconstructed in some sector-level Gacaca hearings (Chakravarty 2006, 28–29). Some survivors have recovered the remains of their loved ones thanks to testimony given before the Gacaca courts. Others have learned more precisely how, when, or where their loved ones were killed. Yet, for many others the truth has remained elusive. The accused were offered reductions in sentences for confessing to their crimes and thousands confessed. However, many Gacaca courts rejected the confessions as incomplete or untrue (HRW 2007, 1; Penal Reform International 2003, 8). Given the benefits of confession, it is understandable that some people might have confessed to less severe crimes than the ones they committed, while others may have confessed to crimes they did not commit so that they could be liberated. In some communities, clandestine groups, referred to as ceceka (meaning "keep quiet"), have organized a code of silence before the Gacaca courts (Reyntjens 2005, 13). Thus, many genocide victims fear the truth will not be restored to them through the Gacaca process.

The accused, prisoners' families, and other Hutu feared that the Gacaca courts would be used for ends other than justice for the genocide. In some communities genocide survivors and others organized themselves to fabricate testimony and evidence against certain people. In some cases, they appeared to be motivated by the desire for reprisal or revenge. They feel as if they know certain people were involved and they want to make sure they are found guilty. In other cases, they fabricated testimony for other purposes, such as to settle disputes over land or other property. Some RPF soldiers whose families were decimated are (understandably) angry and seek revenge through the Gacaca courts against anyone they know who is Hutu.

Another problem is that the *Gacaca* process is perceived as one-sided, as victors' justice (Carroll 2000, 185; HRW 2007, 2). The *Gacaca* law states that the courts only have jurisdiction over crimes related to the genocide, thus killings and other atrocities perpetrated by RPF soldiers, whether during the civil war before 1994, during the genocide and its aftermath in Rwanda, or in Democratic Republic of Congo, are off the table. Although the documentation of RPF abuses committed in 1994 is sparse, several sources report indiscriminate killings of civilians, extrajudicial executions of suspected or accused *génocidaires*, and expropriation of houses, livestock, and other property (Amnesty International 1994; Des Forges 1999, 702–722). As the RPF took control of new areas, it set about separating the civilians from *Interahamwe zariye abantu* (literally "Interahamwe who ate people," meaning "those Interahamwe who killed a lot"). It relocated civilians to camps and then executed the *Interahamwe*. The RPF called these campaigns of indiscriminate killings *gutwika ahantu* (to set a place on fire). When the refugees returned en masse from Zaire and Tanzania in late 1996 and early 1997, the RPF again sorted the *Interahamwe zariye abantu* from the other civilians. Notorious *Interahamwe* were often executed on the spot. As a result of the campaigns to root out "real *Interahamwe*," many Rwandan citizens feel that the "*Interahamwe* among *Interahamwe* are no longer in Rwanda (*Interahamwe nyanterahamwe ntizikiba mu Rwanda*)," meaning that "real *Interahamwe*" are either dead or in exile. Thus to many Rwandans, the people accused in *Gacaca* are not "real *Interahamwe*." At best they are participants who were coerced into action.

Up until 2008, the official language to name the 1994 genocide in Rwanda was *itsembabwoko n'itsembatsemba* (genocide and massacres). This language recognized the thousands of Hutu victims of the genocide. However, a new law passed in 2008 replaced this language with *jenoside yakorewe aba Tutsi* (genocide against the Tutsi), codifying the long-term symbolic erasure of Hutu victims of the genocide from national mourning activities (see Burnet 2009). Beyond their inability to publicly mourn their dead, the families of Hutu victims of the genocide or of Hutu victims of RPF killings face the assumption that their dead were genocide perpetrators (even those who died at the hands of the *Interahamwe* during the genocide. In *Gacaca*, these families often faced accusations that they aided and abetted their so-called genocidal kin.

The Injustices of Local Justice

An important issue that emerged in focus groups conducted in 2007 and that frequently came up in conversations was the problem of integrating released prisoners and *génocidaires* (those who had confessed to and been sentenced for crimes of genocide) into the local community. Following the provisional prisoner releases outlined earlier, releases continued as *Gacaca* courts started operating nationwide in January 2005. During *Gacaca* many more prisoners were convicted and released for time already served.

In preparation for *Gacaca*, the government waged a public awareness campaign to educate the population and the prisoners about the need to accept released prisoners, whether innocent or guilty, back into the community. These types of "sensibilization" campaigns in Rwanda have a long history and are a common technique employed both by the government and by international nongovernmental organizations to change or shape local knowledge. In the focus groups, I frequently heard various versions of the official response to prisoner releases:

> Once they [released prisoners] arrive on the hill, they get along very well. They try to ask for forgiveness from people whose family members they killed. (Female respondent, Southern Province, May 2007)

> The prisoners had received training sessions in *ingando* [reeducation camp] before coming onto the hill. You can see, once he [a released prisoner] arrives on the hill, he has changed a lot. First of all, he prays a lot. You can see that he is truly Christian. Second, he approaches people to talk and to ask forgiveness from people against whom he committed genocide, whose family member he killed. Third, he goes to help others. (Female respondent, Southern Province, May 2007)

> I went to visit a freed man at his home who lived really close to my house, and he came to visit me at home too. We have exchanged ideas and I've seen that this is someone who has totally changed. We should have the courage to approach these people. This man of whom I'm telling you, he killed my family, he asked forgiveness and I forgave him. I find that it's good if someone truly accepts these actions and asks forgiveness, at this time he is relieved and you, too, you feel something like peace in your heart. (Tutsi widow of the genocide, Southern Province, June 2007)

In a focus group in Southern Province with Tutsi and Hutu widows of the genocide and Hutu wives of current or former prisoners, and in another focus group with Tutsi returnees and Hutu women in Northern Province, respondents were very careful to stick to this official, idyllic version of prisoner reintegration. In many cases, the very same respondents would recount an entirely different version of what was happening in more private contexts. Some women waited for others to leave after a focus group so that they could add to or change what they had told me.

In more homogenous groups of women, I heard less rosy depictions of prisoner reintegration. From widows of the genocide (whether Tutsi or

Hutu), they explained the difficulties of accepting known *génocidaires* back
into the local community.

> In general, the prisoners integrate themselves without any trouble.
> But, there is one who did not change. He, he stays at home, he talks to
> no one. Since he did very bad things in the genocide, killed a lot, we
> leave him alone like that. We've put him in quarantine. (Tutsi widow
> of the genocide, Southern Province, May 2007)

> We can't look into the hearts of men, certainly there are those who
> are happy and others who are not happy. In general, we pretend to get
> along. (Female Tutsi genocide survivor, Southern Province, May 2007)

> Some Rwandans are tricky. You hear them on the radio, saying, "The
> man who killed my children came and asked for forgiveness. I gave it.
> Now my daughter will marry his son." That isn't the way it is. Since
> *Gacaca* started, we [genocide survivors] live in fear. . . . Since they
> came home, I can no longer walk every morning by myself. When I
> used to get up at 5 am to walk by myself in nature, I felt confident, I
> felt alive. I had removed the fear. Now, the fear has returned [*putting
> her hand on her chest*]. (Female Tutsi genocide survivor, province with-
> held, June 2009)

The sentiments expressed here are not surprising. It is not hard to imagine
how difficult it must be for genocide survivors to live as neighbors with
people responsible for hunting them like quarry, looting and burning their
homes, or killing their family members.

What I find striking about these cited passages is the subtle differences
in the attitudes behind them. The first statement was made by one of the
key leaders of a church-based women's organization that included widows,
widows of the genocide, and prisoners' wives. She was herself an *inyangamugayo* in the *Gacaca* court in her sector, and she had courageously served as
an unbiased leader in the *Gacaca* process by helping to ensure the innocent
were released and by punishing false testimony. Yet, she freely admitted that
certain *génocidaires* do not have the right to rejoin the community because,
although they asked for mercy (*basabye imbabazi*) before the courts by plead-
ing guilty and admitting the acts they committed, they have not shown
remorse (*batyicuza*).

Many Rwandans, whether Tutsi genocide survivors or Hutu who did not
participate in the genocide, pointed out this qualitative distinction in the
confessions made by *génocidaires*. To confess (*gusaba imbabazi*) before the
courts, receive a reduction in sentence, and be released from prison is not
the same as accepting moral responsibility and showing remorse (*kwicuza*).
Both Kinyarwanda phrases, *gusaba imbabazi* and *kwicuza*, mean to ask for

pardon, but *gusaba imbabazi* is used primarily in the legal arena, whereas *kwicuza* is used among Roman Catholics to refer to seeking pardon in the rite of confession. This distinction underlines the inherent conflict between transitional justice's transcendental promises of peace, justice, healing, and reconciliation and its elision or silencing of alternative mechanisms and coping strategies (see Dwyer, this volume; Drexler, this volume).

The second statement was made by a widow of the genocide in a focus group with two small women's groups from a very rural area of Southern Province. The first group comprised widows of the genocide; the second, Hutu wives of prisoners. During the interview the Hutu women hardly spoke and gave very constrained responses; the leader of the widows of the genocide group did most of the talking. Her earlier statement, especially given that she made it in front of her Hutu neighbors, was intended to underscore the continuing distrust and suspicion among Tutsi genocide survivors. In response to a follow-up question, the same widow returned to the same theme by evoking the lasting trauma (*guhahamuka*) of genocide:

> We cannot forget the wounds that we have in our hearts, but [the] *Gacaca* [process] has warned us to be patient and courageous. If you begin to feel trauma in the *Gacaca* [trial], you cannot get anywhere. . . .
>
> I can't forget that I am left alone. When I don't have water in the house and night is falling, I think that I should have someone to go draw water. When there is no wood for the fire, that reminds me that there should be someone to go and collect wood. When I want this or that, I should have someone to help me. With everything that I do, I am reminded that I am alone. That's how it is, we go to *Gacaca*, we try to be patient, but forget all that; it will never happen.

Her fundamental message is that there can be no justice for genocide survivors. Whether in the *Gacaca* process or any other judicial process, genocide survivors will never have justice because the gaping holes in their lives cannot be filled. No one can bring their dead family members back to life.

The third statement, made by a successful business woman living in a provincial town, directly confronts the disconnect between the official version of the *Gacaca* process and the turmoil in which genocide survivors find themselves: they are forced to live among the people who killed their family members and to live in fear that they may kill again.

Survivors have many different points of view concerning justice, the events of 1994, and the appropriate way to remember the genocide and their lost loved ones. All have been unanimous that dead family members can never be replaced or compensated, but many view justice through the courts (whether national or international) or through *Gacaca* as an important duty—a way to recapture the dignity of those who died in ignominious ways. One widow of the genocide from Southern Province has collaborated extensively over the years with investigators from the ICTR and from foreign governments. She has testified before foreign courts on several occasions, at great emotional cost to herself. Yet, she has undertaken all these activities quietly and discreetly to avoid attracting attention and potential revenge seeking. Also, she has not volunteered to participate in investigations conducted by Rwandan authorities. When I asked her why, she said that she could not work with them because they "were not serious." In other words, she did not have confidence in the Rwandan justice system.

A second issue raised in several conversations and focus group interviews was the problem of new accusations against people who had been living in the community peacefully for the past twelve years. While visiting a family in Western Province in 2007, the conversation fell on the topic of *Gacaca*. Several neighbors and members of the patrilineage had gathered in the living room to receive me in the customary fashion with drinks. The conversation eventually turned to local gossip. One woman asked, "Did you know that —— has become insane?" The others quickly began explaining:

> It's not surprising because we just heard that he, too, killed during the genocide. It's someone who was released from prison thanks to the president of the Republic, who told us that. He said that —— had participated in the genocide. People asked the freed man why he didn't say anything sooner.
>
> [INTERJECTION]: He is ready to denounce him and give all the information if the *Gacaca* court calls him.

While family members and friends were shocked to find out that this particular neighbor had participated in the genocide, they did not feel that the accusations were anything other than factual—the truth. For me, it was a relief to see them discussing *Gacaca* and its complexities without fear and suspicion. In the group there were Tutsi genocide survivors, Hutu former prisoners, family members of former prisoners, Hutu and Tutsi members of the RPF who joined the Front during the civil war between 1990 and 1994, and Hutu supporters of President Habyarimana and the National Republican Movement for Development (MRND). Yet, the ties among them were strong enough to allow for unfettered discussion. The conversation then turned to the dark side of new accusations of genocide:

> WOMAN: I see that —— has been imprisoned again.
> THE OTHERS: This gentleman killed quite a lot of people in the genocide. He admitted it himself. Only, after he was released from prison, that's when he began to lie, denouncing innocent people by saying they had

participated in the genocide. After he had denounced a large number of these people, the population realized that he was lying. He himself said, "No one visited me or ever brought me something to eat when I was in prison. I will take my revenge." After that, people realized that these others were innocent. The population is waiting patiently to see if the *inyangamugayo* are going to do something and if these people will be released from prison.

Confessions have been the foundation of the *Gacaca* process, with prisoners receiving reduced sentences in exchange for their testimony. Prisoners have many motivations to lie. As in the case cited here, some prisoners lie to seek revenge. The theme of revenge is a very strong one in *Gacaca*, and its currents go in many directions. Other prisoners lie because they did not make a full confession and want to cover up the atrocities they committed in the hopes of avoiding more severe punishment.

New accusations disrupt the social fabric that has been tenuously rewoven in certain communities. In a focus group in Southern Province, a Tutsi widow of the genocide explained:

> In *Gacaca* not everything is going well. You see a husband and a wife who have stayed on the hill for thirteen years. We believe they are innocent, and all of the sudden you hear them denounced in *Gacaca*; they did this or that. The family [the husband and wife] is shocked, discouraged, and gets angry, saying that this [the accusations] is motivated by hate. There are interminable conflicts.

Here the speaker leaves the question open whether the accusations are true or false; instead, she highlights that regardless of whether they are true, the family of the accused perceives it as injustice, as the seeking of revenge. To believe that accusations are motivated by revenge is not merely paranoia; these suspicions are often based on known cases of revenge-seeking within the community. The problem is that the legitimacy of *Gacaca* has been so undermined in some communities that residents dismiss all testimony as lies or half-truths.

In my research in 2007, numerous examples of revenge-seeking in *Gacaca* emerged. These cases appear to fall in three main categories: revenge against particular individuals, revenge against particular individuals as representatives of a corporate group, and revenge against a corporate group.

In instances where people sought revenge against particular individuals, they were not necessarily seeking revenge for events that occurred during the 1994 genocide. Sometimes they appeared to be taking revenge for events in the distant past (for instance, previous periods of anti-Tutsi sentiment and violence, such as 1959, 1962–1963, and 1973). Most of these stories are difficult to describe in ethnographic detail because they risk endangering the tellers who are the victims of this revenge-seeking. One Tutsi genocide survivor, Marie,[8] whose husband, Janvier, was Hutu, explained to me the way that another Tutsi genocide survivor, Jeanne, terrorized her during *Gacaca*.

Jeanne frequently appeared before the court and demanded that Marie testify. Marie insisted that she did not witness anything because she spent several months in hiding, moving from house to house among her in-laws, who lived near each other on the hill. Jeanne insisted that Marie was lying, that she knew where victims' bodies were buried. Jeanne repeatedly threatened, "Don't you know what the punishment for lying before the *Gacaca* court is?" As Marie told her story to me, her body trembled, her voice quavered, and tears fell silently from her eyes.

Jeanne and her husband, Patrice (also a Tutsi genocide survivor), had long held a grudge against Marie and her husband. Patrice blamed anti-Tutsi racism for the premature end of his education in 1973 during Tutsi purges from higher education. Patrice eventually focused this anger on Marie's husband, Janvier. In the early 1990s, Janvier was promoted to a leadership position in the regional government; Patrice believed that he had been unfairly passed over for the promotion because of his ethnicity. In the months following the genocide in 1994, Janvier continued to hold this position in the regional government and worked closely with the Rwandan Patriotic Army (RPA) officers stationed in the area. One day as he was walking on the main road into town, a truck transporting prisoners stopped. Without any explanation, Janvier was arrested by the soldiers accompanying the prisoners. It took Marie several weeks to find him in a provincial prison. It took several months to find out that he stood accused of genocide although he did not have a judicial file.

With the loss of her husband's salary, Marie sought to have her children receive assistance from the Genocide Survivors' Assistance Fund (known as FARG [Fonds d'Assistance aux Rescapés du Génocide]), but Jeanne and Patrice, who headed the local genocide survivors' organization, blocked Marie's efforts by refusing to sign the necessary paperwork. Jeanne said to her, "The FARG does not help killers' children!" Although there was no evidence against him, Marie's husband spent seven years in prison under charges of genocide. Marie and her husband believed that Jeanne and Patrice were behind his arrest and imprisonment, but they had no proof.

When Janvier was released in 2001 because of the lack of evidence against him, many (Tutsi) genocide survivors in the community welcomed him back home, as they believed he was innocent. Patrice and Jeanne, on the other hand, harassed the family. On one occasion, Patrice tried to organize a mob to attack Patrice. On other occasions, they threatened that some day soon Janvier would be rearrested. Under great psychological strain, Janvier went to Kigali, hoping to escape the harassment, but it still continued. The family he stayed with began to receive anonymous, threatening phone calls. As a result of the harassment and the strains of readjusting to life outside prison, Janvier became pathologically paranoid, believing that he was constantly being watched and followed. One evening, he was hit by a truck as he was crossing the street. He died from his injuries. While Marie believed that Jeanne and Patrice had something to do with the accident, she had no proof. Police investigators labeled it an accident. A Roman Catholic priest familiar with the case explained, "With this sort of a death there are so many unanswered questions. Maybe it was a simple accident, but Marie will never believe it because of what came before." Trying to support her children alone, Marie hoped that Jeanne and Patrice would leave her in peace, but every time she attended *Gacaca* she faced Jeanne's accusations.[9]

The Rwandan government's genocide commemorations and national mourning practices generate a polarizing discourse that defines all Tutsi as genocide victims and all Hutu as genocide perpetrators (Burnet 2005, 2009). Similar to efforts in Argentina and Chile (see Robben, this volume), Rwandan government memorial practices create master narratives about Rwandan history, the civil war 1990–1994, and the 1994 genocide. Under this logic, certain Tutsi genocide survivors have sought revenge against individual Hutu as a scapegoat for Hutu as a corporate group.

Among women's groupings in Southern Province, several of the Hutu members faced accusations before the *Gacaca* courts. In most cases, the association members, including genocide survivors, conducted investigations to assess the validity of the accusations. They then helped the member launch a defense before the court by locating witnesses and ensuring that the witnesses appeared to testify before the court. However, in a dramatic turn of events one member, a Tutsi widow of the genocide turned against another member, a Hutu widow whose husband had been killed by RPF soldiers in 1995.

AUTHOR: Has the *Gacaca* process had any negative effects on you or your association?

WOMAN: We mustn't lie to you; the *Gacaca* process has had its negative effects. For example, our group leader was imprisoned [*whispering*]. There was an American researcher who came to interview women in the association on the topic of *Gacaca*. In the meeting, Dancille said that there is injustice in *Gacaca* because all the genocide survivors want to make certain that all the Hutu are imprisoned. After [the meeting] Rose [a woman in the association] went to see the *inyangamugayo* in —— to denounce Dancille. She also wrote a letter saying that Dancille had engaged in divisionism.

Dancille was arrested and imprisoned for four months. Because of the accusations of divisionism, the case went all the way to the office of the national prosecutor in the normal courts. When Dancille went before the *Gacaca* court, our group members went to testify on her behalf and said that she hadn't participated in the genocide, that she hadn't divided people, and that she likes peace in the community. Afterward, the prosecutor also made inquiries. In the end, Dancille was released.

AUTHOR: How has all this affected the association?

WOMAN: We had some trouble getting along during that period, but Rose asked forgiveness (*kwicuza*) from all the association leaders and also from Dancille. Now, there aren't any more problems. Dancille forgave Rose, who is still remorseful. We try to show Rose that there is no problem.

Despite these statements, it was clear in my interactions with the members of the association that the story was far from over. Dancille, who had been a vibrant, smiling group leader when I first met her in 2000 had become a shadow of her former self. She walked with her head down, eyes on the ground, and did not say a word. The toll of her time in prison was evident in her gaunt face, worried eyes, and white hair. While she was imprisoned her children had been forced to drop out of school to take care of the family farm and to bring her food and water in prison. Dancille did not say a word in any of the meetings and left the room anytime the subject of her imprisonment and Rose's actions came up. She avoided having any conversations with me.

In a meeting the following week with all of the association leaders, I asked some questions about *Gacaca*. After many women said that *Gacaca* was working well, a Hutu widow of the genocide stood up and said that there was "justice for some in *Gacaca*, but not justice for all." Immediately, Rose stood up and accused the woman of divisionism (a crime under Rwandan law punishable by twenty-five years in prison) in front of everyone. The meeting became very tense, and everyone was upset. Several women spoke in rapid succession, interrupting each other. In the end, a Tutsi widow of the genocide admonished Rose for "restarting her nonsense" and told her that she would be thrown out of the association if she continued.

The statement that had landed Dancille in prison, that some genocide survivors want to imprison all the Hutu through the *Gacaca* courts, was a sentiment that I heard in all three provinces that I visited in May and June 2007. These statements were only made in intimate groups where everyone trusted those who were listening. As illustrated by Dancille's case, making these statements is very risky. In a focus group with a women's association in Northern Province, the members all said that *Gacaca* was working well, that innocent prisoners were being released, and that the perpetrators were being found guilty and sentenced. Following the meeting, a few members lingered to chat. After their colleague, a Tutsi woman who had grown up in Burundi, left, the subject returned to *Gacaca*. The women (all of whom were Hutu) began speaking in low voices so that our conversation could not be overheard. They said that *Gacaca* was not functioning well at all, that it was profoundly dividing the population along ethnic lines.

MEMBER #1: Before, pastoralists and farmers in this region could talk to each other.[10] In 1998, 1999, and 2000, when conflicts arose between them, for instance, when someone's cattle grazed in someone's fields, we could bring them together, negotiate, and settle the problem. Since *Gacaca* has started, both live in fear. They don't talk to each other. In front of each other, we don't say what we really think. That's why we couldn't say what was really happening [before the Tutsi returnee left].

MEMBER #2: What we see now is that the *inyangamugayo* won't stop until all the educated Hutu are in prison with long sentences.

AUTHOR: Are all the *inyangamugayo* Tutsi?

MEMBER #1: Not just Tutsi, they are 59ers.[11]

MEMBER #2: I was an *inyangamugayo*. When I saw people giving false testimony and getting innocent people imprisoned, I denounced it. The other *inyangamugayo* told me to keep quiet, but I went to Kigali and told them [the Ministry of Justice] that the *inyangamugayo* here were not implementing the law correctly. They sent investigators here. Next thing you know, someone is denouncing me in *Gacaca*. I got the message. I resigned, and I kept my mouth shut. No one sang my name in *Gacaca* anymore.

Gacaca has been much touted as a reconciliation mechanism, and indeed its traditional purpose was as a conflict resolution mechanism. However, as it was implemented to try genocide suspects, *Gacaca* deepened cleavages within the communities and sowed mistrust on all sides. Perhaps any justice mechanism would have had the same side effect.

Beyond these injustices, *Gacaca* was also used by some to seek other gains. Stories of people denouncing others before *Gacaca* to take their land are rampant in Rwanda; I heard them in all the communities I visited. Because the story is ubiquitous, it strikes me more as a metaphorical statement about *Gacaca* and its injustices than as an accurate statement about specific cases of land usurping. Yet, in rural Northern Province I encountered detailed statements about land usurping tied to *Gacaca* in former Kinigi commune. Since the RPF victory in 1994, a large number of Tutsi pastoralists moved into Kinigi with their cattle. Between 1997 and 2000, Kinigi was seriously affected by an insurgency that entered Rwanda from Democratic Republic of Congo via the Birunga National Park. As part of its counterinsurgency operations, the Rwandan government forced the population to relocate into internally displaced persons (IDP) camps. Many people were forced to destroy their houses, including brick houses with glass windows and metal doors, before moving into the IDP camp. When I first met this women's group, they were living in deplorable conditions in small shelters made of sheeting that were crowded together at the foot of one of the volcanoes. Since the end of the insurgency, they had not been allowed to return to their houses or parcels. Instead the government forced them to settle in an *umudugudu* (agglomeration) under its villagization policy. In 2007, when asked about the reintegration of released prisoners, the women responded:

> Up until now, we have not yet seen any prisoner releases. On the contrary, many people are being imprisoned. What we see here is a problem of landholdings. Kinigi is inhabited by a lot of Tutsi, and the 59ers want all the land. So, to get the land, the Tutsi and the 59ers who have money, they find Hutu and give them this money so that they can go and give false testimony. Those that they accuse directly are quickly put in prison, and the others take their land, saying that their grandparents lived in these places for a long time. The *inyangamugayo* just discovered this and they said in a meeting that there are people with big bellies [*bafite inda nini*, meaning they are very poor] and they give false testimony to get people arrested for nothing just because of money. They warned us not to start that again.

In other regions I encountered similar stories of people using *Gacaca* to seek other gains, whether land or jobs or to settle family disputes by getting someone else imprisoned. It is not surprising that some citizens are using *Gacaca* as a lever of power to get what they want. This phenomenon has a long tradition in the regular courts as well as in other bureaucratic venues. For instance, in his 1968 monograph, *Remera*, Gravel shows that cases brought before the tribal courts were trials of powers rather than trials of rights, meaning that the winner of court cases was not decided on whose rights had been violated, but rather on whose power within the community was greater. In my own experience with the traditional form of *gacaca* to resolve a conflict with a neighbor in my rural field site in 2001, I encountered a similar result. Although the neighbor was found to be guilty by the hearing and assessed a list of punishments, he did not complete any of the tasks meted out by the *gacaca*. As a permanent resident with kinship ties in the community, and a husband-man (*umugabo*), he had greater power within the community than I, so he was not forced to comply with the decisions. The outcome was a surprise to no one except for me. From this historical perspective, the power plays in *Gacaca* may be yet another example of the vernacularization of local justice in Rwanda (Merry 2006).

power in Gacaca

Gacaca appeared to operate in much the same way in communities around Rwanda. In places where *inyangamugayo* had legitimacy and power within the community, and when they had the will to carry out trials according to legal procedures, *Gacaca* worked well. In conversations and interviews in 2009, residents of these communities recognized that, although imperfect, *Gacaca* had at least returned many men to their homes. There was an improvement in the day-to-day life of people in the community, even if these improvements came with a lot of patience (*ubwihangane*) on the part of genocide survivors. However, in places where the *inyangamugayo* did not have power, or where the power brokers in the community sought ends other than fair genocide trials, *Gacaca* served these other ends and led to many injustices.

Implications of Injustice

In the short term, *Gacaca* destabilized Rwanda and the *Gacaca* courts became arenas where local power relations worked themselves out under the guise of national policy. The central government was well aware of these destabilizing effects, and President Kagame announced in early 2007 that all *Gacaca* trials would be concluded by the end of 2007. In some communities, the work to close their files continued through 2008. Furthermore, the approximately 77,000 accused of category one genocide crimes still await trial before the formal court system, and the possibility of expanding the mandate of the *Gacaca* courts is still being discussed (Hirondelle News Agency 2007a).

Gacaca not only deepened the cleavages between Hutu and Tutsi, but it also made some Tutsi genocide survivors increasingly mistrustful of the current government and the RPF. In December 2007, Benoit Kaboyi, executive secretary of Ibuka, addressed an extraordinary congress of genocide survivors associations and said, "The goal of the gacacas was not to parade people before the courts for form, but to try them well!" (Hirondelle News Agency 2007b). Despite growing criticism, including some public comments such as these, the government of Rwanda continued to support the policy. In reaction to the statements made by Ibuka, the minister of justice, Tharcisse Karugarama, vigorously defended the *Gacaca* courts and said that "all Rwandans should be delighted . . . Those who see things differently are people that are never satisfied" (Hirondelle News Agency 2007d).

Hutu who protected Tutsi during the genocide faced enormous difficulties in *Gacaca*. In hearings, they found their acts of heroism were met with suspicion and often became grounds for accusations against them. If they hid Tutsi in their house for days or weeks but then left them behind to flee the advancing battle lines between the RPF and the FAR, they risked being deemed accomplices to the genocide by the *inyangamugayo*. Beyond these difficulties, they endure discrimination in daily life, where having connections to power (*un piston*) are a prerequisite for access to a job. Among Hutu who supported the Hutu extremists and the genocide, they faced criticism: "we told you they [the Tutsi] would subjugate Hutu as they did under the monarchy" (pers. comm.).

If these conditions were short-term problems, then *Gacaca* could still be the basis for reconciliation, one of the government's key objectives, as stated in the law and in speeches by government officials. Unfortunately, given local perceptions of widespread injustice in the *Gacaca* process, the long-term prospects for a peaceful and just society are not positive. Similar to Drexler's findings in this volume on transitional justice in East Timor, *Gacaca* has delivered justice for some and established at least a partial truth, but it has undermined the rule of law and underscored the impunity for RPF crimes. The "quest to establish 'the truth'" of the genocide through *Gacaca* has been "circumscribed by political considerations" that have limited who was heard, what information was reported, and what the final verdict was (Hinton, this volume). Since the *Gacaca* courts did not always have legitimacy in the eyes of the population, they were often viewed as another imposition of the central government on local communities and as another venue in which local power conflicts worked themselves out while appearing to conform to central government policies.

NOTES

1. In this article, I use "*Gacaca*" (capitalized) to refer to the *Gacaca* courts instituted to adjudicate genocide cases and "*gacaca*" (lowercase) to refer to the informal, traditional conflict resolution mechanism.

2. Unlike Desmond Tutu's characterization of the Truth and Reconciliation Commission as a South African resolution of the South African experience, the Rwandan government emphasized retributive rather than restorative justice (Hinton, this volume).

3. The RPF came to power in July 1994 when it seized the majority of the Rwandan territory and stopped the genocide.

4. For more on the "transitional frictions" (Hinton, this volume) of the ICTR chambers, see Eltringham (this volume).

5. People awaiting trial at the ICTR stay in air-conditioned cells with access to an exercise room and television, whereas detainees in Rwanda face generally miserable conditions without adequate food or water. Until July 2007, when Rwanda abolished the death penalty, the maximum punishment in Rwanda was death, whereas at the ICTR the maximum punishment is imprisonment for life in a prison meeting international standards.

6. As of June 2006, the ICTR had completed the prosecution of twenty-eight defendants; twenty-five were found guilty and three were acquitted. "Achievements of the ICTR," http://69.94.11.53/ENGLISH/factsheets/achievements.htm.

7. See chapter 4, articles 72–75 of Organic Law No. 16/2004 of 19/6/2004 and chapter 4, articles 68–71 of Organic Law No. 40/2000 of 26/01/2001.

8. All names have been changed to hide the identities of informants.

9. Attendance at *Gacaca* is a compulsory, civic duty. On days that *Gacaca* is held, all businesses, schools, and offices close so that everyone can attend. Citizens absent from *Gacaca* face fines and even imprisonment.

10. In this statement "pastoralists" is a euphemism for Tutsi, and "farmers" for Hutu. Many of the Tutsi living in rural areas of Northern Province are predominantly cattle herders with only small garden plots, while the Hutu usually have comparatively large fields and only one or two cows and smaller livestock.

11. In this context, "59ers" refers to the predominantly Tutsi refugees who returned to Rwanda following the RPF victory in 1994. Many of these refugees left Rwanda in 1959, when mass violence targeted members of the Tutsi nobility, or they were the descendants of those who had left in 1959.

REFERENCES

Amnesty International. 1994. *Rwanda: Reports of Killings and Abductions by the Rwandese Patriotic Army, April–August 1994*. New York: Amnesty International.

Burnet, Jennie E. 2005. "Genocide Lives in Us: Amplified Silence and the Politics of Memory in Rwanda." Ph.D. diss., University of North Carolina at Chapel Hill.

———. 2009. "Whose Genocide? Whose Truth? Representations of Victim and Perpetrator in Rwanda." In *Genocide: Truth, Memory, and Representation*, ed. Alexander Laban Hinton and Kevin Lewis O'Neill, 80–100. Durham: Duke University Press.

Carroll, Christina M. 2000. "An Assessment of the Role and Effectiveness of the International Criminal Tribunal for Rwanda and the Rwandan National Justice System in Dealing with the Mass Atrocities of 1994." *Boston University International Law Journal* 18 (2): 163–200.

CBCNews. 2007. "Rwanda Urges Canada to Extradite 'Genocide Masterminds.'" http://www.cbc.ca/world/story/2007/08/31/rwandan-extradition.html.

Chakravarty, Anuradha. 2006. "Local Dynamics of Contention around Genocide Trials in Rwanda." Paper presented at the African Studies Association Annual Meeting, San Francisco.

Des Forges, Alison. 1999. *Leave None to Tell the Story: Genocide in Rwanda*. New York: Human Rights Watch.

Gakwaya, Felin. 2007. "Inkiko za Gacaca zimaze guca imanza zirenga ibihumbi 700." *BBC Great Lakes.com*. December 3. http://www.bbc.co.uk/greatlakes/news/story/2007/12/071203_gacacacourts.shtml.

Gravel, Pierre Bettez. 1968. *Remera: A Community in Eastern Ruanda*. The Hague: Mouton.

Hilhorst, Dorothea, Mathijs van Leeuwen. 1999. *Imidugudu, Villagisation in Rwanda: A Case of Emergency Development?* Wageningen, Netherlands: Disaster Studies, Disaster Sites No. 2.

Hirondelle News Agency. 2007a. "Gacaca Trials Could Continue in 2008." *allafrica.com*. November 21. http://allafrica.com/stories/200711220365.html.

———. 2007b. "Ibuka Draws Up a Negative Assessment of the Gacaca Courts." *allafrica.com*. December 11. http://allafrica.com/stories/printable/200712120624.html.

———. 2007c. "Rwanda Wants to Relieve Congestion in Prisons." *Rwanda Development Gateway*. http://www.rwandagateway.org/article.php3?id_article=7543.

———. 2007d. "The Rwandan Government Refutes Criticism by Ibuka." December 12. http://www.hirondellenews.com/content/view/1354/291.

————. 2007e. "Towards a New Amendment of the Gacaca Law." December 5. http://www.hirondellenews.com/content/view/1316/309/.

Human Rights Watch (HRW). 2001. *Uprooting the Rural Poor in Rwanda*. New York: Human Rights Watch.

————. 2002. *World Report 2002*. New York: Human Rights Watch.

————. 2006. "Rwanda—Human Rights Overview." *World Report 2006*. New York: Human Rights Watch. http://hrw.org/english/docs/2006/01/18/rwanda12286.htm.

————. 2007. "Rwanda—Human Rights Overview." *World Report 2007*. New York: Human Rights Watch. http://www.hrw.org/legacy/englishwr2k7/docs/2007/01/11/rwanda14782.htm.

International Herald Tribune. 2007. "Rwandan Is First to Stand Trial in Canada under War Crimes Act." http://www.iht.com/articles/ap/2007/03/26/america/NA-GEN-Canada-Rwandan-Genocide.php.

IRIN. 2005a. "RWANDA: Release of Suspects in the 1994 Genocide Angers Survivors." *IRINnews.org*. August 9. http://www.irinnews.org/report.asp?ReportID=48504&SelectRegion=Great_Lakes&SelectCountry=RWANDA.

————. 2005b. "RWANDA: Release of Thousands of Prisoners Begins." *IRINnews.org*. August 1. http://www.irinnews.org/report.asp?ReportID=48373&SelectRegion=Great_Lakes&SelectCountry=RWANDA.

Karega, Jyoni wa, Philbert Kagabo, Abbe Smaragde Mbonyintege, Jean Chrisostome Munyampirwa, and Ladislas Twahirwa. 1996. *Gacaca: Le droit coutumier au Rwanda*. Kigali, Rwanda: Nations Unies Haut Commissaire aux Droits de L'Homme Operation sur le Terrain au Rwanda.

Longman, Timothy. 2006. "Rwanda: Achieving Equality or Serving an Authoritarian State?" In *Women in African Parliaments*, ed. H. E. Britton and G. Bauer, 133–150. Boulder: Lynne Rienner.

Mani, Rama. 2008. "Editorial: Dilemmas of Expanding Transitional Justice, or Forging the Nexus between Transitional Justice and Development." *International Journal of Transitional Justice* 2 (3): 253–265.

Merry, Sally Engle. 2006. *Human Rights and Gender Violence: Translating International Law into Local Justice*. Chicago: University of Chicago Press.

Montreal Gazette. 2009. "Historic Genocide Verdict in Canada Due Next Week." *Rwanda News Agency*. May 16. http://www.rnanews.com/index.php?option=com_content&task=view&id=1299&Itemid=47.

Official Website of the Republic of Rwanda. 2001. "Kagame Speaks on the Eve of the Launch of Gacaca Trials." http://www.gov.rw/government/president/interviews/2001/gacaca.html.

Penal Reform International. 2003. *PRI Research Gacaca Report #4: The Guilty Plea Procedure, Cornerstone of the Rwandan Justice System*. London: Penal Reform International.

————. 2006. *Monitoring and Research Report on the Gacaca #8: Information-Gathering during the National Phase*. London: Penal Reform International.

Reyntjens, Filip. 1990. "Le *gacaca* ou la justice du gazon au Rwanda." *Politique Africaine* 40:31–41.

————. 2004. "Rwanda, Ten Years On: From Genocide to Dictatorship." *African Affairs* 103 (411): 177–210.

————. 2005. "Chronique politique du Rwanda et du Burundi, 2003–2005." *L'Afriques des Grands Lacs, Annuaire*, 2004–2005, 1–26.

————. 2006. "Post-1994 Politics in Rwanda: Problematising 'Liberation' and 'Democratisation.'" *Third World Quarterly* 27 (6): 1103–1117.

Schotsman, Martien. 2000. *A l'ecoute des rescapes: Recherche sur la perception par les rescapés de leur situation actuelle.* Kigali, Rwanda: GTZ.

Tsing, Anna. 2005. *Friction: An Ethnography of Global Connection.* Princeton: Princeton University Press.

Uvin, Peter, and Charles Mironko. 2003. "Western and Local Approaches to Justice in Rwanda." *Global Governance* 9:219–231.

Waldorf, Lars. 2006. "Mass Justice for Mass Atrocity: Rethinking Local Justice as Transitional Justice." *Temple Law Review* 79 (1): 1–87.

5

▶▶▶▶▶▶▶▶▶▶▶▶▶▶▶▶ ◀◀◀◀◀◀◀◀◀◀◀◀◀◀◀

Remembering Genocide

Hypocrisy and the Violence of Local/Global "Justice" in Northern Nigeria

CONERLY CASEY

In 1999 and 2000, the transition from Nigerian military to democratic rule, and the implementation of Sharia criminal law in twelve states of northern Nigeria, brought violent conflicts over the legal bounds of identity and citizenship, civility and criminality, with armed youths the new agents of policing. The changes involved the election of President Olusegun Obasanjo, a former military head of state, and the reimposition of Sharia criminal codes that had been in place during the colonial period but excised at independence (Kumo 1993, 7–8).[1] Beyond non-Muslim fears of the Islamization of Nigeria, widely reported in the media, the reimposition of Sharia criminal codes—and the clamor for its implementation in southern areas of the country—are part of widespread religious movements' efforts in Nigeria and around the world to reinsert religion into state politics. From the late 1970s onward, intensified, heated debates in Nigeria about the proper role of religion in politics have led to religious assertions of "moral righteousness" and thus "good politics." This assertion is not new or unique to Nigeria; what is striking, however, is the determination with which Nigerians seek constitutional and judicial reforms to address injustices while simultaneously relying on youth groups to ensure justice, even through violence. At question in northern Nigeria are the possibilities and constraints ushered in with the transitions from Nigerian military to democratic rule, and from state secular law to Sharia criminal law, as well as the gaps between judicial decisions and enforcement. Muslim youths refer to President Obasanjo's forum for transitional justice, the 2002 Human Rights Violation Investigation Commission, or "Oputa Panel," as a "soap opera for the rich," pointing out that the period investigated excluded violations under the Obasanjo military regime and his recent presidency and led to apologies rather than to prosecutions of perpetrators.

I would like to address the possibilities and constraints on transitional justice for Nigerians navigating the local/global frictions (Tsing 2005; see, in this volume, Hinton, Drexler, Wagner, Sanford, and Burnet) of cultural justice during the implementation of Sharia criminal codes in Kano State and in the Human Rights Violations Investigation Commission Report (2002) on the public hearings of human rights violations across Nigeria. My understanding of the frictions of Sharia law, Nigerian federal law, and international law, as well as narratives and enactments of violence as transitional justice, is based on eight years of research between 1991 and 2006 in northern Nigeria.

For Muslim youths, the felt qualities of hypocrisy in state justice reform and violent enactments to enforce "justice" emerge in the historical contexts of liberal universalism, or one law for all people, global ideas espoused by U.S. and western European government officials and Nigerian political elites. In postcolonies such as Nigeria, colonial administrations established citizenship based on race and ethnicity, the legacies of which continue to be felt as differential access to state resources (Mamdani 1996; see, in this volume, Burnet, Woolford, and Hitchcock and Babchuk).

The fervent implementation of Sharia criminal law drew support from a broad spectrum of Muslims who considered it a democratic alternative to, and strong critique of, colonialism and the elitism and corruption of federal and state government officials. Global infusions of neoliberal politics and capitalism, with mediated images of Abu Graib, Guantanamo Bay, and the War in Iraq, revive the ongoing, glaring hypocrisy of espoused liberal universalism, on the one hand, and the violence of local/global inequities and injustice, on the other (Clarke 2009; Mamdani 2009).

The sentiments aroused in young Nigerian Muslims by such blatant hypocrisy from U.S., western European, and Nigerian government officials contribute to what I call "affective citizenship," the feeling of belonging to, and having agency within, the state. Affective citizenship is a fusion of ethnic, religious, and regional citizenship based on ethnic customary law and religious law—and on the historical perceptions of enclosure and exclusion that underpin memories of belonging, which are backed by a law that historically has been arbitrary and violent in its application. Affective citizenship for Muslim youths living in the northern city of Kano is a form of resistance to recolonization and to the war on Muslims through tactical appropriations of liberal universalism by which Kano religious identities are strengthened. This anticolonial, anti-imperial resistance has global applications in the war on Muslims, dividing Nigerian communities. Political religious elites take advantage of these social fissures to gain the support of majority groups, with the consequences for Kano State residents, post-Sharia law, being an increase in rapes, violent attacks on people deemed marginal Muslims, and the May 11, 2004, large-scale massacre of Christians and non-Hausa Muslims

(Casey 2007, 2008, 2009). The felt or affective dimensions of hypocrisy and the material violence of postcolonial local/global "justice" has led to an increase in the use of the term "genocide" to represent large-scale massacres of minorities throughout Nigeria.

Colonialism and Racial- and Ethnic-Based Citizenship

In 1898 Flora Shaw suggested the name "Nigeria" for the British colonial project of uniting "politically neighboring but formerly autonomous states and peoples under imperial rule in one colonial state" (Levin 1997, 135). British administrators arbitrarily established specific territorial units within the colonial state as autonomous, in what Mamdani (1996) refers to as "decentralized despotism," exacerbating ethnic, religious, and regional political tensions. The British takeover of the Royal Niger Company in 1900, indirect rule as the British governing principle in northern Nigeria, and the consolidation of British colonial power under the Sokoto caliphate framed the regional motif of British colonial policy (Last 1967; Levin 1997; Paden 1986). Frictions emerged among the majority Muslim Hausa in the north, Christian Igbo in the southeast, Christian and Muslim Yoruba in the southwest, and the ethnic-religious minorities within these regions, most notably the Ogoni in the oil rich southeast (Crowder 1978; Falola 1998; Okpu 1977; Paden 1973).

The colonial transfer of state power to northern Muslims in 1960 at Nigeria's independence brought with it a renewed interest in world Islamic affairs, grassroots Muslim brotherhoods, and efforts to reimpose Sharia criminal codes that had been excised at independence. The Nigerian civil war in the late 1960s generated thousands of internally displaced persons, requiring state governments to manage disputes about the constitutional and pragmatic rights and protections of displaced people. Nigeria's oil boom in the 1970s and the state's "petro-Capitalism" and "spoils politics" further deepened political antagonisms based on ethnic, religious, and regional interests in the control of Nigeria's land and resources (Watts 2001).

Under General Murtala Mohammed and General Olusegun Obasanjo, political attempts to establish a federal Sharia court of appeal failed, but Sharia courts gained state level appellate status, and this status was incorporated into the 1979 constitution (Williams 1997). These events, coinciding with the 1979 Iranian revolution, emboldened reformist Muslims, who considered the implementation of Sharia criminal law a way to confront Nigeria's political, economic, and social ills.[2] In the 1980s and 1990s, the creation of new states (Levin 1997), the convergence of religious and state politics (Williams 1997), and the introduction of development projects (Ocheje 1997) again displaced large numbers of Nigerians, reviving constitutional disputes over state jurisdictions and the ethnic, religious, and regional dimensions of national and state rights and protections.

Armed Youths and Social (In)Justice

In the past two decades an influx of Nigerian youths into city centers, as well as political economic decentralization and the primacy of the free market, have stimulated parallel economies that support and receive protection from political, economic, and religious rivals. Ethnic and religious vigilantes such as the Yoruba O'odua Peoples Congress (OPC) in the southwest and the Igbo Bakassi Boys of the southeast have received widespread regional support for demanding social justice and government accountability, even when these groups have employed violence as enforcement (Akinyele 2001; Baker 2002; Harnischfeger 2003; Nolte 2004; Smith 2004). Contemporary *'yan daba* (urban ward gang members), *'yan banga* (bodyguards, political vanguards), and Hisba (the enforcing wing of the Sharia Implementation Committee) in northern Nigeria are part of this larger phenomenon.[3] Vanguards in the politics of identity and citizenship, youths police others to assert divergent political imaginings of Nigeria. With demilitarization, deregulation, and the primacy of the market, Nigerian youths use violence to "control the means of coercion," gaining advantage in conflicts over state sovereignty and the appropriation of resources (Mbembe 2001, 78). Violence occurs in the struggle for national and state codification of new rights and privileges, extrajudicial challenges to the international judiciary, the Nigerian nation-state, Nigerian state governments, and corporate elites, whom youths claim turn a deaf ear to the needs of the poor. Mbembe views this as "a process in which international networks of foreign traffickers, middlemen, and businessmen are linking with, and becoming entwined with, local businessmen, 'technocrats,' and warlords, causing whole areas of Africa's international economic relations to be swept underground, making it possible to consolidate methods of government that rest on indiscriminate violence and high-level corruption" (86).

The exploitation of minorities and the poor by wealthy elites and majority ethnic religious groups has become an integral part of postcolonial economies of pleasure and of war. In Nigeria, where national and state governments rely on oil for the bulk of their budgets, government officials silence, and even kill, people who protest unfair state strategies for revenue sharing, corporate hiring practices, and environmental degradation. Ken Saro-Wiwa's *Genocide of the Ogoni People* (1992) is the most notable recording of the Nigerian military slaughter of Ogoni, who protested against Royal Dutch Shell Oil Company and the social and ecological destruction resulting from oil industry exploration, production, refining, and transportation

(Bastian 2000; Saro-Wiwa 1992). Encouraged by the end of the cold war, the increasing attention being paid to the global environment, and the insistence of the European Community that minority rights be respected, Saro-Wiwa made repeated pleas to the United Nations and to the Nigerian government to stop the genocide of the Ogoni people.

In spite of international outcry for the plight of the Ogoni, including an Internet protest with blood spilling over the Shell logo, oil companies in the Niger Delta region of southeastern Nigeria continue to exploit the near absence of regulatory laws to maximize profit at the expense of Nigerians living in these oil rich areas. When villagers protest the pollution or the lack of jobs for locals, or form armed youth groups such as MEND (Movement for the Emancipation of the Niger Delta), oil companies deploy firms of high-priced lawyers or request the Nigerian military to serve as a private security force, with constitutional protection to use violent force in cases of rioting. The Nigerian government essentially forces minorities such as the Ogoni to sacrifice themselves and their ways of life for the state, with the majority ethnic Hausa, Yoruba, and Igbo typically holding state positions of power to regulate and distribute wealth, a colonial legacy.

The Nigerian Constitution and Sharia Criminal Law

Since the Independence Constitution of 1960, Nigerians have written four additional constitutions, in 1963, 1979, 1989, and 1999. There is a sense among Nigerians that a constitution is the only means of guaranteeing equity, social justice, and security in a nation-state with more than three hundred self-identified ethnic groups speaking 262 different languages, with culturally diverse political and religious practices. Ilesanmi (2001, 531) suggests, "Given the historically ambiguous relationship of religion to human rights, globally as well as in the particular context of Nigeria, this romance with human rights language and a constitutional political culture calls for critical probing." In Nigeria, conflicts occur in the gap between theory and practice in accepting the constraints and possibilities of religious pluralism as a normative constitutional principle (Harnischfeger 2008; Ilesanmi 2001).

Ilesanmi, in his assessment of the constitutionality of Sharia criminal law in Nigeria, draws on two constitutional clauses that he describes as the "non-establishment norm" and the "free exercise norm" (2001, 540). During the implementation of Sharia criminal law in Kano State, where Muslim Hausa are a majority of the population, non-Hausa Muslims and Christians tended to use the nonestablishment norm in arguments against the constitutionality of Sharia law as state law, while Muslim Hausa evoked the free exercise norm to legitimate it. The nonestablishment norm, found in section 10 of the 1999 constitution under the title "The Government of the Federation or of a State shall not adopt any religion as State Religion" is as follows: "Every person shall be entitled to freedom of thought, conscience and religion, including freedom to change his religion or belief, and freedom (either alone or in community with others, and in public or in private) to manifest and propagate his religion or belief in worship, teaching, practice and observance."

The prevailing interpretation of the nonestablishment norm by minority non-Hausa Muslims and Christians was that it bestows secularity on the multireligious Nigerian state, neither supporting nor privileging one religion over the others, thus protecting minorities from second-class citizenship. This nonestablishment norm is supplemented by the nondiscrimination principle found in article 26 of the International Covenant on Civil and Political Rights (ICCPR), in section 42 of the 1999 constitution:

> A citizen of Nigeria of a particular community, ethnic group, place of origin, sex, religion or political opinion shall not, by reason only that he is such a person, (a) be subjected either expressly by, or in the practical application of, any law in force in Nigeria or any executive or administrative action of the government, to disabilities or restrictions to which citizens of Nigeria of other communities, ethnic groups, places of origin, sex, religious or political opinions are not made subject; or (b) be accorded either expressly by, or in the practical application of, any law in force in Nigeria or any executive or administrative action, any privilege or advantage that is not accorded to citizens of Nigeria of other communities, ethnic groups, places of origin, sex, religious or political opinions.

Majority Muslim Hausa drew on this nondiscrimination clause to suggest that the underlying premise of secularism, a separation of the individual and the state, of the private and public, and of the spiritual and temporal realms, is incompatible with Islamic theories of government. For Muslim Hausa, secularism is an affront to Muslim affirmations of religious principles, especially Sharia legal codes, as the basis of political legitimacy, creating a barrier for Muslims to be governed by these principles in all spheres of their lives. Secularism thus reduces Muslims to second-class citizenry, impeding them from opportunities to exercise their religious human rights (Ilesanmi 2001).

In the city of Kano, Muslim Hausa 'yan daba joined Hisba in masculine demonstrations of power to establish Sharia criminal codes as state law in Kano State. In the early stages of Sharia implementation, members of both groups cited the nondiscrimination clause of the 1999 constitution, using the language of human rights and what they described as the democratic principle of majority rules to legitimate the implementation of Sharia criminal codes. One member of Hisba said, "We know we are a democracy where the majority are Muslims. We believe in Islam under Islamic law and we believe 100 percent that Islamic injunctions are superior to all other injunctions, and that the Quranic constitution is superior to any other constitution. . . . Hisba is the organization to take care of the law. We are going ahead. The governor is not ready and is going to withdraw all support, so the Hisba are using the truth to stop what we can stop." *'Yan daba* and Hisba regarded Sharia criminal law as the only legal means of radically transforming the corrupt, dysfunctional Kano State into one capable of caring for its citizens.

As Ilesanmi (2001, 542) suggests, while Christians and non-Hausa Muslims tended to see "constitutional democracy as a constraining principle on theocratic ambitions (the priority of the non-establishment norm), Muslims infer from it the moral license to subordinate the state to religious oversight (the priority of the free exercise norm)." The different protections afforded non-Hausa Muslim and Christian minorities and the majority Muslim Hausa, based on interpretations of constitutional law, polarized communities into groups that supported certain forms of cultural justice (see Comaroff and Comaroff 2004). The Sharia Implementation Committee and the Hisba focused on contested cultural issues that had dangerous moral consequences for Muslim Hausa and devastating economic consequences for Christians and non-Hausa Muslims, such as the consumption of alcohol, dancing with mixed genders, and appropriate behavior for women. These three areas of policing created conflicts between Muslims and Christians, and Muslim Hausa and Muslim Yoruba, in which large communities of Christian Igbo and Muslim Yoruba appropriated the nondiscrimination clause to evoke the right to cultural self-determination and religious freedom. Muslim Yoruba argued that they were born into Sharia, and in the words of a Muslim Yoruba female friend, they "did not need Hausa boys telling them how to be good Muslims." Beyond the ideological dimensions of these conflicts, the implementation of Sharia criminal law created severe economic crises for many Christians and non-Hausa Muslims who owned the majority of the city's hotels, restaurants, and bars, where drinking alcohol, listening to music, and dancing were popular ways of relieving the tensions of everyday life.

Excluding Minorities: Democracy as Majority Rules

Though *'yan daba* had played an integral part in forcing Kano State governor Rabiu Kwankwaso to implement Sharia criminal codes, literally threatening to burn down the city with black-market petrol, *'yan daba* became an early focus of Hisba preaching and surveillance. *'Yan daba* and Hisba considered

Sharia law to be a democratic form of governance, but they differed in the emotional attachments they had to democratic values. Hisba continued to equate Sharia law with a democracy of majority rules, while *'yan daba* began to emphasize social justice and individual human rights. For instance, a member of Hisba said, "We are a democracy. We are the majority. . . . So they say it's a government of the people, for the people, by the people—Abraham Lincoln, American President . . . since this is a democracy, we can use it [Sharia] as a political weapon, to make sure that someone who is conscious of Sharia is elected." By contrast, a response I commonly heard among *'yan daba* is reflected by the statement, "We are all Muslims. Sharia will help us to know each other better. In this way, crimes will be reduced and the rich and poor will be the same under the law."

'Yan daba* described their hopes for jobs and schooling, for health care, and for personal reforms in behaviors such as their use of alcohol—forms of idealism reflected in wider discourses of support for Sharia criminal law. However, alongside these public narratives of support for Sharia law, *'yan daba* activities revealed mistrust and feelings of betrayal and anger. *'Yan daba* developed ward lookouts who monitored their neighborhoods for Hisba. Some said discretion was their best protection from Hisba because "Sharia works with eye-witnessing a crime." Others said they would allow Hisba to preach to them, but they would not change. A member of *'yan daba* smoking Indian hemp on the side of a major road joked about Hisba: "These Hisba are hypocrites. They do these things, but they hide in their houses. We do it in the open because we only fear God. We fear God, while they fear other people. We are the only true Muslims."

At the Crossroads of Free-Market Capitalism and Sharia Criminal Law

Since 1991 the numbers of male youths participating in *'yan daba* black market economies in Kano city has increased tenfold ('dan Asabe 1991; Casey 2007, 2008, 2009). *'Yan daba* leaders, with greater incomes and social influence than their parents, invert generational power and emerge as political, economic, and sexual rivals to adult men. Phallic domination and power based on the mobilization of conservative Christian and Muslim foundations of masculinity and femininity has been revived in "postcolonial economies of pleasure where the threat to one's life is not as great as the questioning of a male's ability to demonstrate his virility at the expense of a woman and to obtain its valida-tion from the subjugated woman herself" (Mbembe 2001, 13). Power brokers in illegal and illicit economies, youths such as *'yan daba* engage reforming markets and economies of pleasure, offering themselves and requisitioning the bodies of other youths for labor, pleasure, and war.

In the early stages of Sharia implementation, there was little money for the creation of jobs, social services, or education, other than reformist Islamic education, funded by Saudis, Kuwaitis, Iraqis, and wealthy Nigerians. Instead, the Kano State Sharia Implementation Committee started campaigns against the sale and consumption of alcohol and prostitution, and for marriages of all unmarried Muslim Hausa women. A member of Hisba told me, "Women are the people to bring all moral conduct. It is for them to teach children. They are our mothers, so we like them to be in front. They are the figureheads of everything moral."

Hisba complained that Muslim Yoruba and Christian women not practicing the partial seclusion (*kulle*) of Muslim Hausa women were "too independent" and were available attractions for Muslim men. Among Muslim Hausa, failing to maintain what is considered proper control of one's love, including marital and familial relations, erotic desires, and sexual behavior, is a religious lapse into non-Muslim patterns of indulgence and romanticism (Callaway and Creevey 1994; Wall 1988). Unmarried women who live alone are commonly referred to as *karuwai*, prostitutes bound to men only through sex and money, and are considered potential sources of communal betrayal. During the implementation of Sharia criminal law, *'yan daba* received silent encouragement (or thought they did) from reformist Muslims to frighten and attack Muslim women, married and unmarried, who ventured out of their homes unaccompanied.

Conceptions of reformist interventions in moral social order are widely associated with conservative ideologies of gender and family, yet reformist Muslim groups simultaneously developed strong educational programs for women and persuaded women to participate in politics. Muslim Hausa women, marrying and having babies, were a major front in the domestic politics of democracy as majority rules, but they also participated in protests and other public displays of reformist political affiliation. In December of 2000, thousands of Muslim Hausa women protested in front of the Kano State government house to ask the governor, Dr. Rabiu Kwankwaso, for a stricter implementation of Sharia, believing that the bans on alcohol and prostitution were not strong enough to prevent Muslim Hausa husbands and sons from enjoying these pleasures. Referring to the women's protest, a member of Hisba said, "Politics is there for the religion. All of the questions raised by women were supposed to be raised by men. But, when men start raising an alarm, it won't be looked on with gentle eyes. People would be dead."

At the crossroads of free-market capitalism and Sharia criminal law, efforts to marry or to remove unmarried women from Kano State led to increased rates of rape, particularly of young Muslim Hausa girls selling food on city streets.[4] The intersections of free-market capitalism and Sharia criminal law also led to the emergence of new networks of Eastern European and Middle Eastern sex workers brought into Kano by wealthy businessmen who seem to operate outside of all law. To avoid arrest, middle-class and wealthy Muslims venturing out to consume alcohol changed from Muslim Hausa *riguna* (large robe) into Western-cut shirts tucked into pants, a style Muslim Hausa jokingly refer to as *zanzaro* (wasp), an indication of the immodesty of Christians and Muslim Yoruba who show their bodily contours. Concerned with the "visibility of immorality," Hisba arrested young adults and the poor more often than elders for drinking and wearing Western-style clothing because they were not as likely or able to hide in cars or guesthouses.

Hisba identified the ideologies, practices, and people who might undermine Kano's Sharia state. They ethnicized *ilimi* (religious knowledge) and the Islamic authenticity of signs, people, and practices, and they accused Christians and non-Hausa Muslims, particularly Muslim Yoruba and Bori members,[5] of directly or indirectly patronizing mixed-gender celebrations of false gods where alcohol was served. Because of the closeness of Yoruba deities to the Yoruba institution of kingship, Hisba claimed that Yoruba political leaders promoted polytheism, inebriation, and womanizing under the guise of "culture."

States of Emergency and Cultural Justice

In March of 2001, Dr. Abdullahi Ganduje, the reformist Sunni deputy governor of Kano State, announced an Islamic state of emergency regarding the inability of Sharia criminal law, as it was being practiced in Kano State, to stop prostitution and the sale and consumption of alcohol. In conflict with Governor Kwankwaso, Dr. Ganduje led Hisba on a series of raids of local hotels, restaurants, and "cool spots," where Hisba verbally abused patrons and destroyed millions of dollars worth of alcohol. Because Christian Igbo and Muslim Yoruba owned most of these businesses, the raids bankrupted some and resulted in a mass exodus of Christians and Muslims who feared increased violence. Establishments stayed indefinitely closed or operated odd hours, with armed guards patrolling the gates. Jokes about "dying for a drink" became regular, as did rumors of armed Muslims and Christians. As a result, President Obasanjo called Dr. Ganduje to Abuja, stating in public that the deputy governor had endangered Nigerian state security, thus reframing Kano's Islamic state of emergency as a national state of emergency.

This presidential declaration did little to prevent Kano State Hisba from using force in what Hisba referred to as "emergency conditions," gray areas in the enforcement of Sharia criminal codes. A member of Hisba explained, "Say you have a house where they organize gamblers. You see with this, we talk to the elders. We ask the elders to go and talk to the house owner and this doesn't need any emergency because we can go today, tomorrow or next tomorrow, but if they just do it today only, then we have to make our move. This is an emergency condition." Asked why Hisba attacked people at hotels who drink on a regular basis, he said, "Anyone can make a mistake. But, Hisba are here to stay, and we have 100 percent support from God."

The Oputa Panel

Shortly after the implementation of Sharia criminal codes in Kano State, President Obasanjo established the Human Rights Violations Investigation Commission, popularly referred to as the "Oputa Panel," to investigate human rights violations from January 15, 1966, through May 29, 1999. Chaired by the Honorable Justice Chukwudifu A. Oputa, justice emeritus of the Supreme Court of Nigeria, the Oputa Panel determined that the Nigerian military, oil producers, and civilian collaborators with the military, business, and political elites were directly or indirectly responsible for the overwhelming majority of human rights violations within the period covered by the panel. "During this period, most of our rulers' principal motivation and pre-occupation were not service to country but the accumulation of wealth and personal gratification. . . . Public and private morality reached its nadir; and the casualties included human dignity, human rights and our basic freedoms" (HRVIC 2002, 3). The HRVIC report described the return to democratic civilian rule on May 29, 1999, as an opportunity to rise above the decay, to "forge patriotic zeal," and to benefit from "national catharsis," adding that "we have to confront and resolve a basic paradox in looking at the past: to forget, we have to remember. But remembering the past is one thing and living in the past is another thing. To live in the past is to be a slave to revenge, to retributive recrimination" (4).

Drawing upon observations by the Most Reverend D. M. Tutu, chair of the Truth and Reconciliation Commission of South Africa, the report emphasized the intersections of voice, truth, and narrative: "stories are told and the way they are heard change as the years go by . . . the spotlight gyrates, exposing old lies and illuminating new truths" (HRVIC 2002, 5; see, in this volume, Hinton, Robben, Eltringham, and Dwyer).

The HRVIC report noted that the most common concern across Nigeria was the concept of justice, particularly what constitutes justice and what form of justice Nigerians might expect with the release of the commission's findings. The report indicated that "some Nigerians equated justice with revenge," not unique to Nigeria according to comparative analyses of the work of truth commissions in Argentina, Chile, Guatemala, South Africa, and Uganda (Hayner 2002; Kritz 1995; see, in this volume, Burnet and

Robben). The report also laid out two choices in the aftermath of trauma and unbridled human rights violations—revenge and/or Nuremberg-type trials and forgiveness and reconciliation—observing that only in Argentina were there criminal prosecutions of members of the military junta and their collaborators for human rights violations (see Robben, this volume). In the other four cases, Chile, Guatemala, South Africa, and Uganda, the report suggests that "the aim was for people to know what happened in their respective countries during the dark days of military rule" (HRVIC 2002, 7–8). The commission's mandate from President Obasanjo was forgiveness and reconciliation: "To forgive and to reconcile is not necessarily to deny justice. We should not confuse or conflate justice with prosecution and with criminal or retributive justice. Viewed in the broader perspective of legal theory or jurisprudence as well as moral and political philosophy, reconciliation represents not the antithesis but the triumph of justice" (8). According to the report, to manage the transition from military to civilian government "may require that we sacrifice criminal justice for the higher moral imperative of reconciliation" (8–9).

The report acknowledged British colonialism as the most egregious period of human rights violations, with colonial legacies of regionalism, ethnic religious fissures, and majority/minority marginalization being harmful to the nation of Nigeria: "our national experience with federalism shows that the problem of marginalization is at the bottom of minority ethnic group fears of the curtailment or violation of substantive human rights—the right to self-determination, the right to the promotion of their cultural rights, and their citizenship rights, especially the right to equitable participation in the cultural, economic and political life of the country" (HRVIC 2002, 10–11).

The military takeover of state functions in Nigeria shortly after independence led to what the report refers to as the cult of the head of state, wherein "the personal ambitions of the Head of State, his or her fears and apprehensions; his or her enemies, real or imagined, become matters of State interest and concern, deserving State intervention and State protection, and as borne out by the evidence before us necessitating State-sponsored assassinations, murders and 'disappearances'" (HRVIC 2002, 12–13). According to the report, military heads of state, in making no distinction between themselves and the state, violated the human rights of Nigerians to live under constitutional or limited government; militarized the country; routinized militarized fear, language, and command; and used their positions to coerce ordinary citizens to settle personal scores. It describes the plight of critics of the military—journalists, intellectuals, and human rights activists, among others—who were jailed without recourse to due process in the interest of "state security," and the use of the military by oil industries as private security forces to protect "state interests."

Tackling the interlocking problems of democracy, development, peace, and security in the country, the report focuses on the colonial creation of Nigeria and the difficulty of Nigerian national identification "ultimately bound up with the oxymoronic formulation of the federal idea as unity in diversity" (HRVIC 2002, 17). Rather than dwell on the weakness in the nation, the report suggests Nigerians focus on the strength and vigor with which "Nigerians love their country." The report states generational divides weaken the nation, as Nigerians under forty years of age, disillusioned by the idea of Nigeria, generally blame the political elites for squandering their hopes and futures (18–19).

Considering citizenship and human rights, the report examined the implications of "internationalization" and liberal universalism for Nigeria's human rights domestic law and practice, suggesting that membership in organizations such as the Economic Community of West African States, the African Union (the successor to the Organization of African Unity), and the United Nations impose on their member-states the obligation not only to subscribe to the common values enunciated in the relevant human rights provisions of treaties, conventions, and other international legal instruments, but also to reflect them in their domestic laws and implement them as public policy (see, in this volume, Dwyer and Woolford). The report recognized Sharia law as an integral part of religion and customary law but wrote that the Nigerian constitution is the "supreme law of the land on criminal matters" (HRVIC 2002, 91–92). Although recommendations to establish schools; political space for minorities; fairness in resource generation and allocation; military, police, and judicial reform; and rights to work figured prominently, these efforts, like Sharia law, Nigerian constitutional law, and liberal universalism depend on state government implementation.

State Government Administrations of Justice

Like elsewhere in Nigeria, Kano State government officials cater to majority interests. Of particular concern to them is Muslim Hausa control of state resources, public space, schools, jobs, and public security. A member of Hisba said, "We are over a hundred and we are ready to lose our lives to defend this town." By contrast, a *'yan daba*, skeptical of the Kano State application of Sharia criminal codes, said, "you should remember that if a person is just killed without committing any offense, do you think if the Sharia doesn't do anything about it that we will let the matter rest? . . . The Sharia says if you kill a man, you should be killed too. So why should you kill and not be killed?"

The use of violence to enact cultural justice is further exemplified in the May 11, 2004, *'yan daba* massacre of Christians and non-Hausa Muslims working in the factory areas of Sharada and Challewa and on the Bayero University campus (Casey 2009). *'Yan daba*, with lists of people to kill, attacked their neighbors and fellow residents, calling them *arna* (unbelievers), *Kiristoci* (Christians), and *baki* (strangers). The crisis followed several months of communal violence in Plateau State that Muslim residents of Kano felt had been condoned through the inaction of the Christian governor of Plateau State, Joshua Dariye, and the Christian president Obasanjo (Casey 2009).

In the aftermath of the violence, there was widespread discussion of the violence as retribution for the killings of Muslims in Plateau State and other parts of Nigeria, Iraq, and the Israeli-occupied Palestinian territories. One *'yan daba* said, "if Muslims are not safe in other parts of the country, no one will be safe here." Muslim Hausa *'yan daba* also expressed resentment at the lack of jobs available for them in Kano factories, with the explicit idea that killing and forcefully expelling Christians and Muslim minorities from their jobs would result in greater economic opportunities.

Concluding Remarks

The ongoing crises in the oil-producing Niger Delta of southeastern Nigeria and the May 11, 2004, massacre in Kano reveal the limits of liberal universalism and Sharia criminal law in providing security and opportunities for Nigerians, particularly for minorities and the poor. Youths, the majority of citizens in most countries, are at the forefront of political battles for security and equity in opportunities. Youths enter into relations with new decentralized economic and religious networks and with older centralized state authorities, yet in ways different from that of their parents. In Nigeria, male youths' activities, mobilized around community security and resource control, "combine elements of complicity, insurgency, monitoring and disengagement" in response to state and international business "politics of plunder" (Gore and Pratten 2003). Resurgences of local identities, distinctions between "indigenes" and "strangers," "believers" and "infidels," resulting in large-scale violence, may be understood as affective responses to hypocritical, morally bankrupt adult leaders, local and global, and to new venues of political, economic, and religious participation (Casey 2007, 2008, 2009).

Primitivist, dichotic images and vocabularies of youths as victimized innocents, hypersocialized into market, pleasure, and war economies, and as the new barbarians in need of increased discipline and punishment, do little to help us understand local/global (in)justice. With the rising numbers of youths participating in *daba*, Nigerian adults speak of *'yan daba* and *almajirai* (Quranic students) as "HIV infected," "potential terrorists," "youths on the rampage," withdrawing physical support and empathy. The sentiments aroused by the hypocrisy of espoused liberal universalism in the context of colonialism and imperialism, and the gaps between legal theory and enforcement, encourages violence as a means of ensuring justice. For Kano youths, the violence of local/global justice is the motivation and justification for violent enforcements of cultural justice, justice based on the idea of democratic majority Muslim Hausa rule. It is at the crossroads of liberal universalism, free-market capitalism, and religious orthodoxies where *'yan daba* and Hisba enter the realms of blood sacrifice.

NOTES

I thank Aminu Sharif Bappa, Usman Aliyu, Show Boy, and the *'yan daba*, Hisba, and families who allowed me into their lives. For reasons of confidentiality, they shall remain unnamed, but I greatly appreciate my experiences with them. I also thank Mike Aliyu, Aminu Taura Abdullahi, Abdulkarim 'Dan Asabe, Salisu Abdullahi, Rudi Gaudio, Aminu Inuwa, Brian Larkin, Murray Last, Fatima Palmer, Istvan Patkai, the late Umar Sanda, Shobana Shankar, the late Philip Shea, and Aisha Usman for their important contributions to my thinking about this project. I am grateful to faculty in the departments of psychiatry and sociology at Bayero University and the department of anthropology at University of California, Los Angeles, for research affiliations and a sense of home base. I am indebted to Robert Edgerton, Douglas Hollan, Allen Feldman, Uli Linke, and Alexander Hinton for their mentoring and inspiration. However, the project would have been impossible without the generous support of the Harry Frank Guggenheim Foundation, the skillful guidance of Karen Colvard, and a Fulbright IIE Lecturing/Research Award.

1. Sharia criminal codes were in place under British colonial administrators who outlawed hadd punishments, which they found "repugnant." The civil code of Sharia law, which guides matters such as marriage, divorce, child custody, and inheritance, has been continuously in place since the nineteenth century (Gumi 1992, 50).

2. For historical analyses of religious politics in northern Nigeria and the question of Sharia law, see Christelow (2002), Harnischfeger (2008), Hunwick (1997), Ibrahim (1991), Iman (2002), Kumo (1993), Last (1967), Okunola (1993), Paden (1973, 1986), Sanusi (2000), Umar (1993, 2001), Westerlund (1997), and Yadudu (1993).

3. For historical and contemporary analyses of Kano *'yan daba* and *'yan banga*, see Casey (2007, 2008, 2009), 'dan Asabe (1991), and Ya'u (2000).

4. Some *'yan daba* participate in *'daukar amarya* (literally, to carry a bride), the kidnapping and raping of women whom they feel have "slighted" or disrespected them. *'Yan daba* admit to kidnapping prostitutes from hotels and brutally raping them in uninhabited areas of Kano. Unfortunately, these rapes are rarely reported. According to a magistrate judge in Gyadi-Gyadi, cases of reported rape increased sixfold between the implementation of Sharia law in November of 2000 and January of 2001. The judge (whose name is withheld for safety reasons) attributed this to a decrease in the number of prostitutes available for older men, who had instead begun "turning to young girls" (pers. comm.).

5. Bori is widely regarded as animism or a spirit possession cult predating Islam (Greenberg 1946; Onwuegeogwu 1969; Palmer 1914; Tremearne 1914). Scholars

describe the Bori spirit possession rituals, practiced in northern Nigeria and Niger, as religious opposition to Islam and as alternative or oppositional gender experience and expression (Callaway and Creevey 1994; Masquelier 1999; Onwuegeogwu 1969; Wall 1988). Today, Bori adherents in Kano State consider themselves Muslims, while Kano reformist Muslims variably refer to them as "fallen Muslims," "marginal Muslims," or "pagans."

REFERENCES

Akinyele, R. T. 2001. "Ethnic Militancy and National Stability in Nigeria: A Case Study of the Oodua People's Congress." *African Affairs* 100 (401): 623–640.

Baker, Bruce. 2002. "When the Bakassi Boys Came: Eastern Nigeria Confronts Vigilantism." *Journal of Contemporary African Studies* 20:223–244.

Bastian, Misty. 2000. "Buried under Six Feet of Crude Oil: State Sponsored Death and the Missing Body of Ken Saro-Wiwa." In *Ken Saro-Wiwa: Writer and Political Activist*, ed. Craig W. McLuckie and Aubrey McPhail. Boulder: Lynne Rienner Publications.

Callaway, Barbara, and Lucy Creevey. 1994. *The Heritage of Islam: Women, Religion and Politics in West Africa*. Boulder: Lynne Reinner Publishers.

Casey, Conerly. 2007. "'Policing' through Violence: Fear, Vigilantism and the Politics of Islam in Northern Nigeria." In *Global Vigilantes: Anthropological Approaches to Vigilantism*, ed. David Pratten and Atreyee Sen, 93–124. London: Hurst & Co.

———. 2008. "'Marginal Muslims': Authenticity and Perceptual Bounds of Profiling in Northern Nigeria." Theme issue, "African Youths in the Age of Neoliberalism," ed. Benjamin Soares and Marie Nathalie LeBlanc. *Africa Today* 54 (3): 67–94.

———. 2009. "Mediated Hostility: Media, 'Affective Citizenship,' and Genocide in Northern Nigeria." In *Genocide: Truth, Memory, and Representation*, ed. Alexander Laban Hinton and Kevin Lewis O'Neill. Durham, NC: Duke University Press.

Christelow, Allan. 2002. "Islamic Law and Judicial Practice in Nigeria: An Historical Perspective." *Journal of Muslim Minority Affairs* 22 (1): 185–204.

Clarke, Kamari Maxine. 2009. *Fictions of Justice: The International Criminal Court and the Challenge of Legal Pluralism in Sub-Sahara Africa*. Cambridge, UK: Cambridge University Press.

Comaroff, John L., and Jean Comaroff, eds. 1999. "Introduction." *Civil Society and the Political Imagination in Africa: Critical Perspectives*. Chicago: University of Chicago Press.

———. 2004. "Criminal Justice, Cultural Justice: The Limits of Liberalism and the Pragmatics of Difference in the New South Africa." *American Ethnologist* 31 (2): 188–204.

Crowder, Michael. 1978. *The Story of Nigeria*. London: Faber & Faber.

'dan Asabe, Abdulkarim. 1991. "'Yan Daba: The 'Terrorists' of Kano Metropolitan?" *Kano Studies, Special Issue: Youth and Health in Kano Today* 1:85–112.

Falola, Toyin. 1977. "Nigeria in the Global Context of Refugees: Historical and Comparative Perspectives." *Journal of Asian and African Studies* 32 (1–2): 5–21.

———. 1998. *Violence in Nigeria: The Crisis of Religious Politics and Secular Ideologies*. Rochester, NY: University of Rochester Press.

Gore, Charles, and David Pratten. 2003. "The Politics of Plunder: The Rhetorics of Order and Disorder in Southern Nigeria." *African Affairs* 102:211–240.

Greenberg, Joseph. 1946. *The Influence of Islam on a Sudanese Religion*. New York: J. J. Augustin.

Gumi, Abubakar, with Ismaila Tsiga. 1992. *Where I Stand*. Ibadan, Nigeria: Spectrum Books.

Harnischfeger, Johannes. 2003. "The Bakassi Boys: Fighting Crime in Nigeria." *Journal of Modern African Studies* 41:23–49.

———. 2008. *Democratization and Islamic Law: The Sharia Conflict in Nigeria*. Frankfurt: Campus Verlag.

Hayner, Priscilla. B. 2002. *Unspeakable Truths: Facing the Challenge of Truth Commissions*. New York: Routledge.

Human Rights Violations Investigation Commission (HRVIC). 2002. *HRVIC Report: Conclusions and Recommendations*. Abuja: Nigerian Federal Government.

Hunwick, John. 1997. "Sub-Saharan Africa and the Wider World of Islam: Historical and Contemporary Perspectives." In *African Islam and Islam in Africa: Encounters between Sufis and Islamists*, ed. David Westerlund and Eva Evers Rosander, 28–54. Athens: Ohio University Press.

Ibrahim, Jibrin. 1991. "Religion and Political Turbulence in Nigeria." *Journal of Modern African Studies* 29 (1): 115–136.

Ilesanmi, Simeon. 2001. "Constitutional Treatment of Religion and the Politics of Human Rights in Nigeria." *African Affairs* 100:529–554.

Iman, Ayesha. 2002. "Islam and Women's Rights." http://www.waado.org/NigerDelta/HumanRights/WomenRights/AyeshaIman.html.

Kritz, Neil. ed. 1995. *Transitional Justice: How Emerging Democracies Reckon with Former Regimes*. Vol. 1, *General Considerations*. Washington, DC: United States Institute of Peace.

Kumo, Suleimanu. 1993. "Shari'a under Colonialism—Northern Nigeria." In *Islam in Africa: Proceedings of the Islam in Africa Conference*, ed. Nura Alkali, Adamu Adamu, Awwal Yadudu, Rashid Motem, and Haruna Salihi, 1–22. Ibadan, Nigeria: Spectrum Books.

Last, Murray. 1967. *The Sokoto Caliphate*. Ibadan, Nigeria: Longman Publishers.

———. 2005. "Towards a Political History of Youth in Muslim Northern Nigeria, 1750–2000." In *Vanguards or Vandals: Youth, Politics and Conflict in Africa*, ed. Jon Abbink and Ineke van Kessel, 37–54. Leiden: Brill Academic Publishers.

Levin, Michael. 1997. "The New Nigeria: Displacement and the Nation." *Journal of Asian and African Studies* 32 (1–2): 134–144.

Loimeier, Roland. 1997. "Islamic Reform and Political Change: The Examples of Abubakar Gumi and the 'Yan Izala Movement in Northern Nigeria." In *African Islam and Islam in Africa: Encounters between Sufis and Islamists,* ed. David Westerlund and Eva Evers Rosander, 286–307. Athens: Ohio University Press.

Mamdani, Mahmood. 1996. *Citizen and Subject: Contemporary Africa and the Legacy of Late Colonialism*. Princeton: Princeton University Press.

———. 2009. *Saviors and Survivors: Darfur, Politics, and the War on Terror*. New York: Pantheon.

Masquelier, Adeline. 1999. "Debating Muslims, Disputed Practices: Struggles for the Realization of an Alternative Moral Order in Niger." In *Civil Society and the Political Imagination in Africa: Critical Perspectives*, ed. John L. Comaroff and Jean Comaroff, 219–250. Chicago: University of Chicago Press.

Mbembe, Achille. 2001. *On the Postcolony*. Berkeley: University of California Press.

Nolte, Insa. 2004. "Identity and Violence: The Politics of Youth in Ijebu-Remo, Nigeria." *Journal of Modern African Studies* 42 (1): 61–89.

Ocheje, Paul D. 1997. "Legalizing Displacement: The Legal Order in the Political Economy of Nigeria." *Journal of Asian and African Studies* 32 (1–2): 120–133.

Okpu, U. 1977. *Ethnic Minority Problems in Nigerian Politics 1960–65*. Uppsala: University of Uppsala Press.

Okunola, Muri. 1993. "The Relevance of Shari'a to Nigeria." In *Islam in Africa: Proceedings of the Islam in Africa Conference*, ed. Nura Alkali, Adamu Adamu, Awwal Yadudu, Rashid Motem, and Haruna Salihi, 23–36. Ibadan, Nigeria: Spectrum Books.

Onwuegeogwu, Michael. 1969. "The Cult of the Bori Spirits among the Hausa." In *Man in Africa*, ed. Mary Douglas and Philip Kaberry, 279–306. New York: Tavistock Publications.

Paden, John. 1973. *Religion and Political Culture in Kano*. Berkeley: University of California Press.

———. 1986. *Ahmadu Bello, Sardauna of Sokoto: Values and Leadership in Nigeria*. Zaria, Nigeria: Hudahuda.

Palmer, H. R. 1914. "Bori among the Hausas." *Man* 14:113–117.

Pratten, David. 2005. "Youth, Truth and Trials: The Practice of Nigerian Vigilantism." Paper presented at Global Vigilantes, University of Sussex, July 8–9.

Sanusi, Sanusi Lamido. 2000. "Shariacracy in Nigeria: The Intellectual Roots of Islamist Discourses." http://www.nigerdeltacongress.com/sarticles/shariacracy_in_nigeria.htm.

Saro-Wiwa, Ken. 1992. *Genocide in Nigeria: The Ogoni Tragedy*. London: Saros International Publishers.

Smith, Daniel J. 2004. "The Bakassi Boys: Vigilantism, Violence and Political Imagination in Nigeria." *Cultural Anthropology* 19 (3): 429–455.

Tremearne, A. J. 1914. *Ban of the Bori*. London: Heath, Cranton & Ouseley.

Tsing, Anna. 2005. *Friction: An Ethnography of Global Connection*. Princeton: Princeton University Press.

Umar, Mohammed S. 1993. "Changing Islamic Identity in Nigeria from the 1960s to 1980s." In *Muslim Identity and Social Change in Sub-Saharan Africa,* ed. Luis Brenner, 154–178. Bloomington: Indiana University Press.

———. 2001. "Education and Islamic Trends in Northern Nigeria: 1970s–1990s." *Africa Today* 48 (2): 127–150.

Wall, Louis. 1988. *Hausa Medicine: Illnesses and Well-Being in a West African Culture*. Durham: Duke University Press.

Watts, Michael. 1996. "Islamic Modernities? Citizenship, Civil Society and Islamism in a Nigerian City." *Public Culture* 8:251–289.

———. 2001. "Violent Geographies: Speaking the Unspeakable and the Politics of Space." *City and Society* 13 (1): 85–117.

Westerlund, David. 1997. "Reaction and Action: Accounting for the Rise of Islamism." In *African Islam and Islam in Africa: Encounters between Sufis and Islamists*, ed. David Westerlund and Eva Evers Rosander, 308–334. Athens: Ohio University Press.

Williams, Pat Ama Tokunbo. 1997. "Religion, Violence and Displacement in Nigeria." *Journal of Asian and African Studies* 32 (1–2): 33–49.

Yadudu, Auwalu Hamisu. 1993. "The Prospects for Shari'a in Nigeria." In *Islam in Africa: Proceedings of the Islam in Africa Conference*, ed. Nura Alkali, Adamu Adamu, Awwal Yadudu, Rashid Motem, and Haruna Salihi, 37–58. Ibadan, Nigeria: Spectrum Books.

Ya'u, Yunusa Zakari. 2000. "The Youth, Economic Crisis and Identity Transformation: The Case of the Yandaba in Kano." In *Identity Transformation and Identity Politics under Structural Adjustment in Nigeria*, ed. A. Jega, 161–180. Uppsala: Nordiska Afrikainstitutet and Centre for Research and Documentation.

6

▶ ▷ ▶ ▷ ▷ ▶ ▷ ▷ ▶ ▷ ▶ ▷ ▶ ◁ ◀ ◁ ◀ ◁ ◀ ◁ ◀ ◁ ◀ ◁ ◀ ◁

Genocide, Affirmative Repair,
and the British Columbia
Treaty Process

ANDREW WOOLFORD

This chapter examines the ways in which genocidal violence (understood here as physically, biologically, or culturally destructive violence targeted toward groups) is potentially transformed into symbolic violence through transitional justice processes. The British Columbia Treaty Process, which began in 1992 and has for the past seventeen years made a halting attempt to negotiate treaties between First Nations and the governments of British Columbia and Canada, is used as a case study to illustrate this argument.[1]

A key component of transitional symbolic violence is the failure or refusal to recognize the harms of the past. The British Columbia Treaty Process was established on the pillars of "justice" and "certainty," with the former referring to the need to right past wrongs, while the latter speaks to the desire to create economic and jurisdictional security within the province (BCCTF 1991). However, so far the goal of justice has been treated in a confused and imprecise manner within the process. In particular, the question must be asked, What injustices does the process intend to address? Representatives of the provincial and federal governments often respond to this question by vaguely pointing to the history of unresolved land claims within the province, suggesting the need to settle once and for all questions of ownership of and jurisdiction over lands. However, for First Nations peoples, territorial loss is only one part of a broader history of colonial destruction wrought upon their communities. Indeed, in my interviews with First Nations informants, they did not hesitate to label these injustices "genocide."[2]

Before moving this discussion forward, however, a comment is required on the application of the term "transitional justice" to this process. "Transitional justice" typically refers to justice processes intended to facilitate a societal shift from authoritarianism and mass violence toward democratic rule (as noted by Duthie, this volume). However, such a narrow understanding of transitional justice suggests a certain ethnocentrism that views only nondemocratic nations to be in need of transition. It also limits the notion to a Westphalian framework in which transition is located within the spatial confines of the nation-state. A more capacious notion of transition would enable examination of the ways in which settler societies must also negotiate the existence of self-determining indigenous groups within their midst while at the same time redressing injustices committed against these populations, so as to transition toward new models of confederated association that may indeed burst the Westphalian model.

Without this broadening of the term, transitional justice is rightly subject to the criticisms of teleology and hierarchy that Alexander Hinton identifies in his introduction to this volume. It is also the case that, when addressing matters of transition, scholars must remain attuned to questions of who or what is being transitioned, and on whose terms. The First Nations peoples who are the focus of this chapter have resisted years of transitional justice in the sense that past vehicles for redressing Aboriginal land claims in British Columbia have sought to transition Aboriginal groups toward the economic norms of settler society. This was the case, for example, with the McKenna-McBride Commission (1913–1915), which gathered information about Aboriginal groups that was subsequently used to unilaterally and forcefully fit them into a colonial territorial framework. Such experiences provide an important reminder that societal transition is a constitutive process through which new societal visions and subjectivities are constructed and performed. Moreover, what is built through transitional processes may not amount to a justice that is transformative of the generative conditions of injustice, but rather affirms and reinforces entrenched patterns of power through the offering of merely palliative forms of redress (see also Dwyer, this volume).

Land Claims, Assimilation, and Genocide in British Columbia

When examining the plight of First Nations in what is now British Columbia, it is important to recognize that we are dealing with multiple localities, each possessing regional and cultural variations with respect to their experiences of colonialism. In the northern reaches of the province, for example, First Nations lands were expropriated largely for purposes of resource exploitation and development, whereas First Nations close to the southern cities of Victoria and Vancouver also faced greater degrees of settler encroachment. However, most First Nations groups in the province faced a series of similar damaging events that, because of their cumulative destructive impact on these groups, raises serious questions about what we mean when we use the term "genocide."

Article 2 of the *United Nations Convention on the Prevention and Punishment of Genocide* (1948; hereafter UNGC) reads:

> In the present Convention, genocide means any of the following acts committed with intent to destroy, in whole or in part, a national, ethnical, racial or religious group as such:
>
> (a) Killing members of the group;
> (b) Causing serious bodily or mental harm to members of the group;
> (c) Deliberately inflicting on the group conditions of life calculated to bring about its physical destruction in whole or in part;
> (d) Imposing measures intended to prevent births within the group;
> (e) Forcibly transferring children of the group to another group.

Although several scholars and activists have used this definition to claim that Aboriginal peoples in Canada have suffered genocide (e.g., Annett 2001; Bischoping and Fingerhut 1996; Churchill 2003; Davis and Zannis 1973; Neu and Therrien 2002), the UN template presents several problems when describing the colonial assault on First Nations in British Columbia.

To begin, the UNGC defines the group targeted by genocide as "national, ethnical, racial or religious" in character. This restricted focus has been much criticized in the genocide studies literature for ignoring other collectivities, such as those based upon class and political affiliations (e.g., Kuper 1981; Legters 1984). But it is also problematic in the way that these categories are too often taken to be essential and primordial group identities that are culturally and historically fixed in a near permanent stasis (Powell 2007). This assumed fixity is particularly dangerous when seeking to force First Nations peoples into one of the UNGC's identified group classifications. Thus, although arguments could be made for portraying these collectivities as "ethnicities" or "nations," each of these moves has potential deleterious consequences if done without consideration of the specificity of First Nations groups.

For example, while First Nations have many properties that would allow one to classify them as "ethnic" groups (e.g., shared language, territory, customs, values, and beliefs), this classification is problematic when it is used to portray them as ethnically homogenous. Among the Coast Salish of British Columbia, membership in a First Nation is open to individuals from other Aboriginal and non-Aboriginal communities. Indeed, intermarriages between groups are encouraged to create intergroup ties (Tsleil-Waututh 2000). Such "ethnic mobility" may not be inconsistent with more refined notions of ethnicity (e.g., Eltringham 2004). However, there is a disconcerting tendency to reify ethnic groups—to treat them as coherent and static entities—and this tendency is all too common in applications of the UNGC that seek to protect "stable and permanent" groups (Hinton 2002).

Moreover, as will be suggested below, this reifying tendency could itself have destructive consequences for First Nations peoples.

Sidestepping for the moment the murky issue of ethnicity, one might instead be tempted to classify First Nations as "national" groups, since "nation" appears a potentially more open category. But this classification could also result in a misrepresentation of First Nations peoples. In particular, a national group is often understood to be a group possessing (or deprived of) a definite and bounded territory or homeland. However, although First Nations in British Columbia have long sought recognition of their traditional territories, their concept of territory is much different from that of European nation-states, and we must be careful not to reduce it to the latter form. Again, turning to the worldview of the Coast Salish of British Columbia, territories are not sharply defined; instead, their concept of territory allows for greater freedom of movement, sharing, and multiparty relationships. For this reason, the imposition of national boundaries upon the Coast Salish presents a significant challenge to their self-understanding and group identity. As Thom (2006, 21–22) states, Coast Salish members

> see boundaries and borders as arbitrary and artificial at best, and at worst a part of a recurring colonial mechanism of government to create division between communities and kin and weaken the potential strength of the Coast Salish people as a Nation. These people are concerned that the power of such maps and terms will have the effect of severing their connections to place, framing the future of engagements with the land exercised as rights negotiated under land claims settlements firmly in western ontological terms.

Thus, although the term "Nation" is used here to describe the Coast Salish, it is not a nationhood prescribed by closed territorial space. Indeed, the boundary between the Coast Salish and neighboring Nuu-chah-nulth or Kwakwakw'wakw cannot be drawn as a single line since these borderlands were traditionally spaces of complex interrelationships. In this manner, the term "Nation" is used in this quotation in a relational sense (i.e., relationships between kin and community groups) rather than a rigid spatial sense.

Reflecting on these local understandings of group identity, one can see that attempts to force First Nations to fit one of the group categories identified under the UNGC could potentially encourage a totalization of First Nations lifeworlds. And this in itself represents a threat to the survival of these groups, since this naming effects a subtle shift in their cultural ontology.

This leads to the issue of what it means to destroy such a group. In examining this question in light of the problematics of group definition, it is important to remember that in the process of Canadian colonization Aboriginal communities have suffered because of the ways in which colonial governments have named and categorized them. Indeed, much of this dangerous classification has been carried out through the force of law. Initially misidentified as "Indians," the Aboriginal peoples of Canada subsequently found this label reinforced through various legal mechanisms. Their distinct cultural and linguistic identities were not recognized under Canadian law, whether Cree, Ojibway, Dene, or Coast Salish. Instead, laws, such as Canada's Indian Act (1876), defined them as a single people, transforming them into a governable population while dividing into smaller bands the larger tribal groupings that may have represented a threat to colonial power. Having erased all legal differences among First Nations peoples, Canadian policy makers were then able to attack the imagined general property of "Indianness" through techniques of assimilation.[3] At first, this was attempted through promises of the Enfranchisement Act (1869)—Indians could voluntarily dispossess themselves of their Indian heritage and accept all the supposed benefits of Canadian citizenship. However, when First Nations peoples refused this offer and clung to their indigenous identities, assimilationist policies were intensified, with one of the bleakest forms of deadly governance coming through Canadian residential schools.

Residential schools began operating in the late nineteenth century, drawing on an existing network of Protestant and Catholic schools. These were initially day schools, but their administrators felt it was problematic that the children returned to their parents at the end of each day, thus undoing their day of lessons in the proper conduct of "civilized" persons. In response, the schools began to hold students in residence for most of the year, providing the children sometimes no more than a month in the summer to visit their families. By 1920, these schools were made mandatory for all Aboriginal children.[4] At many of the schools, conditions were so inadequate that large numbers of children died from ill health, exposure to the elements, and poor nutrition (Milloy 1999). Others suffered physical and sexual abuse, as well as a constant verbal assault upon their cultures, traditions, communities, and families. Upon completing their education, many no longer felt at home or welcome in their communities and became divorced from their cultural traditions. Moreover, deprived of the experience of being parented, they later found it a great struggle to raise their own children. Continuing cycles of emotional, physical, and sexual abuse, as well as addiction, suicide, and other markers of intergenerational trauma within Aboriginal communities, are considered residual effects of the residential schooling experience (Haig-Brown 1988; Monture-Angus 1999).

The residential schooling system is an obvious target for application of the UNGC, especially with respect to part (e), "Forcibly transferring children of the group to another group." However, this section of the UNGC captures only a fraction of this destructive experience. In part, what is missing is the fact that through residential schools First Nations peoples were denied their powers of self-constitution. Unable to negotiate their own identity, they were branded inferior, savage, and abject. Moreover, as a result of this branding they were seen as unfit to govern themselves, both at a community and individual level. Their government structures were replaced by those prescribed by the Canadian government, and their children transferred to residential schools to learn not only the dispositions of civilized European society, but also of the inadequacy of their own communal forms of life. Add to this the abuse, neglect, disease, and cultural loss that was suffered through the schools, and one is confronted with a complex network of destructive experiences that is difficult to contain within reductionist juridical terms.

The forms of destruction described in the UNGC are also limited to acts against the human members of the group. This has significant consequences for understanding the harms of land expropriation in British Columbia. In animist cultures, land is not simply a possession of the group to be utilized for purposes of sustenance. It is, in a sense, part of the group, since it is necessarily entwined with processes of group identity formation. As Patricia Monture-Angus (1999, 56) suggests, group identity for many Aboriginal peoples is inextricably entwined with their understanding of territory: "Identity, as I have come to understand it, requires a relationship with territory (and not a relationship based on control of that territory)." Thus, with respect to First Nations, it is insufficient to merely describe territory loss as "deliberately inflicting on the group conditions of life calculated to bring about its physical destruction in whole or in part." Although the removal of First Nations lands in British Columbia and the sequestration of these peoples on tiny reserves did affect their ability to sustain themselves physically, it also attacked their ability to define themselves culturally.[5]

Through this brief discussion, one can see that it is difficult to isolate any definite notion of "intent" to fit the UNGC's specifications. Certainly, government figures voiced their desires to be done with the "Indian problem," both in British Columbia and across Canada. Take for example the following infamous statement made by Duncan Campbell Scott, superintendent of Indian Affairs from 1913 to 1932: "I want to get rid of the Indian problem. Our object is to continue until there is not a single Indian in Canada that has not been absorbed" (Titley 1986, 50). While Scott's words are unambiguous, it would be a disservice to the experiences of Aboriginal peoples to rest too much on such statements, hoping to find in them a teleology of intent. For even individuals who would have been considered the liberal humanitarians of their time called for the assimilation of First Nations peoples (Cairns 2000). For them, this was a means to ensure the physical survival of the First Nations—otherwise they may become extinct from disease and land encroachment. But this was a survival that attempted to deprive them of their ability to continue as groups. Thus, the process of destruction in British Columbia is not a simple matter where a despised identity is targeted for elimination by a perpetrator seized by an irrational hatred. It is more the case, as I have argued elsewhere, of a "catastrophic form of misrecognition, which so devalues a population that assimilation is assumed to be a matter of their general welfare" (Woolford 2009, 92–93).

What the brief discussion above suggests is that the UNGC may itself be part of a tradition, a way of seeing and knowing the world, that is problematic for Indigenous peoples. It is a universalizing logic that often sits tenuously alongside particular experiences of destructive events (see also Wagner, this volume, for further discussion of the tensions between the universal and the particular in transitional justice). Unable to fully grapple with local First Nations understandings of what it means to be a group and how this group might be intentionally destroyed, this template requires that we open it to new and unfamiliar meaning horizons. Moreover, without specific knowledge of the collective context of genocidal destruction, we risk contributing to rather than alleviating the conditions that made this destruction possible.[6] In such circumstances, a poorly conceived transitional justice process has the potential to adapt and advance the project of assimilation, rather than to correct it.

Symbolic Violence and Affirmative Repair

This brings us to the matter of symbolic violence. Symbolic violence has been an ongoing problem in the destructive assault on First Nations in British Columbia since the governments of Canada and British Columbia have historically refused to acknowledge First Nations' understandings of the past. It has, however, been overshadowed by physical, biological, and cultural forms of destruction. It is recently then that the problem of symbolic violence has become magnified under the auspices of "justice," as transitional mechanisms have failed to take into account the very real effects of colonial domination.

Symbolic violence differs from the brute force of physical, economic, or political coercion. Bourdieu (1990, 127) defines symbolic violence as "gentle, invisible violence, unrecognized as such, chosen as much as undergone, that of trust, obligation, personal loyalty, hospitality, gifts, debts, piety, in a word, of all the virtues honoured by the ethic of honour." Symbolic violence arises in situations where the exercise of direct domination or exploitation is likely to be frowned upon and a softer approach to persuasion is needed to confirm or transform a particular vision of the world. It emanates from the social and, in particular, symbolic power of the actor who uses it, who is able to achieve recognition of his or her worldview and to have the practices and rationalities that define this worldview accepted by the addressee as normal, second nature, and/or doxic (Bourdieu 1991). In this sense, symbolic violence takes the appearance of reason, and in being reasonable disguises the interests that lie behind its force, and even the fact that force is being used.

Symbolic violence is thus constitutive in that it allows those with symbolic power to act upon the world and to establish as given what is in fact the arbitrary product of their own particular vision. Law, according to Bourdieu (1990), is the system of symbolic violence par excellence (see also Eltringham, this volume), but symbolic violence is also evident in transitional justice and reparation politics, understood here to include a broad range of activities such as the restitution of stolen money and property, monetary compensation for suffering, commemorative acts to preserve public memory of atrocities, tribunals and other court proceedings designed to punish perpetrators for their crimes, lustration to remove those complicit with the abusive regime from positions of power, and other acts intended to contend with and move a society beyond past harms (see Torpey 2006). These transitional processes are often imbued with power relations, and the most influential among these power relations are those that go unacknowledged—the formal and informal rules that circumscribe what is utterable or demandable within a specific negotiation context.

By limiting justice, symbolic violence can serve to push a transitional process toward "affirmative repair" (Fraser 1997). With affirmative repair the transitional process is structured such that the presuppositions and interests of the dominant group are given priority, which makes it difficult for less powerful groups to state their demands in a reasonable fashion. In the context of modern treaty-making, this involves, in part, enrolling the group into the project of neoliberal governance to an extent that it becomes difficult for the group to assert its difference in any way contrary to the prevailing political and economic norms of local and global markets. Affirmative repair attempts to bracket discussions of justice in the transitional process so as to restrict the process to issues deemed economically and legally feasible. Moreover, when reaching settlements, affirmative repair offers only surface forms of recognition and redistribution that do not threaten to radically transform society; rather, these symbolic and material disbursements are directed toward affirming the prevailing social order (Fraser 1997). More specifically, they require the victimized party to buy in to specific economic and political principles in order to receive the benefits of transitional justice.

The British Columbia Treaty Process and Symbolic Violence

In British Columbia, negotiations have been under way for well over a decade to deal with First Nations land claims. The First Nations peoples of Canada's westernmost province never ceded their territory to the colonial society inserted in their midst in the mid- to late-nineteenth century. Nor did they sign treaties with the federal government, as was the case with First Nations elsewhere in Canada (see, for example, Ray, Miller, and Tough 2000). Instead, as noted above, these peoples were forced onto small reserves, subjected to the rigid controls of the Indian Act, and suffered attempts to legislate (e.g., through the banning of the potlatch) and assimilate (e.g., through residential schools) their culture away. This history of injustice and attempted destruction was long denied and ignored by both the provincial and federal governments, despite the frequent protests, petitions, and court cases launched by First Nations peoples, who have demanded resolution of their outstanding land claims and recognition of their "inherent right" to self-determination since first contact with the colonial powers.

Between 1969 and 1992, the political and legal activism of First Nations in British Columbia created a degree of political and legal uncertainty in the province. Also effective were the road blockades First Nations mounted to disrupt the transport of resources through reserve lands, and the law-suits and court injunctions they filed to challenge government claims to slow down resource extraction activities within Aboriginal traditional territories (Blomley 1996). Similar to the results of the Central Kalahari legal case described by Hitchcock and Babchuk (this volume), however, court cases rarely resulted in outright victories; instead, they affirmed the potential rights of Aboriginal claimants, placing further pressure on gov-ernment to resolve the land question. The economic consequences of these actions were lost investment in the province's resource-based economy and growing public frustration with the provincial and federal governments' reluctance to engage in modern treaty negotiations. In December of 1990, under growing economic, social, and political pressures, the federal and provincial governments at last heeded the requests of First Nations and the tri-partite (Canada, British Columbia, and First Nations) British Columbia Claims Task Force was established. This task force represented the first attempt by non-Aboriginal governments to sit down with First Nations in dialogue to discuss the land question. Together, they examined the history of British Columbia and the harsh impact of colonialism on First Nations peoples in the province; however, the Task Force was careful not to politi-cize this historical record so as not to risk alienating the two non-Aboriginal governments. Indeed, the non Aboriginal governments never officially con-firmed this historical retelling of the province's troubled past—all they agreed to in the end was a process for creating future relationships with First Nations in British Columbia.

On the basis of the British Columbia Claims Task Force report, the Brit-ish Columbia Treaty Commission Agreement was signed on September 21,

1992, and the newly minted British Columbia Treaty Process was operational by December of 1993. The British Columbia Treaty Commission (BCTC), as the keeper of the treaty process, was required to ensure the three negotiating parties' fidelity to the nineteen recommendations of the task force report, which represent the rules for the treaty process, and to act as a guarantor that the negotiations be both fairly negotiated and equitably settled. However, the BCTC lacks adjudicatory or punitive power within the treaty process. Thus, if the BCTC feels a party or parties is acting contrary to the rules of treaty-making, it is limited to moral suasion when encouraging the transgressor(s) to correct this oversight.

This new era of treaty-making was heralded as a means to achieve both justice for the First Nations involved in the process and certainty for government and business. Justice, it was argued, would come in the form of land distribution, resource rights, self-governance, and a "fiscal component" or "capital transfer." Certainty, in contrast, would be the product of a "legal technique that is intended to define with a high degree of specificity all of the rights and obligations that flow from a treaty and ensure that there remain no undefined rights outside of a treaty" (Stevenson 2000, 114). In other words, certainty was envisioned as a legal means for ensuring that treaty negotiations bring finality to First Nations land claims.

Thus, the justice of the British Columbia Treaty Process was to be limited, or some would argue balanced, by a project of certainty-making that would bring an end to the long-standing land claims struggle. However, this balance has not been realized. Certainty has increasingly become the focus of the negotiations, eclipsing the rhetoric of justice (Woolford 2004). Moreover, this quest for certainty often takes an affirmative form, as the non-Aboriginal governments still appear motivated by the unfinished project of colonizing and assimilating resistant Aboriginal lifeworlds.

In its historic treaties with First Nations elsewhere in Canada, the federal government used the language of "extinguishment" to impose certainty on treaty-making; that is, First Nations signatories to treaties were required to "cede, surrender, and release" all heretofore unidentified Aboriginal rights in exchange for the rights defined in the treaty. With this language, the federal government sought to maintain its traditional patterns of colonial control by demanding First Nations surrender to the allegedly superior settler society. First Nations have long resisted this extinguishment clause in treaty-making; they deem it both offensive and as a potential source of uncertainty. Through extinguishment, their Aboriginal rights and title are exchanged for a package of treaty rights that are untested and which may or may not meet the needs of future generations (Stevenson 2000). In support of this Aboriginal perspective, the British Columbia Claims Task Force and the BCTC have both stated that the language of extinguishment is no longer acceptable and a new technique for achieving certainty needs to be found through the negotiation process (BCCTF 1991; BCTC 2000).

Having lost this basic tool of control, the federal and provincial governments have shifted toward less blatant techniques for ensuring the stability of the post-treaty environment. For non-Aboriginal governments, the challenge faced in the British Columbia Treaty Process is to fashion a new language of certainty that will achieve similar results to the language of extinguishment but will not offend First Nations. This has led them to adopt a new strategy of affirmative repair.

In the British Columbia Treaty Process, affirmative repair is mobilized both through micro- and macro-strategies of symbolic violence. At the micro-strategic level, negotiators from the provincial and federal governments employ discourses that categorize Aboriginal statements or justice demands that are contrary to the hegemonic codes as unreasonable or impractical. For example, in several sets of negotiations within the British Columbia Treaty Process, First Nations negotiators have initiated discussions by speaking of the forms of attempted destruction experienced by their communities at the hands of British and Canadian colonialism, and of the toll this legacy continues to exact upon their peoples. To this, the non-Aboriginal negotiators typically respond with the claim that the treaty process is itself an implicit acknowledgment of this unsavory past and therefore there is no need to sink negotiations into the confusion of discussing this history. Instead, they suggest that the parties must focus on the future. As one negotiator said in response to a presentation made by the Tsawwassen First Nation: "I really believe it (the past) is a powerful reminder of why the treaty process is so important. . . . It is important to be educated about the historical, legal, and cultural context of treaty-making. British Columbia's perspective, however, is that while there are legal and historical reasons for being here, the fundamental reason is to look at the future. The past is mired in uncertainty" (provincial representative, July 30, 1999).[7]

In this manner, the non-Aboriginal negotiators sever the reparative gesture of treaty-making from the injustices that are to be resolved. In addition, a clean line is drawn between past and future, evading First Nations peoples' claims that they are still suffering the effects of colonialism—a structure of oppression that is for them a current reality rather than a historical artifact.

Also at the micro-strategic level, non-Aboriginal negotiators, in obedience to the rigid negotiating mandates passed down from the higher echelons of government, have refused to use the term "compensation" to refer to monies distributed through treaty settlement. Indeed, they rebuffed First Nations requests to even discuss this matter for the first decade of the process. First Nations peoples argue that compensation provides necessary symbolic recognition of the harms they have suffered at the hands of Canadian settler society; however, for the non-Aboriginal governments, compensation is a technical term that connotes a willingness to accept liability for these harms. Take the following juxtaposition of statements made by First Nations and government representatives:

> When you look at the issue of compensation, for example, for First Nations that equals a big part of justice. And governments haven't even allowed it to be put on the table. So we can't even explore interests in what we are really looking for in justice . . . B.C. and Canada say, "no, we are forward looking, we are forward looking." . . . What is heard is basically, "when you see what the cash settlement is you will have to factor into it whether or not that is enough to compensate you for past wrongs—but we are not going to talk about it." That's the informal word on the negotiation table. (Tsawwassen representative, June 26, 2000)

> Compensation is due when somebody has done something that is a breach of law, or where there is a compensatory obligation. The Crown has never accepted the First Nations view that we stole the land. The view was that Her Majesty conferred the establishment of Crown land and the Supreme Court has said that, and they refer to Aboriginal interests existing on Crown land. (Federal representative, May 3, 2001)

From the perspective of the federal representative, it is feared that such an admission could later haunt the non-Aboriginal governments, especially if the treaty-making process proves to be unsuccessful and the land claims struggle is returned to the courts. To counteract this fear, the non-Aboriginal negotiators attempt to move First Nations from their demand that monetary settlement be termed compensation for wrongs committed against First Nations peoples, arguing that First Nations are free to privately refer to the monies distributed through treaty however they like, but that non-Aboriginal governments will not accept any final agreement that refers to these monies as "compensation" due to the risks attached to this term. In this sense, they use a "mathematical ethics" (Beck 1992, 99) guided by legalistic concerns to reduce the symbolic scope of treaty negotiations and evade the challenge of contending with First Nations visions of justice. In so doing, they attempt to prevent First Nations from raising serious questions about the past that may have a significant bearing on how the future relationship is defined.

Even when an agreement is finalized, the non-Aboriginal governments have been very cautious with respect to how they discuss the past. The preamble to the Tsawwassen Final Agreement, for example, states: "Canada and

British Columbia acknowledge the perspective of Tsawwassen First Nation that harm and losses in relation to its aboriginal rights have occurred in the past and express regret if any acts or omissions of the Crown have contributed to that perspective, and the parties rely on the Agreement to move them beyond the difficult circumstances of the past" (Tsawwassen Final Agreement 2006, 1–2). During my fieldwork I was often told by non-Aboriginal government officials that an apology would be possible only after a treaty was settled for fear that civil liability would result from any such statement in the event of failed treaty negotiations. However, in this case, one is not quite sure what it is the governments of British Columbia and Canada regret, as the past is held silent and a narrative of treaty negotiations is enforced that fixates solely on the future rather than on identifying past harms (See Dexler, this volume, for further discussion of the use transitional mechanisms for the imposition of specific narratives).

At the macro-strategic level, the question of how certainty will be defined in treaty-making contributes to a pattern of symbolic violence directed toward affirmative repair. Currently a "modification and release" model of certainty is the preferred means amongst non-Aboriginal government negotiators for ensuring economic and legal stability. In the Nisga'a final agreement (signed outside of the British Columbia Treaty Process), and in the agreements in principle and final agreements developed or drafted through the British Columbia Treaty Process thus far, certainty is established through the modification of existing Aboriginal rights into constitutionally protected (section 35) treaty rights, while all undefined Aboriginal rights are released. Many First Nations disapprove of this model of certainty, arguing that it is simply extinguishment by other means (Alfred 2001; Union of British Columbia Indian Chiefs 1998). According to the rules of the British Columbia Treaty Process, each First Nation is entitled to negotiate certainty and could, in theory, propose an alternate definition of this term. However, the non-Aboriginal governments are unlikely to accept the risks of multiple models of certainty since this would increase the likelihood of error in one or another set of certainty provisions, opening the language of certainty to numerous potential points of attack. As one federal government representative told me: "We put a lot of energy and effort into the modification of rights and title that we adopted with the Nisga'a at huge expense and we are not really interested in rediscovering the whole issue of certainty at every table we go to. With certainty, when we have the opportunity to look at the work being done on it, then we look at the proposals made at individual tables, these do not meet a number of legal tests when we examine them" (federal representative, August 29, 2000). In this sense, while the modification language of certainty is not a prerequisite to each individual set of negotiations, the space for variations on this language is severely limited. In effect, early agreement-in-principles and final agreements arrived at through the British Columbia Treaty Process, as well as the Nisga'a settlement achieved outside the process, are being used by non-Aboriginal governments as templates for other sets of negotiations, which amounts to a denial of their cultural distinctiveness and historical existence as fully functioning societies possessed of a different understanding of their relationship to the land.

Another aspect of the certainty sought by the non-Aboriginal governments through treaties is that final agreements represent the "full and final settlement" between the parties (Molloy 2000). In releasing undefined or unarticulated Aboriginal rights through treaty, agreements in British Columbia to date have added a provision stating that the First Nation signatory to the treaty indemnify the non-Aboriginal governments to any later challenges based on Aboriginal rights. That is, if a First Nation member decides to challenge the provisions of the treaty, the First Nation is responsible for settling the matter and providing any costs to Canada or British Columbia. As well, the First Nation agrees not to pursue any future legal claims against Canada or British Columbia with respect to past wrongs relating to interference with or infringement upon the group's Aboriginal rights (Union of British Columbia Indian Chiefs 1998).[8] With this provision, the treaty language realizes the non-Aboriginal governments' goal of dealing with past injustices without the necessity of discussing the nature of these injustices. It ensures that the treaty will bury issues of injustice, leaving them no legal opportunity to resurface.

Undefined Aboriginal rights present government and business with the problem of incalculability. They provide no object on which the techniques and rationalities of governance can operate. Without clear and exhaustive definitions of rights and title, the First Nations may feel less compelled to undertake economically rational self-regulating practices because the hope will remain of further developments in the nature and extent of Aboriginal rights, and non-Aboriginal governments will be less secure in their jurisdiction over nonsettlement lands and resources. For this reason, it is impossible for the non-Aboriginal governments to consider recognizing these rights or to allow them to evolve as the relationship between the two parties develops. As one representative from the province noted:

> The difficulty with that is that if it is a final settlement then it necessarily says that there are no other rights in the future that remain, at least to be exercised. And, of course, that is also fundamental to the notion of economic certainty because as long as there are remaining unstated and unarticulated rights that could be exercised the cloud on title and land necessarily remains. But many First Nations do say that these are rights they have had since time immemorial and "how

can we be asked to surrender these rights? It's not acceptable." And I am afraid I do see that as a hugely difficult problem in terms of achieving treaty settlements. (Provincial representative, May 24, 2001)

Thus, although a discussion is taking place between the parties on the question of certainty, it is clear that the current socioeconomic context of the negotiations limits the possibilities for resolving this issue through any compromise that fully recognizes the alternative rationalities of Aboriginal lifeworlds.

Certainty may, in fact, be a misnomer since there is no necessary course that the relationship between Aboriginal and non-Aboriginal persons in British Columbia will take. Instead, there is a significant degree of indeterminacy that can only be regulated through the imposition of the disciplinary force of uncertainty on First Nations in the form of admitting them into the entrepreneurial arena of market capitalism (see O'Malley 2000). The vagaries of this arena are such that government and third party interests hope treaties will inspire First Nations to successfully employ the entrepreneurial spirit and abide by the norms and rules of the entrepreneurial arena. Indeed, assumptions such as these are at the heart of government studies administered to try to predict the potential effects of treaty settlement on the provincial economy. For example, the province commissioned the accounting firm KPMG to conduct a study of the "benefits and costs of treaty settlement" (KPMG 1996), which was replicated by Grant Thornton Management Consultants in 1999. This study predicts favorable economic returns for the province if treaties are settled, but this finding is predicated on the assumption that First Nations will rationally engage in economic practices in a post-treaty environment. These practices will include the pragmatic management of First Nations settlement lands in a manner that does not disrupt business operation, the wise investment and spending of treaty settlement funds, and a system of community administration that reduces the demand for non-Aboriginal government-sponsored social programs (KPMG 1996, 7–8). Aboriginal self-reliance and autonomy, in effect, are visualized in a manner that does not deviate from non-Aboriginal economic and social practices except in matters of cultural importance that do not impact on economic relations.

The logic of affirmative repair thus brings forward the prospect of assimilation by other means for First Nations communities. Detached from considerations of historical right, ethical obligations, and cultural recognition, settlements threaten to constrain First Nations through the rationality of neoliberal capitalism rather than permitting a return to self-determination. From here the way forward is expressed in terms of the now irrefutable logic of the market. The goal of the non-Aboriginal governments is to dissuade

First Nations from accenting historical injustices and their experiences of attempted destruction, and to instead have them accept the responsibilities attached to distributions of land, money, and governance powers so that they manage their communities in a manner that makes their Aboriginality less uncertain for non-Aboriginal society.

A final problematic area of treaty negotiation is the tension between collective stewardship and individual ownership. Although in the U.S. context collective title to land has not proven to be an obstacle to economic development (Cornell 2001), non-Aboriginal business and government representatives in Canada nonetheless promote fee simple ownership as the most rational means of distributing settlement lands. It is assumed that individual ownership of lands is the most responsive and adaptable to the dynamics of the market economy (Flanagan 2000, 131). Typically, treaties designate a large portion of the land distributed as First Nation fee simple land on which treaty rights and First Nation jurisdiction will apply (e.g., Nisga'a Final Agreement 1998). This does not bring about the individual ownership idealized by groups such as the Canadian Taxpayers Federation, although the First Nation is empowered through treaty to distribute the land in individual fee simple portions if they so desire.

It should be noted, however, that there is still no guarantee that affirmative repair will have its desired effects. Aboriginal peoples have resisted previous attempts at their collective destruction, and, at times, they have subverted the tools of colonialism, such as the Indian Act, to serve their own purposes. In a similar fashion, they may discover new ways to challenge, resist, or transform attempts at symbolic violence, which work best when they are unrecognized.

Conclusion

The potential cacophony and ethical variability of victim demands for justice are too risky for the needs of government and business. For this reason, a risk management focus is becoming more prominent within the field of transitional politics in attempts to reduce victims' needs and desires to a set quantity that can be easily measured and meted out. Moreover, in situations where the claimant group's demands are largely discordant with dominant political and economic codes, symbolic violence and affirmative repair emerge as means to more clearly define the victim, to mark off the boundaries of the victim community (e.g., through eligibility criteria for reparative payment), and to establish a shared normative universe that is predominantly shaped by the criteria of the offending society (e.g., through reparative payments geared toward increasing victim involvement in the mainstream economy). This is achieved not solely through threats or other acts of direct coercion (although these too are present within the British Columbia Treaty Process) but also through the language of alternative dispute resolution, of moving from positions to interests, and reconciliation operating alongside rationalities of economic pragmatism and good governance. Thus, the British Columbia Treaty Process, with its emphasis on achieving certainty and on enrolling First Nations into the project of neoliberal capitalism, illustrates the potential symbolic violence of transitional processes. This is violence directed toward transitioning the victim group to better fit an unjust society, rather than transforming the society itself. Moreover, it is a violence that replicates too much of the destructive violence of the colonial past. By seeking to bound First Nations communities, reify identities, and assimilate them to dominant economic norms, the treaty process does not mark a true break with what was experienced as a genocidal past.

Thus, despite claims that it is a process intended to address past injustices, the British Columbia Treaty Process has allowed visions of certainty to distract it from contending with the destructive experiences of First Nations. So long as First Nations voices at the treaty tables are limited to claims that are acceptable within the limited confines of the provincial and federal government mandates, it will be difficult to achieve proper recognition of the harms suffered by First Nations peoples, let alone ameliorate them.

NOTES

1. As of 2009, only eight First Nations have completed or are near completion of the British Columbia Treaty Process. Fifty-two First Nations remain engaged at earlier stages of the process, and many more have refused participation in it.

2. The term "genocide" is also use by First Nations representatives in their public statements. Arthur Manuel, a critic of the process, recently published a report titled "New Relationship or Final Solution?" in which he pointed out that the new relationship envisioned by British Columbia's government would amount to the assimilation of First Nations peoples to Canadian norms (Manuel 2006). Similarly, Robert Morales, chief negotiator for Hul'qumi'um Treaty Group, stood before British Columbia's parliament on Thursday, December 7, 2006, and read a definition of genocide to illustrate its applicability to First Nations experiences of forced assimilation.

3. Although assimilation was the primary destructive tool of Canadian colonialism, one must also keep in mind the many instances of physical and biological destruction faced by First Nations in British Columbia and Aboriginal peoples across Canada. These instances include the moments of "gunboat diplomacy," forced sterilization, and disease spread.

4. However, it should be noted that Aboriginal peoples in some regions of Canada, such as the Maritime Provinces, were less likely to be forced to attend a residential school (MacDonald 2007).

5. This sentence is in reference to the categories of genocide created by Raphael Lemkin when the United Nations secretariat retained him in 1946 to help draft an international convention. The categories were "physical genocide" (the outright

extermination or imposition of slow death measures), "biological genocide" (the prevention of births among the target group), and "cultural genocide" (destruction of the specific characteristics of the group) (Churchill 2003). However, cultural destruction is understood in this chapter as the interruption of the group's capacity to negotiate and construct its collective identity rather than in the essentialist terms of specific characteristics.

6. This section has focused primarily on the destructive impact of what is often termed "cultural genocide" or "ethnocide." I resist this qualified labeling of the experiences of First Nations in British Columbia because it reduces a complex network of destructive events to those of an assimilative nature. However, it should be noted that the threat of actualization of physical violence was always present behind these assimilative practices. Children who refused assimilation in residential schools could be sent to sleep beside a tuberculosis-infected student or even disappeared. Gunboats were called upon to disperse First Nations peoples from around the early forts when it was assumed they were so unruly or disease-ridden as to pose a threat. In the case of those suffering from diseases such as smallpox, their dispersal from the town and urban areas often resulted in the transport of these diseases to their home communities.

7. Source material and direct quotations in this chapter are largely drawn from research conducted between 1997 and 2002, as well as follow-up interviews and readings since then. During this period I attended public negotiation sessions, public consultation meetings, public information sessions, meetings of the First Nations Summit, as well as treaty table working groups designed to deal with the specific contents of proposed treaties (e.g., fish and wildlife). In addition, fifty-five semistructured interviews were conducted with treaty negotiators, government representatives, First Nations community members, British Columbia Treaty Commissioners, public members of local and province-wide consultation committees, and representatives from the First Nations Summit and the Union of British Columbia Indian Chiefs.

8. This point was also noted in an interview with a representative from the federal government, August 17, 2000.

REFERENCES

Alfred, Taiaiake. 2001. "Deconstructing the British Columbia Treaty Process." *Balayi: Culture, Law, and Colonialism* 3:37–66.

Annett, Kevin. 2001. *Hidden from History: The Canadian Holocaust: A Summary of an Ongoing Independent Inquiry into Canadian Native "Residential Schools" and Their Legacy.* Vancouver: Truth Commission into Genocide in Canada.

Beck, Ulrich. 1992. "From Industrial Society to the Risk Society: Questions of Survival, Social Structure and Ecological Enlightenment." *Theory, Culture, and Society* 9:97–123.

Bischoping, Katherine, and Natalie Fingerhut. 1996. "Border Lines: Indigenous Peoples in Genocide Studies." *Canadian Review of Sociology and Anthropology* 33 (4): 481–506.

Blomley, Nicholas K. 1996. "'Shut the Province Down': First Nations Blockades in British Columbia, 1984–1995." *BC Studies* 111 (Autumn): 5–36.

Bourdieu, Pierre. 1990. *In Other Words: Essays Towards a Reflexive Sociology.* Stanford, CA: Stanford University Press.

———. 1991. *Language and Symbolic Power*. Cambridge, MA: Harvard University Press.

British Columbia Claims Task Force (BCCTF). 1991. *The Report of the British Columbia Claims Task Force*. Vancouver: British Columbia Land Claims Task Force.

British Columbia Treaty Commission. 2000. *What's the Deal with Treaties: A Lay Person's Guide to Treaty Making in British Columbia*. Vancouver: British Columbia Treaty Commission.

Cairns, Alan C. 2000. *Citizens Plus: Aboriginal Peoples and the Canadian State*. Vancouver: UBC Press.

Churchill, Ward. 2003. *Perversions of Justice: Indigenous Peoples and Angloamerican Law*. San Francisco: City Lights Books.

Cornell, Stephen. 2001. "Nation Building and the Treaty Process." Paper presented at "Speaking Truth to Power II: Where Do We Go from Here?" British Columbia Treaty Commission, Vancouver.

Davis, Robert, and Mark Zannis. 1973. *The Genocide Machine in Canada: The Pacification of the North*. Montréal: Black Rose Books.

Eltringham, Nigel. 2004. *Accounting for Horror: Post-Genocide Debates in Rwanda*. London: Pluto Press.

Flanagan, Thomas. 2000. *First Nations? Second Thoughts*. Montreal and Kingston: McGill-Queen's University Press.

Fraser, Nancy. 1997. *Justice Interruptus: Critical Reflections on the "Postsocialist Condition."* New York: Routledge.

Haig-Brown, Celia. 1988. *Resistance and Renewal: Surviving the Indian Residential School*. Vancouver: Tillacum Library.

Hinton, Alexander Laban. 2002. "The Dark Side of Modernity: Toward an Anthropology of Genocide." In *Annihilating Difference: The Anthropology of Genocide*, ed. A. L. Hinton, 1–66. Berkeley: University of California Press.

KPMG. 1996. *Benefits and Costs of Treaty Settlements in British Columbia: A Financial and Economic Perspective*. Vancouver: KPMG.

Kuper, Leo. 1981. *Genocide: Its Political Use in the Twentieth Century*. New Haven, CT: Yale University Press.

Legters, Lyman. 1984. "The Soviet Gulag: Is It Genocidal?" In *Toward the Understanding and Prevention of Genocide: Proceedings of the International Conference on the Holocaust and Genocide*, ed. I. W. Charny, 60–66. Boulder: Westview Press.

MacDonald, David. 2007. "First Nations, Residential Schools, and the Americanization of the Holocaust: Rewriting Indigenous History in the United States and Canada." *Canadian Journal of Political Science* 40 (4): 995–1015.

Manuel, Arthur. 2006. "New Relationship or Final Solution." *First Nations Strategic Bulletin*. December.

Milloy, John S. 1999. *A National Crime: The Canadian Government and the Residential School System, 1879 to 1986*. Winnipeg: University of Manitoba Press.

Molloy, Tom. 2000. *The World Is Our Witness: The Historic Journey of the Nisga'a into Canada*. Calgary: Fifth House.

Monture-Angus, Patricia. 1999. *Journeying Forward: Dreaming First Nations' Independence*. Halifax, Nova Scotia: Fernwood Publishing.

Neu, Dean, and Richard Therrien. 2002. *Accounting for Genocide: Canada's Bureaucratic Assault on Aboriginal People*. Black Point, Nova Scotia: Fernwood Publishing/Zed Books.

Nisga'a Final Agreement. 1998. http://www.aaf.gov.bc/treaty/nisgaa/docs/nisga_agreement .stm.

O'Malley, Patrick. 2000. "Uncertain Subjects: Risks, Liberalism and Contract." *Economy and Society* 29 (4): 460–484.

Powell, Christopher. 2007. "What Do Genocides Kill? A Relational Conception of Genocide." *Journal of Genocide Research* 9 (4): 527–547.

Ray, Arthur J., Jim Miller, and Frank Tough. 2000. *Bounty and Benevolence: A History of Saskatchewan Treaties.* Montreal: McGill-Queen's University Press.

Stevenson, Mark L. 2000. "Visions of Certainty: Challenging Assumptions." Paper presented at "Speaking Truth to Power: A Treaty Forum," British Columbia Treaty Commission, Vancouver.

Thom, Brian. 2006. "The Paradox of Boundaries in Coast Salish Territories." Paper presented at "Indigenous Cartographies and Representational Politics: An International Conference Dedicated to the Critical Examination of Indigenous Mapping and Geographic Information Systems," Cornell University, March 3–5.

Titley, E. Brian. 1986. *A Narrow Vision: Duncan Campbell Scott and the Administration of Indian Affairs in Canada.* Vancouver: University of British Columbia Press.

Torpey, John. 2006. *Making Whole What Has Been Smashed: On Reparations Politics.* Cambridge, MA: Harvard University Press.

Tsawwassen Final Agreement. 2006. *Tsawwassen First Nation Final Agreement.* http://tsawwassenfirstnation.com/treaty/TFN_FA_Dec_1_2006_Final.pdf.

Tsleil-Waututh First Nation. 2000. *Our Land to Share: A Future for the People of the Inlet: A Comprehensive Approach to Settling an Urban First Nation Treaty in British Columbia.* Vancouver: Tsleil Waututh First Nation.

Union of British Columbia Indian Chiefs. 1998. *Certainty: Canada's Struggle to Extinguish Aboriginal Title.* Vancouver: Union of British Columbia Indian Chiefs.

United Nations Convention on the Prevention and Punishment of Genocide. 1948. Adopted by Resolution 260 (III) A of the UN General Assembly on December 9, 1948. Entry into force January 12, 1951.

Woolford, Andrew. 2004. "The Limits of Justice: Certainty, Affirmative Repair, and Aboriginality." *Journal of Human Rights* 3 (4): 429–444.

———. 2009. "Ontological Destruction: Genocide and Aboriginal Peoples in Canada." *Genocide Studies and Prevention: An International Journal* 4 (1): 81–97.

7

▶▶ ▶▶ ▶▶ ▶▶ ▶▶ ▶▶ ▶▶ ◀◀ ◀◀ ◀◀ ◀◀ ◀◀ ◀◀ ◀◀

Local Justice and Legal Rights among the San and Bakgalagadi of the Central Kalahari, Botswana

ROBERT K. HITCHCOCK AND WAYNE A. BABCHUK

The Republic of Botswana in southern Africa has long been regarded as an exceptional African nation-state. Not only has it been democratic for over forty years, with half a dozen open, corruption-free elections, but it has also maintained an active civil society, an independent press, political stability, economic growth, and, until recently, an excellent human rights record (Leith 2005). Unlike some of its neighbors, Botswana did not experience violence and conflict in the transformation from colonial to postcolonial status. While South Africa had a Truth and Reconciliation Commission and Zimbabwe had investigations of human rights abuses in the post-independence period, Botswana has had no large-scale external or internal investigations of human rights violations. There have, however, been charges of human rights violations made against Botswana government officials, police, and the military, especially with regard to the treatment of San (Bushmen, Basarwa) and Bakgalagadi in the past decade (e.g., Mogwe 1992; USDOS 1993, 2003; Good 1993, 1999, 2003, 2009; Cassidy et al. 2001).

The issue that has called into question Botswana's commitment to human rights revolves around the resettlement of over a thousand San and Bakgalagadi residents from the Central Kalahari Game Reserve (CKGR), Botswana's largest protected area. In 1985, the government of Botswana called for a fact-finding mission "to investigate the Central Kalahari Game Reserve problems, with a view to providing information that would facilitate decision making on environmental protection and wildlife conservation on the one hand and the socioeconomic development of the remote area dwellers of the CKGR on the other" (Government of Botswana 1985, vi). In 1986, the Ministry of Commerce and Industry (in which was housed the Department of Wildlife and National Parks, one of the stakeholders in managing protected areas in Botswana) issued a circular that called for the resettlement of people outside of the reserve to promote "development opportunities" (Ministry of Commerce and Industry 1986, 2). This decision, which was not implemented until 1997, set in motion a whole series of efforts by San and Bakgalagadi, and both local and international support groups, to get the Botswana government to change its mind and allow the residents to remain in the Central Kalahari (Corry 2003; Saugestad 2005; Suzman 2002–2003).

Global conceptions of indigenous peoples and minority rights have been drawn upon in some of the debates surrounding the struggles of the San and Bakgalagadi for their land, resources, and cultural identities (Hitchcock 2002; Kuper 2003; Saugestad 2001). At the same time, the San and Bakgalagadi have relied on systems of local justice and have called for recognition of their rights as citizens of the Republic of Botswana. These processes have played out at the same time as San, Bakgalagadi, and other minorities in Botswana have used legal means and negotiating tactics to get access to land and resources. By and large, San and Bakgalagadi in Botswana had not, until recently, resorted to direct action, demonstrations, and strikes to bring attention to the need for land and resource rights.

On December 13, 2006, the San and Bakgalagadi of the Central Kalahari Game Reserve won an important legal victory in the High Court of Botswana after a long and expensive legal case and an extensive negotiation effort. The decisions of the three High Court judges guaranteed that at least some of the people who had been removed from their traditional territories in the Central Kalahari would be allowed the right of return, and they would be able to hunt and gather for their subsistence as long as they had appropriate licenses from the government. Subsequently, the attorney general of the Government of Botswana, Athalia Molokomme, ruled that the people returning to the reserve would not be allowed access to services, including schools, health posts, and water facilities (Molokomme 2006). The question is, Will the San and Bakgalagadi be able to negotiate different terms regarding the occupation of the Central Kalahari with the government of Botswana? If so, it will be necessary for the government to recognize the legal rights of San and Bakgalagadi to represent their own interests. If social justice is to be achieved, consultation will have to take place, and mutually agreed-upon decisions will have to be made.

Social Justice and Land Rights in Botswana

Botswana, like nearly all states in Africa, is a diverse country, with at least twenty-nine different languages being spoken by its citizens. "Botswana" literally means "land of the Tswana," the Tswana being a large tribe or sociopolitical grouping that occupied what is now the Kalahari Desert and adjacent areas in the past two millennia. Some of the earliest residents of what is now Botswana are the San (Bushmen, Basarwa), who claim to be indigenous to the country, though it should be noted that the government of Botswana does not accept that the San are the only indigenous people in Botswana, saying instead that all citizens of the country are indigenous (see Saugestad 2001). Other early residents of Botswana include the Bakgalagadi, Sekgalagadi-speaking peoples who have lived side by side with San in the Kalahari for hundreds of years (for descriptions of Bakgalagadi social, political, and economic systems, see Ikeya 1999; Kuper 1970, 1971; Schapera 1952; Silberbauer and Kuper 1981; Solway 1986; Wynne 1988, 1989). Today, there are some 50,000 San in Botswana and approximately 100,000 Bakgalagadi, spread over a wide area of the country. In the 1990s, approximately a third of the 1,100 residents of the Central Kalahari Game Reserve were Bakgalagadi, while the majority were San from a number of different ethnic groups (G/ui, G//ana, Kua, and Tsila) (Hitchcock and Babchuk 2007).

Historically, the San and Bakgalagadi, like the Kalanga, Mbukushu, Nama, Herero, Yeei, Pedi, and some other minorities in Botswana, were seen as having few rights (for a discussion of minority rights issues in Botswana, see Werbner and Gaitskell 2002). In the past, the San and Bakgalagadi were excluded from land allocation and from the courts because of their being defined as *balata*, or "servile groups." San and other minority groups were required to provide goods and services to members of the Tswana elite and sometimes to other groups of people in the Kalahari and surrounding areas (Schapera 1930, 233–234; 1938, 30–32, 60–68, 250–255). Schapera (1970, 250–253) points out that traditionally San and Bakgalagadi were not allowed to own property. If they were attached to a Tswana family, they could not transfer their allegiance to another person (Schapera 1938, 251–252; 1970, 89). Some of the balata "belonged" to individual families, and the rights to their services were inherited by succeeding generations, a practice that, while uncommon, still existed in the 1970s.

Some members of the Tswana elite did attempt to use their personal influence to promote sociopolitical change, including promoting access to land and resources for minority groups (see, e.g., Parsons 1973, 33–35, 215–216, 316, 325–328; Schapera 1970, 42, 82–91, 161). In many ways, however, their efforts were either incomplete in terms of their implementation, or they had little impact on people living far from the tribal capitals. Cattle owners and others living in remote grazing areas continued to treat San, Bakgalagadi, and other minorities the way that they wished and were relatively assured of impunity.

A prevailing assumption in Botswana government circles was that San communities lacked formal leaders and that they did not have organized political institutions. Discussions with San revealed that virtually all communities had people they respected and listened to. These leaders made decisions, adjudicated disputes, and represented the community in discussions with outsiders. In some cases there were groups of individuals, some of them elderly persons, who formed community councils. These people had a significant say in civil matters, such as handling disruptive individuals and allowing outsiders to use local resources.

Public policy was a product of extensive consultation and discussion among the members of San groups, with all adults and some children having the opportunity to participate, and decisions were made on the basis of consensus. In the San communities, individualism was not only tolerated but also admired. However, disruptive or socially inappropriate behavior (stealing, fighting, adultery, or overuse of resources) was usually dealt with by peers, who intervened and urged the offenders to stop acting in negative ways. Those who continued to act unacceptably were subjected to social pressure, usually in the form of comments and criticisms from the group.

As Marshall (1976, 350) notes about the Ju/'hoansi, San have customs that help them avoid situations likely to arouse ill will and hostility among individuals within groups and between groups. These customs include sharing meat, giving gifts, and hosting extensive public discussions concerning relevant events and issues. The Ju/'hoansi shared the meat of wild animals among members of a group, usually along lines of kinship and friendship. The distribution was usually overseen by the individual(s) who procured the resource, manufactured it, or had possession of it. There were some gender and age differences in who was allowed to get which parts of an animal, and the degree to which there was true equality in sharing and goods distribution has been questioned by some analysts. Nevertheless, most if not all San see sharing as important to maintaining good social relations among people.

Some of the most important sociopolitical institutions in rural Botswana are the tribal offices and the customary courts. As Wynne (1989, 359) notes, the customary court system consists of a hierarchy of graded courts staffed by headmen and chiefs, or, as they are known in Botswana, tribal authorities. There are a number of different types of tribal authorities, including headmen, chief's representatives, senior chief's representatives, deputy chief, and chief. At the community level in Botswana, a significant position is membership in local institutions, notably village development committees (VDCs) and community trust committees or councils.

While the Bamangwato, Bangwaketse, and other Tswana tribes have most or all of these tribal authorities, there are only two tribal authorities found in San communities in Botswana. The lowest ranking, these are the headmen of arbitration and the customary court of record. The headmen of arbitration adjudicate disputes but do not handle criminal cases. The headmen of the customary court of record, on the other hand, handle criminal cases, levy fines, and oversee the activities of tribal policemen and court clerks assigned to the community. Both types of headmen are paid for their work by the Ministry of Local Government. An assessment of the lists of warranted customary courts in Botswana, combined with interviews of members of local communities and tribal authorities, provides an indication of the number and distribution of official headmen in remote areas.

According to the commissioner of customary courts in the Ministry of Local Government, San communities have been involved in electing headmen for more than thirty years. Some of these headmen have been recognized officially by the tribal administrations in their respective districts, and their statuses have been confirmed by the minister of local government under the Customary Courts Act (1975) and the Chieftainship Act (1987). There are a number of cases, however, where headmen have been elected in communities but have yet to be recognized officially. There were also cases in which nonlocal people had become headmen, sometimes to the chagrin of resident members of the community. It is important to note, however, that there have been relatively few instances in which the elections of headmen have been challenged. This is the case in spite of the fact that sometimes the government of Botswana has appointed outsiders, most of whom are non-San, as headmen in communities where the majority of residents are San.

One of the criteria for becoming a headman in Botswana is the ability to read and write, which was problematic for the many nonliterate San. Nevertheless, some San groups found innovative ways to get around this issue. For example, a young nonliterate San at Ka/Gae was appointed headman in the late 1980s in the Ghanzi District, but his close adviser was a well-respected elder. The government also relaxed its requirements in some cases.

The commissioner of customary courts and the tribal authorities in each district assisted the Remote Area Development Program in informing locals on how to elect effective headmen. Through *kgotla* (community council) meetings and small group gatherings, the tribal administration personnel and district commissioners explained the process of electing leaders and taking care of community management responsibilities (Kann, Hitchcock, and Mbere 1990).

Prospective San headmen went to villages and towns to observe official headmen at work. In a few cases, the district commissioner debriefed the headmen prior to their taking up their positions. A few San headmen said they had problems getting people to listen to them because their appointments had yet to be announced by government officials. Judging from information obtained during interviews in 1988, 1990, 1995, 1999, 2001, and 2005, San headmen in general did a fairly good job handling court cases. Most group members said the headmen were fair, but a few said the fines and other penalties were too stiff. In one case, fines were levied on non-San cattle owners for damage done by their cattle to the crops of San. When the defendants protested the amounts of the fines, the San headman refused to back down. There were also cases in which San headmen faced inordinate amounts of pressure to drop criminal cases against non-San, something which did, in fact, occur on occasion. The argument given was that San headmen did not have the authority to assess the actions of non-San.

Some of the leaders elected by San communities have been very effective at representing their constituents. For example, the headman of Ka/Gae sent letters to the Ghanzi District council complaining of problems caused by cattle in two nearby boreholes. When nothing was done, he organized a deputation of community members who went to the district council meeting and complained formally. The result was that the Ghanzi council passed a resolution stating that the cattle would be removed from the boreholes, in spite of the fact that some of the district councilors had cattle that were being watered at those places.

However, in other communities San leaders have not been recognized by tribal authorities. In Kgatleng District, for example, the chief of the Bakgatla refused to acknowledge the leadership of a community of San at Kgomodiatshaba. There has been a long-standing struggle over the San's rights to reside in this location, which according to the chief and other influential Bakgatla is a grazing area. The San, who were seen by some members of the Kweneng District council and tribal administration as nontribesmen, were told by the chief and the district council to leave the area. The San appealed the case to the minister of local government and lands, but nothing was done officially to reverse the chief's decision. In early 1990, the council decided not only that the San should move, but also that the facilities constructed for them under the Remote Area Development Program should be dismantled.

Similar recommendations were made by central government officials for settlements in Ghanzi District, including Bere, East Hanahai, and West Hanahai. These decisions were opposed by local headmen, who were able to get their opinions heard in the Ghanzi District council and to have the resettlement decision put off, at least for the time being. In New Xade, on the other hand, the traditional authority in the settlement, who had been appointed by government rather than elected, was reasonably certain that the district council and the central government authorities were not going to relocate people elsewhere. Clearly, the issues of leadership capacity, decision making, and legitimacy of traditional authorities are serious in Botswana (for further discussions of traditional leadership in Botswana, see Holm and Botlhale 2008; Holm and Molutsi 1989; Kuper 1970, 1971; Schapera 1970).

Tensions in the Central Kalahari Region

In the 1980s and 1990s, a number of issues arose concerning populations in the CKGR. One major issue was the high concentration of people living around water points in Xade. At various times in the 1980s the population there was over a thousand people, and, according to ecologists and Department of Wildlife officials, the landscape showed evidence of environmental degradation. Also of concern was the issue of wildlife loss in the Central Kalahari. Wildlife department officials and safari companies attributed the decline to overhunting, even by individuals with special game licenses in the remote areas of Botswana.

In the early 1990s, numerous *kgotla* meetings were held in the Ghanzi District and in the Central Kalahari by Botswana government personnel, urging the residents to leave the reserve so they could have direct access to services and, as was said repeatedly, "develop themselves." Local people pointed out that the government had been providing services, including health, education, and water, in the Central Kalahari since the 1970s. There were rumors that the slow delivery of services (e.g., food commodities for drought relief and diesel for water pumps) was deliberate to force people out of the Central Kalahari. Some felt they could only move into already overcrowded or inaccessible locations. Of those who actually left, many returned, saying that the availability of land and natural resources was minimal.

It was clear from events in the early 1990s that all was not well with San and Bakgalagadi land rights in Botswana. In March 1992, the permanent secretary of the Ministry of Local Government, Lands, and Housing, in a letter to the director of the Department of Wildlife and National Parks stated, "The remote area dwellers who reside within the CKGR have agreed to be resettled at Xade in the Ghanzi District." But many of the reserve residents claimed they had made no such agreement. Tensions rose, and local people talked about taking matters into their own hands. What exactly they would do was unspecified, but it was clear that the people of the Central Kalahari wanted action and to maintain their homes in the reserve.

On April 13–15, 1992, the Botswana Society sponsored a workshop on "Sustainable Rural Development" in Gaborone, where Komtsha Komtsha, a Nharo San from D'Kar in Ghanzi District, along with Roy Sesana, a G//ana San from Molapo in the CKGR, and other people spoke out on the problems of the Botswana San. Participants decried the widespread poverty, exploitation, alienation from land and natural resources and the lack of equal access to development assistance for people in remote areas.

After a rural development workshop on May 18, 1992, a meeting was held between San representatives and officials in the Ministry of Local Government, Lands, and Housing in Gaborone. The San called for the creation of new types of representative structures, including a San national council, and for the representation of San in the Botswana House of Chiefs. In addition, they asked for a vote (a financial commitment by government) to be set aside to cover consultations in order to establish the council.

The ministry personnel's responses to these requests were less than positive. Some of the officials at the meeting said the San were attempting to obtain self-determination (self-rule) and were seeking to secede from Botswana. The permanent secretary of Ministry of Local Government, Lands, and Housing said, "Botswana owns the Basarwa and it will own Basarwa until it ceases to be a country; they will never be allowed to walk around in skins again." She also said the San's demand for self-rule was instigated by nongovernmental organizations and donor agencies from outside the country.

The San decried the fact that the meeting was held in Setswana, which meant that some of the San participants could not understand the discussions. As a result, they came away from the meeting feeling that not only had they been insulted but also that the government of Botswana was not serious about engaging in negotiations with them and promoting their social, economic, and cultural rights.

From 1992 to 1997, the government of Botswana increased the pressure on CKGR residents. Through a series of visits to CKGR communities, radio broadcasts, and *kgotla* meetings in Ghanzi and Kweneng Districts, residents were encouraged to leave. In May–June 1997, 1,739 people, mainly G/wi and G//ana San and Bakgalagadi, were relocated in trucks by government officials. They were taken to two large settlements, one in eastern Ghanzi District (New Xade) (also known as K'goesakeni), and the other in northeastern Kweneng District, not far from the gate to Khutse Game Reserve, Kaudwane. The government claimed that the move was carried out humanely and with the agreement of the people involved. However, some local people said they were forced onto trucks and moved against their will; in some cases, members of the same family were taken to different settlements hundreds of kilometers apart.

Some compensation was paid to people when they resettled, although the amounts were small and many were left out. The Botswana government saw compensation as one means of ensuring social justice for people whose assets and land rights were being taken away. The total compensation paid to 730 households (1997–2002) amounted to P4,400,000 (at that time, US$900,000), as well as a disturbance allowance for each household, calculated at 10 percent of the total compensation. Compensation ranged from P1,000 (US$220) per household to P100,000 (US$22,000). According to Botswana government figures, compensation paid to people was also done in kind, with 2,300 cattle and 2,018 goats given to 602 people (5 head of cattle and 15 goats per beneficiary) (see http://www.gov.bw/index.php/). Interviews of resettled San and Bakgalagadi revealed that many of them felt that cash and in-kind compensation was not a substitution for the loss of their lands and resources.

In response to the CKGR resettlement, various San-related nongovernmental organizations led by First People of the Kalahari (FPK), along with Kuru Development Trust (KDT) (now the Kuru Family of Organizations [KFO]), the Working Group of Indigenous Minorities in Southern Africa (WIMSA), and several Botswana-based nongovernmental organizations (e.g., the Botswana Centre for Human Rights [DITSHWANELO], the Botswana Council of Non-Government Organisations [BOCONGO], and the Botswana Christian Council [BCC]) established a consultative group—the CKGR Negotiating Team—to carry out negotiations with the government of Botswana on the future of the people of the CKGR. The team held its first meeting at D'Kar, Ghanzi District, Botswana on June 16–17, 1997. Local representatives of San and Bakgalagadi communities met with members of the negotiating team and provided their perspectives on land and resource rights issues and the justice system as they saw it in and around the Central Kalahari.

The CKGR Negotiating Team attempted to consult and negotiate with the government of Botswana from 1997 to 2001. In fact, there was some consultation, but little real negotiation. Representatives of the CKGR Negotiating Team met with various ministers and high government officials. There was also a meeting in the United States held by John Hardbattle and Roy Sesana, of First People of the Kalahari, with Botswana President Sir Ketumile Masire in March 1998 in Washington, D.C., at the Botswana Embassy. In July and September of 1999 the negotiating team met with the minister of Local Government, Lands, and Housing, Daniel Kwelagobe. At the September 1999 meeting, Minister Kwelagobe stated that "the Government of Botswana would not recognize rights to land in a game reserve but would only grant ownership of land to Basarwa who moved out of the CKGR and into New Xade and Kaudwane."

At the local level, San and Bakgalagadi residents of the Central Kalahari sought audiences with government officials. They requested fair treatment before the law in cases where individuals were arrested for violating Botswana government wildlife legislation. There were numerous complaints to government ministries and international visitors (e.g., members of the diplomatic services of the United States, the United Kingdom, and the European Union) that San and Bakgalagadi were not being treated the same way as members of other groups living outside of the Central Kalahari; for example, they noted that jail sentences and fines for hunting violations and livestock theft were much higher for Central Kalahari San and Bakgalagadi than for other people.

Although there had been numerous protests by local people about the government's decision regarding the Central Kalahari, government officials did not take these protests seriously. In some cases, this was because the *kgotla* meetings in Botswana consisted mainly of government officials putting forth their views. Local people felt they had little, if any, opportunity to respond openly to the officials. Spokespersons for the government presented the official line, which essentially was that people had no choice in the matter regarding resettlement. From the Botswana government's perspective, the residents had to leave the Central Kalahari and reestablish themselves in government-sponsored settlements on the peripheries of the reserve.

In these settlements, people felt that there was little in the way of local justice; decision-making was handled by government-appointed headmen and the rule of law was enforced by tribal or government police officers and, in some cases, by representatives of the Department of Wildlife and National Parks. As a number of informants pointed out, traditional systems of justice did not operate effectively in the new settlements. Arrests for entering the Central Kalahari Game Reserve without a permit occurred, as did arrests and beatings for subsistence hunting or gathering. Suspects were subjected to harsh and degrading treatment by officials, resulting in calls for official investigations of human rights violations. At one point, after the arrest, detention, and alleged mistreatment of more than a dozen San and Bakgalagadi in the Molapo area of the Central Kalahari, the government claimed that a formal investigation had been conducted in which members of the police and the Department of Wildlife and National Parks were interviewed, but no official report was ever made public. Local people asked for an apology by the government of Botswana for the treatment of the residents of the Central Kalahari, but the Botswana government has thus far refused to issue any apologies.

Further Removals from the Central Kalahari

In January 2002, the Botswana government informed the remaining residents of the CKGR that they were shutting down the wells and stopping all food deliveries inside the reserve. In February, the Botswana government and two district councils, Ghanzi and Kweneng, began moving people and their possessions out of the Central Kalahari. By March, 2002, it was estimated that there were fewer than two dozen people remaining in the reserve.

On February 19, 2002, the lawyers for the people of the Central Kalahari, John Whitehead, Glyn Williams, and Rahim Khan, filed a legal case in the High Court of Botswana (*Roy Sesana, Kiewa Setlhobogwa, & 241 Others v. the Attorney General of Botswana*, case no. 52 of 2002). However, shortly afterward the case was dismissed on a technicality by the High Court. The dismissal of the case was appealed, and it was ruled that the case should be heard in the High Court.

The Central Kalahari legal case began with hearings at New Xade in Ghanzi District in July 2004. Only three witnesses gave testimony in the initial phase of the trial, including two San and George Silberbauer, at that time a retired anthropology professor living in Australia. The case was continued until November 2004 in part because the legal team ran out of funds. In the July–November period, discussions were held among some of the applicants (those who brought the case before the court). The discussions were held by the lawyers and members of San organizations in and around the Central Kalahari. Local people were able to express their opinions and make recommendations as to how the case should be pursued. Similar discussions were held at the local level (e.g., in New Xade), at the district level (e.g., in Ghanzi), and at the national level (in a series of meetings held in Gaborone). Eventually it was decided that new lawyers were necessary and that additional funds and support had to be sought from the international community to pursue the balance of the case.

A second phase of the legal case began on November 5, 2004, with some new lawyers on the side of the people of the Central Kalahari, one of whom was Gordon Bennett, an international lawyer from the United Kingdom, and another was Gideon Duma Boko from Botswana. Support for this phase of the case was provided by Survival International, a human rights organization based in London. On the government side was lawyer Sidney Pilane. Issues that were heard in this phase of the case revolved around the length of time that the San and Bakgalagadi had resided in the Central Kalahari, the use of wildlife resources inside the boundaries of the Central Kalahari, land use patterns of local people, and the ways in which people depended on natural resources in the settlements surrounding the Central Kalahari, including the ones that contained the people who had been resettled out of the reserve in the late 1990s through 2002.

From the perspective of Central Kalahari residents and former residents, the removals of people from their land and their means to earning a livelihood amounted to the denial of basic human rights. While many people appreciated the fact that the Botswana government provided services outside of the reserve, they noted that they still faced problems of poverty, lack of employment, and development assistance. According to some residents the conditions in the resettlement villages were problematic, with poor health conditions, hunger, and social tensions.

There were also strong opinions about distributive justice, with local people expressing concerns about the ways in which the government of Botswana, the district councils, and district administration personnel (the district commissioners and their staffs) were treating local people in cases involving land, livestock, labor, and wildlife. Some San individuals noted that members of non-San groups had an easier time getting arable land allocated to them by the land boards in Central, Ghanzi, and Kweneng Districts. They also noted that while the government said that under the constitution all individuals had the right to land, in practice, a number of

San and Bakgalagadi who applied for arable, grazing, and residential land did not receive the land they requested. As one man from Metsiamonong in the Central Kalahari put it, "We are not being treated fairly by the government or the district councils when we request land for our families." There was also a sense in the communities surrounding the reserve that the government was encouraging in-migration of nonlocal people, many of them neither San nor Bakgalagadi, in order to change the power relations at the local level.

Violent Confrontations between Local People and the State

In September 2005, some two dozen San who were from the Central Kalahari in Botswana had a confrontation with government officials and police in the CKGR. The government of Botswana had announced in early September 2005 that the CKGR was off limits to people. On September 12, 2005, armed police and Department of Wildlife and National Parks officers entered the reserve and told people living there to leave. People allegedly were prevented at gunpoint from hunting and gathering, and dozens of people were loaded onto trucks and removed from the reserve against their will. People suspected of hunting illegally were beaten and tortured. In one case a man was shot in both legs while standing unarmed with his arms raised.

On September 24, 2005, a group of armed police and wildlife officers opened fire with rubber bullets and tear gas on a group of twenty-eight San men, women, and children attempting to enter the reserve to bring food and water to their relatives and friends. Three people were hit with rubber bullets, one of whom was wounded seriously and was hospitalized. A number of the people involved in the confrontation, including four members of First People of the Kalahari (FPK), a San advocacy group, were arrested, allegedly beaten, and kept in jail for several days. The entire group, including the FPK representatives, was charged with unlawful assembly.

In the latter part of September and October, people living in the reserve and some in the settlements outside of the reserve said that they were harassed and intimidated by armed police. Some individuals reported receiving death threats; in one case the threats came directly from police officers. In early November 2005, an elderly San woman, Qoroxioo Duxee, was found dead in the reserve. An autopsy revealed that she had died of "dehydration, starvation, and shock."

In response to this series of events, Steven Corry of Survival International made the following statement:

> The Botswana government doesn't care about its own courts or the rule of law and least of all about its indigenous people. All minorities there must feel under severe threat. We will ensure the international

community doesn't forget the Bushmen and what they are suffering. The outside world would turn a blind eye to the destruction—which is now tantamount to genocide. Tourists to Botswana and those who buy diamonds from De Beers are also complicit in this, the greatest of crimes. (Corry 2005)

Representatives of nongovernmental organizations accused the Botswana government of "ethnic cleansing," "slow genocide," "cultural genocide," and acts "tantamount to genocide" (Isaacson 2002). San and Bakgalagadi supporters at the international level argued that that forced resettlement and mistreatment of individuals and groups represented what in effect was "slow genocide." Evelyne Arce-Whyte, the executive director of International Funders for Indigenous Peoples, said, "There is a largely unpublicized genocide occurring in Botswana." Survival International said about the San: "They have experienced a genocide which has almost completely been ignored." Mike Lavene, a historian at Southampton University, asked, "Can Botswana be charged with genocide?" (Levene 2002).

In November 2005, Paul Kenyon, host of a British Broadcasting Corporation Radio 4 program entitled "Crossing Continents," raised questions about the accuracy of the term "genocide" to describe a situation in which few people have died (Kenyon 2005). He pointed out that in Botswana, representatives of local nongovernmental organizations expressed the opinion that while there were human rights violations going on in the Central Kalahari, to call this situation genocide was overstating the case. Some observers said that the tactic of calling what was going on in the Central Kalahari genocide was aimed at embarrassing the government and forcing the government's hand independently of the legal case.

The Botswana government categorically rejected the charges of genocide, forced removals, and ethnic cleansing. Government spokespersons stated repeatedly that the relocations of people from the Central Kalahari were voluntary and that they were done with the full consent of the people concerned after extensive consultations and *kgotla* meetings. The United Nations Genocide Convention (Article II) defines genocide as follows:

In the present Convention: genocide means any of the following acts committed with intent to destroy, in whole or in part, a national, ethnical, racial, or religious group, as such:

(a) Killing members of the group;

(b) Causing serious bodily or mental harm to members of the group

(c) Deliberately inflicting on the group conditions of life calculated to bring about its physical destruction in whole or in part;

(d) Imposing measures intended to prevent birth within the group;

(e) Forcibly transferring children of the group to another group

A number of representatives of San support organizations in Botswana say that the claim that genocide occurred and that San and Bakgalagadi were killed deliberately because of who they were is a severe overstatement. They point out that practically no deaths have occurred in or around the Central Kalahari. There have, however, been allegations of torture and mistreatment that appear to be substantiated (see, e.g., Mogwe 1992), though few governmental inquiries have been carried out to indicate whether or not people were tortured.

In May 2006, it was estimated by FPK that 10 percent of the original applicants in the legal case had died since the case began in July 2004. At least a dozen people were arrested in or near the boundaries of the CKGR in 2005–2006. This added to the more than seventy-five people arrested for hunting since the case began in 2004. It is important to note that some of the hunters were in possession of special game licenses, which were given by the Botswana government to subsistence hunters; thus, from a legal perspective, the hunters were hunting legally. While some of the individuals charged with contravening Botswana wildlife legislation had the charges dismissed, arrests and detentions of people engaged in subsistence procurement have continued to the present. San and Bakgalagadi community members said repeatedly that one of the most urgent issues they faced was the right to earn a living, something they felt was difficult to do in the settlements on the peripheries of the Central Kalahari, which they saw as "places of poverty and disease."

One argument put forth by the lawyers of the San and Bakgalagadi was that the people of the Central Kalahari had legal (*de jure*) as well as customary (*de facto*) rights to land and resources in the Central Kalahari. The lawyer for the government of Botswana, Sidney Pilane, argued that the people of the Central Kalahari did not have legal rights to land and resources, including water, nor the right to social services and development assistance. Some international civil society groups recommended that Botswana be brought before the International Criminal Court (ICC) for failure to observe the rights of indigenous peoples. However, Botswana was not a signatory to Convention 169 of the International Labour Organization Concerning Indigenous and Tribal Peoples in Independent Countries, the only international convention on the rights of indigenous people. In fact, no country in southern Africa is a signatory to this convention.

On December 13, the same day the results of the Central Kalahari trial were read, Botswana's minister of Minerals, Energy, and Water Resources, Charles Tiboni, said, "The United Nations Declaration on the Rights of Indigenous People, in its current form, would not see the light of day." A month before that, the Botswana ambassador to the United Nations, Samuel Outlule, said in a speech to the United Nations that the government of

Botswana had problems with the draft of the Declaration on the Rights of Indigenous People on a number of grounds, including a lack of clarity on the definition of "indigenous people." The Botswana ambassador said in his address that "Africans and citizens of Botswana are, with a few exceptions, all indigenous to the country and the African continent." Nevertheless, on September 13, 2007, the Botswana government, in spite of its reservations about the Declaration on the Rights of Indigenous Peoples, voted in favor of it, along with all of the other southern African states. San and Bakgalagadi from the Central Kalahari expressed their appreciation to the government for a bold step in recognizing the rights of indigenous peoples. At the same time, members of civil society organizations in Botswana argued that Botswana should not only ratify the Declaration on the Rights of Indigenous Peoples, but that it should change the constitution to recognize explicitly that minority and indigenous groups exist in the country and have the same rights as other people.

The Conclusions of the Central Kalahari Legal Case

When the final results of the Central Kalahari case were read by the three High Court judges on December 13, 2006, 130 days had been spent in court since the case began, and there were 19,000 pages of trial transcript. The three judges disagreed on a number of issues, but there was unanimity on the issues of the land rights of Central Kalahari residents at the time of the relocation and that the government had acted wrongfully in stopping subsistence hunting licenses.

Justice Maruping Dibotelo, the first High Court judge to give his opinion, concluded that the termination of services in the Central Kalahari was lawful and that people had been consulted sufficiently prior to the termination of those services. Justice Unity Dow, the next High Court judge to speak, concluded that consultations had been inadequate, that the principles of compensation had not been explained to the residents of the Central Kalahari sufficiently, and that the cessation of services to the residents was unlawful. She went on to say that indigenous people had rights, the removals were unlawful, and so too was the elimination of special game licenses for purposes of subsistence hunting. As the High Court ruling on the case stated, "There were, in fact, no compensation negotiations, only a one-sided process. The whole process was top down in its execution, and was conducted as just one more step to go through in getting the task at hand, which was relocation, executed" (Government of Botswana 2006, 242).

The final High Court judge to speak, Justice Mpaphi Phumaphi, concluded that the government had tried to persuade people to relocate outside of the reserve for a decade, that provision of services was expensive, and that the restoration of services would cause problems. He also said that the residents of the reserve had prior rights to occupation of the land, that the residents were deprived of their rights "wrongly and without their consent," that the government had not acted legally in stopping the distribution of special game licenses, and that the residents of the reserve had the right to enter the reserve without having to seek permits from the Department of Wildlife and National Parks. The judgment of the High Court was that the government was not required to restore services in the reserve, the stopping of services was lawful, and the removals of people and denial of their land and subsistence rights in the Central Kalahari were unlawful (Government of Botswana 2006).

The day after the High Court ruling on December 14, the Botswana attorney general issued a statement that outlined the position of the Botswana government on how the court's decisions would be implemented. The statement held that only the 189 surviving individuals on the original court case, along with their children, could return to the Central Kalahari, that services would not be restored, that domestic animals would not be brought into the Central Kalahari, and that people choosing to return to the reserve would still need to apply to the Department of Wildlife and National Parks for special game licenses. Subsequently, on December 19, 2006, the Botswana government announced that it would not appeal the decision in the Central Kalahari case. Forty people returned to the Central Kalahari on January 20, 2007, and began the process of establishing new homes.

As of May 2009, there are some 120 people residing in the CKGR. Some of them spoke to S. James Anaya, the special rapporteur on the human rights and fundamental freedoms of indigenous peoples of the United Nations, saying that they wanted social justice and fair treatment and that they wanted their legal rights to land and resources recognized by the government of Botswana and local authorities. Some residents of the Central Kalahari have spoken to DITSHWANELO, the Botswana Centre for Human Rights, and other civil society organizations in Botswana, saying that they would like to see efforts made to ensure transitional justice after the conflicts they have experienced in the Central Kalahari over the past two decades (for discussions of transitional justice, see Hinton, this volume; Hughes, Schabas, and Thakur 2008; Quinn 2009; Roht-Ariaza and Currena 2006).

Many questions remain as a result of this case. Is it indeed a "landmark decision for the indigenous peoples of Africa," as was argued in some media statements? Will those who return to the CKGR be able to sustain themselves economically in the absence of services, including the provision of water? Will people other than the 189 surviving applicants in the legal case be allowed the right to return without having to seek special permission from the government of Botswana? Most important, will the San and Bakgalagadi be able to exercise freely their basic human rights to self-determination, dignity, and identity both inside and outside of the CKGR?

From the perspective of FPK and many former residents of the Central Kalahari, the CKGR legal case sets an important precedent for indigenous peoples' rights, not just in Botswana but around the world. Whether or not this happens depends on how the government of Botswana and the people of the CKGR work out agreements concerning land and resources in and around the Central Kalahari.

A crucial question is this: Will the San and Bakgalagadi be able to negotiate different terms than the High Court decided regarding the occupation of the CKGR? It is unlikely that this will be possible, according to Botswana government officials. Some civil society groups in Botswana, on the other hand, believe that it will be possible to get the government of Botswana to allow residents access to water and to at least some social services. If this is to occur, it will be necessary for the government of Botswana to recognize fully the legal rights of San and Bakgalagadi in the CKGR to water, game, wild plants, and land. At the same time, the government of Botswana will have to accord full rights to public participation and decision-making to the organizations and individuals representing San and Bakgalagadi interests, not just in the Central Kalahari but throughout the country.

NOTE

Support for the research this paper is based upon was provided by the Remote Area Development Program of the government of Botswana, the United States Agency for International Development, the Norwegian Agency for International Development (NORAD), and the Danish Ministry of Foreign Affairs. We would like to thank the government of Botswana and the San and Bakgalagadi communities in and around the Central Kalahari for their assistance, ideas, and information. We would also like to thank the various civil society organizations in southern Africa and Europe for their willingness to answer questions on the issues raised by the Central Kalahari legal case.

REFERENCES

Albertson, Arthur. 1998. *Traditional Land-Use Systems of Selected Traditional Territories in the Central Kalahari Game Reserve*. Ghanzi, Botswana: First People of the Kalahari.

Arce-Whyte, Evelyne. 2004. "Funding Indigenous Conservation: International Funders for Indigenous Peoples Strives to Protect Pristine Environments." http://www.internationalfunders.org/images2/conservation.pdf.

Cassidy, Lin, Ken Good, Isaac Mazonde, and Roberta Rivers. 2001. *An Assessment of the Status of the San in Botswana*. Windhoek, Namibia: Legal Assistance Center.

Corry, Stephen. 2003. "Bushmen—The Final Solution and Blaming the Messenger." *Before Farming* 2 (14): 1–4.

———. 2005. "Bushmen's Last Stand as Armed Police Raid Reserve." *Survival International*. September 12. http://www.survival-international.org/news/1014.

Good, Kenneth. 1993. "At the Ends of the Ladder: Racial Inequalities in Botswana." *Journal of Modern African Studies* 31 (2): 211–216.

———. 1999. "The State and Extreme Poverty in Botswana: The San and Destitutes." *Journal of Modern African Studies* 37 (2): 185–205.

———. 2003. *Bushmen and Diamonds: (Un)Civil Society in Botswana*. Nordiska Afrikainstitutet Discussion Paper 23. Uppsala, Sweden: Nordiska Afrikainstitutet.

———. 2009. *Diamonds, Dispossession and Democracy in Botswana*. Johannesburg: James Currey and Jacana Media.

Government of Botswana. 1985. *Report of the Central Kgalagadi Game Reserve Fact Finding Mission*. Gaborone: Government of Botswana.

———. 2006. *Ruling, in the High Court of Botswana Held at Lobatse, Misca. No. 52 of 2002, in the case of Roy Sesana, Keiwa Seglhobogwa and Others and the Attorney General*. Gaborone: Government of Botswana.

Hitchcock, Robert K. 2002. "'We Are the First People': Land, Natural Resources, and Identity in the Central Kalahari, Botswana." *Journal of Southern African Studies* 28 (4): 797–824.

Hitchcock, Robert K., and Wayne A. Babchuk. 2007. "Kalahari San Foraging, Land Use and Territoriality: Implications for the Future." *Before Farming: The Archaeology and Anthropology of Hunter-Gatherers* 3:169–181.

Hitchcock, Robert K., and John D. Holm. 1993. "Bureaucratic Domination of Hunter-Gatherer Societies: A Study of the San in Botswana." *Development and Change* 24 (2): 305–338.

Holm, John D., and Emmanuel Botlhale. 2008. "Persistence and Decline of Traditional Authority in Modern Botswana Politics." *Botswana Notes and Records* 40:74–87.

Holm, John D., and Patrick Molutsi, eds. 1989. *Democracy in Botswana*. Gaborone: Botswana Society.

Hughes, Edel, William A. Schabas, and Ramesh Thakur, eds. 2008. *Atrocities and International Accountability: Beyond Transitional Justice*. Tokyo and New York: United Nations University Press.

Ikeya, Kazonobu. 1999. "The Historical Dynamics of the Socioeconomic Relationships between the Nomadic San and the Rural Kgalagadi." *Botswana Notes and Records* 31:19–32.

Isaacson, Rupert. 2002. "Last Exit from the Kalahari: The Slow Genocide of the Bushmen/San." *openDemocracy*. August 28. http://www.opendemocracy.net/globalization-africa_democracy/article_267.jsp.

Kann, Ulla, Robert Hitchcock, and Nomtuse Mbere. 1990. *Let Them Talk: A Review of the Accelerated Remote Area Development Program*. Gaborone, Botswana: Ministry of Local Government and Lands and Norwegian Agency for International Development (NORAD).

Kenyon, Paul. 2005. "Row over Bushmen 'Genocide.'" Crossing Continents, British Broadcasting Corporation. November 6.

Kuper, Adam J. 1970. *Kalahari Village Politics: An African Democracy*. Cambridge: Cambridge University Press.

———. 1971. "The Kalahari Lekgota." In *Councils in Action*. Ed. Audrey Richards and Adam Kuper, 80–99. Cambridge: Cambridge University Press.

———. 1982. "Social Aspects of Kgalagari Settlement." In *Settlement in Botswana: The Historical Development of a Human Landscape*, ed. R. R. Hitchcock and M.R. Smith, 258–263. Marshalltown: Heinemann.

————. 2003. "The Return of the Native." *Current Anthropology* 44 (3): 389–411.

Leith, J. Clark. 2005. *Why Botswana Prospered*. Montreal: McGill-Queens University Press.

Levene, Mark. 2002. "Can Botswana Be Charged with Genocide?" *Mmegi Reporter*, October 4.

Marshall, Lorna. 1976. *The !Kung of Nyae Nyae*. Cambridge: Harvard University Press.

Ministry of Commerce and Industry. 1986. *Report of the Central Kalahari Game Reserve Fact Finding Mission*. MCI Circular No. 1 of 1986. Gaborone, Botswana: Ministry of Commerce and Industry.

Mogwe, Alice. 1992. Who Was (T)here First? An Assessment of the Human Rights Situation of Basarwa in Selected Communities in the Gantsi District, Botswana. Gaborone: Botswana Christian Council.

Molokomme, Athalia. 2006. "Attorney General's Statement on the Outcome of the Case of *Roy Seasana and Others vs. the Attorney General*." Attorney General's Chambers, Government of Botswana, Gaborone. December 14.

Parsons, Quentin Neil. 1973. "Khama III, the Bamangwato, and the British, with Special Reference to 1895–1923." Ph.D. diss., University of Edinburgh, Scotland.

Quinn, Joanna R. 2009. *Reconciliations: Transitional Justice in Post-Conflict Societies*. Montreal: McGill-Queens University Press.

Roht-Ariaza, Naomi, and Javier Moriez Currena, eds. 2006. *Transitional Justice in the Twenty-First Century: Beyond Truth versus Justice*. Cambridge: Cambridge University Press.

Saugestad, Sidsel. 2001. *The Inconvenient Indigenous: Remote Area Development in Botswana, Donor Assistance, and the First People of the Kalahari*. Uppsala, Sweden: Nordic Africa Institute.

————. 2005. "'Improving Their Lives': State Policies and San Resistance in Botswana." *Before Farming* 4:1–11.

Schapera, Isaac. 1927. "Bows and Arrows of the Bushmen." *Man* 27 (71–72): 113–117.

————. 1930. *The Khoisan Peoples of South Africa: Bushmen and Hottentots*. London: Routledge and Kegan Paul.

————. 1938. *A Handbook of Tswana Law and Custom*. London: Frank Cass.

————. 1943. *Native Land Tenure in the Bechuanaland Protectorate*. Alice, South Africa: Lovedale Press.

————. 1952. *The Ethnic Composition of Tswana Tribes*. London: London School of Economics and Political Science.

————. 1970. *Tribal Innovators: Tswana Chiefs and Social Change, 1795–1940*. London: Athlone Press.

Silberbauer, George B. 1965. *Report to the Government of Bechuanaland on the Bushman Survey*. Gaborone: Bechuanaland Government.

————. 1981. *Hunter and Habitat in the Central Kalahari Desert*. Cambridge: Cambridge University Press.

Silberbauer, George B., and Adam J. Kuper. 1966. "Kgalagari Masters and Bushman Serfs: Some Observations." *African Studies* 25 (4): 171–179.

Solway, Jacqueline S. 1986. "Commercialization and Social Differentiation in a Kalahari Village, Botswana." Ph.D. diss., University of Toronto.

————. 1994. "Drought as a 'Revelatory Crisis': An Exploration of Shifting Entitlements and Hierarchies in the Kalahari, Botswana." *Development and Change* 25:471–495.

Suzman, James. 2002–2003. "Kalahari Conundrums: Relocation, Resistance, and International Support in the Central Kalahari, Botswana." *Before Farming* 4 (12): 1–10.

Taylor, Julie J. 2007. "Celebrating Victory Too Soon? Reflections on the Outcome of the Central Kalahari Game Reserve Case." *Anthropology Today* 23 (5): 3–5.

Totten, Sam, William S. Parsons Jr., and Robert K. Hitchcock. 2002. "Confronting Genocide and Ethnocide of Indigenous Peoples: An Interdisciplinary Approach to Definition, Intervention, Prevention, and Adequacy." In *Annihilating Difference: The Anthropology of Genocide*, ed. Alexander Labhan Hinton, 54–91. Berkeley and London: University of California Press.

U.S. Department of State (USDOS). 1993. *Country Reports on Human Rights Practices for 1993*. Washington, DC: Government Printing Office.

———. 2003. *Country Reports on Human Rights Practices for 2003*. Washington, DC: Government Printing Office.

Valiente-Noailles, Carlos. 1993. *The Kua: Life and Soul of the Central Kalahari Bushmen*. Amsterdam: A. A. Balkema.

Van der Merwe, Hugo, Victoria Baxter, and Audrey R. Chapman, eds. 2009. *Assessing the Impact of Transitional Justice: Challenges for Empirical Research*. Washington, DC: U.S. Institute for Peace Press.

Werbner, Richard, and Deborah Gaitskell, eds. 2004. *Minorities and Citizenship in Botswana. Journal of Southern African Studies* (Special Issue) 28 (4): 671–841.

Wynne, Susan G. 1988. "Institutional Resources for Development among the Kgalagadi of Botswana." In *Rethinking Institutional Analysis and Development: Issues, Alternatives, and Choices*, ed. Vincent Ostrum, David Feeny, and Harmut Picht, 213–246. San Francisco: Institute for Contemporary Studies Press.

———. 1989. "The Land Boards of Botswana: A Problem in Institutional Design." Ph.D. diss., Indiana University, Bloomington.

PART THREE

Voice, Truth, and Narrative

8

▶▷▶▷▶▷▶▷▶▷▶▷▶▷▶▷ ◀◁◀◁◀◁◀◁◀◁◀◁◀◁◀◁

Testimonies, Truths, and Transitions of Justice in Argentina and Chile

ANTONIUS C.G.M. ROBBEN

After General Reynaldo Bignone passed the sash and baton of authority to Raúl Alfonsín on December 10, 1983, and left the presidential palace at the Plaza de Mayo in Buenos Aires through the rear exit, he found himself face to face with Argentina's most vexed question: "Cain, where is thy brother?" This chilling message was left on a scrap of paper stuck under the windshield wiper of the car that sped the ex-dictator away from the crowd celebrating the return to democracy after seven years of military rule (CISEA 1984, 534). The message referred of course to the 10,000–30,000 Argentines who had disappeared between 1976 and 1983, but alluded as well to the fratricide within the nation and the many lives sacrificed for a more just Argentina.[1] The note had been written by the Mothers of the Plaza de Mayo, who had courageously protested the disappearances during the dictatorship, and we can safely assume that the message hinted as well at the military's oath to uphold the constitution and be the nation's keepers instead of grabbing power through a coup d'état and slaughtering the political opponents.

Did the note's biblical connotations also foreshadow the predicament of General Bignone and the Argentine military? Would Bignone, like Cain who received God's protection from vengeance, not be held accountable for his deeds? Or did the message contain the warning that the military would be pursued relentlessly, despite their self-decreed immunity from prosecution and, as Cain, would never find rest in this world? What forms of justice, other than bringing perpetrators to court, could the Argentine people expect?

The fate of Argentina's disappeared was foremost in Alfonsín's mind when he assumed the presidency in December 1983 because there were persistent rumors that many disappeared continued to be held captive by the military. Furthermore, several abducted children had been found alive, and this raised the hope of other searching grandparents. One of Alfonsín's

179

first acts in power was therefore to create the National Commission on Disappeared Persons or CONADEP (Comisión Nacional sobre la Desaparición
de Personas). The truth commission's findings were anxiously awaited by a
nation held hostage by the disappearances.

Nothing of this urgency surrounded the Chilean National Commission
on Truth and Reconciliation (Comisión Nacional de Verdad y Reconciliación)
installed in March 1990 by Patricio Aylwin, Chile's first president after seventeen years of dictatorial rule by General Augusto Pinochet. Chileans were
more informed about military repression in 1990 than Argentines were in
1983. The Chilean truth and reconciliation commission, generally known
as the Rettig commission after its president Raúl Rettig Guissen, put truth-
finding in the service of national reconciliation. Instead, the Argentine
CONADEP focused on the past to uncover the truth, while national reconciliation only became an issue after justice had been served.

The pursuit of either truth or reconciliation provides different kinds of
justice, as has been the case in Chile and Argentina, but the two may also be
aspired together, as was the goal of the South African Truth and Reconciliation Commission. Reconciliation departs from the premise that the harm
inflicted on individuals, groups, and societies has to be healed, and that
victims and perpetrators need to be reintegrated into society by "building
or rebuilding relationships today that are not haunted by the conflicts and
hatreds of yesterday" (Hayner 2001, 161). Such restorative justice is "constructive and transformative rather than punitive and retributive" (Daly and
Sarkin 2007, 15).

The Chilean state and broad layers of society have dealt in circumspect
ways with the dictatorial past, afraid to rock the boat of reconciliation.
Instead, the incessant search for truth in Argentina by the human rights
movement, vocal political leaders, and critical lawyers and judges, as well as
the public dissemination of survivor narratives, have postponed reconciliation because the revelation of so many horrendous truths made criminal
prosecution almost inevitable and led to the repeated failure of amnesty legislation to turn the page on the past. A focus on the testimonial voices and
narratives of victims and survivors in Chilean and Argentine commissions
and trials investigating human rights violations, and their manifestation in
local discourses, practices, and sites of memory will bring these different
types of justice to light.

Testimonies and local forms of justice played other roles in Chile and
Argentina because of the different objectives, political contexts, and discursive politics of the various contesting groups and adversarial public
players in each country. As Hinton argues in this volume's introduction:
"this intersection of justice and locality . . . is concerned with the ways in
which justice is experienced, perceived, conceptualized, transacted, and

produced in various localities." The continued influence of the Chilean military on national politics, the divided public opinion about the dictatorship, and the desire of the military and many Chileans to silence the past resulted in the Chilean government's reluctance to prosecute perpetrators and pursue restorative justice instead. Even though Chile and Argentina suffered a similar state repression with disappearances, massive torture, assassinations, and an overall culture of fear, the Argentine approach to human rights violations has differed considerably from that of Chile. The defeat of the Argentine military, the abhorrence at the state terror inflicted on the Argentine people, the military's denial of the disappearances, and the public call for accountability made the Argentine authorities bring the military to court, and made many Argentines demand retributive justice. The different Chilean and Argentine responses to similar gross human rights violations, and the respectively restorative and retributive justice pursued, have influenced the function, rendition, and meaning of the testimonies given and have resulted in irreconcilable positions among victims, perpetrators, survivors, and special interest groups about how justice has to be served.

Truth, Denial, and Accountability in Argentina

Western cultures entrust the judiciary with the administering of justice even though it can never entirely satisfy people's sense of justice. People's sense of justice is larger than the courtroom, not only in its different appraisal of reparative, restorative, retributive, or punitive justice, but especially in terms of a notion of personal fairness based on a cultural understanding of society's social contract, as Rawls (1973) has argued persuasively. This feeling of fairness is all the more strongly felt when a society has survived grave human rights violations. Here, tensions can easily arise between what people consider fair and which types and degrees of justice are feasible in a transitional democracy. "By the principle of fairness it is not possible to be bound to unjust institutions, or at least to institutions which exceed the limits of tolerable injustice" (Rawls 1973, 112). If people, including opposed interest groups, believe that the judiciary is not dispensing justice, then they might pursue other routes to satisfy their sense of justice.

Not surprisingly, the Argentine military felt they were being treated unfairly when the Alfonsín government ordered the military supreme court on December 13, 1983, to try the nine former junta commanders, and on top instituted the CONADEP commission two days later, as if distrusting the truth investigated by the defendants' peers. The military's sense of injustice was founded on the following master narrative: (I) the Argentine military fought an antirevolutionary war against a tenacious guerrilla insurgency, supported by Cuba and the Soviet Union, at the cost of hundreds of lives; (2) the military government prevented the political disintegration of Argentina, jumpstarted the economy, and abolished corruption and nepotism; (3) the antirevolutionary war was fought within the letter of the law, while torture and disappearances were the inevitable excesses of war; and (4) the Argentine armed forces had a historical bond with Argentine society, from the independence wars against the Spanish colonizers in the 1810s to the war against the unpatriotic guerrilla insurgents of the 1970s (Robben 2005b, 130–131). This master narrative implied that the Argentine military troops sacrificed their lives in a just war, saved the country from ruin and revolution, and therefore should be praised for its victory instead of prosecuted and questioned about its successful military strategy. The accusations about disappearing 30,000 Argentines were unfounded, according to the military, and the rumors about torture centers were false.

Facing this master narrative and the dismissal of systematic disappearances, the CONADEP truth commission immediately solicited oral and written testimonies in Argentina and abroad; visited military bases, police stations, prisons, psychiatric hospitals and former secret detention centers; examined the records of morgues and cemeteries; and carried out forensic exhumations. There was much trepidation about the commission's findings. A mass grave found in October 1982 with four hundred unidentified bodies foreshadowed a fate that might have befallen other disappeared.

When the material proof of the disappearances became overwhelming through exhumations and the analysis of cemetery records, the military began to discredit the forensic methodology and the quality of the evidence. Exhumations seldom revealed the identity of the manslayers, even though the bullets from Itaka submachine guns found amidst the skeletal remains pointed at the Argentine military. The military maintained, however, that these dead had been killed in internal disputes of the guerrilla organizations. Testimony became therefore the primary source to interpret forensic evidence. Furthermore, these testimonies became important because in April 1983 Bignone had ordered the armed forces to destroy incriminatory documents (*Ejército Argentino* 1984, 4524:673). The testimonies and their rendition in the CONADEP's final report became influenced by the military's denial that they had carried out the disappearances.

Oral testimony was given by survivors of secret detention centers, relatives of the disappeared, and eyewitnesses. They sensed the impact of their words through the reactions of CONADEP's civil servants. Many early staff members could not stand listening to the stories of torture and humiliation and resigned (CONADEP 1986, 430). These understandable reactions, when little was known about the brutal torture regime, had a profound effect on the witnesses and their testimonies. A clerk's emotional collapse could make witnesses doubt whether the truth commission could really help them in having their stories believed by their countrymen. The testimonies were thus constructed in a context of denial and disbelief.

How to convince the truth commission and Argentine society that the horrible experiences had really taken place? As declarations, these testimonies have a stream of consciousness narrative and visual quality that maximized the empathy of the listener and produced a shared emotional truth in the interlocutors. Much attention was paid to describing the excruciating pain endured and the length of the suffering. Take, for example, the description by César Casalli Urrutia of his abduction by a task group:

> On 10 June I was kidnapped from my house in Martín Coronado. About ten men broke in and, pressing a revolver to my head, began to wreck the house looking for arms. At one point, they threw me to the floor and began to torture me with the cable from an electrical appliance. My wife was also being badly treated and beaten in another room. After an hour and a half in my house, they took me out and made me lie on the floor of a car while they went to look for a friend of mine. (CONADEP 1986, 18)

Testimonies by torture victims may satisfy at least two aspects of personal justice: reconstructing the voice shattered during torture and recovering the truth concealed or distorted by a repressive state (Phelps 2004, 44–45). The recovery of language and the retelling of the experiences are forms of restoration and retribution that are emotionally and politically rewarding. However, as I have pointed out earlier, such narratives are often influenced by competing narratives in the public domain. Here, the acknowledgment of the testimonial voice as official truth becomes important to personal justice. The brandishing of survivors of torture and disappearance as subversives is unmade, and the perpetrators are denounced before society for their aberrant acts. The circumstances under which testimonies are taken, which truths are acknowledged, how these are used by truth commissions, and how they appear in final reports are thus important in satisfying people's sense of fairness and personal justice, as an examination of the Argentine and Chilean truth commission reports will reveal.

"Many of the events described in this report will be hard to believe. This is because the men and women of our nation have only heard of such horror in reports from distant places," so read the opening sentences of the Argentine CONADEP report (CONADEP 1986, 9). The report is constructed in such a way as to disprove the denial by the military that they were responsible for the disappearances and that widespread torture took place. The report was to turn the unbelievable into the credible through a narrative organized around the dynamic of denial versus testimony.

The 482-page text consists of three main chapters followed by three small chapters that take up only forty pages, or 8 percent, of the volume.[2] The three large chapters ("The Repressive Action," "Victims," and "The Judiciary during the Period in Which the Forced Disappearance of Persons Occurred") are based on empirical evidence acquired through firsthand observations, depositions, public statements, and documents. Chapter 1 comprises the book's largest part, 278 pages, or 58 percent. It takes the reader step by step through the disappearance process, from abduction to torture to disappearance into the secret detention centers, which are described one by one and occasionally visualized by photographs and hand-drawn illustrations. Chapter 1 ends with a description of how the military junta tried to cover up the disappearances and reaped the material benefits through theft. Chapter 2 describes the victims by social category (infants, adolescents, families, handicapped individuals, the clergy, conscripts, journalists, unionists), while chapter 3 shows how this repression was carried out with impunity because the judicial process became inoperative and the right of habeas corpus was trampled. The last three small chapters ("Creation and Organization of the National Commission on the Disappeared," "The Doctrine behind the Repression," and "Recommendations and Conclusions") contextualize the previous chapters respectively: the present, the past, and the future. In sum, the report's organization emphasizes the harrowing personal testimonies of the victims in the first three chapters and then treats the ideological and political context in three short, matter-of-fact chapters.

Never Again (Nunca Más), the first published report by a truth commission worldwide, set the standard and style for other countries.[3] The literary hand of the commission's president, the prominent Argentine novelist Ernesto Sábato, can be seen in the way the testimonies are woven through a master narrative emphasizing the agency and purpose of military repression. Teresa Phelps (2004, 90) characterizes its style as a sustained tension between, on the one hand, testimonies "which are stories of disorder and chaos, of a world in which nothing was predictable," and on the other, a master narrative that imposes order on the survivor accounts to reveal a premeditated plan of state terrorism.

According to the commissioners, the quotations were used "solely in order to substantiate and illustrate our main arguments" (CONADEP 1986, 7). This reason undervalues their impact in eliciting the readers' empathy for the survivors. Indented from the main text, the report's rhetorical weight rests on the testimonies and therefore turns the victims into the report's main focus. The testimonies also deconstructed the military master narrative by demonstrating that many disappeared were not the feared subversive enemies trying to install a communist regime. One of the most shocking revelations of the testimonies was that the interrogators were not after pressing intelligence to detect bombs or prevent assassination attempts but that many captives were women and children tortured without apparent reason and without being asked a single question for hours on end.

The CONADEP's reconstruction of the dirty war revolved around the moral question of innocence. The innocence of the victims is contrasted starkly with the willful abuse by the state authorities, as if the commission feared that the testimonies would be discredited by mentioning the victims' political affiliation. The argument that the absence of due process made such information unbecoming ignored that now the Argentine people were dumbfounded about the rationale of all this suffering and that the Argentine military apparently were insane killers. This picture was reinforced by the Mothers of the Plaza de Mayo, who maintained that their disappeared sons and daughters had not been involved in politics at all.

CONADEP's master narrative stood diametrically opposite from the military's narrative: the *Never Again* report portrayed the dirty war as the systematic persecution of an idealistic younger generation by an evil military apparatus, whereas the military had always described their counterinsurgency war as the legitimate defense of Argentina's sovereignty against revolutionary subversives. The Manichaeism of both narratives was criticized by president Alfonsín's party. According to congressman Leopoldo Moreau, there "has been an armed struggle between two sectors to take power in which both equally demolished ethical values and were not fighting for democracy" (Areas 1984, 11). This so-called two-demon theory made the Argentine government pursue the prosecution of military officers and guerrilla commanders alike. The transitional justice of turning a dictatorship into a stable democracy consisted of bringing both violent parties to court and thus cleaning the slate of collective guilt (Robben 2005a, 321). The CONADEP report left an indelible image on a considerable segment of Argentine society and made a majority favor the culprits' prosecution. The CONADEP recommended "that the courts process with the utmost urgency the investigation and verification of the depositions received by this Commission" (CONADEP 1986, 446).

The CONADEP report was of course not accepted by the military, and its dismissal has persisted to this day. They regard its use in educational programs as a Gramscian strategy to indoctrinate Argentina's youth against the military with a distorted version of Argentine history. They produce books and documentaries denying the testimonies about disappearance and torture and praise the Argentine armed forces for destroying the guerrilla insurgency (e.g., AUNAR 1999; Etchecolatz 1988; Foro de Generales Retirados 2004; Márquez 2004). One such group consists of the youth organization Argentines for a Complete Memory (Argentinos por la Memoria Completa), which dedicates itself "to the men and women who wore a uniform during the 1970s to defend the Fatherland. Because we have collected the blood of our martyrs to raise the Argentine flag and because we are committed to our prisoners of war" (http://www.memoriacompleta.com.ar). Pro-dictatorship interest groups condemn the political trials carried out by a partisan judiciary. They contest the testimonies accepted by the courts and dismiss forensic evidence as manipulated, forged, and misinterpreted.

Although the CONADEP commission did not have the mandate to prosecute perpetrators, its findings did provide enough information to indict the nine junta members who reigned between 1976 and 1982. The justice done by the CONADEP truth commission did not preempt the possibility of other forms of justice, be they trials, amnesties, and presidential pardons, because justice does not have one form and is not a discrete event that culminates in the pronunciation of a verdict; instead, it is "an ongoing, dynamic process, of which storytelling is a vital part" (Phelps 2004, 9). The horrendous tales of torture and suffering in the commission's report, the appearance of survivors in the media, and the denial of the Argentine military that these human rights violations had taken place, prepared a public platform for the 1985 trial against the commanders.

Given the persistent denial of human rights violations by the retired military, Argentine society had no position to fall back on other than retributive justice if testimony after testimony was dismissed as false. Victims and witnesses know that testimonies are constructions that can be easily dismissed as fabrications by political opponents. Public truths carry less weight than judicial truths in people's perception because of a belief in the judicial verification process. The Argentine truth commission gave recognition to the testimony of lived experiences but had limited means to establish their veracity. Subsequent court room testimonies have made credible incursions into the continued denials of the human rights violations.

Most witnesses for the prosecution were survivors of secret detention centers and mothers searching for their disappeared children. Many of them had already made depositions to the truth commission but now faced defense lawyers who questioned the veracity of their testimonies and judges who wanted factual accounts, as is clear in the following exchange on April 29, 1985, between judge Guillermo Ledesma and Adriana Calvo de Laborde. Adriana Calvo de Laborde is telling about a man brutally tortured for hours to make him say that his mother was "a bitch's daughter" (*una hija de puta*). She apologizes to the judge for saying these words and then adds:

CALVO DE LABORDE: But I believe that this is important because here [in this court room] they're talking about excesses and supposedly these are excesses. The rest, the cold and cruel torture was an act of service, was due obedience.

LEDESMA: I ask you, madam, that you tell facts without qualifications.

CALVO DE LABORDE: Sir, this was a fact.

LEDESMA: I take your emotion into account. There is no doubt that the fact was real, but we are talking about your qualification afterwards.

CALVO DE LABORDE: I apologize, your honor. ("Testimonia" 1985, 31)

The following rendition of what must have been emotionally the most conflictive and indelible day in her life illustrates the difference between a testimony before a truth commission and a tribunal. Adriana Calvo de Laborde was abducted by policemen on the morning of February 4, 1977, in the town of Tolosa. Seven months pregnant with her third child, she was taken to a police station in La Plata, where her husband was also being held. On April 15, as she was taken by police car to another location by two policemen and a collaborating disappeared captive called Lucrecia, Adriana went into labor. She pleaded with them to take her to a hospital because the baby was about to be born. The policemen just laughed and told her that it did not matter because they were going to kill her and her child anyway. Blindfolded and handcuffed, she succeeded in removing her underpants and gave birth:

> Thanks to the forces of nature, the birth was normal. The only assistance I received was when "Lucrecia" tied the umbilical cord which was still linking me with the child as there was nothing to cut it with. No more than five minutes later we drove on, supposedly in the direction of a hospital. I was still blindfolded and my child was on the seat. (CONADEP 1986, 291)

In the trial against the commanders, she gave the following rendition of her ordeal:

> My baby was born well, she was very tiny, she was hanging from the umbilical cord because she had fallen from the seat. She was on the floor. I asked them to, please, hand her to me so that I could have her with me, but they didn't give her to me. Lucrecia asked for a rag to the one sitting in front, who cut a dirty rag and with that they tied the umbilical cord, and continued on their way. Three minutes had passed. My baby was crying, I continued with my hands behind my back, with my eyes covered. ("Testimonia" 1985, 32)

The differences in tone and detail are remarkable, especially when we take into consideration that the first testimony was relayed in a personal encounter with a staff member of the benign truth commission, whereas the second testimony was given in an adversarial environment of inquisitive judges and hostile defense lawyers. The first testimony was given in 1984,

when much was unknown about the abuse, and survivors seemed incredu-
lous. The second testimony was given one year later in a court of law in
the awareness of the persistent denial by the military. The trial testimony's
minute description of the birth is given with the utmost attention to details
to enhance its truth value by trying to stay as close as possible to the facts.
Many court testimonies were very precise about date, time, and location
and, whenever possible, the (nick)names of the torturers and the military
unit that held them captive.

The conviction of five of the nine junta members on trial in 1985 raised
hopes that the more than 2,000 complaints filed against more than 650
defendants would also result in many convictions. Trying to appease the
growing discontent among the Argentine military, president Alfonsín passed
two amnesty laws in 1986 and 1987 that greatly reduced the number of defendants. Intent on bringing about a national reconciliation, Alfonsín's successor president, Menem, pardoned hundreds of indicted officers and guerrillas
in 1989 and released the five convicted junta members in 1990.

Menem's strategy seemed to work initially, as the first half of the 1990s
was relatively calm in terms of human rights protests, but the unresolved
issue of the disappeared remained present in Argentine society. Exhumations exposed new mass graves, grandmothers searched for their abducted
grandchildren, memorials were inaugurated, retired military officers continued to justify the dirty war, and former captives published personal accounts
of their hardships. The 1995 confession of a naval officer about his role
in throwing sedated captives from planes flying across the South Atlantic
stirred up calls for punitive justice that remained unanswered because of
the amnesty laws.

Frustrated about the impunity, an organization called Children for
Identity and Justice, against Oblivion and Silence or HIJOS (Hijos por la
Identidad y la Justicia, contra el Olvido y el Silencio) organized in December
1996 its first of many *escraches*. These street happenings were intended to
shame perpetrators of the dirty war publicly. Justice was brought literally to
the door step of amnestied torturers and pardoned repressors. Their homes
were spray-painted with slogans, their pasts were revealed by indictments
read by megaphone, and street signs were posted with texts such as "Here
lives a murderer." The accusations were raised beyond the confines of the
courtroom, where justice could not be found according to the protesters.
These young adult children of the disappeared said that "without justice,
there will be escraches" (De Mano en Mano 2002, 35). They developed a form
of local justice that aimed at ostracizing the perpetrators from Argentine
society until the day when all of them would be in prison. As they declared
during the *escrache* of a torturer, they wanted the neighborhood to shut him
out, so that "tomorrow, the newsstand decides not to attend to him, the taxi

driver decides not to take him, the baker chooses not to serve him, and the newsboy refuses him a paper" (De Mano en Mano 2002, 47). The escrache tried to involve the community in the process of denouncement, sentencing, and stigmatization, turning perpetrators into social outcasts and meting out punishment beyond the judiciary. The mobilization of the community in exacting this popular justice was done through public denunciations that escaped judicial sanctioning, and whose truth was moral and historical rather than juridical.

Impunity took a radical turn in 1998 when army commander General Balza declared that the armed forces had a standard operating procedure of separating captives from their children. Within days, former dictator General Jorge Videla was taken in preventive custody on baby theft charges. Admiral Massera, like Videla, who was pardoned in 1990 while serving a life sentence, was detained six months later. As congressional and judicial steps were undertaken to abrogate the amnesty legislations and apply punitive justice, another legal route to truth finding was developed within the judiciary. This new approach had its origins in the witness testimony of Admiral Massera in a case before a federal court in 1996.

Massera's appearance in court emboldened human rights organizations in La Plata, the capital of Buenos Aires Province, to initiate in 1998 a "historical truth trial" (*juicio por la verdad histórica*). The trial's objective was not accountability but truth finding, not punitive but restorative justice. Protected from criminal prosecution by amnesty laws, alleged perpetrators were summoned to give testimony under oath about the cause of death and the destination of the remains of disappeared captives. The La Plata initiative encouraged truth trials in a half dozen major Argentine cities. Several officers decided not to appear in court because they were afraid of being accused of perjury and thus risking a four-year sentence. They were subsequently arrested, charged with the obstruction of justice, given a forty-eight-hour arrest to reconsider their refusal, and then convicted to thirty days in prison if they continued to remain silent. Some officers appealed these convictions successfully. Higher courts argued that suspects had the constitutional right to refrain from self-incriminatory testimonies. Even though many truth trials were inconclusive because most military officers and civilian collaborators denied any knowledge of the disappearances, the trials kept the issue of the disappeared on the public agenda and maintained the pressure on Congress to undo the amnesty legislation (Boschi 2000; Comisión de Educación 2004, 38–39).

The truth trials were an important means of local justice in which different testimonial voices were heard than those in the national CONADEP truth commission and the federal trial against the junta commanders. First, justice was localized by taking place in the cities and provinces where the disappearances had taken place. Argentina was subdivided into 117 areas to repress the insurgency and political opposition. Each area was the operational territory of a task group that hunted after their targets and often ran its own secret detention centers (Robben 2005a, 193–197). Truth trials allowed searching relatives to come face to face with the alleged perpetrators and led to acts of popular justice. For instance, the widow of Pablo Balustro, who had been executed in October 1976, spat in the face of Corporal Miguel Angel Pérez, and one person insulted and tried to hit Major Gustavo Adolfo Alsina, who was suspected of spiking a naked captive to the ground in the courtyard of a prison in Córdoba (Garcia 2000). Second, amnestied perpetrators and former disappeared shared a different relation than in a criminal trial. Ostensibly, they were equal witnesses before a court that was only interested in truth finding, but their testimonies occurred during pending appeals of the amnesty laws and thus discouraged most perpetrators from speaking openly. The pitting against one another of two opposed truths verbalized by interlocutors equal before the court, but at opposite ends before the crime, became a contest of credibility in which voice and silence meant the same to the audience of mostly searching relatives and former disappeared.

The growing unrest among the Argentine military raised by the truth trials made army commander Lieutenant General Ricardo Brinzoni in mid-2000 suggest a round-table dialogue (*mesa de diálogo*) shaped after a similar initiative begun the previous year in Chile. These meetings were to be composed of members of the armed forces and human rights organizations, under the chairmanship of the Roman Catholic Church, to resolve the issue of the disappeared and bring about reconciliation. Nora de Cortiñas, a leading member of the Mothers of the Plaza de Mayo Founding Line association, declared that "in no way whatsoever, we are going to sit with the military, with *genocidaires* and repressors," and she added that the military should go to court if they have information to offer, because "we believe that truth and justice always go together" ("Para los familiares" 2000; "La Corte" 2000). One congressional representative proposed a truth commission instead in which priests would take the confession of perpetrators to guarantee the anonymity of their information. The two proposals amounted to nothing because the derogation of the amnesty legislation was imminent.

A federal judge declared in March 2001 that the 1986 and 1987 amnesty legislation were unconstitutional, and Congress followed suit in 2003. The Supreme Court overturned the amnesty laws in June 2005, and the 1989 and 1990 presidential pardons were ruled unconstitutional in April 2007. By December 2008, there were 385 suspects in protective custody and 46 fugitives from justice. Many of the 44 convicts received sentences from twenty-five years to life (CELS 2009, 71).

Testimonies contributed in Argentina to the realization of different kinds of justice—namely, national and local, as well as transitional, punitive, restorative, and personal. Witnesses made their voices heard in the different contexts and settings where justice was at stake. These different kinds of justice overlapped partially but still required different narratives. Argentina's emphasis on truth, guilt, accountability, and punishment contrasts with Chile's search for reparation, reconciliation, and atonement after the dictatorship ended in 1990.

Reparation and Reconciliation in Chile

The CONADEP report became a bestseller, with over 300,000 copies sold in Argentina. In stark contrast, the report of the Chilean National Commission on Truth and Reconciliation was printed in a limited edition and was only available to the general public through inserts in *La Nación* newspaper (Hayner 2001, 34–37), while there was a fifty-year embargo on the confidential testimonies. The two commissions were of course operating in different political contexts. Whereas the CONADEP commission faced a defeated military and was supported by a strong popular mandate, the Rettig commission had to navigate among a confident military that had given itself amnesty and voluntarily handed over power. Furthermore, the Chilean president was concerned about the viability of Chile's transitional democracy, and Chilean society was more deeply divided over its past than Argentina. From a discursive perspective, the Argentine CONADEP commission was steered by the public contest of testimony versus denial, between survivors and perpetrators of state terror, while the Chilean Rettig commission was influenced by a tension between testimony and silence.

In July 1985, at a time when Argentina was in the midst of public hearings during the trial against the junta commanders, Chilean politicians formulated a national accord to initiate a return to democracy and demand the prosecution of human rights violators within the letter of the law and the spirit of national reconciliation (Ensalaco 2000, 170). Accountability and reconciliation were thus of central concern in imagining a post-Pinochet Chile. Therefore, it came as no surprise when president Patricio Aylwin created on April 25, 1990, the National Commission on Truth and Reconciliation based on the idea that "only upon a foundation of truth will it be possible to meet the basic demands of justice and create the necessary conditions for achieving true national reconciliation" (Chilean National Commission 1993, 1:5).

To preempt the accusation that the commission was biased against the military, as occurred in Argentina, Aylwin appointed four Pinochet supporters and four members of the political opposition, of whom former senator Raúl Rettig Guissen was appointed as the commission's president (Hayner

2001, 35). For reasons of expediency, the Chilean investigation was limited to the investigation of disappearances and deaths inflicted by both the Chilean military and the guerrillas (Chilean National Commission 1993, 1:6). They were thus defined as equitable suspects, even though the first were state representatives, while the second were private citizens, a distinction made by Argentina's CONADEP commission.

The political reality of 1990 made it appear that everybody was responsible for the military dictatorship. Allende's electoral victory, the expropriation of large estates, the radicalization toward socialism, the deteriorating economy, and the growing political polarization within Chilean society had been the responsibility of all Chileans, who were therefore as much to blame for the coup d'état of September 1973 as Pinochet and his coconspirators. According to the Rettig report, the political climate preceding the coup could never justify human rights violations, but it "enabled such violations to take root" (Chilean Commission 1993, 1:23). Another indication of the collective responsibility for the dictatorship was the premise that officials and civilians, either as state employees or guerrilla combatants, could be held responsible for human rights violations (Chilean National Commission 1993, 1:31), while the CONADEP held to the more common position that only states could be charged with human rights violations. Implicitly, there was a collective responsibility for the Chilean state terror, even though individual perpetrators were largely found among the Chilean military and police.

Given the restriction to examine only disappearances and violent deaths during the dictatorship, the commission drew primarily on the testimony of relatives, eyewitnesses, and government agents, even though some site visits were made, and documents, court records, and autopsy and human rights reports were also examined. The names of victims were requested from a large number of organizations, including the armed and guerrilla forces, after which around 3,400 cases were selected for further examination. All testimonies were cross-checked with earlier testimonies submitted elsewhere, notably with the Vicariate of Solidarity, established by Chile's Roman Catholic Church. The commission had to walk a political tightrope because the presidential decree forbade it from mentioning suspected perpetrators by name, as that would be an encroachment on the judiciary. Only the military unit, police precinct, or guerrilla organization involved, and not individuals, were mentioned in the Chilean report (Chilean National Commission 1993, 1:43). By contrast, the Argentine CONADEP report identified perpetrators by name in its testimonial excerpts.

In February 1991, the Rettig commission presented its report to president Aylwin. Heaping case upon case, the report painted a dictatorship in which the armed and security forces, the intelligence services, and the courts cooperated in the systematic violation of the human rights of Chilean civilians through torture, summary executions, disappearances, and arbitrary imprisonment. The report concluded that the detained-disappeared were dead. Their bodies had been thrown into the sea, were secretly buried, or had been disposed of in other ways (Chilean National Commission 1993, 1:44). The Rettig commission arrived at 2,298 confirmed dead and disappeared and 2,188 unresolved cases. Its unfinished work was completed by a follow-up commission, presided by Alejandro González Poblete, which raised the total number of dead and disappeared to 3,197 (Corporación Nacional 1996, 1:535). The 1996 Poblete report used the same narrative rendition of testimonies as the Rettig report: the testimonies were decontextualized, written in third person, and did not identify repressors.

The Rettig commission's master narrative was that Chilean society had become enwrapped in a process of political polarization instigated in the late 1950s by a global movement propagating new societal models and a growing belief in armed struggle, especially after the 1959 Cuban revolution, the violence of the guerrilla organization MIR (Revolutionary Left Movement), the armed response from right-wing organizations, and the 1970 electoral victory of Allende and the Popular Unity (Unidad Popular). The political climate of strikes, kidnappings, assassinations, illegal land seizures and the violent recovery of their properties by landowners, the nationalization of businesses, and the failure of the national government to curb the armed violence "led to a climate that by 1973 was objectively favorable to civil war" (Chilean National Commission 1993, 1:53). The Rettig report attributed the military coup to this threat of a civil war, for which the civilian government and polarized civilian groups were responsible. The truth and reconciliation commission did not attribute the political violence to identifiable groups in Chilean society, as did the CONADEP commission for Argentina, but dissipated the responsibility among a worldwide zeitgeist and national political developments. The human rights violations by military and police during the dictatorship were directed by the intelligence community and supported by the highest military ranks.

The Chilean military reacted immediately to the report. The Chilean army stated that the report distorted historical truth by selectively using testimonial sources, ignored the political violence and human rights violations preceding the September 1973 coup, and disregarded that Chile had been in a state of war and that the armed forces had the legitimate right to protect the nation by force from a communist takeover. Furthermore, the Rettig report failed to mention that peace and democracy had returned to Chile thanks to the military. Worse even, the Rettig commission incited animosities within the nation and destabilized the internal order. Silence about the past would be the best way to achieve reconciliation in Chile: "History and personal and social experience prove that situations of great turmoil are not overcome by reconstructing the events that caused the conflict. It interrupts the pacifying passage of time which tempers animosities and leaves behind affronts" (Ejército de Chile 1991, 7; Marchesi 2005).

One month after the Rettig report appeared, President Aylwin asked, "in his capacity as president, speaking on behalf of the entire nation, and in the name of the nation, to request pardon from the families of the victims" (Ensalaco 2000, 213). Thus, Chile's president adopted the commission's rendition of the political violence and state terrorism, assumed the state's guilt for the suffering of its citizens, and accepted responsibility for repairing the damage done.[4] Although this gesture seemed magnanimous, it was troubling for the victims because the democratic state assumed guilt without authorial agency and offered reparation without retribution.

Human rights organizations saw this injustice also reflected in the disturbing omission of verbatim testimonies, often given under great emotional duress, from the Rettig report, which consists of three volumes. The first two volumes contain four parts, each subdivided into a handful of chapters. The third volume is a 400-page alphabetical list of the victims of human rights violations, each with a short biography and an account of the circumstances of their death or disappearance. Preceded by Presidential Decree 355, which installed the commission, part 1 describes the investigative methodology and defines the principal legal concepts. Part 2 analyzes the political context at the time of the September 11, 1973, coup; the legal and institutional frameworks in place; the war tribunals; and the conduct of the courts toward human rights violations. Part 3 documents the human rights violations between September 11, 1973, and March 11, 1990; describes their impact on family relations; and lists unresolved cases. Part 4 contains proposals for the reparation of the suffering endured by the relatives of the disappeared and assassinated; makes legislative, institutional, and educational recommendations for the prevention of human rights violations; and draws a general conclusion about truth and reconciliation.

For this chapter's purposes, the report's treatment of testimony is particularly relevant. Which place are victim and survivor testimonies accorded in the Rettig report as compared to the Sábato report? The substantive volumes 1 and 2 are 1,030 pages long. The cases of executed or disappeared victims in part 3 take up 86 percent of the text. Although percentage-wise larger than the 58 percent of the CONADEP report, the narrative structure of the Rettig report is substantially different. The CONADEP's narrative is interspersed with heart-wrenching testimonies that illustrate the state repression vividly, while the Rettig report describes cases chronologically, intermingling victims of the military, the police, and guerrilla organizations in legalistic language. For example:

On September 19, 1973, **Julio Esteban HENRIQUEZ BRAVO**, 37, a merchant, was arrested along with another person by members of the investigative police in the Plaza de Armas [town's main square] and taken to the regiment, according to what the family was told. Witnesses say that he was seen at that installation until the end of September and that he had been beaten and tortured. Since that time he remains disappeared; he did not return home, has not conducted official business, nor is he registered as having left the country. Since it is sufficiently established that he was arrested, this Commission holds the conviction that Julio Esteban Henríquez suffered a human rights violation at the hands of government agents who after arresting him caused him to disappear. (Chilean National Commission 1993, 1:371)

There are no testimonial narratives in the report that define the place, time, and personal circumstances of the events, but only cases that read like a dispassionate legal record. This narrative rendition undermines the testimony's credibility by reducing the lived experience to a decontextualized legal case stripped of the particular time, location, and emotional state conveyed in the self-referential witness testimony.

The only two exceptions are a five-page description of torture and execution methods interspersed with anonymous quotations, and the twenty-page chapter "Impact of the Most Serious Human Rights Violations on Families and Social Relations," which contains statements from relatives about their suffering.[5] Still, these statements are not testimonial narratives but brief decontextualized quotations; for instance, "I had to explain to my five-year-old son that, just like animals and flowers, human beings sometimes kill human beings" or "They brought my son to my cell, unconscious and all bruised from torture" (Chilean National Commission 1993, 2:779, 782). Much pain hides behind these anonymous quotations, which comprise only 2.5 percent of the report and thus fail to have the rhetorical impact so striking in the Argentine CONADEP report. Even though the Rettig report acknowledges the suffering of the Chilean people as a whole, the surviving relatives are done little justice because the report fails to restore their lives shattered and voices muted by state terror.[6]

As Phelps (2004, 96) has observed, the quotations about the sequels of human rights violations are arranged from despair to hope, ending with the quotation, "I don't want revenge. I only want peace. I want to rest and so I have to know the truth. We don't want to get revenge, and we don't want others to suffer what we've suffered" (Chilean National Commission 1993, 2:800). Rhetorically, the report mutes survivor narratives and works toward the national reconciliation desired by the state. Historical and legal truths are emphasized at the expense of experiential truth to achieve that goal.

Justice for the people most directly affected by state terror—namely, the relatives of the disappeared and assassinated—is restricted to restorative justice, made subservient to the greater good of national reconciliation, and narrowly defined as personal and symbolic reparation.

Reparation became the preferred way "to bring society together and move toward creating conditions for true reconciliation" (Chilean National Commission 1993, 2:837). The same even-handedness that characterized the appointment of commission members from opposed political sides, and the equitability of the Chilean armed forces and the guerrillas as violators of human rights, was also dispensed in the reparation measures. Victims and perpetrators were equally awarded assistance in a spirit of forgiveness: "we want to point to the need to serve the health needs of those persons who have been involved in practicing torture in detention sites and to those who have acknowledged their participation in actions whose grave results we have investigated" (Chilean National Commission 1993, 2:846). The state preempted the active participation of perpetrators and victims in the reconciliation process and turned it into an administrative procedure, unlike the South African TRC, which required a public confession to allow forgiveness and truthfulness to receive amnesty, and made reparations in full awareness of their inadequacy in repairing the harm done (Minow 2002, 23–24; Sarkin 2008).

The Chilean commission recommended the restoration of the victims' good name and dignity, symbolic reparation (monuments, memory parks, and cultural events), solutions to legal issues for relatives of deceased victims, special legislation about the presumption of death of the disappeared, and social welfare (pensions, health care, housing, debt cancellation, exemption from military service, and scholarships) (Chilean National Commission 1993, 2:837–851). Medical and psychological assistance occupied a central place in the commission's 1991 recommendations. Since 1997, nearly 5,000 Chileans have received monthly checks of $345–$482 (Hayner 2001, 172–173), while by 2001 more than 32,000 persons have received psychotherapeutic assistance (Lira and Gómez 1996, 135; Lira and Loveman 2005, 388). Social suffering became individualized, and healing Chilean society was pursued through personal reparation, albeit with mixed results. People were treated for their mental demons, but such care medicalized and individualized their suffering instead of politicizing and socializing their plight.

Restorative justice was more important for the Chilean state than retribution. It would be the tenacious pursuit of Latin American dictators by Spanish judge Baltazar Garzón that would place accountability on the national agenda. In October 1998, Augusto Pinochet was arrested in Great Britain on genocide and terrorism charges (Roht-Arriaza 2005, 34–36). As supporters and opponents of Pinochet were battling each other in the media and through public demonstrations in Santiago and London, the Chilean government reacted with a reconciliatory initiative. Between August 1999 and May 2000, meetings were held between representatives of the armed forces, human rights organizations, the church, universities, and political parties. This round-table dialogue addressed major sores in Chilean society, notably the predicament of the disappeared, and revealed the potential benefits for the interlocutors. Relatives and human rights organizations wanted to know the truth about loved ones. The military tried to prevent criminal prosecution, and the government hoped for a renewed step toward national reconciliation. These gains were sufficiently promising to create a common ground for dialogue. This common ground did not exist in Argentina because of moral objections and was also rejected in Chile by a critical younger generation.

In October 1999, young activists organized the first *funas,* or street protests of public shaming, modeled after the Argentine *escraches,* as "acts of social justice that try to unmask before society those who participated in human rights violations during the dictatorship."[7] The protesters were inspired by Pinochet's arrest in London and bemoaned the reigning impunity, the amnesty legislation, and the complacency of the human rights movement. They regarded their protests as an alternative to institutional justice because the *funas* "do not delegate the power of the desire for justice but transform it in the construction and creation of an alternative way of experiencing justice" (Sandoval and Ortolani 2002, 50). The Chilean authorities were less tolerant of the *funas* than the Argentine. *Funas* were repressed in 2001 by the police with tear gas and mass arrests, but they have continued into the present (De Mano en Mano 2002, 57).

The general clamor for the truth had its effects. In January 2001, the armed forces clarified 200 disappearances and revealed that 130 disappeared had been thrown into the Pacific Ocean and Chile's open waters (Aguilar 2002). This admission was interpreted by the Chilean Roman Catholic authorities as a reconciliatory gesture, and Cardinal Errázuriz suggested that the military should only be prosecuted for the most notorious forced disappearances, while the rest would be pardoned (Aguilar 2002, 423). Meanwhile, after having been medically declared unfit to stand trial, Pinochet returned to Chile in March 2000 but was eventually held accountable in August 2004.

Pinochet's arrest in London led to many accusations against Chilean officers and policemen. Only a dozen of the most notorious perpetrators were convicted by 2004, while more than 300 cases remained pending in court (Lira and Loveman 2002, 387–393; Roht-Arriaza 2005, 94–96). The Chilean government lacked the will to press forward on the accountability issue and instead broadened its reparation measures to bring about the desired national reconciliation.

A new truth commission was the government's answer to the call for truth and justice for all victims of state terrorism. President Ricardo Lagos created in November 2003 the eight-member National Commission about Political Imprisonment and Torture (Comisión Nacional sobre Prisión Política y Tortura), under the chairmanship of Sergio Valech Aldunate. This commission was to investigate the interrogation and incarceration regime under the Pinochet dictatorship. The tens of thousands of Chileans who had survived torture and captivity in police stations, prisons, and military bases had not fallen within the investigative mandate of the 1991 Rettig commission. Survivors felt a great injustice about not having been able to tell their story and hoped that the Valech commission was to make good.

The political composition and premises of the Rettig and Valech commissions were different. Whereas the National Commission on Truth and Reconciliation went out of its way to emphasize its neutrality by appointing an equal number of members pro- and contra-Pinochet, and treated human rights violations by the Chilean military and the guerrillas equally, the Valech commission included two persons who had been tortured and stated from the outset that government agents had violated the dignity of their victims (Comisión Nacional 2004, 9). The 1998 arrest of Pinochet, the 1999–2000 round-table dialogue, the 2001 admission of disappearances by the military, and several convictions of perpetrators resulted in the general opinion that the dictatorship was responsible for the human rights violations and that the principled even-handedness of the Rettig commission could now be abandoned.

The Valech commission took more than 35,000 testimonies, of which nearly 28,000 were accepted as having sufficient ground. The interviews lasted on average one hour and were held throughout Chile and abroad. In a clear breach with the narrative of the Rettig report, the Valech report reproduced lengthy quotations from the testimonies of anonymous victims of torture, including the month of detention, detention center, and state branch involved.

> Woman, detained in May 1975. Account of her internment at the DINA quarters in Villa Grimaldi, Metropolitan Region: *when we arrived at the place, they threw me from the pick-up truck on the ground and immediately subjected me to interrogations by [name omitted] who humiliated me verbally. Then they took me to the "Corvi houses" (boxes in which one could only remain standing). They always kept me blindfolded, hands tied and naked. They applied electric shocks. I was a victim of fondling and dishonest abuses, many blows and a mock execution at the edge of the swimming pool.* (Comisión Nacional 2004, 277)

The 660-page report, presented to president Lagos in 2003, consists of ten chapters, of which the forty-three-page chapter 5 ("Torture Methods: Definitions and Testimonies") and the twenty-eight-page chapter 8

("Consequences of Political Imprisonment and Torture") contain lengthy contextualized testimonies of torture, suffering, trauma, and mourning.

Still, the Chilean government was careful not to polarize Chilean society with the Valech report. Its findings were not to lead to the systematic prosecution of perpetrators, but to "create the conditions to restore our collective memory . . . dignify the victims" by acknowledging their suffering, and "heal the wounds of our national soul" (prologue by president Ricardo Lagos, Comisión Nacional 2004). As a telling sign of the state's resolve to achieve reconciliation, victims were awarded state pensions and health services. Aside from excerpts reproduced in the report, their testimonies were to remain confidential for fifty years. Testimony thus served mainly to verify the claims for reparation payments. Victims and perpetrators remained anonymous for society, and both the acknowledgment of their suffering and the accountability of their deeds were prevented. The Chilean government was thus actively shaping a counter master narrative of the military narrative through two truth commissions that only partially satisfied the victim's sense of justice: "To replace one oppressive master narrative with a different one does not empower the victims and, worse, it threatens to perpetuate the oppression, only in another, perhaps more benign, form" (Phelps 2005, 50).

As if he knew the intentions of president Lagos, the Chilean army commander General Cheyre accepted the institutional responsibility for the dictatorship's human rights violations just weeks before the Valech report appeared (Agüero and Hershberg 2005, 8). The report did not lead to an acceleration of the court cases pending against suspected perpetrators, let alone against their commander Augusto Pinochet. Pinochet died on December 10, 2006. His death seemed to open the way for truth and retribution. Human rights organizations became more determined to press charges against perpetrators, and Chilean president Michelle Bachelet promised, after an emotional visit in October 2006 to the former torture center Villa Grimaldi, where she and her mother had been held in 1975, to respect the ruling by the Interamerican Court of Human Rights that Chile's 1978 amnesty law was in violation of international legislation. The law has remained in place till the present, but individual courts have prosecuted perpetrators nevertheless on the argument that the amnesty does not apply to gross human rights violations.

In February 2009, 257 officers and national policemen were convicted (FASIC 2009, 15). Still, the mild sentences for violations comparable to those in Argentina revealed Chile's continued desire for restorative justice. Sentences were lowered upon the Supreme Court's call for "justice with clemency" because of the passage of time since the violations had taken place (FASIC 2009, 2–3). The Chilean state, with its military and judicial institutions in front, continued on the path of reconciliation despite the persistent clamor for truth, remembrance, and accountability by survivors, relatives, and human rights organizations.

The court cases and the Valech commission have provided a greater openness to the voices of the survivors of state terror, but these national fora have been unable to fully satisfy the need for personal and local justice. These victim-survivors have therefore produced testimonial literature and pursued the construction of memorial museums to preserve the memory of their predicament. Voices materialize in sites of memory whose reconstruction is made on the basis of survivor testimonies. Furthermore, local justice is achieved by representing suffering in a specific place set in a guilty landscape. The Villa Grimaldi Peace Park is the most developed memory site in Chile. This former torture and detention center in Peñalolén, an Andean foothill outskirt of Santiago, caught the attention of a survivors organization in 1991, was opened to the public in 1994, and became an official memory site in 1997.

Villa Grimaldi was the most important interrogation center of the Chilean National Intelligence Directorate (DINA). It consisted of office buildings, torture rooms, and three different facilities to hold captives, of which the water tower was the most feared. The Rettig report states: "Inside it there were ten tight spaces for holding prisoners, about 70 by 70 centimeters [two square feet] and two meters high with a tiny door at the bottom which one had to enter on one's knees. . . . Apparently those who were taken to the tower were prisoners of some importance whose period of intensive interrogation was over. Many of those held in the tower were never seen again" (Chilean National Commission 1993, 2:486).

The wooden tower is the most prominent structure at the Villa Grimaldi Peace Park. There is considerable personal justice for the survivors in rebuilding Villa Grimaldi, which the military sold to a project developer who leveled the place to build condominiums. The testimonies of the few captives who survived the tower cannot be read in the 1991 Rettig and 1996 Poblete reports because they are restricted to the dead and the disappeared. Even the 2003 Valech report gives scant information, as in the case of a female prisoner who in February 1975 "*was subjected to . . . total isolation in the tower of Villa Grimaldi, in a small cell, without ventilation, without light, without a door and with a small opening through which one entered and left, crawling*" (Comisión Nacional 2004, 285). Detailed accounts can only be found in Chilean testimonial literature, as in the following excerpt from *The Inferno* by Luz Arce, who was forced to spend twelve days penned up in the tower and survived with the help of several guards.

> I didn't feel my legs. The truth is I didn't feel anything, except the inner edge of my foot and my right leg where I suffered from

hypersensitivity. . . . Days and hours didn't exist for me, only a permanent stupor. The few conscious moments were strange too. I felt like
the guards did what they could, but I was incapable of anything. I just
looked at them and said, "Thanks." . . .

The pain was different too. I could feel its constant presence, but
I wasn't suffering. It was as if the pain had crossed the threshold that
a human being can endure, as if it had vanished, disappeared. I was
beyond pain. One day I asked myself, is it possible to die from pain?
I felt that more than anything I wanted to die, that a haze had taken
over everything. (Arce 2004, 86)

The difference between the quotations from the Valech report and Luz
Arce's autobiography demonstrates that testimonies occupy the narrative
spaces accorded by their contexts and that these different voices address
different kinds of justice. Luz Arce exploits this freedom to the fullest in
a carefully constructed story of redemption. She tells about her journey
from Allende's inner circle, via her torture by, collaboration with, and
resignation from Chile's secret service, to her conversion to Catholicism.
Arce symbolizes the many Chileans who were forced to collaborate, and
she found personal justice in the public confession about her dark past.
Her confessional account "emblematizes and echoes the utopian discourse
of reconciliation that has been the hallmark of Chile's transition" (Lazzara
2006, 71).

Reconciliatory discourse has also found its way into the Villa Grimaldi
Peace Park, whose name projects into the future the interrogation center's
meaning and contrasts with Argentina's Memory Park, whose name points
to the past (for a related discussion, see Dwyer, this volume). The spatial
outlays of both parks reflect nationally dominant discourses. The Chilean
Peace Park was designed in the shape of a cross made by two diagonal paths.
"With its double meaning, death and resurrection, the cross with two axes at
the center of the park encompasses a fountain that is a place of encounter
and orientation where it is possible to enter into contact with the water"
(Lazzara 2006, 138). The Argentine Memory Park, along the riverbank of the
Rio de la Plata in Buenos Aires, has a striking monument to the victims of
state terrorism in the shape of a sinuous fissure that traverses part of the
fourteen-hectare park "designed as a cut, an open wound, in a lawn hill,
stripped of all other elements. The landscape and the layout recreate the
effort required to build a fairer society and the wound caused by the violent
acts perpetrated by the State" (Comisión Pro Monumento 2005, 62). These
two parks demonstrate how testimony and politics meet in the symbolism
of the cross and the open wound, and manifest the types of justice desired
in Chile and Argentina when they were designed.

Conclusion: Restorative versus Retributive Justice

This chapter has indicated that Argentine society has been pursuing truth finding and retributive justice, despite occasional attempts at turning the page of history, whereas Chile has been trying to achieve restorative justice and national reconciliation, even though perpetrators have been eventually prosecuted. Testimonies by survivors of abduction, torture, and disappearance, as well as by perpetrators, have time and again been crucial in changing the legal and political parameters of justice in Chile and Argentina, because justice is not confined to the judiciary and because "transitional justice mechanisms almost always have unexpected outcomes that emerge out of the 'frictions' between these global mechanisms and local realities" (Hinton, this volume).

Truth commissions and courts have different relations to justice. Both use testimony to discover human rights violations, but the first centers on doing justice to survivors while the second focuses on prosecuting perpetrators. Truth commissions in Chile and Argentina showed compassion for the victims of state terrorism and morally condemned the perpetrators, while courts sought to redress legal grievances by putting the accused on trial as a demonstration of people's equality before the law. The types of justice have multiplied in the Southern Cone of Latin America, next to those provided by courts and truth commissions, through autobiographies, documentaries, street protests, forensic investigations, museums, and memory sites. Justice became an increasingly layered phenomenon as the decades passed. Each country bore its own stamp. The different post-dictatorial trajectories of Chile and Argentina demonstrate that atonement and accountability, as well as reconciliation and retribution, evoke different types of justice, yield different forms of testimony, and give different legitimacies to survivors and perpetrators.

Chilean society has largely supported the state's pursuit of restorative justice and national reconciliation, despite the protests of the human rights movement and the political opposition. Successive governments have not proactively tried to annul the amnesty legislation but have placed much effort on reparations, while the courts have produced many convictions but given mild sentences. Argentina has been on a roller coaster of prosecution and amnesty. The persistent political mobilization by the human rights movement, critical lawyers, judges, and politicians has resulted in lengthy prison terms for perpetrators.

Former president General Bignone was one of the perpetrators who never found rest after he handed power to president Raúl Alfonsín in December 1983. He was arrested in January 1984 in relation to two disappearances in 1976 at the Military College when he was its director. Bignone was imprisoned for six months, and the case dismissed in July 1987. In 1999 he was charged with the abduction of nine babies, for which he was sentenced house arrest rather than imprisonment because of his advanced age. In 2004, on the twenty-eighth anniversary of the March 1976 military coup, Argentine president Kirchner ordered the removal of Bignone's portrait from the Military College. In October 2005, Bignone's house arrest was lifted because the court was taking too much time to formally accuse him. In late 2007, Bignone faced a new charge. He was accused of the illegal detention of fifteen persons and sentenced to house arrest. In January 2009 the seventy-nine-year-old Bignone was formally accused of the abduction and torture of thirty-six physicians and nurses at the Posadas Hospital in the town of Haedo.

NOTES

Research in Argentina was made possible by grants from the National Science Foundation and the Harry Frank Guggenheim Foundation. A field trip to Chile was funded by Utrecht University and the Netherlands Organisation for Scientific Research. I thank Katrien Klep of Utrecht University and the anonymous reviewers for their perceptive and constructive comments.

1. The Argentine Forensic Anthropology Team (EAAF) holds that 9,000–10,000 Argentines disappeared during the military regime, whereas most Argentine human rights organizations maintain that 30,000 people disappeared (Argentine Forensic Anthropology Team 2007, 21).

2. These figures and comments refer to the original Argentine edition of the CONADEP report (CONADEP 1984).

3. The 1974 Ugandan and the 1982–1984 Bolivian truth commissions investigated disappearances in Uganda and Bolivia, but the findings were never published (Hayner 2001, 52–53).

4. The Rettig report could please neither the Chilean military and chief justices nor the human rights organizations. The Chilean military were upset by the conclusion that they had not been engaged in a war but had been attacking unarmed people (Chilean National Commission 1993, 1:33); the Supreme Court dismissed the report's accusation of collaboration with the dictatorship and unwillingness to honor habeas corpus requests and prosecute members of the armed and security forces. Finally, human rights organizations deplored Aylwin's appeal to forgiveness on behalf of the nation and declared that they were unwilling to forgive the military (Ensalaco 2000, 213–224).

5. I disagree with Phelps (2004, 97) that "the stories of the victims . . . dominate the report." They do so in terms of the space allotted to the case descriptions, but these fail to stand out above the general text because of their legalistic, third-person rendition of the victims' predicament.

6. This calculation is based on the 1996 edition of the 1991 Rettig report, available on the Web site of the Chilean government's Human Rights Program (http://www.ddhh.gov.cl). The 1996 edition was supervised by Alejandro González Poblete and involves some minor corrections to the original report.

7. http://funachile.cl/index.php?option=com_content&task=view&id=800&Itemid=32.

REFERENCES

Agüero, Felipe, and Eric Hershberg. 2005. "Las Fuerzas Armadas y las memorias de la represión en el Cono Sur." In *Memorias militares sobre la represión en el Cono Sur: Visiones en disputa en dictadura y democracia*, ed. Eric Hershberg and Felipe Agüero, 1–34. Madrid: Siglo Veintiuno de España Editores.

Aguilar, Mario I. 2002. "The Disappeared and the Mesa de Diálogo in Chile 1999–2001: Searching for Those Who Never Grew Old." *Bulletin of Latin American Research* 21 (3): 413–424.

Arce, Luz. 2004. *The Inferno: A Story of Terror and Survival in Chile*. Madison: University of Wisconsin Press.

Areas, Tabaré. 1984. "Sábato enfrentó a Alfonsín: El shock de 'Nunca más.'" *Somos* 8 (408): 6–11

Argentine Forensic Anthropology Team. 2007. *2007 Annual Report: Covering the Period January to December 2006*. Buenos Aires: EAAF.

Asociación Unidad Argentina (AUNAR). 1999. *Subversión: La historia olvidada*. 2nd ed. Buenos Aires: Asociación Unidad Argentina.

Boschi, Silvana. 2000. "Por qué siguen y qué puede pasar con los juicios a militares." *Clarín*, July 23.

Centro de Estudios Legales y Sociales (CELS). 2009. *Derechos humanos en Argentina: Informe 2009*. Buenos Aires: Siglo Veintiuno Editores.

Centro de Investigaciones Sociales sobre el Estado y la Administración (CISEA). 1984. *Argentina 1983*. Buenos Aires: Centro Editor de América Latina.

Chilean National Commission on Truth and Reconciliation. 1993. *Report on the Chilean National Commission on Truth and Reconciliation*. 2 vols. Notre Dame: University of Notre Dame Press.

Comisión de Educación. 2004. *Memoria y dictadura: Un espacio para la reflexión desde los derechos humanos*. Buenos Aires: APDH.

Comisión Nacional sobre la Desaparición de Personas (CONADEP). 1984. *Nunca Más: Informe de la Comisión Nacional sobre la Desaparición de Personas*. Buenos Aires: EUDEBA.

———. 1986. *Nunca Más: The Report of the Argentine National Commission on the Disappeared*. New York: Farrar Straus Giroux.

Comisión Nacional sobre Prisión Política y Tortura. 2004. *Informe de la Comisión Nacional sobre Prisión Política y Tortura*. Santiago: Ministerio Secretaría General de Gobierno.

Comisión Pro Monumento a las Víctimas del Terrorismo de Estado. 2005. *Proyecto Parque de la Memoria*. Buenos Aires: Gobierno de la Ciudad de Buenos Aires.

Corporación Nacional de Reparación y Reconciliación. 1996. *Informe sobre calificación de víctimas de violaciones de derechos humanos y de la violencia política*. Santiago: Corporación Nacional de Reparación y Reconciliación.

Daly, Erin, and Jeremy Sarkin. 2007. *Reconciliation in Divided Societies: Finding Common Ground*. Philadelphia: University of Pennsylvania Press.

De Mano en Mano. 2002. *Situaciones 5: Mesa de escrache popular*. Buenos Aires: Ediciones De Mano en Mano.

Ejército Argentino. 1984. "Incineración de documentación estadística." *Boletín público ejército Argentino* 4524 (November 8): 673.

Ejército de Chile. 1991. *El Ejército, la verdad y la reconciliación*. Santiago: Ejército de Chile.

Ensalaco, Mark. 2000. *Chile under Pinochet: Recovering the Truth*. Philadelphia: University of Pennsylvania Press.

Etchecolatz, Miguel O. 1988. *La otra campana del nunca más.* Buenos Aires: privately printed.

Fundación de Ayuda Social de las Iglesias Cristianas (FASIC). 2009. "Balance de Derechos Humanos, Año 2008." http://www.fasic.org/doc/Microsoft%20Word%20-BALANCE%202008.pdf.

Foro de Generales Retirados. 2004. *Las Fuerzas Armadas y la crisis militar.* Buenos Aires: Foro de Generales Retirados.

Garcia, Fabián. 2000. "Detienen a tres militares en una causa sobre la represión ilegal." *Clarín,* April 25.

Hayner, Priscilla B. 2001. *Unspeakable Truths: Confronting State Terror and Atrocity.* New York: Routledge.

"La Corte deberá decidir sobre la situación de los militares." 2000. *Clarín,* July 12.

Lazzara, Michael J. 2006. *Chile in Transition: The Poetics and Politics of Memory.* Gainesville: University Press of Florida.

Lira, Elizabeth, and Elena Gómez. 1996. "Reparación y salud mental: Programa PRAIS." In *Reparación, derechos humanos y salud mental,* ed. Elizabeth Lira and Isabel Piper, 123–146. Santiago: ILAS.

Lira, Elizabeth, and Brian Loveman. 2002. "Derechos humanos y 'paz social.'" In *Chile 2001–2002: Impactos y desafíos de las crisis internacionales,* ed. FLACSO-Chile, 149–172. Vitacura: FLACSO-Chile.

Marchesi, Aldo. 2005. "Vencedores vencidos: Las respuestas militares frente a los informes 'Nunca Más' en el Cono Sur." In *Memorias militares sobre la represión en el Cono Sur: visiones en disputa en dictadura y democracia,* ed. Eric Hershberg and Felipe Agüero, 175–210. Madrid: Siglo Veintiuno de España Editores.

Márquez, Nicolás. 2004. *La otra parte de la verdad: La respuesta a los que han ocultado y deformado la verdad histórica sobre la década del '70 y el terrorismo.* Mar del Plata, Argentina: privately printed.

Minow, Martha. 2002. "Breaking the Cycles of Hatred." In *Breaking the Cycles of Hatred: Memory, Law, and Repair,* ed. Martha Minow and Nancy L. Rosenblum, 14–76. Princeton, NJ: Princeton University Press.

"Para los familiares solo vale la justicia." 2000. *Clarín,* July 11.

Phelps, Teresa Godwin. 2004. *Shattered Voices: Language, Violence, and the Work of Truth Commissions.* Philadelphia: University of Pennsylvania Press.

Rawls, John. 1973. *A Theory of Justice.* Oxford: Oxford University Press.

Robben, Antonius C. G. M. 2005a. *Political Violence and Trauma in Argentina.* Philadelphia: University of Pennsylvania Press.

———. 2005b. "How Traumatized Societies Remember: The Aftermath of Argentina's Dirty War." *Cultural Critique* 59:120–164.

Roht-Arriaza, Naomi. 2005. *The Pinochet Effect: Transnational Justice in the Age of Human Rights.* Philadelphia: University of Pennsylvania Press.

Sandoval, Rodrigo, and Diego Ortolani. 2002. "De escraches y funas." In *Situaciones 5: Mesa de escrache popular,* ed. De Mano en Mano, 48–52. Buenos Aires: Ediciones De Mano en Mano.

Sarkin, Jeremy. 2008. "An Evaluation of the South African Amnesty Process." In *Truth and Reconciliation in South Africa: Did the TRC Deliver?* ed. Audrey R. Chapman and Hugo van der Merwe, 93–115. Philadelphia: University of Pennsylvania Press.

"Testimonia de la señora Calvo de Laborde, licenciada en Física." 1985. *El diario del juicio* 1 (June 4): 29–33.

9

▶▶▶▶▶▶▶▶▶▶▶▶▶ ◀◀◀◀◀◀◀◀◀◀◀◀◀

Judging the "Crime of Crimes"

Continuity and Improvisation at the International Criminal Tribunal for Rwanda

NIGEL ELTRINGHAM

Courtroom III of the International Criminal Tribunal for Rwanda (ICTR), Arusha, Tanzania, in 2006. A protected Rwandan prosecution witness is being cross-examined by an American defense lawyer.[1] The witness has been on the stand for eight days, the court sitting from 9:00 A.M. to 5:30 P.M. with two hours for lunch. It is now around 5:00 P.M. The defense counsel presses the witness on whether he made notes when he gave his statement and whether he has been consulting those notes in the evenings. The presiding judge asks the defense lawyer to explain the relevance of this line of questioning.

DEFENSE COUNSEL: Mr. President, if the witness has been reviewing documents concerning the events that he's testified about, that affects his credibility; his memory is being enhanced. And the defense is entitled to see those documents he has been reviewing.

CO-JUDGE: But he said these were his own notes.

DEFENSE COUNSEL: Yes, and if he's relying on notes to refresh his memory, the defense are entitled to see those notes.

CO-JUDGE: You're saying you're entitled to his own private notes?

DEFENSE COUNSEL: Yes. If he's used them to refresh his memory. Isn't that common practice in every jurisdiction, that a witness who's used material to refresh their memory has to produce that material?

PRESIDING JUDGE: I'm not aware of that rule. I'm not aware of any control over what he reads when he's not in the witness box.

DEFENSE COUNSEL: So if a witness has prepared some kind of document and uses that in the evenings, it's your understanding that it's only disclosable if he brings it to court with him? Maybe it's my national practice that I'm betraying knowledge of, but I'm not aware of that distinction.

PROSECUTION COUNSEL: I think in that regard it must be a Californian practice because I practiced in New York and I've never heard an application
quite like this one. In any case, I would suggest that there's nothing in
our rules that require disclosure of a witness's own memoranda.

PRESIDING JUDGE: We rule that the witness's own notes are not disclosable.

Another trial. A defense lawyer has just completed the examination-in-
chief of a another protected Rwandan witness. It is about 3 P.M.

DEFENSE COUNSEL: Mr. President, I don't know what the situation is for you,
but here it's intolerable. It's very, very humid here. There's something
wrong in this courtroom and it's very, very difficult for us to work under
these conditions.

PRESIDING JUDGE: Yes. Madam Registrar, could you give us a report on what
happened today.

REGISTRAR: Thank you, Mr. President. They told us that they had resolved
the situation. And after the morning coffee break, I believe the place
was cool enough. I don't know what has happened now after the lunch
break. We will call them to come back again during the tea break.

PRESIDING JUDGE: Mr. —— [prosecution counsel], is it any better on your
side?

PROSECUTION COUNSEL: Not at all, Mr. President. Certainly less than the
situation on Mr. ——'s [defense lawyer] side because he's talking. But
when I start talking, I too will be sweating and I will be spending a lot of
energy, and I will probably feel the same way as him. So I totally agree
with him that something should be done about the problem.

PRESIDING JUDGE [*to the Prosecution Counsel*]: May the uncomfortable conditions cause you to speak a bit less? [*generalized laughter in the courtroom*].

The first episode illustrates that while international criminal courts
are formally "hybrids" of civil and common law procedure, the negotiation of hybridity continues in the courtroom. While legal practitioners may
cultivate the illusion that a court's foundational texts (the Statute and the
Rules of Procedure and Evidence) are comprehensive, the enactment of
international criminal law is a daily process of challenging habitual practice,
revealing discordant assumptions, negotiating novelty, and developing new
configurations. As a defense lawyer commented:

In a domestic jurisdiction there is a systemic structure. Each case is
different, but that structure works to contain and guide each case.
But, at the Tribunal that does not exist. An innovation has to be made
to account for something particular. A lot of the time it's a gut-check,
we take something out of our pocket and see how it fits. The judiciary

may give the impression that there is a standard guiding them, they give that appearance, but the idea found in common law of centuries of practice, that's not there. Judges try to be sincere, but it's very individuated, the decisions they make. There's no systematic structure, we're literally bringing it into existence in the courtroom.[2]

He is describing a process of localized adaptation, of "vernacularization," but it is not one in which a static, identifiable text (such as the Universal Declaration of Human Rights) is "mediated, appropriated, translated, modified, misunderstood [or] ignored" ("Introduction," this volume; see Merry 1997, 2006), but a process in which otherwise implicit assumptions brought by lawyers and judges from myriad national jurisdictions (assumptions refracted through individual biographies) are voiced, assessed, adopted, rejected, or syncretized. As a prosecution lawyer observed, "What we would normally take for granted, we would never even discuss it, but here, every tiny thing has to be discussed. We're actually creating law." Furthermore, lawyers and judges do not necessarily display a parochial conservatism, keen to preserve their own practices. Rather, there is an openness to creative adaptation. In the opening episode, the prosecution lawyer disavows parochialism, saying, "In any case, I would suggest that there's nothing in *our rules* that require disclosure of a witness's own memoranda." Likewise, a defense lawyer observed that "[practicing here] makes you think about what you are doing, how you do things. It makes you open to the fact that just because we have one way of doing something doesn't mean it's better," and, according to a prosecution lawyer, "you can be very creative in an institution in which there is no set way of doing things." As one judge said to me, "Who the hell cares how things are done in the old country." For legal practitioners, the transition in "transitional justice" is a matter of reflection on prior assumptions and reformulating their procedural and performative preferences (see Eltringham 2008, 316–317).

This localized negotiation is effaced in much commentary on the ICTR, where the focus is on *purposes* and *products*, on the "liberal normative goods" ("Introduction," this volume) of "retribution"; "accountability"; "deterrence"; "ending impunity"; "reconciliation" (see, e.g., International Crisis Group 2001). While these "liberal normative goods" are found in the preamble to the tribunal's Statute,[3] and are continually reiterated by tribunal officials, a focus on *results achieved* in relation to *promises made* contributes to the portrayal of the tribunal as "a being unto itself, animated with a will and mind of its own" (Taussig 1992, 112).

But, just as the judgment of a precursor institution, the Nuremberg Tribunal, stated that "Crimes against international law are committed by men, not by abstract entities" (International Military Tribunal 1947, 223), so, in turn, such crimes are tried by persons in a specific site. Transitional justice may seek static texts (judgments or substantive reports), but these are a residue of dynamic, situated encounters (see Robben, this volume; Buur 2003, 67n8). As the second illustration above demonstrates, the courtroom is a place where people are positioned, where people sweat, expend energy, and where the sequencing of prohibited and required movement transforms a room into a courtroom and provides a grammar for interaction. Again, divergent assumptions brought from domestic jurisdictions regarding bodily performance must be negotiated. And yet the prominence of bodily performance in this space is matched only by incessant attempts to *dis*-embody and *de*-localize authority in symbols and supposedly authorless texts.

What follows is a discussion of place, *dis*-placement, and the negotiation of sanctioned kinetics within that space.

Context

The ad hoc International Criminal Tribunal for Rwanda was established on November 8, 1994, by the United Nations Security Council (Resolution 955) as a response to the 1994 Rwandan genocide, during which (according to a 2001 census) an estimated 937,000 Rwandans were killed between April and July, the majority ethnic Tutsi (see Burnet, this volume). The tribunal investigates, and puts on trial, *any person* accused of committing the following in Rwanda in 1994: one of five acts of genocide (as defined by the 1948 United Nations Convention for the Prevention and Punishment of the Crime of Genocide), crimes against humanity (a widespread or systematic attack on a civilian population), and war crimes (Article 3 common to the 1949 Geneva Conventions). In addition, Rwandan citizens who committed any of these crimes in neighboring countries in 1994 can be indicted.[4] The seat of the tribunal and its four courtrooms are located in Arusha, Tanzania. The tribunal has three principal organs: the office of the prosecutor, which investigates allegations, issues indictments, and prosecutes the case in court; the registry (administration); and three trial chambers composed of seven judges nominated by their home state and elected by the United Nations General Assembly. In addition, up to twelve *ad litem* judges may serve at the tribunal at any one time. Three judges sit in each trial. There is no jury; the three judges assess the evidence and issue a judgment. There is, in addition, an appeals chamber consisting of seven judges that is shared with the International Criminal Tribunal for the Former Yugoslavia (ICTY). By 2007, around 1,500 witnesses (80 percent under a witness protection scheme) had testified at the tribunal. Currently, forty-seven cases have been completed (including six acquittals), twenty-three accused are on trial, five accused are awaiting trial, and thirteen indicted remain at large. In 2008, the United

Nations Security Council called on the ICTR to complete all trial activities by the end of December 2009 (see United Nations 2008).

The Theater of the Courtroom

Whereas description of the courtrooms as spaces are largely absent from existing commentary on the ICTR, it is a prominent element in eye-witness accounts of precursor institutions: the Nuremberg Tribunal (see Neave 1978, 47, 253, 263; Taylor 1993, 224–231; West 1984, 7) and the trial of Adolf Eichmann (see Arendt 1994, 3; Gouri 2004, 144, 171, 297). At the ICTR, one is struck by the elongated shape of Courtrooms I, II, and III created by knocking down internal office walls. The *consecrated* space of the court is separated from the public gallery by a tinted (bullet-proof) glass wall, a *rood screen* separating the profane *nave* of the public gallery from the sacred *chancel* of the judicial space (Garapon 2001, 34). The three judges sit on a *raised* podium against the center of the back wall, flanked by two stenographers (French and English); the judges' assistant legal officers (ALO) and registry staff sit immediately in front, and in front of them is the witness box. The three desks of the defense are to the left; the two desks of the prosecution are to the right. Serving a practical purpose, the desks also prevent anyone from "escaping from the place he [*sic*] is allocated by the judicial liturgy" (Garapon 2001, 36) initiated by the entrance of judges (see figure 9.1).

The judges are framed by a large, firmament-blue UN-emblem on the back wall. This emblem creates "an axis of symmetry with the person of the judge[s]" (Garapon 2001, 28), so that the "distribution of space, of roles, of functions, the gestures of the judicial debate, take meaning in relation to that major axis" (Jacob 1994, 13). The UN emblem, designed in 1945 by Donal McLaughlin, chief of the Graphics Presentation Branch of the United States Office of Strategic Studies, is a map of the world "inscribed in a wreath consisting of crossed conventionalized branches of the olive tree" (United Nations 1946). The prominence of this emblem in the courtroom implies the presence of "affronted humanity," evoking the amphitheater trial of *A Matter of Life and Death* (Powell and Pressburger 1946). The same wreath appears on the tribunal's own seal (the scales of justice superimposed on a dove of peace). All official documents are stamped with a wet seal, while written judicial decisions are stamped with an embossed dry seal (see figure 9.2). It is the superimposition of the judges onto the UN emblem that creates an axis around which courtroom exchange is orientated. Placed behind the judges, the UN emblem takes the place of, for example, a county seal in the United States or the Royal Coat of Arms in the United Kingdom. The UN emblem inherits the role played by these domestic objects, indicating a *delegation/transference* of authority from an exterior foundation of justice ("the

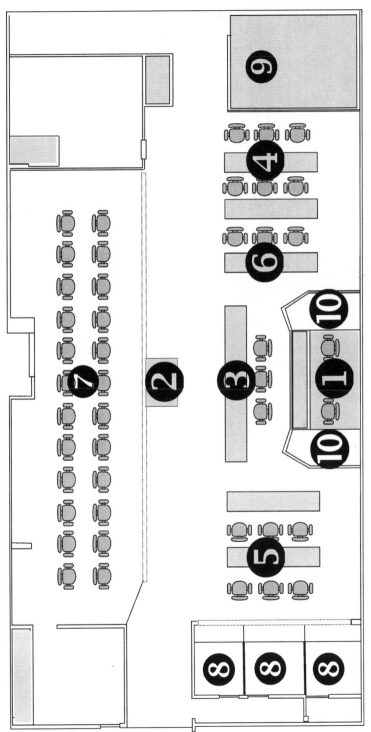

FIGURE 9.1 Inside a courtroom at the ICTR. Key: (1) judges, (2) witness box, (3) registry officials, (4) accused, (5) prosecution team, (6) defense team(s), (7) public gallery, (8) interpreters, (9) technical control room, (10) stenographers.

Source: Adapted from ICTR 2005, 16.

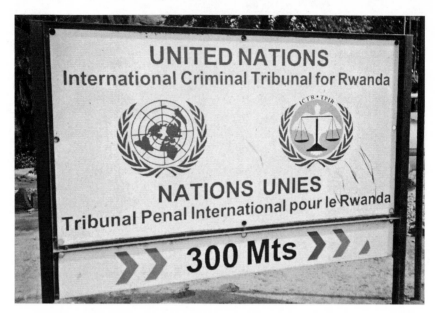

FIGURE 9.2 The UN emblem and the seal of the ICTR.

people," "the monarch") to the judges. At the ICTR, certain people bow in the direction of the judges when entering and leaving the courtroom, most notably Tanzanian registry officials. Others, such as French lawyers, do not bow. An American assistant legal officer and an American stenographer explained to me that there is no bowing in U.S. courts and that this is a "British Tanzanian thing." In the United Kingdom, when one bows to a judge one is primarily showing deference to the presence of the monarch in the form of the Royal Coat of Arms, rather than the monarch's delegate, the judge. From 1919, the Royal Coat of Arms would have been behind or above judges with jurisdiction over Tanganyika. It appears a residual disposition remained following independence in 1961. In regard to the UN emblem behind the judges, an ICTR intern asked, "Who are people bowing to, the International Community?" On one hand, people's relation to the emblem indicates a particular residue of local Tanzanian courts,[5] but it also indicates the preservation of a more general form found in many domestic jurisdictions, the presence of an emblem behind judges that indicates that they are delegates of a transcendent justice that is "somewhere else [which] cannot be contained in laws or confined totally to persons" (Garapon 2001, 28).

The courtroom's elongated form makes manifest that this is an ad hoc tribunal, an unsuitable space lacking ergonomic sensitivity that is adapted for an unintended purpose (see figure 9.3). One defense lawyer described

FIGURE 9.3 Courtroom I at the ICTR.
Source: Courtesy of the ICTR.

the courtroom as being like "a bowling alley." When a protected witness gives testimony, UN-blue curtains are pulled across the middle section of the glass wall. Forced to sit at either end of the public gallery, one sees only the prosecution or the defense. There are closed-circuit television systems in three of the four courtrooms (with four to five cameras mounted to the ceiling), and the images broadcast to screens on lawyers' and judges' desks, to monitors in the public gallery, and to offices throughout the building. Audio is relayed directly through wire-free headsets (with channels for Floor, French, English, and Kinyarwanda interpretations).

Obstructed lines of sight, interpreted and amplified speech, and the instantaneous *paring* (and interpretative mediation) of movement through closed-circuit television images generate multiple aural and visual centers that compete for attention. None of this is conveyed by the transcripts globally accessible on the tribunal's Web site. For example, given the requirement for simultaneous interpretation, all speakers must use microphones. The frequent failure to activate microphones necessitates repetition. Wild hand gestures by lawyers and judges indicate that witnesses should stop speaking or slow down to enable interpretation and stenography (judges and lawyers monitor the transcript on their laptops through real-time transcript software; see Eltringham 2009, 67–69). Documents are held aloft to confirm shared reference, while rejected/depleted documents are violently thrown aside. Protected witnesses are asked to write information to conceal identity, and long periods pass in silent hiatus, save for the amplified scratching sound of a pen. The transcripts omit all this texture and contain only a spectral residue of what is dense, disjointed, disorienting activity (see Clifford 1988, 290).

Haim Gouri (2004) chooses to distill his experience of watching the 1961 trial of Adolf Eichmann into the phrase "facing the glass booth."[6] While "a pane of glass" can be metaphor for what divides "civilization from barbarism" (Buchan 1915, 211), glass also immobilized, protected, and displayed one accused of "barbarous acts" (United Nations 1948).[7] And yet, at the ICTR, the combination of the glass wall of the public gallery, the glass booth of the closed-circuit television technicians, and the glass booths of the interpreters create an impression that it is observers who are encased in glass. Only the presence of those outside these glass enclosures is recorded in the daily case minutes and transcripts. And yet, while visitors in the public gallery ask, "Can they see us?" a judge commented, "We are like fish, people looking at us," and a defense lawyer stated, independently, "It's a little disconcerting having someone watching the fish in the goldfish bowl. This is our water, this is our world."

This is a space that undergoes a ritual of transformation. Before a session, people mill around, wave at acquaintances in the public gallery, adjust their robes, struggle with the unwieldy curtains, untangle translation headsets, and fiddle with air-conditioner controls. Lawyers freely cross to their counterparts' desks ("the prosecutors come and talk to my client about all manner of things, they laugh and joke," a defense lawyer complains).

But this is transformed by the entrance of the judges. Before a curtain is drawn back at the entrance and the judges enter, lawyers, stenographers, and the witness must be in their places and *seated*, for only then can they display deference by standing when the judges, led in by an usher, enter the courtroom. This practice is strenuously enforced. A witness stands in the witness box waiting for the judges to enter. The prosecution counsel, sitting, mouths to the witness to "sit down." A few minutes later, everyone notices the movement of the curtain at the entrance and they stand. But, the usher exclaims, *"Le témoin?"* The witness has gone to the toilet. The curtain remains open, the judges stand at the entrance, everyone in the courtroom is standing. There is laughter, and the witness runs in from the right. Then the usher shouts "all rise," and the procession enters.

The judges' entrance transforms the space into a courtroom. As a defense lawyer commented, "I cannot when the judges are present cross over the courtroom and talk to the prosecution. I cannot go and shake hands with the judge, even if he is a good friend. I cannot pass documents to the judges or prosecution. If I want to speak to the prosecution, I need to ask the judges' permission. When the judges are in the room, it is a courtroom; when they leave, it is just a room."

The transformative effect of the judges' movement, their embodiment of an authority that transforms a room into a courtroom, is matched only by a language which seeks to dis-embody and de-localize authority. On an initial encounter, one assumes that the chamber is the physical courtroom itself. Officially, however, a chamber indicates the triumvirate of judges. For example, the daily case minutes read:

TRIAL DAY 256

1. Remarks / *Remarques*
   a. The Chamber announced that it was still sitting pursuant to Rule 15-bis of the Rules of Procedure and Evidence . . .
2. Decisions & Orders rendered orally / *Décisions & Ordnances rendues oralement* The Chamber reminded the Parties that any cross-examining Party, before conducting its cross-examination, should disclose to the other Parties the documents it intends to use during the cross-examination.

This metonym of three judges as "the Chamber" is not restricted to texts, but is maintained in courtroom exchanges where actors reify the judges as "the chamber," "the court," or "the tribunal." A lawyer may confront a witness by saying that she or he has given testimony "To this Chamber on your oath" or "You have taken an oath before this International Criminal Tribunal to tell the truth." The lawyer may continue by referring to documents "in front of the court" and then ask a witness, "Could you give the Trial Chamber some insight into where you were?" and then, "Chamber, just excuse me, I need to find a name."

But, judges also disassociate themselves from individual authority. Judges form a huddle and then the presiding judge announces, "This will be the ruling of the trial chamber." A witness may query the relevance of a lawyer's question and the presiding judge will interject, "That may be well, Mr. Witness, but the relevance has got to be determined by the trial chamber." A presiding judge may ask a witness, "What should the chamber be aware of now? What is the point?" When a witness has finished testimony, the presiding judge will state, "The chamber does not have any questions." While judges may use alternative metonyms, there is always externalization:

PRESIDING JUDGE: Witness, you see the questions being asked by counsel are asked in order to enable the Bench [*he hesitates and corrects himself*] the Trial Chamber to understand the events as are told by witnesses who lived through the events.

This disassociation is not simply because one person speaks for three. This conflation of three persons into a depersonalized one indicates judicial collusion in creating an image of "transcendent justice" (see "Introduction," this volume), the notion that "justice itself is somewhere else: it cannot be . . . confined totally to persons" (Garapon 2001, 28). Shifting the annunciative locus away from *persons* conveys a sense of a presence that transcends those individuals. The insinuated location of that presence is always elsewhere, always beyond an individual speaker, passed in relays from lawyers to judges and from judges to "somewhere else, always out of reach" (Feldman 2004, 193), a presence *without* a locale.

Legal Accretion

The same illusion of *dis*-locating authority is seen in the Rules of Procedure and Evidence. In the opening epigraph, the prosecution lawyer states, "I would suggest that there's nothing in our rules that require disclosure of a witness's own memoranda," and the daily case minutes quoted earlier refer to "Rule 15-*bis* of the Rules of Procedure and Evidence." These rules are a prominent feature of courtroom exchange. For example, a witness appealing to the presiding judge (regarding questions posed by a cross-examining lawyer) will be told that "one of the functions of the trial chamber is to ensure that the questions put to you by counsel conform with the rules which govern our proceedings." Likewise, a prosecution lawyer contests the alleged nondisclosure of documents to the defense by invoking Rule 66;[8] when a presiding judge asks the defense lawyer whether a document is a judicial record, the prosecution lawyer will invoke Rule 98.[9] Debates concerning Rule 89 ("Rules of Evidence") are a daily occurrence. All in the courtroom exhibit submission to "the cult of the text" (Bourdieu 1987, 851), all evoke the rules.[10] Although only judges possess authority to resolve conflicts of application, all in the courtroom appeal to the rules, with the consequence that the judges' resolutions do not appear as "naked exercises of power," but as the necessary result of a principled interpretation of a unanimously accepted text (Bourdieu 1987, 818; see Woolford, this volume), a text immune from the vagaries of individual arbitrariness. This emulates domestic jurisdictions where legal practitioners defer to an inherited rule system, allowing them to maintain the appearance that they are implementing neutral, impersonal principles. However, as others (see Falk-Moore 2000, 9, 11; Humphreys 1985, 253) have observed, legal rule systems are, in reality, the outcome of continuous, adaptive, piecemeal accretion, although the idea of "core principles" is maintained in order to preserve the aura of consistency.

The same process takes place at the ICTR, but in a highly compressed form. Article 14 of the 1994 Statute reads:

Rules of procedure and evidence: The judges of the International Tribunal for Rwanda shall adopt, for the purpose of proceedings before the International Tribunal for Rwanda, the rules of procedure and evidence for the conduct of the pre-trial phase of the proceedings, trials and appeals, the admission of evidence, the protection of victims and witnesses and other appropriate matters of the International Tribunal for the former Yugoslavia with such changes as they deem necessary. (United Nations 1994, 9)

Although inherited from the ICTY, the rules are constantly revised by the ICTR judiciary at an annual plenary session. Although the number of rules has remained constant at 126, the English translation has, since 1995, expanded from 11,000 to 25,000 words. These amendments are justified as expediting proceedings (see Moghalu 2002, 34), modifications being made in response to omissions/contradictions encountered in the daily practice of the court (see also United Nations 1999). But the judges' need for an autonomous referent is accomplished by the (re)constructive work of the judiciary itself. It is, as anywhere, incremental accretion, not systematic planning, that has generated the Rules of Procedure and Evidence. Pragmatic modifications of the rules are portrayed not as creations, but as clarifications; not as innovations, but revelations of immanent principles. The rules are treated as a consistent whole that existed prior to any amendment, a comprehensive logic awaiting discovery. This systematization creates the appearance of a transcendental basis and the illusion that "all new rules are somehow logically related to old ones, either consciously or unconsciously playing out certain themes throughout . . . The whole then becomes as apparently logical as if it had been intentional" (Falk-Moore 2000, 10).

In this way, the tribunal perpetuates, in compressed microcosm, a feature of domestic jurisdictions. The Rules of Procedure and Evidence are used by all in the courtroom as if they were static and authorless, when in reality they contain formalizations of *their* courtroom practice, formalized by the same judges who evoke the rules as if they were entirely autonomous.[11]

Hybrid Practice

Although the tribunal's Statute and Rules of Procedure and Evidence are formally a hybrid of common/adversarial/Anglo-Saxon and civil/inquisitorial/Continental practice (in the latter, the judge actively interrogates witnesses and defense/prosecution lawyers play a relatively passive role), the rules are essentially adversarial, with trials taking a form almost identical to that in the United Kingdom, other Commonwealth countries, and the United States (see Apuuli 2009, 15–17). Legal practitioners are, however, drawn from both legal systems. Judges must represent the "principal legal systems of the world" (United Nations 1994, article 12c), while defense lawyers must only fulfill the criteria of having been "admitted to practice law in a State, or is a professor of law at a university or similar academic institution and has at least 10 years relevant experience" (ICTR 2004, article 13[1]). The common law form of trials does not, however, appear to concern civil law practitioners (see Eltringham 2008, 314–316). For example, a judge drawn from a civil law jurisdiction observed, "You know, as a boy I used to watch Perry Mason and he would say 'objection' and the judge would say 'sustained' or 'over-ruled.' Now, I do it even though it's not part of the civil law system of my country and it gives me great pleasure. There's an objection and there are those two catch phrases, 'sustained' and 'over-ruled,' it's very efficient so why not use it?"

However, the technical, rule-centered dilemmas that hybridity raises have been the subject of extensive discussion (Ambos 2003; Ellis 1997; Nice 2001; Tochilovsky 2004; United Nations 1999, paragraph 82). These debates concentrate on civil law features in this predominantly common law/adversarial court. For example, that a presiding judge may order a party to shorten the estimated length of the examination-in-chief of witnesses (Rule 73*bis*C and 73*ter*C); that a judge may question a witness at any time (Rule 85B); that presiding judges may summon their own witnesses or order a party to produce additional evidence (Rule 98); that the judges may admit any relevant evidence they consider to have "probative value," including hearsay evidence (Rule 89). For some, this textual syncretism has been unproblematic, that at the "level of international criminal procedure, the common–civil law divide has been overcome" (Ambos 2003, 34). This upbeat assessment is borne out by judges at the tribunal:

> It's astonishing, there's so little tension. People are coming from different legal, cultural and linguistic backgrounds, it's amazing. What people say about the civil and common law traditions, that it's a war, is myth. In all my time here, none of the difference of opinion [between judges] was based on where we came from: a civil or common law background. You have to leave your luggage at the doorstep and go through that door with an open mind. It's the differences that create the richness. (Judge, civil law)

> The most fascinating and challenging aspect of working here are the various backgrounds of the judges: the common law and civil law approaches. When we first started in 1996, when there were deliberations, one could see that each person brought their own baggage, their own background. But, there was a give and take element when we gave each other the opportunity. This was most surprising, we approached an issue differently, but the end results were the same. I

cannot really explain it, you have to live through it. I don't even think about it now. (Judge, common law)

Such apparent accommodation leaves unconsidered issues regarding the manner in which hybridity is negotiated and embodied performatively in the courtroom. Beyond the mutually acknowledged texts to which practitioners refer, the "judicial field" is also organized around a legal *habitus*. In domestic legal systems, practitioners have in common both the "written and unwritten laws" of the judicial field where the latter refers to acquired, intuitive dispositions that constitute an embodied competence (see Bourdieu 1987, 831, 820; Woolford, this volume).[12] This intuitive legal *habitus* is present (although in different forms) in all legal systems and sustains the self-conception, self-recognition, and self-reproduction of legal professionals. Under normal circumstances, these dispositions are not explicitly acknowledged.[13]

At the ICTR, however, diverse provenance reveals divergent assumptions. In the opening illustration, the prosecution counsel said, "it must be a Californian practice, because I practiced in New York and I've never heard an application quite like this one." While this draws attention to diversity within formal, common law procedure, common law lawyers also suggest there is a difference in disposition:

> Mr. —— [UK prosecution lawyer] and I are very different in the way we practice law, but in the eyes of civil law lawyers it's very different again. In the U.S. we're aggressive, litigious, it's not elegant, it's in your face. Whether the court likes you is not important. Mr. —— [U.S. defense lawyer] insults the bench, but it's not deliberate. We do that all the time in the U.S. In contrast, Mr. —— [prosecution lawyer] is very gentile, solicitous of the bench. (Prosecution lawyer, common law)

> Among American lawyers, there's a lack of due deference towards the judges, a feeling of trying to get around them, rather than defer to them, not in some English obsequious way, but to realize that they make the decisions and if you push them they will push back. You must find the right tone or it sounds like you're treating them like idiots. You say something like, "Your honor may have thought," goes down better to show that it was their idea. It has more elegance, adds to the sanctity of the proceedings. (Prosecution lawyer, common law)

Although one should remain aware that when asked to externalize intuitive behavior, lawyers may propose stylized versions of their practice that are akin to "folk models" of legal practice (see Comaroff and Roberts 1981, 9; Just 1986, 60n17), the lawyers quoted earlier are implying that divergence within common law practice is as much about deportment as procedure. Equally, where practitioners drawn from the same common law tradition

(United Kingdom) describe "their" practice and its emulation by others, it is by means of somatic performance resistant to precise description. This is illustrated by comments of three British barristers on the influence of a fourth British barrister on the courtroom:

> In our trial, the Americans and French have adopted Crown Court etiquette. Part of the reason was Mr. —— [UK defense lawyer]. He imposed it by doing it with authority and attractively rather than by dint of commanding it. If you try to operate to high standards with a few demonstrations, by dint of influence and example, you can affect the people around you. (Defense lawyer, common law)

> The whole feeling of the courtroom was different when he was there, the way in which his behavior, his way of acting, had an effect on the whole defense, even on the prosecution and the judges themselves. Everyone responded to the way he acted. (Defense lawyer, common law)

> Those sort of people, they have the ear of the court. There's a social dynamic. Others watch someone who has the ear of the court. It brings everyone else's game up. It's like playing with a great footballer. People follow the game of a good person. (Prosecution lawyer, common law)

What legal practitioners themselves state regarding disjuncture, negotiation, and emulation of practice is important, but more important is what they do (see Holy and Stuchlik 1983, 11). An illustration is the seemingly mundane practice of standing, for it is considered by some to be an enactment of a common law ethos (Bourdieu 2003, 77), sine qua non:

> Generally, in Commonwealth countries, two counsel are not on their feet at the same time. An English barrister will expect to sit down when someone else rises to speak. But the French will continue to stand and even address the court sitting down. You never address the court if not on your feet, the court would never hear it. The French counsel do not have that etiquette. In court one expects good manners, to listen to one person at a time; otherwise, you don't know who to pay attention to. (Judge, common law)

> Etiquette is very important in the common law tradition I am used to. For example, we have to tell lawyers that when their opposite is speaking you must sit down. These are important etiquette matters. It looks offensive to us.[14] (Judge, common law)

At the first trial I attended in 2005, the presiding judge, prosecution lawyer, and defense lawyer were English-trained barristers. During the cross-examination of a prosecution witness by the defense lawyer, the prosecution lawyer stood up to object to a particular question. The defense lawyer refused on this occasion to yield, saying, "I am not going to talk across the court," at which point the presiding judge said, "I will not have two counsel on their feet at the same time." This established in my mind that the tribunal had adopted the common law principle by which standing simultaneously indicates the desire to speak and grants permission to speak once a speaking opponent sits. The act of standing is synonymous with speaking. For example, a common law judge admonishing a lawyer she considers to be objecting prematurely says, "you get to your feet too frequently"; another common law judge says, "Documents must be disclosed before a cross-examiner gets to his feet." Likewise, a civil law defense lawyer says, "I see my learned friend is on his feet," and then sits down; a civil law judge commented, "Telling them to sit down is also a message to shut up." This metaphorical language and somatic movement appeared to have been universally adopted.

As my experience of trials grew, however, my assumed nexus of standing and speech was challenged. During a two-hour session in October 2006, presided over by three judges all from common law jurisdictions, the defense and prosecution lawyers stood and conducted a direct discussion across the room. There was, unlike in 2005, no censure from the presiding judge. The following day I attended a different trial with a common law presiding judge. At one point a U.S. (common law) defense lawyer made an objection, but the U.S. prosecution lawyer did not sit down, brushing the objection aside. Again there was no censure from the presiding judge. In a third trial, however, the two opposing U.S. lawyers enacted the etiquette faultlessly.

This suggested that the linking of speech and standing was a negotiable feature of common law etiquette. I was, therefore, struck by the following incident. The court convened around 8:45 A.M. The two co-judges were both Commonwealth (common law), while the presiding judge, although civil law, had on previous days acknowledged a lawyer's desire to speak by saying, "Mr. —— is on his feet." While this implied adoption of the speech/standing nexus, the U.S. prosecution lawyer, who had examined a prosecution witness over the last couple of days, never sat down when the Commonwealth defense lawyer rose to make an objection. On this day, it was the Commonwealth defense lawyer's turn to cross-examine the same prosecution witness. After a few minutes, the defense lawyer's co-counsel rose to assist his colleague, at which point the following dialogue ensued:

CO-JUDGE: Mr. ——, just for good order, courtroom order, isn't it possible that when you want to stand up, you let Mr. —— sit down and when you want to sit down, you let . . .

DEFENSE COUNSEL: No. No. Let me explain . . .

CO-JUDGE: I mean, if you are sharing it question by question, that's fine. But let us know who is on their feet.

DEFENSE CO-COUNSEL: [*explains he is assisting his colleague*].

CO-JUDGE: I have grown up in the common law tradition, and there courtroom practice requires that there is always one counsel on his feet, never two counsels.

While this censure was clearly inconsistent given the earlier behavior of the common law (U.S.) prosecution lawyer, the real significance of this statement is that the judge would make it at all. The very act of explicitly articulating the principle suggests a consciousness of a breakdown in habitual practice, an anxiety to reestablish a norm. This need to explicitly appeal to what was assumed to be implicitly shared was also enacted by lawyers. For example, an English defense lawyer said to an African (Commonwealth) prosecution lawyer, "I was on my feet first and in courtroom etiquette whoever is on their feet first continues, and he knows that, and he knows that he should not interrupt counsel on their feet."

All involved in this, and the previous, incident are Commonwealth-trained lawyers. The axiom of standing/speaking is, it appears, only evoked among affiliates. The confrontation is among those who emanate from domestic systems where this etiquette is normally enacted intuitively. While the amorphous notions of "elegance," "tone," "influence," and "whether the court likes you" do not lend themselves to the enforcement of habitual practice; the somatic act of standing does. Habitual practice must be maintained by those from whom it is expected in the midst of those from whom it is not. A supposedly successful textual hybridity of formal procedural rules does not suppress a desire to enforce habitual embodied acts and the preservation of judicial *habitus*.

Summary

The ICTR is considered to be a central feature of an emerging "global architecture of international criminal justice" (Moghalu 2002, 39). Such notoriety, however, relies on the local micro-architecture and micro-practices of the institution itself. As discussed, naturalized cultural forms adopted from noninternational judicial contexts continue to be called upon to symbolically and discursively create a sense of transcendent justice. The disjunctures of intuitive (often embodied) practice affirm that "international justice" remains a social activity dependent on socially acquired assumptions and expectations, that enacting law and generating global judicial commodities requires human agents. As Antoine Garapon (2001, 45) notes, "[The court] only exists by the life that we give it. Without judges and lawyers, without skills, without its density of emotion, without that concentration of anguish and at times joy, without that race for notoriety, advancement or successful outcome, without hurried, worried or idle people, the court does not exist." Given that the "genocidal mentality" (Lifton and Markusen 1990) forcibly naturalizes constructs, obliterates indeterminacy, projects innate predispositions immune to reformation, and, in so doing, rejects the situated acts by which humans negotiate their social reality, an appreciation of human agency is undoubtedly appropriate in a site where crimes that have "outraged the conscience of mankind" are considered (United Nations 1948).

NOTES

I am grateful to the Nuffield Foundation (SGS/32034) and British Academy (SG-47168) for supporting this research. Research was conducted under COSTECH (Tanzanian Commission for Science and Technology) Research Permit No. 2006-304-CC-2006-122. Thanks to the anonymous reviewers for their comments.

1. Protection measures are found in Rules 69 and 75 of the tribunal's rules of procedure and evidence: "Rule 75(B)i (a) Expunging names and identifying information from the Tribunal's public records; (b) Non-disclosure to the public of any records identifying the victim."

2. All quotations are taken from interviews conducted by the author in Arusha between 2005 and 2007.

3. "*Determined* to put an end to such crimes . . . *Convinced* that . . . the prosecution of persons . . . would enable this aim to be achieved and would contribute to the process of national reconciliation and to the restoration and maintenance of peace, [and] the prosecution of persons . . . will contribute to ensuring that such violations are halted and effectively redressed" (United Nations 1994, 1–2).

4. The criteria by which accused are selected has evolved through a pragmatic shift, from an initial maximalist criteria that "the [ICTR] shall have the power to prosecute persons responsible for serious violations of international humanitarian law" (United Nations 1994, article 1) to "the Prosecutor's strategy is to prosecute . . . those persons bearing the *highest responsibility*" (United Nations 2003, 6; emphasis added).

5. As Paul Connerton (1990, 72) observes, "Many forms of habitual skilled remembering illustrate a keeping of the past in mind that, without ever adverting to its historical origin, nevertheless re-enacts the past in our present conduct. In habitual memory the past is, as it were, sedimented in the body."

6. "The glass separating him from us is now, once again, just bulletproofing, after a terrible, prolonged attempt to turn it into a reducing lens" (Gouri 2004, 245).

7. As Lawrence Douglas (2001, 145) suggests, "the glass booth is transformed from a structure intended to protect the accused into a cage, a structure meant to confine and render available for scrutiny a dangerous and alien creature."

8. Rule 66: Disclosure of Exculpatory and Other Relevant Material.

9. Rule 98: Power of Chambers to Order Production of Additional Evidence.

10. As Paul Connerton (1989, 97) suggests, "A legal system has to be made concretely valid in the present by being interpreted."

11. Rules thus remove "norms from the contingency of a particular situation [and] authorizes and fosters the logic of precedent upon which specifically juridical thought and action are based" (Bourdieu 1987, 845).

12. As Bourdieu (2003, 72n1) notes, "The word *disposition* seems particularly suited to express what is covered by the concept of habitus . . . a *way of being, a habitual state* (especially of the body) and, in particular, a *predisposition, tendency, propensity, or inclination.*"

13. Erving Goffman (1959, 108) makes a similar observation: "In the study of social establishments it is important to describe the prevailing standards of decorum; it is difficult to do so because informants . . . tend to take many of these standards for granted, not realising they have done so until an accident, or crisis, or peculiar circumstance occurs."

14. As Pierre Bourdieu (2003, 78) notes, "Habitus which have been produced by different *modes of generation* [impose] different definitions of the impossible, the possible, and the probable, cause one group to experience as natural or reasonable practices or aspirations which another group finds unthinkable or scandalous, and vice versa."

REFERENCES

Ambos, Kai. 2003. "International Criminal Procedure: 'Adversarial,' 'Inquisitorial' or Mixed?" *International Criminal Law Review* 3 (1): 1–37.

Apuuli, Kasaija Phillip. 2009. "Procedural Due Process and the Prosecution of Genocide Suspects in Rwanda." *Journal of Genocide Research* 11 (1): 11–30.

Arendt, Hannah. 1994. *Eichmann in Jerusalem: A Report on the Banality of Evil.* Harmondsworth: Penguin.

Bourdieu, Pierre. 1987. "The Force of Law: Toward a Sociology of the Juridical Field." *Hastings Journal of Law* 38 (5): 814–853.

———. 2003. *Outline of a Theory of Practice.* Cambridge: Cambridge University Press.

Buchan, John. 1915. *The Power House.* London: Thomas Nelson and Sons Ltd.

Buur, Lars. 2003. "Monumental History: Visibility and Invisibility in the Work of the South African Truth and Reconciliation Commission." In *Commissioning the Past: Understanding South Africa's Truth and Reconciliation Commission,* ed. Deborah Posel and Graeme Simpson. Johannesburg: Witwatersrand University Press.

Clifford, James. 1988. *The Predicament of Culture: Twentieth Century Ethnography, Literature and Art.* Cambridge, MA: Harvard University Press.

Comaroff, John L., and Simon Roberts. 1981. *Rules and Processes: The Cultural Logic of Dispute in an African Context.* Chicago: University of Chicago Press.

Connerton, Paul. 1990. *How Societies Remember.* Cambridge: Cambridge University Press.

Douglas, Lawrence. 2001. *The Memory of Judgment: Making Law and History in the Trials of the Holocaust.* New Haven, CT: Yale University Press.

Ellis, Mark. 1997. "Achieving Justice before the International War Crimes Tribunal: Challenges for the Defense Counsel." *Duke Journal of Comparative and International Law* 7 (2): 519–536.

Eltringham, Nigel. 2008. "'A War Crimes Community': The Legacy of the International Criminal Tribunal for Rwanda *beyond* Jurisprudence." *New England Journal of International and Comparative Law* 14 (2): 309–318.

———. 2009. "'We Are Not a Truth Commission': Fragmented Narratives and the Historical Record at the International Criminal Tribunal for Rwanda." *Journal of Genocide Research* 11 (1): 55–79.

Falk-Moore, Sally. 2000. *Law as Process: An Anthropological Approach*. 2nd ed. Oxford: James Currey.

Feldman, Allen. 2004. "Memory Theatres, Virtual Witnessing, and the Trauma-Aesthetic." *Biography* 27 (I): 163–202.

Garapon, Antoine. 2001. *Bien juger: Essai sur le rituel judiciare*. Paris: Éditions Odile Jacob.

Goffman, Erving. 1959. *The Presentation of Self in Everyday Life*. New York: Doubleday Anchor.

Gouri, Haim. 2004. *Facing the Glass Booth: The Jerusalem Trial of Adolf Eichmann*. Trans. Michael Swirsky. Detroit: Wayne State University Press.

Holy, Ladislav, and Milan Stuchlik. 1983. *Actions, Norms and Representations: Foundations of Anthropological Inquiry*. Cambridge: Cambridge University Press.

Humphreys, Sally. 1985. "Law as Discourse." *History and Anthropology* I (2): 241–264.

International Criminal Tribunal for Rwanda (ICTR). 2004. *Directive on the Assignment of Defence Counsel*. Arusha: ICTR.

———. 2005. *Testifying before the International Criminal Tribunal for Rwanda*. Arusha: ICTR.

International Crisis Group. 2001. *International Criminal Tribunal for Rwanda: Justice Delayed*. Brussels: International Crisis Group.

International Military Tribunal. 1947. *Trial of the Major War Criminals before the International Military Tribunal*. Vol. I. Nuremberg: International Military Tribunal.

Jacob, Robert. 1994. *Images de la Justice: Essai sur l'iconographie judiciaire du Moyen Âge à l'Âge classique*. Paris: Le Léopard d'Or.

Just, Peter. 1986. "Let the Evidence Fit the Crime: Evidence, Law, and 'Sociological Truth' among the Dou Donggo." *American Ethnologist* 13 (I): 43–61.

Lifton, Robert Jay, and Eric Markusen. 1990. *The Genocidal Mentality: Nazi Holocaust and Nuclear Threat*. London: Macmillan.

Merry, Sally Engle. 1997. "Legal Pluralism and Transnational Culture: The Ka Ho'okolokolonui Kanaka Maoli Tribunal, Hawai'i, 1993." In *Human Rights, Culture and Context: Anthropological Perspectives*, ed. Richard Wilson. London: Pluto Press.

———. 2006. "Transnational Human Rights and Local Activism: Mapping the Middle." *American Anthropologist* 108 (I): 38–51.

Moghalu, Kingsley Chiedu. 2002. "Image and Reality of War Crimes Justice: External Perceptions of the International Criminal Tribunal for Rwanda." *Fletcher Forum of World Affairs* 26 (2): 21–46.

Neave, Airey. 1978. *Nuremberg: A Personal Record of the Trial of the Major Nazi War Criminals*. London: Hodder and Stoughton.

Nice, Geoffrey. 2001. "Trials of Imperfection." *Leiden Journal of International Law* 14:383–397.

Powell, Michael, and Emeric Pressburger. 1946. *A Matter of Life and Death*. London: Archers.

Taussig, Michael. 1992. *The Nervous System*. New York: Routedge.

Taylor, Telford. 1993. *The Anatomy of the Nuremberg Trials: A Personal Memoir*. London: Bloomsbury.

Tochilovsky, Vladimir. 2004. "International Criminal Justice: 'Strangers in the Foreign System.'" *Criminal Law Forum* 15 (3): 319–344.

United Nations. 1946. *Report of the Secretary-General: Official Seal and Emblem of the United Nations*. New York: United Nations.

———. 1948. *Universal Declaration of Human Rights*. New York: United Nations.

————. 1994. *Statute of the International Criminal Tribunal for Rwanda.* New York: United Nations.

————. 1999. *Report of the Expert Group to Conduct a Review of the Effective Operation and Functioning of the ICTY and the ICTR.* November 11. UN Doc. A/54/634. New York: United Nations.

————. 2003. *Letter dated 3 October 2003 from the Secretary-General addressed to the President of the Security Council.* October 6 . UN Doc. S/2003/946. New York: United Nations.

————. 2008. *Security Council resolution 1824 (2008).* July 18. UN Doc. S/RES/1824 (2008).

West, Rebecca. 1984. *A Train of Powder.* London: Virago.

10

▶▶▶▶▶▶▶▶▶▶▶▶▶▶▶ ◀◀◀◀◀◀◀◀◀◀◀◀◀◀◀

Building a Monument

Intimate Politics of "Reconciliation" in Post-1965 Bali

LESLIE DWYER

What are the politics of speaking the violent past, of investing it with social form and force in the search for a different kind of future? How are ideas of justice evoked in motion, apprehended in their travels across national, cultural, gendered, and generational divisions, and made to speak to particular kinds of experience? And where might anthropology position itself in the contested aftermath of violent conflict, where weighty terms like "history," "victimization," and "reconciliation" occupy the horizons of political attention? In this essay, I draw upon long-term ethnographic fieldwork with survivors of the 1965–1966 state-sponsored anticommunist massacres in Bali, Indonesia, to think through these issues. Describing some of the heated debates provoked by a project to memorialize the violence, I explore how globalizing discourses of truth, peacebuilding, community, and social repair are shaping intimate practices of narrating personal and familial histories in Bali, and how these localized contests might speak to broader efforts to counter the long-term effects of conflict.

Since the fall of former president Soeharto's thirty-two-year-long dictatorship in 1998, Indonesia has joined the growing ranks of nations seen to require transitional justice efforts. Dubious of the ability of Indonesia's judicial system to hold figures of the former regime to account, national and international organizations have called upon Indonesia's government to form a Truth and Reconciliation Commission, to revise the national history curriculum to acknowledge political abuses during the Soeharto era, and to restore the civil rights of former political prisoners and those with familial ties to alleged communists. Across the archipelago, nongovernmental organizations have also promoted programs to collect oral histories from survivors of violence, to create support groups where experiences of suffering can be shared, and to enact conflict resolution initiatives in regions with legacies of bloodshed.[1] As an anthropologist conducting research on the charged aftermath of violence in Bali, both my fieldwork trajectories and the political concerns I shared with many of my interlocutors brought me into close engagement with these emergent discourses of transitional justice and the relationships between anthropology and powerful globalizing frameworks for knowing and doing. Working in partnership with a Balinese anthropologist/human rights advocate, and building ties with both Indonesian activists and survivors of violence, I have grown increasingly supportive of intellectual work in solidarity with social justice claims—of what the late Pierre Bourdieu called "a scholarship with commitment" (2003, 17). Yet at the same time, I recognize that such a pathway is not always clear. Postconflict social landscapes frequently tend to be fraught and treacherous, marked not only by lingering wounds of violence but also by competing interpretations and interests, making solidarity a necessarily partial alignment. Aftermaths of violence are also often arenas organized by what I think of as deflective terms—key words such as "peace," "justice," "reconciliation," and "healing" that possess a potent ability to divert critical engagement with their premises, genealogies, and uses. Yet it is precisely the power of such terms to resist analysis by painting it as cynical, undermining, and (over) intellectually elitist that I suggest needs to be more rigorously examined, and where I believe anthropology can provide especially relevant insights.

These deflective terms flourish in the field of transitional justice, and it is perhaps unsurprising that anthropology's position vis-à-vis its discourses— including the ideological assumptions and institutional habits encoded in calls for democratization, postconflict reconciliation, psychosocial repair, recovery from trauma, capacity-building, and civil society development— has been a complex and often troubled one (see Hinton, this volume). Although there is by now a vital and growing stream of anthropological work explicitly committed to an "engaged" (Bourgois 2006; Sanford 2006; Smith 1999; Warren 2006) or "public" (Borofsky 2004) stance, transcending older disciplinary dichotomies between theoretical and applied work, intellectual and political rapprochement between anthropologists and those professionals charged with programming social change is still often tenuous and hesitant. Anthropologists have frequently been suspicious of the one-size-fits-all character of programs that assume, for instance, that truth commissions based on the 1994 South African model (Coxshall 2005; Shaw 2005, 2007) or clinical interventions to treat post-traumatic stress disorder among victims of violence (Breslau 2004; Dwyer and Santikarma 2007; Kleinman 1995) are necessary or beneficial in all settings, showing little regard for local understandings of truth and justice (Goodale 2009; Goodale and Merry 2007; Theidon 2007) or local politics of speaking, subjectivity, or individual and social well-being. Anthropologists have also, from their vantage points on everyday social life and community concerns, often questioned the wisdom of programs that prioritize attention to formal political structures—which in Indonesia have focused on constitutional and judicial reform, government transparency, free and fair elections, and increased autonomy of provinces vis-à-vis the central state—rather than to the informal social networks, political narratives, and enactments of symbolic violence that structure ongoing inequalities despite institutional realignments and legislative changes (see Sanford and Burnet, this volume). With their commitments to conversing with nonelites in their own languages, anthropologists are also more likely to encounter the critical perspectives of those who are the objects of such interventions—which for many of my interlocutors in Indonesia have included not only a continuing ambivalence about the social, political, and economic ramifications of speaking of the past, and a critique of oversimplistic models of culture and community, but also a keen suspicion that transitional justice is "third world justice," one that accepts a lack of government accountability for past abuses in the name of consolidating peace and democracy and channeling flows of capital (see Drexler, this volume).

For their part, policymakers and program specialists have often bemoaned what is frequently seen as anthropology's haughty intellectualist—or naive populist—disregard of the practical exigencies of social and political transformation, or its tendency to undermine aid efforts through deconstructive readings of program goals that dead-end into the unhelpful evocation of complexity. Despite increasing programmatic emphasis on cultural sensitivity and local participation in transitional justice efforts, anthropologists themselves are often critiqued for a hesitancy—sometimes interpreted as an ornery refusal—to speak in prescriptive terms. Such critiques may constitute an important push toward more collaborative and accountable anthropological practices, but they may also be used to justify a comfortable lack of engagement with the difficult translations anthropological perspectives demand, with a director of a U.S. Agency for International Development division recently warning anthropologists that their critical ambivalence about universalist human rights paradigms risks rendering them of diminished relevance to human rights work (Hyman 2006).

It is tempting—and quite typical, I think—to try to resolve such divisions by resorting to platitudes about the importance of cross-disciplinary conversations and collaborations, or to draw upon metaphors of bridge-building and cross-pollination. Yet simply splitting the difference—asking anthropologists to contribute their "local knowledge" (Geertz 1983) to attempts to ameliorate injustices instead of disinterestedly describing them, or demanding that policymakers seek more fluent understandings of cultural difference to better implement their projects—often ends up reifying problematic distinctions between the local and the universal, or analyzing and doing, or academia and activism—and fundamentally misrepresenting what many of us actually *do*. Within such framings, anthropologists are left with their small-scale communities and their obscure cultural concerns, while practitioners and policymakers are positioned at the macro edge of an imaginary scale of influence, engaged in world-shaping work. Rather than perpetuate such distinctions by framing anthropology's role mainly as a translator of local cultures into universally relevant terms, to be taken up by expert institutions and actors, I am more interested in questioning the definitions of "doing" implicit in such divides. Viewing the production and circulation of discourses and the population of zones of debate as activist endeavors, one of my interests here is in tracing how the stories Balinese do and do not tell about their pasts and their futures shift the social and material worlds available to them. In other words, rethinking what we mean when we speak of justice, or reconciliation, or culture, is itself a crucial political intervention. It is in this spirit that I read Balinese engagements with transitional justice ideas, attending to how survivors of violence are called upon to become the kinds of speaking, participatory subjects, reconciled with each other and with the state, appropriate to a postdictatorship democracy and a liberalized tourist economy, and how the Balinese I know have incorporated, dodged, and critiqued these portrayals and the places they offer for new national subjects.

Genealogies of Remembering

July of 2005 marked almost forty years since state-sponsored violence led to the deaths of some half to one million Indonesians—including 80,000–100,000 Balinese, or 5–8 percent of the island's population—and the imprisonment, surveillance, and curtailment of civil rights for hundreds of thousands of other alleged communists.[2] During the long decades of Soeharto's rule (1966–1998), official histories of the violence described it as a necessary defense against an antinational leftist threat, with alternate narratives risking harsh repression by the military-backed state apparatus. In Bali, the tourist center of the nation, tales of the terror and its lingering legacies were especially absent from the public domain, seen as challenging not only to state control but also to the smooth flow of foreign exchange. Yet with the end of the Soeharto era, new political possibilities seemed to open. In a village on the edge of Bali's capital city of Denpasar, a group of young students and activists whose parents and grandparents had lived through the violence decided to construct what they called the "1965 Park." This small square of lawn and concrete in the midst of their extended family compound was, to my knowledge, the first such effort in Indonesia to materially memorialize the experiences of those who had been targeted by the state in 1965. Inspired by transnational discourses of transitional justice and reconciliation that stress the importance of publicly articulating the truths of the past, these young people hoped to create a monument to a community's suffering that could act as a catalyst to local political transformation and as a liberatory challenge to erasure of the massacres from official Indonesian histories.

Yet, as I detail, this project to commemorate and consolidate a community through explicit reference to a violent past soon proved to be far more complex than the park's planners had first envisioned. What emerged from this project was not a collective social memory standing outside of, and in resistant opposition to, state history. Nor was it a brave breaking of the silence, a straightforward challenge to power that could coalesce political will. Instead, the park provoked claims and counterclaims over suffering and its representation, memory and its multiple forms, and the possibilities and limits of community after violence. The youth of this family, in their attempts to create a space for reflection on history and a reimagination of the future, faced questioning and often opposition from those less persuaded by the promise of truth-telling condensed in calls for reconciliation. By building a monument to what they saw as a common traumatic legacy, they ended up exposing the fault lines that underlie postconflict community, forcing a local rethinking of a generic subject of suffering and ultimately creating incentives for moving beyond a binary politics of perpetrators and victims, remembering and forgetting, and memory and its repression or recuperation to articulate hybrid notions of justice.

Before telling the story of the 1965 Park and the debates that it provoked, I want to first note that this space, novel as it certainly was, possessed a particular genealogy. This might seem self-evident: that reflections on a past are social practices that emerge historically and in often-critical relation to other ways of imagining and engaging. Yet it seems necessary to stress this, given the political work that has been tasked to a concept of collective memory and to its presumed location in a closed store of shared experience. Postconflict programs to promote psychosocial repair or community reconciliation in the wake of violence have become increasingly concerned with their cultural sensitivity—a laudable corrective to generic peace-building programs and policies that were critiqued for having imposed top-down models on diverse histories of conflict. Yet an enthusiasm to enact a cultural mandate may override sensitivity to how a sense of community may often be one of the first casualties of violence—and to how contests over the boundaries and definitions of community and culture may have helped to funnel state terror deep into intimate domains of life. Postconflict interventions that identify and target communities for civic empowerment or the resolution of social tensions may also work to detract attention away from broader political inequalities to the extent that they legitimize outsourcing of states'

responsibilities for the well-being of their citizens and leave ongoing officially sanctioned physical or structural violence outside of their program
purviews (Cruikshank 1999; Li 2007; Paley 2001; Rose 1999). In this case, the
Balinese youth who founded the 1965 Park were not enacting a spontaneous
local cultural response to a history of violence and injustice. Nor were they
representing a bounded community's position on a past. Rather, they consciously drew upon what they had seen or heard of projects to memorialize
violence elsewhere, as well as on a history of contested claims about Balinese
culture and its ability to account for violence and give power to new kinds
of futures.

Many of the park's planners had, as schoolchildren, visited or read
about the New Order's monumental Museum of the Indonesian Communist
Party's Treachery in Jakarta, which concretized an official history of the military's triumph over leftist threat in celebratory statuary, gruesome dioramas, and a blood-red reconstruction of the infamous "Crocodile Hole" well
(*Lubang Buaya*), where communist coup plotters were said to have dumped
the bodies of six Indonesian generals on September 30, 1965, provoking the
patriotic defense of the nation.[3] All of them had also heard the public calls
to commemorate with a monument the victims of the 2002 Bali bombings,
those 202 mainly foreign tourists who had perished in the terrorist attack
that the then-governor of Bali termed "the worst tragedy the island had ever
experienced."[4] The 1965 Park was to be, they explained, a kind of counter-
monument to these suspect framings of the past that, in their eyes, concealed far more than they revealed in their hard stone surfaces. For them,
the Jakarta museum wrote a teleology of a triumphant nation, set against
the subversive figure of the "communist" whose alleged atrocities could be
safely contained by the state's glass-encased dioramas. In contrast, the 1965
Park would remember those denied not only citizenship but a recognition
of humanity, challenging the regime's claims to represent its people. And
where the Bali bomb memorial called for the mourning of an innocent island
of peace and social harmony senselessly attacked by Islamist outsiders, the
1965 Park would draw aside the curtain of Bali's exoticism, exposing internal
histories of terror and betrayal that challenged the touristic commodification of silence about past violence. And in distinction to both of these
monuments, the 1965 Park would be designed not as an authoritative text to
be passively read, but as a space that, once empty, could now be filled by a
community's active engagements with its experiences and with each other.

Yet by choosing to approach the past through the medium of a memorial park, these young Balinese set in place certain social framings. Like
most monuments, the park did not simply condense a particular version of
the past in built form. The gestures of memorials are not only temporal but
also spatial and social in the sense of mapping out an imagined audience of

those who experienced history and those who read it for traces of a future. They are not simply mimetic of a shared community consciousness, collective memory, or cultural trauma, but interpolative, positioning subjects in particular postures of grief and outrage, and orienting activists in ways that sometimes obscure the powers that mediate public inscription. And in the tense aftermath of violence, where suspicion and surveillance have been embedded in social life, this process of delineating a community defined by shared origins in and perspectives on the past faced multiple challenges.

Negotiating Claims to the Past

One of the most powerful questions the presence of the 1965 Park provoked was what it meant to mark off a social and political category of victim of violence whose suffering should be acknowledged. Since the 1998 fall of Soeharto's regime and the slow emergence into Indonesian public culture of stories of state-sponsored terror and repression, those who had been targeted as communists or labeled as having an "unclean [political] environment" (*tidak bersih lingkungkan*) due to their familial or associational ties to alleged leftists have had the opportunity to recast their identities as victims (*korban*). National organizations such as the Foundation for Research on Victims of Massacre (Yayasan Penelitian Korban Pembantaian or YPKP) and the Organization for Victims of the New Order (Paguyuban Korban Orde Baru or PAKORBA) have carved a space (albeit small) out of the public domain through which to circulate pamphlets, books, and conference papers; to advocate for changes in legislation that continue to discriminate against those with alleged communist ties;[5] and to gather those who were impacted by the 1965–1966 violence. While in Western activist circles, the term "victim" has often been denigrated as denying the agency of survivors of violence, this new marker of identification has been felt as empowering by many Indonesians, who have used this designation to claim rights that had been unjustly abrogated by the state, to form social links among those who had been alienated from full national or local belonging, or to create shared languages to describe experiences that were felt to exceed the bounds of commonplace speech. Indeed, I frequently heard those who had attended the sporadic meetings of the small-scale "victims of 1965" advocacy organization in Bali say that they had found these gatherings crucial for providing a sense of identity and acknowledgement that had been shattered by the New Order state, whose vast bureaucratic apparatus of identity cards, official "letters of good behavior" and mechanisms of monitoring had reached deep into hamlets and families to deprive those alleged to have communist ties of both citizenship and social acceptance. In addition to evoking these national efforts, the statements made by the 1965 Park youth about their determination to create "a space for victims to share their experiences" were also comfortably resonant with powerful globalizing assumptions about the prerequisites for social repair, which stress the importance of attending to victims' voices, and with posing an inherent connection between talking about the past and personal or communal healing.[6] Yet at the same time, by using this potent language to speak of and as victims of violence, these young Balinese were asserting a social and political identity that privileged certain kinds of historical narratives.

Once the 1965 Park had been planted with lush grass and the low concrete wall surrounding it set with stones arranged to shape the numbers "1965, 1965, 1965," its planners held an open discussion to lay out their aims. Their enthusiasm was palpable but not universally shared. Out of the several dozen attendees at the first planning meeting, held on the open lawn of the park, many remained silent. Meanwhile, almost a hundred other inhabitants of the 150-plus member family compound chose not to attend, either remaining in their individual houses or walking quickly past the park, catching snippets of the conversation before moving on. At first, I was unsure if their nonattendance had signaled tensions within the family about the park's presence or if these absences expressed a tacit decision to let the youth proceed on their course. A few days after the meeting, however, I spoke with Madé,[7] one of the young people who sat in silence as his peers spoke of the need for victims to tell their stories. He told me how the talk brought his memories back to when he was a young boy and had caught a fascinating glimpse of his grandfather's sword, hidden in the recesses of a cabinet. He said he had not thought much about it until the park's inauguration, when he felt called upon to take up the name of victim. The next day, he visited his grandparents and heard their reluctantly told story of how his grandfather had joined an anticommunist militia, helping to slaughter residents of a neighboring village, in what he claimed was an attempt to ensure the safety of his immediate family. Madé's grandfather had insisted that he too was a victim, forced to shed blood in the service of the state, which then abandoned him to face the suspicion of his neighbors and his own disturbing guilt. "What kind of victims are we? And how can I tell this story to those whose family members were killed?" Madé asked me, sharing a deeply painful sense that the 1965 Park's narratives could not easily ascribe him a political position as supportive of truth-telling, yet torn by his love for and desire to understand his grandfather. Not everyone, his story suggested, could be easily cast as the same kind of victim. Not everyone, he implied, could sit easily in the space that was being called community. And Madé's story was not the only such talk to emerge.

As the 1965 Park project got further under way, tensions over how to make sense, identity, and political practice out of the past also translated into divisions along generational and gendered lines, sparking questions about what it meant to claim the past as one's own and how to address competing notions of justice and social repair. As it became clearer that not all of the family members were convinced of the park's liberatory promise, many of the children and grandchildren of survivors of the violence began increasingly to speak of 1965 as "their history" as well as their elders', despite the fact that most of them had been born after the violence. Many of these younger people described how their planning discussions for the park allowed them to assert an origin point for certain aspects of their selves, helping them to restructure personal biographies that had often been marked by struggles for social acceptance, foreclosed educational or economic opportunities, and confusion about the secrets that seemed to saturate their family histories. Gedé, a twenty-seven-year-old whose grandfather was killed in 1965, spoke about growing up with an unspoken prohibition against socializing with the children of the family compound next door, whom he learned as an adult were suspected of having used their Nationalist Party affiliation to gain political prestige by informing on alleged communists in 1965. For Gedé, claiming 1965 as his history not only allowed him to make sense of a childhood he described as full of uncertainty over what had really happened in the village, but also legitimized his desire to move past legacies of violence to ensure new forms of social cohesion among neighboring youth. If 1965 was his history, he could claim the right to work through it and revise it in an active engagement and choose to ultimately dismiss its power to determine his future. For him and the youth who agreed with him, this recognition of having been shaped by the official designation as "*anak PKI*," or "children of the Indonesian Communist Party," was a powerful move, one that worked against state aims of fragmenting potentially resistant solidarities. Where the state had attempted to alienate survivors of violence from each other by monitoring public speech and recruiting citizens through fear and indoctrination to self-surveil their communities, staking an identity in a shared relationship to the past raised the possibility of directing suffering that was at once widespread and socially fragmented into focused political energy.

At the same time, by claiming 1965 as their history, as a kind of cultural property in which they held equal share, paid for in the currency of pain, these young people often ended by ironically reproducing some of the ideological supports of the very same powers they purported to resist. One of the first projects the youth planned for the park was a photograph exhibit of the family members killed in 1965 and 1966. This idea was appealing to them both because they had seen images of similar displays from post–9/11 New York and Dirty War–era Argentina, and because they felt it would encourage the participation (*partisipasi*)—a term familiar to those who had engaged in student activism influenced by languages of community development—of the entire extended family, bringing them together in an articulation of shared loss. They also hoped that the process of collecting these photographs from older family members would enable them to gather histories of the violence, closing the gaps they perceived among those who had experienced the violence directly and those who would have the responsibility of preserving these memories in the future. And at first, the project seemed to go smoothly. Family members sought out old black-and-white photos of those who had been killed, releasing their smiling young faces from the hidden niches where they had been kept safe from a public eye that scanned for signs of subversive tendencies. Some of the older people explained that exposing the photographs was frightening; nevertheless, they were prepared to explain their decision by drawing on a religious language of ancestral respect and the popular practice of displaying photographs of the deceased in preparation for rituals that ensure their well-being in the afterlife. But if family elders were willing to have their losses visualized—indeed, many grew concerned that their own close family not be excluded—they were much less eager to narrate the details of the past. Many of the young people grew extremely frustrated with those elders they saw as reluctant to tell them about what they had experienced in linear, expository form, using a language of "rights" and "responsibilities" to attempt to elicit oral histories from those in the family who had witnessed the violence firsthand.

As this struggle continued, it seemed to resonate closely with what I had seen happen in the immediate aftermath of Soeharto's regime, when human rights activists began "fact-finding" projects to uncover a history they saw as having been hidden under the repressive silence of three decades of dictatorship. Relatives of those who had been killed as communists, including residents of the 1965 Park family compound, were subject to structured questionnaires that often mimicked the interrogation practices of military intelligence, asking about the formal political affiliations of the deceased, what mass organizations they had been active in, and the times and places they had last been seen alive. I had heard how these efforts had caused fright and worry among family members. I had also worked with some of the activists to consider ethnographic methods that entailed more sustained and respectful engagement with people's diverse ways of remembering. I found that even for those who did not experience oral history gathering as a painful reminder of experiences of interrogation, these calls to narrate and witness through the excavation and articulation of a linear, realist form of memory were often received with discomfort or disinterest. Those who had felt terror firsthand had, over the decades, found ways of expressing it that posed less risk of arousing the wrath of the state and less chance of antagonizing neighbors who had either themselves participated in the violence or had gained power through manipulating the potent symbol of communist threat. Indeed, these survivors were not, as their children often assumed, simply silent, muted by power and awaiting the release of their words. Older family members were often suspicious of the genre of courageous "testimony" against state atrocities, wary of what they saw as all-too-easy reassurances that the post-Soeharto regime change had really changed the standards for safe public enunciation. They also doubted that their children and grandchildren could be trusted to read the local social landscape with canniness and care, avoiding speech that could spark tensions among those who had lost family members and those suspected of having collaborated with or benefited from the violence. But their stance was not simply one of fear-provoking silence, but also of practiced familiarity with less positivist articulations of the past. They had long used Balinese languages of karmic justice to whisper of the misfortunes of killers or the corruption of the judiciary, or communicated with those who had been executed through the medium of ritual trance, or engaged in psychic divinations to discover who had reincarnated in their families' children. Women had whispered stories of their suffering while doing their daylong work of weaving ceremonial offerings, and men had commented obliquely on how perpetrating violence had called forth the fate of an early demise while gathering at the late-night wakes of the village's dead. Yet such work of remembering, so often inflected by the otherworldly, was often discounted by the young activists, for whom religious and ritual discourse seemed backward and old-fashioned, politically defeatist, or uncomfortably resonant with state attempts to control Balinese subjectivities by asserting an apolitical cultural traditionalism that could be used to maintain social order and to sell Bali to foreign tourists.

The young people's language of "choice" in relation to their history was also interpreted as presumptuous and naive by many of the older residents of the family compound. For them, the violence was not an event, distantly bracketed, against which one could take a purposeful stance. It was not something that one intentionally chose to either remember by way of oral history projects, truth commissions, or an updated national history curriculum, or to forget by way of erasure from public discourse or more personal attempts to deny or disregard. It was not, as some Western psychological models might have it, an experience located safely in historical remove, recovery from which involves a working through or letting go of a destructive past, the arrival at closure through an imposition of meaningful narrative on the chaos of pathologically insistent and fragmentary memory. Rather, in their eyes, the events of 1965–1966 continued to channel and dam possibilities for speech, political action, and cultural meaning, shaping the terms of local social engagement. In fact, this language of agency over the past sparked some of the most heated commentary on the park, captured by the words of one older woman, Gung Biang Putu, who stood up at one of the youth's meetings to tell them, "If you want to do this, go ahead, but don't say that it's for me. I don't need a park, or photographs, or speeches to remember. Whether I want to or not, I remember every day."

As these divergent understandings of the social life of history sharpened generational gulfs, they also marked off gendered divisions, when women who showed ambivalence about openly sharing their memories were cast by the younger people as ignorant of politics or trapped by a misplaced maternal protectiveness inherent to a feminine self. That there were stories these women did not desire to tell was difficult for the park's planners to accept, and difficult for these women to communicate when they felt there was no language in which to speak—especially stories of the sexual assaults many of them had suffered at the hands of local militias. Woman who had lived through examinations for bodily signs of communism—searches by military or militia personnel for a fantasized hammer and sickle tattoo on the vagina or lower abdomen, which were often followed by rape (cf. Dwyer 2004)—did indeed say they wished to protect their sons and grandsons from the knowledge of their abuse, less out of a feminine shame or self-blame than out of a concern that this information would spark retaliatory violence in the neighborhood. But they also explained that newly popular discourses of transitional justice, which called on Indonesians to decry state violations of human rights and to resolve legacies of conflict among neighbors, seemed to offer them little space for their own stories. While the gendered violence of 1965 was enabled by military propaganda that demonized women's political participation as a transgression against sexual order (Dwyer 2004; Larasati 2006; Wieringa 2002,), it was also deeply embedded in structural inequalities that have continued to shape Balinese gender relations, marginalizing women from formal political participation and offering them unequal access to inheritance, rights within marriage, and custody of their children. To the extent that their stories refused a conciliatory stance with such inequalities, and exposed the implication of cultural values in violence, they were much harder to read as heroic local resistance or compromise-based peace-building (see also Sanford, this volume).

Ironically, even when many more older women than men showed support for the youth's efforts, providing coffee and food for their meetings, and taking breaks from their daily activities to sit and listen to their discussions, they were generally still assumed to be there primarily to care for their children, rather than demonstrating a real engagement with the park's aims. The few suggestions for the park I heard women make, including the idea that a Balinese *pelinggih*, or ancestral shrine, be erected in the corner, were immediately dismissed as insufficiently political—this despite the fact that for women, the domain of reincarnation and deification of the dead was one of the major sites where they contested the New Order state's attempts to erase

alleged communists from national memory (Dwyer 2004; Dwyer and Santikarma 2006). The naturalized exclusion of women from an arena marked
political became especially apparent when a plainclothes agent from the
local military intelligence unit visited the park, asking the young planners
questions about upcoming events and who would be attending them. The
young people insisted that they were not afraid of such surveillance; they
had nothing to hide, and, besides, it was now a new era in Indonesia, when
they knew their rights and were prepared to defend them. What they worried
about, they said, was the possibility of a traumatic impact upon the older
women who had lived through the violence, whom they saw as needing to be
sheltered from awareness of the park's potential repercussions. "If they knew,
they wouldn't be able to handle it," worried Gedé, his genuinely heartfelt concern seeming to overshadow his awareness of just how much these women
had already handled. Indeed, the discourse of victimhood these young people were operating within seemed to offer two gendered polar positions for
postconflict subjects: the heroic, masculinized victim, who finds a political
identity in the resistant articulation of experience, and the tragic, feminized
victim, whose inability to utter the past leaves her trapped in a voiceless,
vulnerable state of trauma.[8]

The tensions between the youth and the older men of the family took
a strikingly different form, with men's opposition to the park explained in
much more antagonistic terms. For those men who had spent decades struggling to downplay their political marginalization as "ex-communists" within
village economic and political structures, the attempts of their sons to cast
1965 in concrete in the space of their home's courtyard seemed foolhardy
at best and treacherous at worst. Like the older women, they doubted the
ability of their children to navigate the fraught local landscape of memory,
and to avoid resurrecting issues that could be used against them, as their
communist links had been manipulated in the years after 1965 to force them
to labor on public works projects and to deprive them of a number of tracts
of family land. Those men who had been barred from the vast civil service
due to their political stigmatization, and who had later found a modicum of
success in the private tourism sector, were especially ambivalent about the
benefits of articulating the violent past. They knew quite well that Balinese
tourism is driven by images of harmonious, aesthetically appealing culture,
not by memories of mass killings and protests against human rights abuses.
To them, the park seemed to challenge the choices they had made to keep
their families safe, and to be moved by a naive, thrill-seeking resistance
that claimed erroneously to speak on behalf of a community. For their
part, the young park planners saw their elders as ensnared in the past and
bounded by the circumscribed space of the village, unaware of the cosmopolitan currents now flowing through Indonesia to bring new options for

addressing political matters. "They haven't even read Pramoedya!" one of them exclaimed, referring to Indonesia's most famous novelist, the Nobel-nominated Pramoedya Ananta Toer, who spent fourteen years in detainment after 1965, and whose books were banned by the Soeharto regime as promoting "Marxist-Leninist ideology," only to become inspirational bestsellers in the post-Soeharto era. "They don't even know the word *rekonsiliasi*," another complained before launching into a parody of an imaginary Balinese peasant trying to pronounce the unfamiliar Indonesianized English term. Inasmuch as the youth perceived transitional justice ideas to have originated in a modern, elite, educated international space, they could draw upon their self-positioning as conceptual gatekeepers to ascribe to themselves a privileged status in hierarchies of progress and sophistication.

Soon, however, these tensions grew even more heated, as some supporters of the 1965 Park started to see the opposition of older men not simply as an old-fashioned conservatism but as a potential sign of complicity with power. Middle-aged Ketut, who had taken a central role in the park's creation, donating the small portion of space within the family compound he had inherited when his father was killed in 1965, began to suggest that concerns about the park could in fact represent screens erected to hide people's hidden histories. Earlier, one of Ketut's uncles had suggested that if Ketut really wanted to talk about 1965, he should build a park at the new, separate house he had constructed for his nuclear family, not in the shared space of the family compound where he no longer resided. Community, this uncle stated, is built on consensus, and if some do not agree with the park, it should be dismantled. But these comments on community only served to rouse Ketut's anger. "I think it is very possible that those who disagree with the park are trying to hide their own involvement in 1965," Ketut said, referring to the long-standing rumors that moved surreptitiously through the family compound concerning who might have informed on their relatives in order to maneuver themselves into positions of local power, or to deflect threats to their own lives at a time when military propaganda made it clear that those who failed to cleanse communists from the nation were subversives themselves. "You know, we can use the 1965 Park as a kind of 'diagnostic tool' (*alat diagnostik*) to discover the truth of the past," Ketut claimed. "Those who are against it, we should ask if they have something to hide." What the park's presence had diagnosed, he continued, was a particularly pathological effect of violence. "Our real enemy is not the state," he said, "it is our own families."

Anthropologies of and for Justice

What then might we learn from these debates and tensions? Certainly an anthropology that would work in support of social justice cannot end by simply—or complexly—critiquing initiatives to seek justice. As important as it is to be what one of Anna Tsing's Indonesian interlocutors calls "a hair in the flour," someone who can confound the easy inscriptions of power by challenging rigid interpretations of possibility, to conclude with the evocation of contest and contingency would do little justice to my Balinese interlocutors, who welcomed me into their enthusiastic projects and emotional engagements with the hope that anthropology might contribute to their struggles (Tsing 2004, 205).

One crucial point I would suggest these stories speak to is the necessity of looking closely at those figures that haunt the edge of narration (see also Robben and Eltringham, this volume). The widespread euphoria that followed Soeharto's resignation, when the public domain seemed willing to accommodate a plurality of political viewpoints, in fact often served to mask the marginality of those who told their tales in culturally unrecognizable or politically perilous languages. Even with the emergence of grassroots organizations to document and disseminate evidence of human rights violations and the testimony of victims, there is much that still cannot be heard about 1965 in Bali. For example, stories of women's experiences of sexual violence, or of the intimate betrayals and suspicion that have marked families, or of the ritual work of recalling the dead through processes of divination, death ceremony, and reincarnation, have thus far failed to attract the audiences that can shape survivors' experiences into movements for social change. Here I suggest that it is crucial to think about mainstream human rights discourses and the victims' narratives they select to voice as particular genres that may work not only to spread awareness of conflicts but also to situate unruly experiences in what anthropologist Joao Biehl has called "zones of social abandonment" (2005), molding spaces of political recognition and effecting whose pain will be recognized and whose denied. This is less a plea for attention to a more representative victim's position—clearly there is none—or for inclusion of the voices of the marginalized in ethnographies and programs, than it is a call to recognize how advocacy depends upon particular genres of expression and how exhortations to bear witness and testify to a violent past may delineate their own margins where other more indirect, uncanny, or troubled ways of enunciating go unheard.

These stories also underscore the point that for many survivors of violence, recalling and representing the past evoke far more complex issues than calls to empower sufferers to gain conscious control over history, and to compose narratives that can challenge power, might have it. As a process that is fundamentally semiotic and political, memory is not simply a matter of individual agency, but rather is embedded in past and present social relations. Contemporary Balinese are not living in a post-1965 landscape, where neoliberal languages of choice and mastery can be easily applied to one's relation to the past, but in a social world where patterns of personhood, speech, and interaction have been fundamentally shaped by the violence. In part, and as many scholars of Indonesian politics have noted, this endurance of the events of 1965–1966 has been an effect of the Indonesian state's persistent attempts to promote its version of history to authorize ongoing political oppression and to vigorously animate the specter of communist threat to enhance its nation-building aims (Heryanto 1999; Honna 1999). And, indeed, fear of attracting the attention of authorities was one aspect of the ambivalence about the promise of public speech those concerned with the 1965 Park expressed. But as the tensions over the park exposed, the continuing power of the violence to shape Balinese social life and subjectivity has also been an artifact of the context in which the killings and their aftermath were embedded in Bali. Violence became entangled in local communities and kin groups as neighbors killed neighbors and relatives killed relatives, and the very assumptions and expectations brought to bear on social life shifted. Narrating and remembering, in such a case, must be understood in the context of ongoing social relationships among those who participated in violent events. Given such a context, working through or speaking of memory is a highly complex cultural and political negotiation, rather than a self-evident goal (see also Burnet, this volume). Moving past memory to a state that could be termed peace is not always even necessarily desirable. As one Balinese member of the same family, who lost his brother to the violence and was himself imprisoned for three years for membership in a leftist high school organization, told me after I apologized for asking him questions that I thought might have brought traumatic memories to the surface, "It's not you who has made me remember. I will have these memories until I also am dead. It is these memories that make me know I'm still alive." Just as memory in this case can be understood to entail a deeply ethical position essential to the construction of selfhood, it must also be seen as something that takes place in engagement with one's everyday social world and those who inhabit it, but not always in linear, representational narrative. For most Balinese, memory emerges not in abstract, realist form but in relation to a social landscape, as victims of violence encounter those they believe responsible for their suffering in regular community interaction. The maintenance of memories of 1965–1966 is often seen as essential for navigating a social terrain made treacherous by the open possibility of violence. At the same time, memory and the emotions it entails are often socially managed through strategies of temporary concealment that rarely reach a state of closure or a homogenous sense of community.

These particular configurations of violence have helped to create the context in which memory might now be articulated in Bali. To the extent that narrating one's experiences involves positioning oneself as a subject of and in the past, it evokes far more ambivalence for those who can neither imagine themselves as having been unequivocally victimized nor victimizing. The modern juridical language of perpetrators, victims, and witnesses, which presumes certain consistent subject positions, or the appeal for truthtelling and national reconciliation, which holds as its premise a transparent notion of historical narrative and as its goal the recovery of national subjects who can be brought together into a shared symbolic community, often falls far short of being able to encompass memory, its articulation, and the contemporary politics in which it is embedded. Certainly for someone like Madé, the painful questioning the park provoked was not simply a matter of situating himself against a past, but of how to orient himself intellectually and emotionally in a political moment whose categories of identity and interest felt troublingly limited. For a man like Ketut, a monumental diagnostic tool would refuse to whitewash history, rejecting realist models of reconciliation or conflict resolution that stress compromise with power in the service of peace, even as they reproduced marginalizing languages of social pathology that reroute attention away from state abuses and responsibilities. And for a woman like Gung Biang Putu, whose memories arise in the everyday, and in the uncanny ritual movements between past and present, memorializing violence is a need only of those who do not know its weight.

By highlighting the tenacity of violence in social life, and the slippages and abrasions between different imaginations of and strategies for effecting postconflict futures, my goal is not to cynically dismiss the possibility for peace in Indonesia—to paint it as the misplaced dreamwork or directive of those ignorant of the challenges Balinese face in imagining and enacting something that could be called reconciliation. The stories I have briefly told—stories of activist determination, stories of mistranslations, and stories, ultimately, of the importance of learning to better listen in unexpected semiotic spaces—offer as much hope as they do caution, if we believe that only a deep and committed engagement with the perspectives of those who live with violence can pave the way for truly effective and collaborative responses to their predicaments. I do not see anthropology's role as choosing between these competing perspectives. I am interested in using a critical anthropology, conscious of how the stories we tell about violence help to shape the possibilities for peace, to reimagine and rework a social field. Stories of communist threat, resistant heroism, and the promise of reconciled national subjects that are told to young Indonesians—as well as stories of marginalization, madness, terror, and rape that are told and not heard, or that move outside of speech—are stories that can indeed wound and kill. But stories of harmonious Balinese at ease with their past and with each other, participating in a new nation while conserving their precious, harmonious culture—and marketing it to those travelers seeking respite from their own violent worlds—do not always sound like liberation to those who have heard words like "peace," democracy," and "culture" used to corner them discursively by obscuring their pain, anger, ambivalence—and longing. The late Clifford Geertz once said that what anthropologists do is write. This may seem a pale form of politics. But by telling old stories in crosswise ways, by telling new stories that speak afresh to old concerns, and by highlighting how any real reconciliation will require not only new laws and new commissions, but also a revaluation of the terms and grammars we use to apprehend Bali, violence, and the work of the past, we may move toward an anthropology that can speak awkward plural truths to power.

Dancing through History

Indeed, it would be presumptuous of me to offer a definitive conclusion, for this story of the 1965 Park, and of the possibilities and limits of narrating the violent past in order to forge a different kind of future, is still very much ongoing. On Indonesia's national stage, debates over reconciliation have recently reached a tense crossroads, where suggestions by government elites that truth might in fact be an impediment to reconciliation and economic progress grind harshly against hopes for justice. Intellectual and political caution is necessary in such a setting, where languages of populism and democracy have been used to delegitimize activists' attempts to urge official investigations of the violence, with some government figures arguing that history should be left to a public to diversely interpret and unravel in the course of time. When in December 2006 Indonesia's Constitutional Court struck down legislation authorizing a National Truth and Reconciliation Commission—earning Indonesia the dubious distinction of being the first country to authorize, and then cancel, such a body—many in the international community began speaking of Indonesia as a transitional justice failure, where their efforts to implement postconflict programming could not convince the state to hold itself to account. Some Indonesian activists who had been critical of the proposed commission worried that it would distract from a push for human rights tribunals or silence social justice advocates by telling them in the aftermath of its operation that they should now be quiet after having had their turn to speak, began—like I myself did—to question whether they should have softened their critical stance to ensure that *something* happened.

But in this family compound in Bali, where the most painful questioning has been less about a state's inhumanity or an international community's indifference and failure than about how to live together with the social legacies of violence, the young promoters of the 1965 Park have been trying to turn contest into productive tension. Moving among diverse visions of past and future, memory and history, remembering and forgetting, and the ambivalent attraction of public speech, they have worked—not always well, and not always smoothly, but with hope and determination—toward a more reflective apprehension of the multiple stakes of engaging violence. Two years after the park's inauguration, photocopies of the photographs of the dead still hung on a wall bordering the park, but they were joined by an art exhibition by a young member of the 1965 Park Collective. The works—an outline of Bali with a razor blade through its heart, a smiling young woman whose lips are sealed by a question mark, a tenant farmer whose rice land is being sold to build a golf course—called on Balinese to reconsider their long-running performance of touristic images of peace and social harmony, and to acknowledge the ongoing structural violence against Bali's poor, its immigrants, and the women whose ritual labor underlies the commodification of Bali's alluring exoticism. Exposing these parallels between the erasure of past violence from Bali's globalized image and the forces that promote contemporary inequalities, the park's proponents are trying to create more inclusive narratives of suffering and social justice that rely not on homogenous categories of victimhood but on a collaborative mapping of diverse experiences of power. And inspired by the work of young Muslim activists in Java who have gathered children of perpetrators and victims of the 1965–1966 violence to speak against the determinism of such categories, Madé has made a tenuous peace with his past and his peers, encouraging the opening of a space for the sharing of more complex narratives by publishing his story in the park's new community newsletter. And most recently, a group of older women survivors of 1965 began to gather for a new daily aerobics class on the park's lawn. It was difficult, one young activist acknowledged to me over the phone, for the park's creators to consider knee bends and toe-touching the kind of political act they had envisioned this space being used for. "*Aduh*, Tante Leslie," he exclaimed to me. "They were dancing to *dangdut*," referring to the hip-shaking mélange of Arabic pop and Bollywood tunes popular among Indonesia's working class, which he saw as equally inappropriate for an activist soundtrack or an elderly woman's exercise. Yet when his grandmother took the phone to say hello, I heard another story. "*Politik, politik, politik*," she exclaimed. "They think they know what's *politik*." She continued. "According to Soeharto and the militias, we were all supposed to be dead. That I didn't die, that I had my children, that means, at the very least, that they failed. If these aerobics help us to stay alive longer to prove that they didn't win, that's *politik* too, isn't it?" I could only agree.

NOTES

This essay is based on more than forty-eight months of collaborative ethnographic research, carried out in partnership with Degung Santikarma. I gratefully acknowledge support from a John D. and Catherine T. MacArthur Research and Writing Fellowship, an H. F. Guggenheim Foundation grant, a grant from the U.S. Institute of Peace, and a grant from the Haverford College Faculty Research Fund. For critical engagement with ideas expressed in this essay, I thank Gung Ayu Ratih, John Roosa, Agung Putri, Hilmar Farid, Diyah Larasati, Dag Yngvesson, Anita Isaacs, Elizabeth Rhoads, A. A. Ngurah Termana, A. A. Gede Putra, A. A. Mayun Karmadi, and the Rumah Barat and Taman sixty-five participants. I am especially grateful to Alex Hinton for his support, encouragement, and patience.

1. For an overview of some of these efforts, see Zurbuchen (2002) and ICTJ (2004).

2. The exact number of Indonesians killed is unknown and will likely remain so, despite recent efforts at fact-finding by victims' advocacy groups. Estimates have ranged from around 300,000 deaths to as many as 3 million, with a figure of 1 million frequently cited in academic and journalistic accounts of the violence. The politics of numbering the dead is, of course, far from straightforward, speaking both to the state's desire to block access to nonofficial historical research and to activists' desires to ground calls for attention to the violence in statistical claims of its significance.

3. For more on the "Crocodile Hole" monument and the Museum of the Indonesian Communist Party's Treachery (Museum Penghianatan G/30/S-PKI), see Schreiner (2005). This memorial complex, which is still functioning and open to the public today, was central to the New Order state's production of nationalism through the evocation of threat and the erasure of its bloody origins by reference to a mythic history of heroic triumph over communism.

4. The governor of Bali offered this characterization of the bombings, failing to mention the much greater loss of life that occurred in 1965–1966, in a speech to an international convention in 2002 (Berata 2002).

5. For more information on the range of legislation discriminating against alleged communists, former political prisoners and their families, see ICTJ (2006).

6. For critiques of an assumed direct link between speaking of the past and individual or social recovery, see Dwyer and Santikarma (2007); Langer (1997); Shaw (2005, 2007).

7. All of the names used in this essay are pseudonyms.

8. I thank Gung Ayu Ratih for insightful conversation on this point, based on her experiences working with women survivors of 1965 and with young woman human rights activists who at first assumed their advocees to be fragile, delicate figures reluctant to speak and in need of protection.

REFERENCES

Berata, Dewa. 2002. "The Kuta Tragedy and the Present-Day Bali (A Report by the Governor of Bali)." Paper presented at the ASEAN + 3 NTO meeting. Depasar, Bali, December 11–12.

Biehl, Joao. 2005. *Vita: Life in a Zone of Social Abandonment.* Berkeley: University of California Press.

Borofsky, Robert. 2004. "Conceptualizing Public Anthropology." http://www.publicanthropology.org/Defining/definingpa.htm.

Bourdieu, Pierre. 2003. *Firing Back: Against the Tyranny of the Market 2.* New York: Verso.

Bourgois, Philippe. 2006. "Foreword: Anthropology in the Global State of Emergency." In *Engaged Observer: Anthropology, Advocacy, and Activism*, ed. Victoria Sanford and Asale Angel-Ajani, ix–xii. New Brunswick: Rutgers University Press.

Breslau, Joshua. 2004. "Introduction: Cultures of Trauma: Anthropological Views of Posttraumatic Stress Disorder in International Health." *Culture, Medicine, and Psychiatry* 28 (2): 113–126.

Coxshall, Wendy. 2005. "From the Peruvian Reconciliation Commission to Ethnography: Narrative, Relatedness and Silence." *Political and Legal Anthropology Review* 28 (2): 203–222.

Cruikshank, Barbara. 1999. *The Will to Empower: Democratic Citizens and Other Subjects.* Ithaca: Cornell University Press.

Dwyer, Leslie. 2004. "The Intimacy of Terror: Gender and the Violence of 1965–66 in Bali." *Intersections: Gender, History and Culture in the Asian Context.* http:/intersections.anu.edu.au.

Dwyer, Leslie, and Degung Santikarma. 2007. "Posttraumatic Politics: Violence, Memory and Medical Discourse in Bali." In *Understanding Trauma: Integrating Biological, Clinical and Cultural Perspectives*, ed. Lawrence Kirmayer, Robert Lemelson, and Mark Barad, 403–432. New York: Cambridge University Press.

———. 2006. "Speaking from the Shadows: Memory and Mass Violence in Bali." In *After Mass Crimes: Rebuilding States and Communities*, ed. Beatrice Pouligny, Albrecht Schnabel, and Simon Chesterman, 190–214. Tokyo: United Nations University Press.

Geertz, Clifford. 1983. *Local Knowledge: Further Essays in Interpretive Anthropology.* New York: Basic Books.

Goodale, Mark. 2009. *Human Rights: An Anthropological Reader.* Malden, MA: Blackwell.

Goodale, Mark, and Sally Engle Merry, eds. 2007. *The Practice of Human Rights: Tracking Law between the Global and the Local.* New York: Cambridge University Press.

Heryanto, Ariel. 1999. "Where Communism Never Dies: Violence, Trauma and Narration in the Last Cold War Capitalist Authoritarian State." *International Journal of Cultural Studies* 2 (2): 147–177.

Honna, Jun. 1999. "Military Ideology in Response to Democratic Pressure during the Late Suharto Era: Political and Institutional Contexts." *Indonesia* 67:77–126.

Hyman, Gerald. 2006. "Ambivalence Leads to Limited Relevance." *Anthropology News* 47 (4): 7–8.

International Center for Transitional Justice (ICTJ). 2004. "The Struggle for Truth and Justice: A Survey of Transitional Justice Initiatives throughout Indonesia." ICTJ Occasional Papers. January.

———. 2006. "Neglected Duty: Providing Comprehensive Reparations to the Indonesian '1965 Victims' of State Persecution." ICTJ Occasional Papers. November.

Kleinman, Arthur. 1995. *Writing at the Margin: Discourse between Anthropology and Medicine.* Berkeley: University of California Press.

Langer, Lawrence. 1997. "The Alarmed Vision: Social Suffering and Holocaust Atrocity." In *Social Suffering, ed.* A. Kleinman, V. Das, and M. Lock, 47–65. Berkeley: University of California Press.

Larasati, Diyah Rachmi. 2006. "Dancing on the Mass Grave: Cultural Reconstruction Post Indonesian Massacres." Ph.D. diss., University of California, Riverside.

Li, Tania Murray. 2007. *The Will to Improve: Governmentality, Development, and the Practice of Politics.* Durham, NC: Duke University Press.

Paley, Julia. 2001. *Marketing Democracy: Power and Social Movements in Post-Dictatorship Chile.* Berkeley: University of California Press.

Rose, Nikolas. 1999. *Powers of Freedom: Reframing Political Thought.* New York: Cambridge University Press.

Sanford, Victoria. 2006. "Introduction." In *Engaged Observer: Anthropology, Advocacy, and Activism*, ed. V. Sanford and A. Angel-Ajani, 1–15. New Brunswick: Rutgers University Press.

Schreiner, Klaus. 2005. "Lubang Buaya: Histories of Trauma and Sites of Memory." In *Beginning to Remember: The Past in the Indonesian Present*, ed. M. Zurbuchen, 261–277. Seattle: University of Washington Press.

Shaw, Rosalind. 2005. "Rethinking Truth and Reconciliation Commissions: Lessons from Sierra Leone." United States Institute of Peace Special Report No. 130, Washington, DC.

———. 2007. "Displacing Violence: Making Pentecostal Memory in Postwar Sierra Leone." *Cultural Anthropology* 22 (1): 66–93.

Smith, Gavin. 1999. *Confronting the Present: Towards a Politically Engaged Anthropology*. London: Berg.

Theidon, Kimberly. 2007. "Transitional Subjects: The Disarmament, Demobilization and Reintegration of Former Combatants in Columbia." *International Journal of Transitional Justice* 1 (1): 66–91.

Tsing, Anna Lowenhaupt. 2004. *Friction: An Ethnography of Global Connection*. Princeton: Princeton University Press.

Warren, Kay. 2006. "Perils and Promises of Engaged Anthropology: Historical Transitions and Ethnographic Dilemmas." In *Engaged Observer: Anthropology, Advocacy, and Activism*, ed. V. Sanford and A. Angel-Ajani, 213–227. New Brunswick: Rutgers University Press.

Wieringa, Saskia. 2002. *Sexual Politics in Indonesia*. New York: Palgrave Macmillan.

Zurbuchen, Mary. 2002. "History, Memory and the '1965 Incident' in Indonesia." *Asian Survey* 42 (4): 564–581.

Afterword

The Consequences of Transitional
Justice in Particular Contexts

ROGER DUTHIE

The field of transitional justice has developed over the past two decades as a particular approach to addressing the legacies of massive human rights abuses or atrocities (see Arthur 2009). The primary measures that make up what might be called the tool box of this approach are criminal prosecutions of perpetrators, truth-telling initiatives such as truth commissions, reparations for victims, certain institutional reforms such as vetting, and memorialization efforts. Transitional justice measures are generally applied in countries emerging out of armed conflict or authoritarian rule, and the goals that have been ascribed to them include making contributions to democratization, the prevention of the recurrence of abuses, and reconciliation. There are good reasons to think that transitional justice measures may indeed make such contributions (see, for example, Aspen Institute 1989; de Greiff, forthcoming; Méndez 1997).

One of the things that the different chapters in this volume demonstrate clearly, however, is that the application of transitional justice measures in specific contexts and places—when we move from, for example, the global to the local, the universal to the particular, or discourse to practice—in pursuit of such goals often leads to a number of unintended consequences.

Some Unintended Consequences
of Transitional Justice Efforts

"Even as they may be initiated with the best of intentions," emphasizes Alex Hinton in the introduction of this volume, "transitional justice mechanisms almost always have unexpected outcomes that emerge out of the 'frictions' between global mechanisms and local realities." The types of unintended consequences that the application of transitional justice measures might lead to are broadly described throughout the case studies in this volume in various ways.

Leslie Dwyer, for example, in examining the politics surrounding the building of a monument in Bali, Indonesia, highlights "the overlaps and frictions that occur as transitional justice discourses are translated into Balinese practice." She also looks at the "challenges and possibilities" that emerge out of the process of a "local rethinking of a universalist subject of suffering, the 'grieving victim,'" which leads to "hybrid notions of 'justice.'" Sarah Wagner points to the use of DNA-based technology to identify the mortal remains of missing persons in Srebrenica in order "to examine how internationally accepted universals intersect with particular circumstances," how the "universal 'right to know'" relates to the "particular ethno-national political forces in Bosnia." Beth Drexler seeks to situate international transitional processes in East Timor and Indonesia on the ground, arguing that "the very distinction between international and local justice may be producing unintended consequences that ultimately may foreclose possibilities for accountability and resolution of past violence." Other chapters look at the application of transitional justice measures and concepts in the particular contexts of Rwanda, Chile, Argentina, Canada, Botswana, and Nigeria.

One of the often stated goals of transitional justice processes, especially truth-telling efforts, is the establishment and acknowledgment of a more accurate record of the events of the past (see, for instance, Hayner 2002, 24–27). Attempting to do so can generate positive results, as in Bali, where, according to Dwyer, the opportunity for survivors of the massive violence in 1965 and their children to recast their identities as victims "has been felt as empowering by many Indonesians, who have used this designation to claim rights that had been unjustly abrogated, to form social links among those who had been alienated from full national or local social belonging, or to find shared languages to describe experiences." The experiences of these Indonesians within the previous government narrative involved limited social acceptance and educational and economic experiences, as well as confusion about their past.

In painting a particular picture of the past, however, there may be complex elements of local dynamics during conflict for which transitional justice measures are unable to account in their narratives. This may lead to unintended consequences. As Dwyer explains, in local contexts "where suspicion and surveillance have been embedded in everyday social life, this process of circumscribing a community defined by shared origins in and orientations to the past faced multiple challenges." In the Bali example, survivors of the violence in 1965 lived through decades of the state's attempts to alienate them from each other through monitoring and community self-surveillance; in response, they developed forms of expression concerning their painful experiences that "posed less risk of arousing the wrath of the state than straightforward, public recountings of the past," such as rituals. For such survivors, "calls to narrate and witness were often received uncomfortably." The resulting tensions even lead to intrafamily violence. "Narrating and remembering," concludes Dwyer, "must be understood in the context of ongoing social relationships."

Similarly, in East Timor, where the Indonesian occupation employed an intelligence system that drew in civilians from within each community, "ordinary interactions and daily life were restructured by suspicion and the possibility of betrayal." In a context in which the line between victim and perpetrator has blurred over many years, establishing an agreed-upon narrative is difficult. "The morally ambiguous situations generated by years of intelligence operations," argues Drexler, "have not been, and cannot be, resolved with clear narratives of culpability and victimization." The result is the continuing proliferation of local rumor, suspicion, and mistrust.

The process of developing a new narrative may become problematic at the local political level in other ways as well, such as when it runs up against competing or conflicting narratives, or when the new narrative is or is seen to be one-sided or exclusionary. In Bosnia, for example, writes Wagner, by intervening in a context with "competing historical accounts of the region and its victims" in such a way as to appear to support one narrative (the Bosnian one) over another (the Bosnian Serb one)—through identifying bodies and prosecuting war criminals—the international community has "effectively polarized Bosnian Serb and Bosniak reactions," even playing a role in the rise of "new forms of ethnonationalism."

In Rwanda, conflicting narratives can be seen regarding the effectiveness of the *gacaca* process to integrate released prisoners into local communities. The Rwandan government, writes Jennie Burnet, pushes an "official, idyllic version" of things, one which members of focus groups agreed with in public, while in private recounting "an entirely different version." The government's narrative—to which *gacaca* contributes—generally portrays Tutsi as victims and Hutu as perpetrators; it is part of a "polarizing discourse," which, rather than leading to reconciliation, contends Burnet, is "deepening cleavages within the communities and sowing mistrust on all sides."

Andrew Woolford, in his chapter on the British Columbia Treaty Process in Canada, argues that this process is "hampered by the lack of shared understanding" between the First Nations of British Columbia and the provincial and federal governments concerning "the injustices that need to be resolved." On the one hand, he writes, the Aboriginal groups seek a process that addresses the socially destructive experience of colonialism (which their members often label "genocide") and its legacy; while, on the other hand, the non-Aboriginal governments want to limit the focus of negotiations to resolving land claims and reducing political and legal uncertainty in the province. The restricted forms of justice and reparation sought by the governments, Woolford contends, by failing to recognize the harms done to the victim groups, constitute an act of "reparative symbolic violence" that amounts to a new type of injustice in itself.

The narratives that emerge out of transitional justice efforts can also be limited and shaped in particular situations by international politics, again leading to unintended consequences. In East Timor and Indonesia, for example, suggests Drexler, "transitional institutions enforce particular narratives so that they have social and political consequences and exclude other narratives so that pervasive patterns of violence are excluded from prosecutorial and social visibility." What is excluded from the narrative in this case is the role of the Indonesian military in designing the system of occupation and in the violence following the 1999 referendum, as well as the role played in the conflict by global geopolitics during the cold war— precisely the least local of issues. Similarly, argues Wagner, the international community's interventions in postwar Bosnia demonstrated its intention "to control the manner in which these injustices were addressed, ensuring that their own complicity or inaction remained safely outside the realm of scrutiny or required redress." In neither Bosnia nor East Timor, then, according to these authors, does the narrative produced by transitional justice measures accurately portray the international context of the conflict in which abuses occurred. The result, according to Drexler, is a legally constructed narrative that differs from the one that the public believes to be true, which ultimately undermines the legitimacy of the legal institutions involved and the rule of law itself.

Considering the Unintended Consequences

I do not want to dispute the broad claim that justice efforts may lead to unintended consequences, which is highlighted in different contexts by the authors throughout this volume. The pursuit of justice in the aftermath of atrocities may indeed confront competing narratives of the past, which may very well generate local and/or ethnic disputes, instability, polarization, and even new injustices, and which may undermine goals such as the strengthening of the rule of law and reconciliation. This will be the case particularly when local political, social, and economic contexts are not taken into account. I do, however, want to make two related points that should inform our consideration of such unintended consequences. Both have to do with expectations. The first point is that some unintended consequences of transitional justice efforts should be expected. They can then be assessed in terms of the specific risks they may give rise to in a given context, and, where appropriate, steps can be taken to minimize negative consequences and maximize potentially positive ones. The second, broader point is that the overall goals and expectations that we hold regarding transitional justice measures should be modest and realistic.

Expected Consequences

While it is clear that transitional justice efforts may lead to unintended consequences, we should distinguish between those that may to a certain extent be foreseen and short term, those that are more fundamentally problematic and may in fact undermine the long-term goals of justice, and those that are the result of processes that, strictly speaking, may not qualify as transitional justice measures. To begin with, certain outcomes may be viewed as unintended or negative but should nevertheless be expected. Transitional justice measures are inherently political. They involve particular ways of effecting particular kinds of change in societies. Some resistance, competing narratives, and disagreement is inevitable and perhaps even desirable. Conceptions of justice, for example, will never be shared by all. In his chapter comparing the experiences of Argentina and Chile with truth-telling exercises, for example, Antonius Robben observes that personal testimony is but "one form of justice next to other forms existing on many distinct social levels, such as states, societies, groups, families, and persons. People's sense of justice is thus composed of a complex of partially overlapping justices ranging from punitive to restorative, and retributive to reparative justice at each social level." This is true at the global level as well; there are, for instance, fundamental disagreements within the field of transitional justice around understandings of justice and reconciliation (see de Greiff, forthcoming; Teitel 2000), as well as around the appropriate balance between the pursuits of peace and justice (see Ambos et al. 2009). Furthermore, if levels of resistance and disagreement remain below a certain threshold, it could be argued that achieving long-term goals—such as reconciliation and sustainable peace and democratization—may be worth taking some short-term risk. That the revelation of the truth may provoke immediate unpleasant reactions or divisions within society may be a trade-off worth making.

It may also be the case, however, that transitional justice measures are designed or implemented in such a way as to lead to unintended consequences that may ultimately undermine sustainable peace and democratization or to create risks than simply are not worth taking. As Hinton points out, friction in the extreme can lead to "new sorts of violence and impunity." This is precisely the argument that Burnet makes concerning Rwanda. "Increased ethnic cleavages in the short term would not necessarily be a negative outcome if the long-term prospects for building a peaceful society were good," she writes. "Unfortunately, given local perceptions of widespread injustice in the *Gacaca* process, the long-term prospects for a peaceful and just society are not positive." If that is indeed the case, then the trade-off may not be worth it. Similarly, Drexler argues that the effect of transitional justice measures in Timor has been to increase impunity for Indonesian military leaders, and that their unintended consequences may "ultimately foreclose possibilities for accountability and resolution of past violence."

Woolford argues that the British Columbia Treaty Process in Canada is aimed at "reproduc[ing] the dominant social order" rather than effecting change for the better, at "shaping the victim group to better fit an unjust society, rather than transforming the society itself." In other words, to Woolford the process does not just risk certain negative outcomes, but rather is in itself a form of injustice. (This would be in this view, then, not really an unintended consequence.) Regardless, it is important to point out that the treaty process as a whole is broader than most understandings of a transitional justice process; it involves a complicated negotiation over issues such as land distribution, resource rights, self-governance, and capital transfer. And perhaps of even greater significance (from the perspective of examining the unintended consequences of transitional justice efforts) is the fact that the capital transfer element of the process may not qualify as reparations. As Woolford points out, the two sides of the negotiations do not agree on the use of the term "compensation" to refer to money that is distributed; for the First Nations, the term would provide "necessary symbolic recognition of the harms they have suffered at the hands of Canadian settler society; however, for the non-Aboriginal governments, compensation is a technical term that connotes a willingness to accept liability for these harms." The governments may indeed see the process as a whole as an "implicit acknowledgment" of an "unsavory past"; but a reparations effort requires more than that—specifically an explicit acknowledgment of wrongs committed and an acceptance of responsibility. As Pablo de Greiff articulates the point, for reparations programs, "it is precisely because the benefits are given in recognition of the (violated) rights of citizens that this general aim of recognition is related to justice" (de Greiff 2008).

Modest and Realistic Expectations

A related but somewhat broader point is that the expectations of transitional justice measures should be modest and realistic. There may be a tendency of both transitional justice practitioners themselves and observers to expect too much, especially from a single measure. Wagner is critical, for example, of the rhetoric of the chairman of the International Commission on Missing Persons, who claimed that the identification of victims' remains in Bosnia helps "to bring a sense of closure for their families." As Wagner points out, for many families the process of hearing what actually happened to a missing son or husband "opens, rather than closes off, a whole range of new and disturbing facts, images, and experiences for the surviving families." Closure for a society as a whole is even more unlikely. Burnet frames her chapter as an exploration of whether or not *gacaca* is achieving its primary goals to (quoting Rwandan president Paul Kagame) "end impunity" and establish the "real truth of what happened during the Genocide." And Woolford negatively characterizes the British Columbia Treaty Process as one of "affirmative repair," which "offers only surface forms of recognition and redistribution that do not threaten to radically transform society."

Criticisms of these measures may all be valid; my point is simply that bringing closure, ending impunity, and radically transforming society are most likely beyond the reaches of transitional justice. Transitional justice measures should therefore not be evaluated based on whether or not they alone achieve such goals. In fact, there is an acknowledgment within the field that the type of justice that transitional justice may help to bring about will always be imperfect or incomplete justice. This is even more the case when speaking of individual measures of transitional justice, such truth-telling or criminal prosecutions or reparations programs. Truth-telling exercises may have some benefit beyond just revealing the truth, but they will not bring closure to all victims or to society. Successful prosecutions may hold some perpetrators criminally accountable, but they will not completely end impunity for massive human rights violations. Reparations programs may symbolize the government's recognition of victims as both victims and citizens, but they will never fully repair the damage done to those victims. In fact, it is precisely the individual weakness of each measure taken on its own that strengthens the argument for a holistic approach to transitional justice, in which the different measures are employed in an integrated manner (de Greiff 2008). But even a holistic approach calls for modest expectations and recognition of the need for change in other areas as well. As Hinton observes in the introduction, scholars of transitional justice have argued that criminal tribunals "often fall short of their goals because expectations for them are too high and they are not accompanied by a matrix of other strategies meant to facilitate social repair," including changes in the much broader fields of institutional reform, development, and social justice (de Greiff and Duthie 2009; Mayer-Rieckh and de Greiff 2007).

It is clear from Victoria Sanford's chapter in this volume, for example, that a truth commission alone cannot establish the rule of law or break a continuum of violence against women. In Guatemala, where the truth commission acknowledged that in the 1980s the state trained its soldiers and agents to rape and terrorize women, mortality rates of women today are close to the high levels seen during the genocidal war. If the truth commission report had been accompanied by the prosecution of those responsible for this violence during the war, however, then the culture of impunity might not be so strong today. Ultimately, though, broad reform of the current justice and security system is needed. Sanford offers an analysis of the killing of women in Guatemala that is "grounded in present and past practices of the state and its security institutions."

Transitional justice efforts make up but one set of tools for effecting social change in a particular context, one that on its own can make an important contribution to but will not bring about a radical transformation of society.

REFERENCES

Ambos, Kai, Judith Large, and Marieke Wierda, eds. 2009. *Building a Future on Peace and Justice: Studies on Transitional Justice, Peace and Development: The Nuremberg Declaration on Peace and Justice.* Heidelberg: Springer.

Arthur, Paige. 2009. "How 'Transitions' Reshaped Human Rights: A Conceptual History of Transitional Justice." *Human Rights Quarterly* 31 (2): 321–367.

Aspen Institute. 1989. *State Crimes: Punishment or Pardon.* Papers and report of conference, November 4–6, 1988. Wye Center, MD: Aspen Institute.

de Greiff, Pablo. 2008. "Addressing the Past: Reparations for Gross Human Rights Abuses." In *Civil War and the Rule of Law: Security, Development, Human Rights*, ed. Agnes Hurwitz and Reyko Huang, 163–189. Boulder, CO: Lynne Rienner Publishers.

———. Forthcoming. "Theorizing Transitional Justice." In *Transitional Justice*, ed. Melissa Williams and Rosemary Nagy. New York: New York University Press.

de Greiff, Pablo, and Roger Duthie, eds. 2009. *Transitional Justice and Development: Making Connections.* New York: Social Science Research Council.

Hayner, Priscilla. 2002. *Unspeakable Truths: Facing the Challenge of Truth Commissions.* New York and London: Routledge.

Mayer-Rieckh, Alexander, and Pablo de Greiff, eds. 2007. *Justice as Prevention: Vetting Public Employees in Transitional Societies.* New York: Social Science Research Council.

Méndez, Juan E. 1997. "Accountability for Past Abuses." *Human Rights Quarterly* 19 (2): 255–282.

Teitel, Ruti. 2000. *Transitional Justice.* Oxford: Oxford University Press.

CONTRIBUTORS

WAYNE A. BABCHUK is a lecturer and adjunct professor in the Department of Anthropology and the Department of Sociology at the University of Nebraska–Lincoln and in the Department of Sociology and Anthropology at Nebraska Wesleyan University. Additionally, he serves as research associate for the Kalahari Peoples Fund in conjunction with the Department of Anthropology at Michigan State University.

MÔ BLEEKER is a political anthropologist who serves as a senior adviser in the Swiss Federal Department of Foreign Affairs, in charge of dealing with the past and prevention of genocide. She has produced documentaries and published numerous articles and reports on dealing with the past and conflict transformation.

JENNIE E. BURNET is assistant professor of anthropology at the University of Louisville. She has been conducting research on Rwanda since 1996. Her research interests include gender, ethnicity, and race in postconflict societies, development, human rights, peace, and reconciliation.

CONERLY CASEY is an associate professor at the Rochester Institute of Technology. Her research and publications include the topics of (post)colonial violence and subjectivity, religious heterodoxy, memory and mediated emotion, and (in)justice and human rights.

ELIZABETH F. DREXLER is director of Peace and Justice Studies and associate professor of anthropology at Michigan State University. Her research in Indonesia and East Timor explores how societies address the legacies of past violence. She is author of the award-winning *Aceh, Indonesia: Securing the Insecure State* and coeditor of *Aftermaths of Violence: Institutions of Truth and Memory* (University of Pennsylvania Press).

ROGER DUTHIE is a senior research associate at the International Center for Transitional Justice in New York. His publications include "Toward a

Development-Sensitive Approach to Transitional Justice," *International Journal of Transitional Justice* 2, no. 3 (2008); and *Transitional Justice and Development: Making Connections* (Social Science Research Council, 2009).

LESLIE DWYER is an assistant professor of conflict analysis and anthropology at the Institute for Conflict Analysis and Resolution at George Mason University. Her research interests include violence, gender, memory, ritual, and the social implications of globalizing discourses of trauma and psychosocial repair.

NIGEL ELTRINGHAM is senior lecturer in the department of anthropology at the University of Sussex, United Kingdom. He has published extensively on the Rwandan genocide and is the author of *Accounting for Horror: Post-Genocide Debates in Rwanda* (Pluto, 2004).

ALEXANDER LABAN HINTON is director of the Center for the Study of Genocide, Conflict Resolution, and Human Rights (CGCHR) and professor of anthropology and global affairs at Rutgers University, Newark. He is the author of the award-winning *Why Did They Kill? Cambodia in the Shadow of Genocide* (University of California Press, 2005) and editor or coeditor of six other volumes.

ROBERT K. HITCHCOCK is professor of geography and an adjunct faculty member in the Department of Anthropology at Michigan State University in East Lansing. He is the coauthor (with Megan Biesele) of *The Ju/'hoan San of Nyae Nyae and Namibian Independence: Development, Democracy, and Indigenous Voices in Southern Africa* (Berghahn Books, 2010).

MARTHA LINCOLN is a doctoral candidate in anthropology at City University of New York Graduate Center. She has published on human rights, biopower, and violence in *American Anthropologist*, *Anthropology Now*, *Daedalus*, *Discourse*, and *Socialism and Democracy*. She is currently researching public health policy in Vietnam.

ANTONIUS C.G.M. ROBBEN is professor of anthropology at Utrecht University, the Netherlands. Two of his most recent books are the edited volume *Iraq at a Distance: What Anthropologists Can Teach Us About the War* (University of Pennsylvania Press, 2010) and the award-winning ethnography *Political Violence and Trauma in Argentina* (University of Pennsylvania Press, 2005).

VICTORIA SANFORD is associate professor of anthropology at Lehman College, City University of New York, and a member of the doctoral faculty at CUNY Graduate Center. She is the author of *La Masacre de Panzos—Etnicidad, Tierra y*

Violencia en Guatemala (F & G Editores, 2009) and coeditor (with Asale Angel-Ajani) of *Engaged Observer: Anthropology, Advocacy and Activism* (Rutgers University Press, 2006).

SARAH WAGNER is an assistant professor of anthropology at the University of North Carolina at Greensboro, and the author of *To Know Where He Lies: DNA Technology and the Search for Srebrenica's Missing* (University of California Press, 2008). Her research interests include identification technology, missing persons and the politics of memory, postconflict social reconstruction, and forced migration.

ANDREW WOOLFORD is associate professor of sociology at the University of Manitoba. He is coauthor (with R. S. Ratner) of *Informal Reckonings: Conflict Resolution in Mediation, Restorative Justice and Reparations* (Routledge-Cavendish, 2008) and author of *Between Justice and Certainty: Treaty Making in British Columbia* (University of British Columbia Press, 2005).

INDEX